Jewish Christians
in Puritan England

Jewish Christians
in Puritan England

AIDAN COTTRELL-BOYCE

☙PICKWICK *Publications* · Eugene, Oregon

JEWISH CHRISTIANS IN PURITAN ENGLAND

Pickwick Publications
An Imprint of Wipf and Stock Publishers
199 W. 8th Ave., Suite 3
Eugene, OR 97401

www.wipfandstock.com

PAPERBACK ISBN: 978-1-7252-6141-9
HARDCOVER ISBN: 978-1-7252-6140-2
EBOOK ISBN: 978-1-7252-6142-6

Cataloguing-in-Publication data:

Names: Cottrell-Boyce, Aidan, author.

Title: Jewish Christians in Puritan England / Aidan Cottrell-Boyce.

Description: Eugene, OR: Pickwick Publications, 2021 | Includes bibliographical references and index.

Identifiers: ISBN 978-1-7252-6141-9 (paperback) | ISBN 978-1-7252-6140-2 (hardcover) | ISBN 978-1-7252-6142-6 (ebook)

Subjects: LCSH: Jewish Christians—Europe—History | Puritans—England—History—17th century | Christianity and other religions—Judaism | England—Church history—17th century

Classification: BX9334 C68 2021 (print) | BX9334 (ebook)

DECEMBER 10, 2020

For Anna

Contents

Introduction

DURING THE FIRST DECADES of the seventeenth century in England, a remarkable number of small religious groups began to adopt elements of Jewish ceremonial law. In London, in South Wales, in the Chilterns and the Cotswolds, congregations revived the observation of the Saturday Sabbath.[1] Thomas Woolsey, imprisoned for separatism, wrote to his co-religionists in Amsterdam to 'prove it unlawful to eat blood and things strangled.'[2] John Traske and his followers began to celebrate Passover seders.[3] Thomas Tillam announced the restoration of the practice of circumcision.[4] James Whitehall was sent down from Oxford for holding 'Jewish errors' before later reappearing in Wexford, still 'infected' with these opinions.[5] Anne Curtyn practiced circumcision on 'young boys.'[6] Hamlet Jackson travelled to Amsterdam to be circumcised by a *mohel*.[7] Robert Bacon, encountered a group of pilgrims on the road to Marlborough who also believed that they 'must be circumcised.'[8] William Everard and Abiezer Coppe referred to

1. Ball, *English Connection*, 1–22; *Seventh-Day Men*, 1–30; Katz, *Sabbath and Sectarianism*, 1–21; Parker, *English Sabbath*, 161–64.

2. Reynolds, *Godly Reformers and Their Opponents*, 92.

3. See Traske, *Christ's Kingdome Discovered*; *Treatise of Libertie from Iudaisme*; *True Gospel Vindicated*; Pagitt, *Heresiography*, 163–214; Falconer, *Briefe Refutation of John Traskes*; Fuller, *Church-History of Britain*, 17:76–77; Greene, 'Trask in the Star-Chamber, 1619,' 8–14; Como, *Blown by the Spirit*, 138–75; McDowell, 'Stigmatizing of Puritans as Jews,' 348–63; Smith, 'Christian Judaizers in Early Stuart England,' 125–33.

4. Katz, *Sabbath and Sectarianism*, 21–48; *Philo-semitism and the Readmission of the Jews*, 33–34; Tillam, *Banners of Love*; *Temple of Lively Stones*; Whitley, 'Rev. Colonel Paul Hobson,' 307–10; Goadby, *Bye-paths in Baptist History*, 22, 251; Kenworthy, *History of the Baptist Church at Hill Cliffe*, 43–49; Payne, 'Thomas Tillam,' 61–66; National Archives, SP 29/181 f. 150; SP 29/236, f. 28.

5. National Archives, SP 14/180, f. 133; SP 63/237, f. 142.

6. 'Recognizances and Indictments from the Sessions of the Peace Rolls,' 186–87.

7. Pagitt, *Heresiography*, 181; Sprunger, *Trumpets from the Tower*, 71.

8. Bacon, *Taste of the Spirit*, 41.

themselves as 'Jews,' while Thomas Totney identified himself as 'a Jew of the tribe of Reuben.'[9] Seventeenth-century Judaizing, James Shapiro writes, was 'a new and unprecedented phenomenon.'[10] Lamenting this trend in 1642, the pseudonymous puritan 'T. S.' wrote:

> Have you ever heard such a thing? That necessary truths having lyen hidden sixteen-hundred years, should after be revealed and preached by witnesses?[11]

These developments took place in the context of a Godly revolution in devotional practice, a revolution that led to some of the Godly being labelled by their contemporaries as 'Jews.' While the first generation of Puritans were identifiable with the political project of fully reforming the Elizabethan Church, the Puritanism of the early Stuart period had become an identity, constructed from a variety of ritual, dramaturgical, discursive materials, which rendered the Godly themselves identifiable and (as the Laudian crisis emerged) deviant. In the context of the rise of Laudianism, a Puritan public sphere began to emerge, a culture within which a variety of theological positions were entertained. For Peter Lake and David Como, it was this 'public sphere,' which provided the context for the emergence of, what some scholars have described as, the radical Puritanism of the interregnum. Throughout this period, Puritanism was associated in English culture with Judaism. For Shapiro, this 'labelling' process, spoke to 'deep, cultural anxieties' about difference and cohesion.[12]

The question, posed by 'T. S.,' retains some validity today. Why, after one and a half millennia of dormancy, was the spectre of 'Judaizing' awakened in England in the seventeenth century? Focusing on three illustrative examples—John Traske, Thomas Totney and Thomas Tillam—this book attempts to provide an answer to this question. In doing so, it will uncover the complex and profound affinities these figures had with each other, despite more superficial differences on matters of ecclesiology. As such, it will describe Judaizing—not as a 'shopping list' of different doctrinal

---

9. Whitelock, *Memorials of the English Affairs*, 383; Coppe, *Some Sweet Sips, of Some Spirituall Wine*, A2r–3r; Tany, *Nations Right in Magna Charta Discussed*; *Theauraujohn His Aurora in Tranlogorum in Salem Gloria*, 9, 28, 42; *Theauraujohn His Theos-ori Apokolipikal*; *Theauraujohn High Priest to the Jewes*; *I Proclaime from the Lord of Hosts the Returne of the Jewes*; *Second Part of His Theos-ori Apokolipikal*; *High-Newes for Hierusalem*; *My Edict Royal*; *Tharam Taniah*; Smith, *Perfection Proclaimed*, 56, 190–92, 304–7; Gibbons, *Gender in Mystical and Occult Thought*, 129–39; Hessayon, *Gold Tried in the Fire*.

10. Shapiro, *Shakespeare and the Jews*, 8.

11. Pagitt, *Heresiography*, 168.

12. Shapiro, *Shakespeare and the Jews*, 8.

positions—but rather as an identity, a culture, 'constructed,' like Puritanism itself, 'out of a variety of discursive materials by a number of different groups and individuals.' The development of Judaizing 'the thing,' I contend, was a process, which intertwined with the development of Judaizing 'the label,' the latter creating 'resources' that could be 'reconstructed and redeployed by those whom the very terms had been intended to marginalize and defame.'[13]

At the heart of most accounts of the development of Judaizing in seventeenth-century England is the assumption that Judaizers were—to a greater or lesser degree—philo-semitic.[14] This has been attributed to a number of factors: the renewed presence of 'real-life' Jews in England; renewed awareness of Jews in foreign countries via the medium of travel literature; renewed interest in Judeocentric eschatology; renewed interest in Hebrew texts arising from Renaissance humanism; a more literalist understanding of the biblical Law; a more typological understanding of the topos of Israel. Each approach takes for its starting point the presumption that Judaizers like John Traske, Thomas Tillam and Thomas Totney thought positively of the Jews and because of this chose to appropriate 'Jewish' practices. This study takes an alternative approach, examining Judaizers (to paraphrase Peter Lake) through the lens provided by anti-Judaizers.[15] I contend that the Judaizers understood the pejorative meaning of such practices and adopted them as a designation of difference or resistance. Judaism, as we shall see, functioned as a cipher for otherness in this period. At times, the otherness of the Jewish people contributed to philo-semitic feeling, at other times it was manifest in anti-Semitic feeling. At all times, it was manifest in allose-mitic feeling.[16] The pervasiveness of allosemitism in early modern England has been explored in detail, in recent times by Andrew Crome.[17] In other words, Judaizers adopted Jewish practices in part *because* they knew that Jewish practices were considered 'deviant' not in *spite of* this fact. Moreover, I argue that the practices adopted by Tillam, Totney and Traske—circumcision, Sabbatarianism and the 'division of meates'—all functioned (both

13. Lake, 'Anti-Puritanism,' 86–87.

14. Philo-semitism, it has been suggested in recent scholarship, is something of a misnomer. Certainly the positivity of feeling that various Christian groups have historically exhibited towards Jews—which has been referred to as 'philo-semitic'—is not an uncomplicated phenomenon. Nonetheless, its usage is descriptive. For the purposes of this study, I will use the word to refer to a trope, defined by Adam Sutcliffe and Jonathan Karp as 'a tendency towards the admiration of the Jews,' which is nevertheless frequently combined with a 'conversionist desire ultimately to erase Jewish distinctiveness altogether' (Sutcliffe and Karp, *Brief History of Philo-semitism*, 1–4).

15. Lake, 'Anti-Puritanism,' 85.

16. Bauman, 'Allosemitism,' 143–56.

17. Crome, *Christian Zionism and English National Identity*, 11, 22, 24.

intrinsically *and* historically or circumstantially) to denote separation, and difference. As such, Judaizing functioned as a component of a typically Godly 'ethic of social separation,' or, to use a form of expression proper to the period, an ethic of 'singularity.'[18] This dimension is evident in the literature produced by the Judaizers themselves. John Traske looked for the 'general separation of the saints.'[19] Thomas Tillam spoke of the 'virgin train of separated saints.'[20] Thomas Totney enjoined his reader to 'seperate, seperate, seperate, seperate, separate, seperate, seperate.'[21]

It is notable that the concatenation of practices collectively referred to as 'Judaizing,' emerged from a variety of different sectarian settings. The same could be claimed for the practices which were associated with 'Puritanism.' In the Stuart period, the term 'Puritan' denoted those who were concerned ultimately with maintaining distinctiveness between themselves and a majority that they presumed to be reprobate. Often this process involved the active inhabitation of the role of the oppressed minority.[22] This was a presumption that they shared with the originators of Jewish ritual practices, the authors of the Holiness code, and with successive generations of practitioners. In each generation, the practices of Judaism became more and more freighted with association with 'singularity' and distinctiveness. When the Godly appropriated these practices, they too were labelled as outsiders by their peers. They were 'plaguy people,' who 'for feare of infecting others' were 'carefully to be secluded.'[23] As such, mimesis is too superficial a word to describe the deep and complex affinities that the Godly Judaizers felt for these practices. In order to fully 'see things their way,' we must seek to understand the complex matrices of meaning that these rituals communicated.[24] Before exploring *this* approach, however, we must briefly survey the variety of *existing* approaches to the analysis of Puritan Judaizing.

---

18. Milton, 'Religion and Community in Pre-Civil War England,' 70. For examples of the pejorative use of the term 'singularity,' see Ormerod, *Picture of a Puritan*, 33; Burroughs, *Excellency of a Gracious Spirit Delivered in a Treatise*, 151; Baxter, *Non-Conformity without Controversie*, 38.

19. Traske, *Power of Preaching*, A2v.

20. Tillam, *Temple of Lively Stones*, 220.

21. Tany, *My Edict Royal*, 27.

22. Collinson, 'Cohabitation of the Faithful with the Unfaithful,' 56; Spraggon, 'Puritan Iconoclasm in England,' 18; Cambers, *Godly Reading*, 13–14, 22; Walsham, 'Happiness of Suffering,' 56, 58.

23. Falconer, *Briefe Refutation*, 6.

24. Skinner, *Visions of Politics*, 3.

FAMILIARITY AND MIMESIS

William Davies of Hereford, in 1597, prayed that 'England never be defiled by Pope, Turk or Jew.'[25] But it was already too late. Jews—as Cecil Roth and Lucien Wolf demonstrated almost a hundred years ago—began to make their homes in England in the sixteenth century for the first time since the expulsion of 1290. A brief hiatus in the aftermath of the Roderigo Lopes scandal preceded a slow but steady, informal readmission starting in the 1630s.[26] As the seventeenth century wore on, calls from financiers (like Thomas Shirley), jurists (like John Selden) and millenarians (like John Dury) brought about a distinct softening in English attitudes towards the Jews, such that a readmission was all but granted in 1655.[27] This cultural shift facilitated the unveiling of London's small, secret Jewish congregation. On March 24, 1656, a petition was submitted to Cromwell for the liberty of conscience of the Jews of London. It was signed by seven members of the Jewish community—including Menasseh ben Israel—and asked (amongst other concessions) for permission to create a Jewish cemetery.[28] Menasseh ben Israel himself had become a public figure and had spoken at the White-hall conference, supported by Samuel Hartlib, John Dury and Henry Jessey.[29] He had even been accommodated at Cromwell's behest in a house opposite the New Exchange on the Strand.[30] The emergence of this enclave—even of such small number—allowed an equally small number of English Protestants a peek at the ritual life of Judaism.

At the same time, 'real-life' Jews began to appear in travel journals and newsbooks.[31] Thomas Coryat's records of his travels in 1610 included a first hand account of a synagogue service held in Venice and of a circumcision rite held in Istanbul.[32] Coryat's work went into meticulous detail, describing the fabric from which the prayer-shawls in the Venetian synagogue were

25. Davies, *True Relation of the Travailes*, E1r.

26. Endelman, *Jews of Britain*, 18; Wolf, 'Jews in Tudor England,' 73–90; Roth, *History of the Jews in England*, 136–44; Katz, *Jews in the History of England*, 1–14, 49–64, 107–45.

27. Samuel, 'Sir Thomas Shirley's Project for the Jews,' 195–97; Rosenblatt, *Renaissance England's Chief Rabbi*, 49; Guibbory, 'England, Israel, and the Jews,' 31; Popkin 'Can One Be a True Christian,' 44.

28. National Archives, SP 18/101, f. 237.

29. Crome, 'English National Identity,' 281–83; Popkin, *Third Force in Seventeenth-Century Thought*, 94–95; Katz, 'Menasseh ben Israel's Christian Connection,' 117–38.

30. Wolf, *Menasseh ben Israel's Mission to Oliver Cromwell*, xxxvii.

31. Holmberg, *Jews in the Early Modern English Imagination*, 53–105.

32. Coryat, 'Master Thomas Coryates,' 1.10:1825.

made, the brass and pewter of the candlesticks.[33] John Sanderson, meanwhile, travelled to Ottoman Galilee and offered accounts of Jewish life there.[34] Samuel Fisher, a little later in the century, travelled 'from synagogue to synagogue,' around Europe.[35]

In the period spanning the end of the sixteenth and the first decades of the seventeenth century, Englishmen also came into contact with Jews on the continent. In Amsterdam, a growing community of English Separatists rubbed shoulders with a community of Sephardi Jews seeking toleration in the United Provinces.[36] Indeed, many expatriated Puritans—including Hugh Broughton, Henry Ainsworth, and John Paget—actively sought out Jews in order to learn Hebrew and to engage in theological discussion. Ainsworth even used rabbinic literature to inform his exegetical works.[37]

A fourth and more dubious source of information about 'real' Jews came from the fantastical claims of Thomas Thorowgood and of the anonymous authors of the 'Catzius fantasy.' The former claimed that the lost tribes of Israel had been discovered among the natives of North America. The fantastical notion that an army of Jews was being raised by 'Josias Catzius' in 'Illyria, Bithinia and Capadoccia' first appeared in a pamphlet entitled *Doome's Day* in London in 1647.[38]

Some scholars have endeavored to draw a correlation between the reappearance of Jews in English life and letters, and the emergence of Judaizing practices. Bernard Glassman identifies 'contact between Christian and Jews' as a key factor in the emergence of Judaizing. He cites John Traske as an example of this phenomenon.[39] Glassman's claim is that renewed contact between Jews and English Protestants, and the sympathy this contact elicited, created a desire—in some—to become more like Jews, and so to adopt some of their ritual practices. Keith Sprunger has drawn a connection between Traskism and the meetings of Jews and Christians in Amsterdam. 'Judaizing,' writes Sprunger, 'was an unintended consequence' of these interactions.[40]

---

33. Coryat, *Coryat's Crudities*, 232.

34. Sanderson, 'Sundry the Personal Voyages performed by John Sanderson,' 2.9:1614–40.

35. Popkin, 'Spinoza and Samuel Fisher,' 230.

36. Sprunger, *Trumpets from the Tower*, 60–74.

37. Ainsworth, *Annotations* 5v.

38. Thorowgood, *Jewes in America*, 3; *Doomes-day*, 1.

39. Glassman, *Anti-Semitic Stereotypes without Jews*, 78.

40. Sprunger, *Trumpets from the Tower*, 70.

It is certainly true that Thomas Tillam and Thomas Totney *were* in-terested in 'real-life' Jews, *were* moved by their plight and *were* intrigued by their rituals. The presence of Jews in England and the emergence of records of Jewish life in Europe more widely fed into this fascination. Thomas Tot-ney, for example, wrote to express empathy with the Jews of Amsterdam.[41] Thomas Tillam *believed* that he had met a Jew, before it transpired to be the 'false Jew,' Thomas Ramsay.[42] Moreover, he confessed that he 'trembled' when he read a correspondent's account of the Jewish congregation in London.[43]

Overall, however, this analysis is incomplete. Firstly, it fails to account for the Judaizing practices of Glassman's primary exemplar. At the time of John Traske's activities, the entire Jewish population of London almost certainly numbered less than one hundred. In fact, as far as most people knew 'there were no Jews in England.' Katz writes that the only Jews that English people encountered were either literary, biblical or imaginary.[44] It is unlikely that Traske would have directly encountered Jews during his so-journ in London, let alone during the time that he spent in Somerset and Cambridgeshire. Whilst he did, later, become associated with Henry Jessey (an advocate of Menasseh ben Israel's) the chronology does not support this being a source of his Judaizing practices.

It is possible that Totney, Tillam and Traske may have *read* about Jews in travel accounts, but even if they had encountered Jews in this way, it does not by any means account for a dramatic shift in attitude towards a posi-tive appraisal of Jewish ritual observation. As Holmberg has demonstrated, even the most curious of observers wrote excoriatingly of Jewish rituals. Thomas Coryat declared Jewish worship to be carnal and irreverent.[45] As Eliane Glaser has demonstrated, the topos of Talmud, rediscovered during this period by Christian apologetes, was co-opted as a rhetorical device with which to stigmatize and delegitimize 'carnal' Catholicism and Laudianism.[46] The 'impious blasphemies' of the Talmud were, for Christians, evidence of the 'depth of divine vengeance, which in this blinded Nation wee may *heare and feare.*'[47] Such texts *accentuated* rather than mitigating the other-ness of Judaism.

41. Katz, 'Restoration of the Jews,' 187–93; Tany, *High News for Hierusalem*, 12.

42. Tillam, *Banners of Love*, 11.

43. Tillam, *Seventh-Day Sabbath*, 51.

44. Katz, *Jews in the History of England*, 107–9.

45. Coryat, *Coryat's Crudities*, 231.

46. Glaser, *Judaism without Jews*, 66, 76.

47. Purchas, *Purchas His Pilgrimage*, 160.

Traskites did travel to Amsterdam in order to seek out contact with Jews and in order to be circumcised.[48] However, this contact does not explain the fact that the Traskites were already Judaizing before they travelled to Amsterdam. Indeed, their tendency towards adopting Jewish ritual provided the impetus for the journey. Moreover, the attitude of the English Calvinists in Amsterdam towards Jews and Jewish ceremonies did not appear to facilitate irenic interaction. Both Broughton and Paget were interested in engaging with Jews but grew increasingly intolerant when they encountered a lack of enthusiasm for abandoning rituals. It appears that their interactions were characterized by a mutual antagonism, rather than osmosis. Broughton 'confronted' Jews with Christian apologetics and found to his chagrin that the Jews responded by 'speaking openly against Christianity.'[49] Broughton apparently encountered the same response that George Whitehead did when he attempted to convert an 'assembly' of Jews at 'Bevers Marks' and that Coryat received when he confronted the Jews of Venice with their denial of Christ.[50] The perceived intransigence of the Jews led Broughton and Paget to the conclusion that the Jews were even *more* irredeemable, even more alien than they had previously thought. In this, their journey mirrored that of Luther's fifty years previously.[51] The Jews were 'obstinate' Paget wrote.[52] They were 'dogs,' thought Broughton.[53] Thirdly, as Katchen has noted, the interest in Hebrew texts that the Amsterdam Separatists exhibited, made them particularly wary of the charge of Judaizing.[54] This claim is corroborated by the record of an interaction between Ainsworth and the imprisoned, English Judaizer Thomas Woolsey. Woolsey had been a hero of the Separatist movement in the years before the exodus of 1585. But when he began to argue for the 'separation of meates' he was sternly castigated and anathematized by his erstwhile co-religionists.[55] Overall, the experience of the Separatists at Amsterdam appears to have hardened, rather than softening, the division between Jews and Christians.

In the Commonwealth period, those who advocated for the readmission of the Jews did so not in principled defence of the liberty of conscience,

48. Pagitt, *Heresiography*, 180.

49. Israel, *European Jewry in the Age of Mercantilism*, 84.

50. Whitehead, 'For the Jews,' 63; Coryat, *Coryates Crambe*, D4r; *Coryate's Crudities*, 236.

51. Roper, *Martin Luther*, 391–97.

52. Paget, *Arrow Against the Separation of the Brownistes*, 26.

53. Lightfoot, 'Preface Giving Some Accompt of the Authours Life,' B1v.

54. Katchen, *Christian Hebraists and Dutch Rabbis*, 9–10.

55. Moody, 'Thomas Woolsey'; Reynolds, *Godly Reformers*, 92; Ofwod, *Advertisement to Ihon Declcluse*, 40–41; Ainsworth et al., *Seasonable Treatise*, 2.

but rather in the cause of conversion. As such, whether or not they truly 'loved' Jews, their interest was in the *retreat*, rather than the *advance*, of Jewish ceremonies. Thomas Collier welcomed the readmission in the hope that the 'leprosy' of Judaism, could be 'washed away' by exposure to English Protestantism.[56] Even John Dury was convinced that the Jews, upon their readmission, would need to remain ghettoized and sequestered from the Christian population to prevent the spread of Judaism.[57] Thomas Barlow, the late seventeenth-century Bishop of Lincoln, was, by the standards of the day, a champion of philo-semitism. He lamented that 'the Jews' had been 'inhumanly and barbarously used' and advocated for their readmission.[58] His primary concern, however, was not that Jews should be allowed to practice Judaism on British soil, but rather that they should be invited to be a captive audience for Christian apologetes. '(The Jews) should be enjoyned,' he wrote, 'to admit of friendly Collations and Disputation. ... For there will be little hopes (or possibility) of their Conversion, if they be permitted obstinately to refuse all means of doing it.'[59] Those who resisted conversion should be sequestered, ghettoized, separated and rendered 'singular' using the same methods as those used on pre-expulsion Jewry. Their freedom was to be 'reduced' said Barlow. Jews should 'not be permitted to wear Garments exactly of the Christian Fashion, but are to have distinct Habits, that all might know them to be Jews.'[60] He advised that the Jews should not be allowed 'to come abroad on Good Friday.'[61] They were not to be allowed to be doctors or soldiers. 'They should not,' wrote Barlow 'be allowed to carry any dignity.'[62]

David S. Katz concluded that the impetus for the readmission project was to remove a stumbling block to the conversion of the Jews.[63] As such, Judaizing could be seen as a mirror image of this process. But desire for the conversion of the Jews was just one amongst many reasons for the renewed focus on Jews in England during the mid-seventeenth century. James Shapiro has argued that the primary function of the readmission debate was to bolster the salience of English national identity in the context of

56. Collier, *Brief Answer to Some of the Objections*, 12.

57. Dury, *Case of Conscience*, 8–9.

58. Barlow, 'Case of the Jews,' 8.

59. Barlow, 'Case of the Jews,' 73.

60. Barlow, 'Case of the Jews,' 67, 71.

61. Barlow, 'Case of the Jews,' 71.

62. Barlow, 'Case of the Jews,' 72, 68.

63. Katz, *Philo-Semitism*, 166.

the perceived threat of 'cultural miscegenation' (and social disintegration).[64] Where Ranulf Higden used anti-Jewish myths to bolster a sense of national coherence in the aftermath of the Baron's War, William Prynne rehearsed precisely the same myths in the aftermath of the Civil War.[65] Captain Francis Willoughby feared that the Westminster Conference would lead to the conditions whereby 'another nation' would be 'suffered to live amongst us.'[66] Eliane Glaser offers a similar thesis, accentuating the role of Judaism as theoretical leverage in intra-Protestant, ecclesiological debate.[67] Andrew Crome has posited a third factor, placing emphasis on the dissemination of Judeocentric eschatology during this period. Millenarians were concerned to preserve the otherness of the Jews *in lieu* of their repatriation. As part of this process, English Protestants would play a providential role—helping to facilitate the restoration—but would not be the lead actors in the apocalyptic denouement. Crome argues that for this reason the *advocates* of readmission served to 'fetishize' the Jew and—in doing so—'emphasized the otherness of the Jew just as much as the opponents of readmission.'[68] All three of these explanations suggest an 'othering' of Judaism in early-modern English culture. For Katz's conversionist philo-semites, Jewish ritual represented a 'stumbling block to the conversion of the Jews.' For those who 'fetishized' the Jew—whether as an eschatological 'type' or as the antithesis to 'Englishness'—Jewish ritual itself was a designation of 'otherness.'

Awareness of Jews—and being confronted with the *humanity* of Jews, therefore—did not lead ineluctably to sympathy for the Jews. Nor, as we have seen, did sympathy for the Jews necessarily lead to the admiration of their ceremonies. Indeed, the opposite was usually the case. Certainly, admiration for—or fascination with—Jewish ceremonies did not necessarily lead to their adoption. Whilst the readmission debate did capture the imaginations of many, it did not directly 'cause' the 'new and unprecedented phenomenon' of Judaizing.[69] This question requires a consideration of what these Jewish ceremonies *meant* to early modern English Protestants.

---

64. Shapiro, *Shakespeare and the Jews*, 40, 43, 88, 189.

65. Bale, 'Framing Antisemitic Exempla,' 19–47; Prynne, *Short Demurrer to the Jewes*, 35.

66. National Archives, SP 18/102, f. 33.

67. Glaser, *Judaism without Jews*, 127–29.

68. Crome, 'English National Identity,' 280–301 (quotation at 299).

69. Shapiro, *Shakespeare and the Jews*, 8.

JUDAIZING AND TURNING THE WORLD UPSIDE DOWN

'Judaizing,' Christopher Hill wrote, 'meant looking back to the customs and traditions of a tribal society, still relatively egalitarian and democratic.' This act of 'looking back' allowed some of the Godly to develop 'destructive criticisms of the institutions that had been built up in medieval society.' As the seventeenth century wore on, Hill observed, the charge of 'Judaizing' became a slander used as a 'religious expression . . . of political theory.' He cited the use of the word 'Judaizing' by Sir Robert Berkeley to denote 'utter ruin and subversion.' Accusing an interlocutor of being a Jew or of Judaizing—for Hill—had 'political as well as theological connotations.'[70]

Aspects of this analysis are fruitful. It is clear, for example, that Judaizing was considered intrinsically threatening to the status quo. Bishop Morton urged his ministers to 'observe' those 'as are said to encline to Judaisme.'[71] The anxiety that gave rise to the anti-Sabbatarianism of James I's reign shows that Judaizing was seen as a subversion of secular and ecclesiastical authority.[72] Nicholas McDowell's analysis of the Traskite controversy confirms the association of Judaizing with 'sedition.' The Stuart authorities, McDowell argues, weaponized this association in an attempt to further marginalize Puritan opponents of the *Book of Sports.* The trial of Traske before the Star Chamber was a 'public spectacle of state discipline.'[73] Crome makes a similar point in relation to the accusations levelled at Henry Finch.[74] Even if not in quite the sense that Hill intended, it is true that Judaism was in some sense analogous to insubordination, and was treated as such by the authorities in Stuart England.

It is also true that, during the period of the Civil War, Parliamentarians saw the association of their political philosophy with Hebraic models of governance as a way to undercut Royalist claims of longevity and, therefore, of legitimacy. Thomas Harrison's proposal that the Barebones Parliament be organized on the model of the Sanhedrin was received favorably.[75] James Harrington's *Oceana* (in its 1656 edition) was approved by Cromwell.[76] More radical elements also used this typology. William Everard

---

70. Hill, *Society and Puritanism in Pre-Revolutionary England*, 204–5.

71. Tait, 'Declaration of Sports for Lancashire,' 561–68.

72. Parker, *English Sabbath*, 139–61.

73. McDowell, 'Stigmatizing of Puritans as Jews,' 348–63 (quotation at 349).

74. Crome, 'Proper and Naturall Meaning of the Prophets,' 734.

75. Katz, *Sabbath and Sectarianism*, 2.

76. Harrington, *Oceana*, A2r.

drew clear associations between the 'Diggers' and 'the Jews'.[77] Whether this tendency can be attributed to a 'primitivist' impulse or to a euphemized but 'destructive criticism' is up for debate. The assertion that Judaizing denoted an eschatological view of history, and as such functioned as a form of 'resistance' is certainly valid. The use of eschatological history as a discursive form of resistance is an identifiable characteristic of innumerable religious phenomena. Demonstrative identification with an historical, mythologized polity problematizes the necessity of the individual's obedience to authorities and renders the necessity of that power *itself* temporal and, implicitly, contingent. This was true not only of the *readers* of the Biblical apocalypses, but also, as Anathea Portier-Young has shown, of their *authors*.[78]

In this sense, Hill is correct to identify Judaizing with an attitude of opposition towards the status quo. Where this study parts ways with his analysis, however, is in his understanding of this opposition as 'criticism.' Criticism is a form of action oriented towards facilitating *change* in the interlocutor. The figures with whom this study is concerned were not primarily concerned with affecting change in the actions of the majority. They were concerned with distinguishing themselves *from* the majority.

Others have claimed that Judaizing formed part of a Godly theology of liberation, in the context of the Parliamentary struggle. Quentin Skinner argued that the foremost concern of the Godly party in 1642 was 'classical Liberty.' Drawing on a distinctively Roman conception of liberty—'that what takes away your liberty is the mere fact of living at the mercy of someone else'—a number of apologists for the Parliamentary cause published texts in the early 1640s which (on this basis) legitimized insurrectionary action against the monarch. The most 'sophisticated' of these was the anonymously published *Vindication* of 1642 which depicted a monarch convinced that he 'could do what he list' and therefore was worthy of the name tyrant.[79] John Morrill, meanwhile, famously argued that the English revolution was the 'last war of religion.' It was 'the force of religion that drove minorities to fight,' Morrill argued, not 'the localist and the legal-constitutionalist perceptions of misgovernment.'[80] Members of the Parliamentary forces were motivated by the desire to establish 'true religion' in England, threatened as

77. Whitelock, *Memorials*, 383; Jowitt, 'Consolation of Israel,' 87–100.

78. Murrell and Williams, 'Black Biblical Hermeneutics of Rastafari,' 326–49; Carter, 'James C. Scott and New Testament Studies,' 81–94; Portier-Young, *Apocalypse Against Empire*, 202–17.

79. Skinner, 'Classical Liberty,' 26–27; Ward, *Vindication of Parliament and Their Proceedings*, 6.

80. Morrill, 'Religious Context of the English Civil War,' 157.

it was by Laud, the Spanish match, and any number of Baalish practices.[81] More recently, John Coffey has attempted to synthesise these two perspectives, exploring the notion of a seventeenth-century 'liberation theology.' Coffey suggests that the English revolution was indeed a war of religion, fought by zealots.[82] Crucially, however, he portrays these zealots as being motivated by a Biblical concept of freedom from enslavement. This concept, Coffey argues, emerged from the mythology of Exodus and the ministry of Jesus, rather than the 'neo-Roman understanding of civil liberty.'[83] Coffey acknowledges a debt to Michael Walzer who, thirty years ago, claimed that the Exodus narrative was the basis for—as he called it—'Puritan Judaizing.' The Exodus narrative functioned as a grounding of religion in politics, Walzer argued. In seeking a 'carnal' Kingdom of God, the Puritan revolutionaries mirrored the concerns of their Hebrew antecedents.[84] For Walzer, the concept of Godly revolution found its first iteration in Calvinist thought, which shifted political thought away from the prince and towards the saint. This process would be capitalized on by revolutionary political thinkers of the enlightenment and beyond. 'What was said of the saints,' Walzer writes 'would later be said of the citizens.'[85]

Coffey's understanding of the Liberationist elements of Godly thought in the Commonwealth period is instructive. Nonetheless, his analysis does not fully explore the reasons *why* those texts which celebrated liberation were embraced by the Godly, nor what the meaning of Judaizing rituals— other than as a form of mimesis—was for the Godly Judaizers themselves. The longitudinal nature of Walzer's study aptly demonstrates the many examples of Exodus based 'liberation theologies' that did not result in Judaizing, as such demonstrating that one does not necessarily lead to the other. It would be difficult to argue that the rituals themselves *intrinsically* denote a political notion of liberty. I want to argue, following Coffey's analysis, that the Godly were informed by their theological convictions in their desire to denote liberation and autonomy in their devotional practices. However, I will argue that the roots of this desire lay in a profound and far reaching need to 'resist': to demonstrate their *distinctiveness from* the majority, rather than to '*criticize*' the majority. This was both a circumstantial *and* an intrinsic valence of the practices themselves.

81. Morrill, *Nature of the English Revolution*, 68.

82. Morrill, 'Liberation Theology?,' 27–48.

83. Skinner, *Liberty Before Liberalism*, ix.

84. Walzer, *Exodus and Revolution*, 123.

85. Walzer, *Revolution of the Saints*, 2.

HEBRAISM AND MIMETIC PHILO-SEMITISM

A quite different explanation for the emergence of Judaizing Puritanism can be found in the work of the intellectual historians David S. Katz and Richard Popkin. Katz and Popkin argue that Puritan Judaizing was an outgrowth of early-modern Hebraism. During the period of the interregnum, figures like William Gouge, Samuel Hartlib, John Dury, John Selden and Henry Jessey learnt Hebrew, sought Jewish interlocutors and studied Jewish books of jurisprudence, ethics and mysticism. And when discussion arose regarding the readmission of the Jews, they were at the forefront. They admired and befriended Menasseh ben Israel and sponsored his celebrity.[86] Most of all, they desired for the repair of relations between Jews and Christians. 'Jews,' Katz writes 'were presented . . . in a very favourable light' by Protestant Hebraists of this period.[87] At the same time, as Popkin demonstrated, Jews engaged with Christian scholars and participated in the process of generating an irenic, enlightened and nomothetic approach to ethics. This *positivity*, this 'philo-semitism,' provided the basis for the emergence of Judaizing practices, they claim.

Some European Jews were engaged in messianic expectation during this period and they anticipated that the coming of the messiah might resolve the fundamental sticking point between Jews and Christians: the ultimacy of the incarnation. Rabbi Nathan Shapira—who travelled to Europe in 1657 in order to raise funds for the Jews of Jerusalem—was described in a pamphlet by John Dury as a promising candidate for conversion to a kind of 'Jewish-Christianity.' According to Dury, Shapira believed that the messiah had appeared many times and in many forms, including in the form of Jesus of Nazareth. Moreover, Shapira believed that the faith of the Jews *and* of the millenarian Christians would lay the foundations for the future coming of the Jewish messiah. Dury interpreted this to mean the Second Coming.[88] The refocussing of attentions towards a millenarian future, and the concern to reduce religion to morality, allowed figures like Jean Bodin and Baruch Spinoza to occupy an irenic space between Judaism and Christianity.[89] For

---

86. Popkin, 'Christian Jews and Jewish Christians,' 57–72; 'Christian Interest and Concerns about Sabbatai Zevi,' 91–107; Katz, 'Jewish Sabbath and Christian Sunday,' 119–30; 'Menasseh ben Israel's Christian Connection,' 117–38; *Philo-semitism*, 216–20; 'English Redemption and Jewish Readmission,' 73–91; 'Popkin and the Jews,' 213–28.

87. Katz, *Jews in the History of England*, 112.

88. Dury, *Information Concerning the Present State*, 17; Popkin, 'Rabbi Nathan Shapira's Visit to Amsterdam,' 185–205.

89. Popkin, 'Christian Interest and Concerns about Sabbatai Zevi,' 91–107.

Popkin, the Naylerite moment and the rise of Sabbateanism further opened the door to a millenarian future of Judeo-Christian irenicism.[90]

Popkin claims that the emergence of a secular morality and the privatization of religion was spurred, in part, by this millenarian turn in the seventeenth century. Figures like Moses Germanus, described as a 'Christian, who had become a Jew and [who] offered a Jewish way of accepting part of Christianity, namely Jesus as an important ethical teacher,' loom large in Popkin's analysis.[91] This tendency filtered through the culture via the media of popular literature—most obviously through fantastical travel journals. Here, English Protestants read about encounters with Caraites, with practitioners of 'pure Judaism,' and with Siberian Jews who 'knew nothing of the Talmud' but whose religion was founded on a simple, nomothetic principle: 'to live according to reason . . . sufficient lawgiver, rabbi and interpreter to themselves.'[92] These philo-semitic 'discoveries'—prompted in part by the allure of a long-awaited reconciliation between Jews and Christians—caused (and were caused *by*) a drift towards the kind of secularism and privatization of religion that Popkin identified in the work of Spinoza and Bodin. 'Jewish Christianity,' therefore, was 'not just an oddity or curiosity.' Rather it 'increased the drive towards a more tolerant world' and transformed Christianity and Judaism 'into ethical views, thereby creating modern liberal outlooks.' Tillamism and Traskism, the adoption by Christians of 'Jewish' rituals, according to this reading, are nothing more than 'unintended consequences,' 'blind alleys and religious lunacies,' bi-products and misapprehensions.[93]

Popkin and Katz's analysis comes close to conflating philo-semitism and Judaizing. But as Aaron Katchen has noted, philo-semitic Hebraists were often amongst those most 'on their guard' against Judaizing.[94] Philo-semites

90. Popkin, 'Christian Interest and Concerns About Sabbatai Zevi,' 91–107; *Third Force*, 125, 364; Scholem, *Sabbatai Sevi*, 461–591; Damrosch, *Sorrows of the Quaker Jesus*, 115–322.

91. Popkin, 'Christian Jews and Jewish Christians,' 69.

92. Popkin, *Third Force*, 365; Marana, *Letters Writ by a Turkish Spy*, 104. Caraism was used for rhetorical, millenarian, and political purposes by these scholars but the existence of Caraism in early modern Europe was not itself 'fantastical.' A number of Christian scholars during this period offered serious analysis of Caraite writings. The most notable example of this in the seventeenth century was Richard Simon, a Catholic Priest who acquired and studied Aaron ben Joseph's commentary on the Pentateuch, *Sefer ha-Mivhar*, but Dury's correspondent, Johannes Rittangel, also made contact with Caraites in Poland (Fenton, 'European Discovery of Karaism,' 3–7; Berg, *Religious Currents and Cross-Currents*, 48).

93. Popkin, 'Christian Jews and Jewish Christians,' 69; Katz, *Philo-Semitism*, 107–10.

94. Katchen, *Christian Hebraists*, 9.

like John Dury, William Gouge, and John Selden—who sought out Jews and Jewish learning—were actively averse to the adoption of elements of the ceremonial law. Selden's 'central intellectual project' was to demonstrate that Natural Law was revealed (as opposed to innate) whilst maintaining that it was revealed to all humanity through Adam.[95] Thus, drawing on the Talmudic concept of the Noachide covenant, Selden delineated a greater distinction between the ceremonial law—revealed to Moses—and the moral law, revealed to Adam. For all his appreciation of Jewish jurisprudence, Selden saw it as a facility of the *separateness* of the Jews, writing that 'God at the first gave Laws to all Mankind, but afterwards he gave peculiar Laws to the Jews.'[96] Jewish law was intended for '*the land of Canaan*,' for '*the Jewes and their brethren only.*'[97] As Sutcliffe has shown, Selden's 'love for *halacha*' had 'very little to do with relations between Christians and Jews.' Rather, it was motivated by Selden's interest in identifying the *distinctions* between Jewish and English jurisprudence.[98] Selden was almost uniquely tolerant in his attitude towards the Jews but, nonetheless, he was critical of Jewish rituals, *especially* when he saw them mimicked by the Godly. There was 'no superstition more truly and properly so called,' he wrote than 'observing the Sabboth after the Jewish Manner.'[99]

When Lancelot Andrewes denounced John Traske in the Star Chamber, he critiqued Traske's Judaizing using a *reductio ad absurdum*. If Traske honored Jewish ceremonies, Andrewes argued, he should also honor the practice of circumcision. Selden agreed. Those who wished to adopt Judaizing practices, he argued, should first be circumcised.[100] This action would render the actor as outside of the structures of Christian Law and within the structure of Jewish Law. It would separate the actor. Selden himself recognized the interplay between Jewish 'singularity' and anti-Judaic malice.[101]

Those who *were* enamoured of the project of reuniting 'enlightened' Jews and Christians around a 'natural,' moral, religion were equally disdainful of the kind of ceremonies that Traske, Totney and Tillam adopted. John Dury expressed affection for Jews. But the topos of 'the Jew' was bifurcated in Dury's thought. He avowed his admiration for Jewish wisdom whilst at the same time denouncing Judaism as a religion 'full of superstitious imaginary

---

95. Somerville, 'John Selden,' 437–47.

96. Selden, *Table Talk*, 69.

97. Selden, *Tyth-gatherers*, 17.

98. Sutcliffe, 'Philo-Semitic Moment?,' 78–80.

99. Selden, *Table Talk*, 166; Rosenblatt, *Renaissance England's Chief Rabbi*, 176–80.

100. Selden, *Tyth-gatherers*, 21.

101. Selden, *Table Talk*, 69.

conceits.' Like many of his contemporaries, Dury postulated the existence of two discrete Judaisms, each corresponding to these different elements. The 'Caraites' drew out 'necessary and profitable duties' by 'comparing one text with another.' They were concerned with the 'inward,' whilst the 'Pharisees' were 'outward' in their worship and in their ethics. The Pharisees practiced usury, the Caraites did not. Whilst the Caraites engaged in discourse with their Christian peers, the Pharisees are sequestered, separated.[102] William Gouge, a figure who—along with Henry Finch—was closely associated with millenarian philo-semitism during this period, was equally critical of the Judaizing tendency as he perceived it. In a sermon, delivered before the Long Parliament in 1645, Gouge described 'Jewish Christians' as 'conformers to that servile pedagogy':

> For what fish, fowl and beast were then forbidden, they still hold unlawfull to be eaten, though God hath forbidden us to call that unclean which he hath cleansed. . . . The last day also of the week they still keep for their *Sabbath*.

Gouge feared that such practices *prevented* the reconciliation of Christians and Jews:

> These *Jewish Christians* doe both justifie the poor blinde Jews . . . and also doe harden their hearts, and make them bold in cleaving to their Law, when they see such as professe themselves Christians, come so near there unto.[103]

Gouge would later attempt to rescue Mary Chester from the Traskites.[104] Jeremiah Ives shared these fears, expressing concern that Jews encountering Sabbatarianism would consider Christians 'mad.' Sabbatarianism, he feared, would prevent the 'conversion of the world.'[105]

In other words, whilst Ives, Gouge and Dury's understanding of Judaism can be assimilated into a broader pattern of 'millenarian philo-semitism,' it was a far cry from those Puritans who actively adopted the 'traditions and ceremonies, and foolish curiosities' of the 'Pharisees.' In Dury's terms, Thomas Tillam and John Traske were closer to being 'Pharisees,' than 'pure Jews.' Moreover, 'philo-semites' specifically rejected Judaizing, on the grounds that it was deleterious to the progress of the conversion of the Jews and that it jeopardized the pristine outsiderliness of the Jews. A straight line,

102. Dury, 'Epistolicall Discourse,' C2r, 2v, 3r; Berg, *Religious Currents*, 48–50.

103. Gouge, *Progresse of Divine Providence*, 23–24.

104. Pagitt, *Heresiography*, 193.

105. Ives, *Saturday No Sabbath*, a2v.

therefore, *cannot* be drawn between affinity for Hebrew, or sympathy for the Jews, and the desire to adopt Jewish ritual customs.

There is an even more fundamental problem with using the same analytical tools to address millenarian philo-semites (like Dury and Selden and Gouge) and the phenomenon of Judaizing. The philo-semitic tendency, as described by Popkin, was informed by a desire to develop a collective, consensual, enlightened and nomothetic morality. For the key figures of *this* study, on the other hand, the objective was almost diametrically opposite. Far from engaging in practices that they believed would facilitate consensus, Tillam, Traske and Totney actively and strenuously asserted an ethic of 'singularity.' They desired, by their practices, *not* to build bridges, but rather to build walls, to create churches 'compassed round with walls of fire': to create a form of religion defined by its being 'different to the religion of most people.'[106]

In his essay, 'Allosemitism: Premodern, Modern and Post-modern,' Zymgunt Bauman notes the confluence of philo-Semitism and anti-Semitism in the Christian tendency towards allosemitism. Whilst Christians sometimes express sentiments of positivity towards 'the Jews,' and at other times trade in anti-Judaic canards, both activities serve only to accentuate the otherness of the Jew. Popkin and others might be correct in suggesting that the early modern period in Europe saw a surge in philo-semitic sentiment, but the claim that this served to perforate the boundary between Christians and Jews is superficial.

A deeper and unresolved question remains from this discussion. It concerns the fundamental role of the figure of the Jew and Judaism in early modern millenarian thought. It is to this discussion that we turn next.

THE ESCHATOLOGICAL ROLE OF THE JEWS

A significant shift occurred in the reading of the apocalyptic texts of the New and Old Testaments in the late sixteenth and early seventeenth centuries. New attention was paid to those passages—Ezekiel 37, Romans 11, Revelation 7—that appeared to explicitly place the Jews at the center of the eschatological drama. This shift, signalled by the commentaries of John Napier, Henry Finch, John Archer, William Aspinwall, Thomas Tillinghast, Joseph Mede, Thomas Goodwin and—perhaps most significantly—Thomas Brightman, was to usher the Jews to the forefront of the English

---

106. Traske, *Heaven's Joy*, 149; Collinson, 'Godly Preachers and Zealous Magistrates,' 9.

popular imagination.[107] Reflecting on this, some commentators have drawn a connection between Judaizing modes of Godly devotion—as exhibited by Traske, Tillam and Totney—and the Judeocentric turn in Reformed Protestant eschatology.[108] There is significant merit in exploring the connection between these two trends and there are profound interactions between the apocalyptic and the Judaizing impulses. However, this analysis will stop short of claiming that new 'admiration' for the Jews, elicited by Judeocentric eschatology, was the direct cause of the Judaizing phenomenon.

Amillenialism, from the patristic era until the end of the sixteenth century, represented the mainstream of eschatological thought within Christianity. Augustine had claimed that the concept of a terrestrial millennium, as described in the twentieth chapter of Revelation, was a figurative one and that the millennium described by John was already being fulfilled in the advance of Christianity.[109] The Protestant Reformation did little—at first—to shift this consensus. The thought-leaders of the Reformation, both in England and on the continent, refuted the doctrine of millenarianism. It was condemned in the Augsburg Confession, the Second Helvetic Constitution, and the Fourty-Two Articles.[110] As they debunked the notion that there would be a thousand-year reign of the saints on earth, so they rejected—in full—the corresponding prophecies relating to the Jews.[111] The notion that a millennial reign of the saints would dawn, that the Jews would be repatriated to Jerusalem and that they would be converted *en masse*, was—to use Howard Hotson's phrase—an 'error almost universally condemned.'[112]

In the seventeenth century, nonetheless, large numbers English Reformed Protestants began to turn towards millenarianism.[113] 'The first Englishman' to adopt the Judeo-centrist view was Thomas Brightman.[114] Brightman's commentaries on Revelation and the Canticles prognosticated the triumph of the converted Jews over the Turks and the restoration of Israel to Jerusalem. The Jews would become the 'Kings of the East.'[115] Henry

---

107. Cogley, 'Fall of the Ottoman Empire,' 304–32; Toon, 'Latter Day Glory,' 23–42.

108. Katz, *Philo-Semitism*, 107–20.

109. Augustine, *City of God* 20.7–8; Cohn, *Pursuit of Millennium*, 29.

110. Hotson, *Paradise Postponed*, 3.

111. Crome, 'Proper and Naturall Meaning,' 728; Toon, *Puritans, the Millennium and the Future of Israel*, 19.

112. Hotson, *Paradise Postponed*, 3.

113. Firth, *Apocalyptic Tradition in Reformation Britain*; Ball, *Great Expectation*; Bauckham, *Tudor Apocalypse*; Cogley, 'Fall of the Ottoman Empire,' 306–7; Bozeman, *To Live Ancient Lives*, 202–12; Cohen, 'Two Roads to the Puritan Millenium,' 322–38.

114. Bozeman, *To Live Ancient Lives*, 206.

115. Brightman, *Commentary on the Canticles*, 1051; *Revelation of the Apocalypse*,

Finch's *The World's Restauration*, published in 1620, went further, claiming that the political hegemony of millenarian Jewish rule would extend across the globe.[116] The latter claim, in particular, inflamed a political controversy and landed Finch in prison.

The development of Judeocentric eschatology, during this period, has been read in light of a variety of wider religious, political and cultural developments. In part, according to Peter Toon, the emergence of Judeocentric eschatology can be attributed to 'interest in the Hebrew Language . . . interest in Jewish studies . . . and the developing conviction that the Bible . . . was the Word of God.'[117] The link between 'philo-semitism' and Judeocentric eschatology is a tenuous one, however. Brightman and other Judeocentrists expressed plainly anti-Semitic and anti-Judaic sentiments. As such, Philip Almond contends that anti-Catholicism and 'anti-Islamism,' rather than philo-Judaism, provided the basis for Brightman's innovations.[118] In addition to Almond's claims, Nabil Matar emphasized the importance of Judeocentric millenarianism in the development of British imperialist ideology.[119] This second interpretation has been refuted in the work of both Richard Cogley and Andrew Crome. For Cogley, the proto-imperialist reading of Brightman and Finch misapprehends—and indeed under-estimates—the role given to the Jews in these texts. Instead, Cogley situates Judeocentric millenarianism in the context of the primitivist turn.[120] Judeocentrists, he argues, 'understood the millennium as the re-creation of the apostolic church,' a resumption of the earliest form of Christianity in Palestine.[121] Andrew Crome offers a third alternative, suggesting that Brightman's innovation was hermeneutic. The shift towards the 'literal' reading of sacred texts that played such a fundamental part in the emergence of Puritan practical divinity, also played a role in changing the way figures like Brightman, Thomas Draxe, Henry Finch and others read prophetic texts. It led them to 're-literalize' prophecy.[122] As such, according to Crome, the Judeo-centrism of Brightman and others should not be read as a cipher for wider political or religious concerns but rather should be taken at face value.

116. Finch, *Worlds Great Restauration*.
117. Toon, 'Latter Day Glory,' 23–24.
118. Almond, 'Thomas Brightman,' 3–25.
119. Matar, *Islam in Britain*, 167–83.
120. Bozeman, *To Live Ancient Lives*, 193–226.
121. Cogley, 'Fall of the Ottoman Empire,' 330.
122. Crome, 'Proper and Naturall Meaning of the Prophets,' 737.

The emergence of this specifically millenarian form of Judeo-centrism has been associated by some scholars with the Judaizing turn. The argument follows that Brightman and Finch had offered such a positive appraisal of the role of the Jews in the eschatological drama that some of the Godly sought to fulfil that role themselves. Thomas Totney, David Katz suggests, was so smitten with the eschatological topos of 'the Jew' that he sought to take on the role, becoming circumcised, announcing his own Jewish identity and initiating the restoration in his final ill-fated mission.[123] 'The forewarnings of the Old Testament and St. John's vision of the 144,000,' Ariel Hessayon writes 'helped stress the identification of God's elect with Israel.'[124] This, it is suggested, formed a scriptural basis for Judaizing.

Andrew Crome disputes this link. Judeocentric eschatology, he demonstrates, served to buffer rather than to perforate the membrane between Judaism and Christianity. The maintenance of distinct prophecies for Christians and for Jews better served to demonstrate that God worked through nations his wonders to perform.[125] Brightman's hermeneutic innovations led the Godly reader towards the commitment that 'the Jews were to have promises *entirely separate* to those made to Christians.' Christianity and Judaism, in the context of Brightman's eschatology, were 'sharply divided.' Certainly Judeo-centrist millenarians did not 'call for Gentiles to follow Jewish laws.' Brightman himself responded to this suggestion with a curt 'God forbid.'[126] But much more fundamentally, the Judeocentric, eschatological approach *precluded* such a move. It served to deepen, to ontologically reduce, the distinction between Jews and Christians. As such, Brightman's reasoning made Judaizing 'an impossibility.'[127] Postmillennialist and amillenialist readings of Romans 11:26 *had* allowed for a degree of fluidity in the relation between Jews and Christians. Calvin believed that the text denoted 'spiritual Israel . . . the elect of all ages, places and nationalities.'[128] The authors of the Geneva Bible commentaries believed that 'the nation of the Jewes' but 'not every [Jew]' would be converted in the end times.[129] For these figures, the topos of Israel denoted the people of God: a confluence of the 'Old Testament saints' and the 'Gospel saints.' Even those who believed

---

123. Katz, *Philo-Semitism*, 107–110.

124. Hessayon, *Gold Tried in the Fire*, 134.

125. Crome, *Christian Zionism and English National Identity*, 11, 22, 24.

126. Crome, 'Proper and Naturall Meaning of the Prophets,' 735–36; Brightman, *Commentary on the Canticles*, 1060.

127. Crome, 'Proper and Naturall Meaning of the Prophets,' 735.

128. Gribben, *Puritan Millennium*, 38–40.

129. *Bible and Holy Scriptures*, TT2v.

in the mass conversion of the Jews envisioned that event as a subduction of Judaism itself. John Weemes described the Jews as a 'people dwelling by themselves.'[130] But he foresaw that the millennial conversion would *end* the distinctiveness of the Jews so that 'the name of Jew and Gentile [would] no more be heard.'[131] It was Brightman's great innovation—later followed by Finch, Mede, Tillinghast, Nicholas and others—to claim that *after* their conversion, the Jews would *retain* their irreducible otherness, would *remain* a people set-apart. While Weemes saw the singularity of the Jews—a people 'separate and set apart'—as a temporary and lamentable condition, Brightman saw it as a 'thing truly wonderfull marvellous.'[132]

Brightman's *Revelation of the Apocalyps* features a lengthy repudiation of the eschatological claims of the Jesuit commentator Robert Bellarmine. Where Bellarmine had claimed that the anti-Christ would be a Jew, Brightman suggested that the Jews would *lead* the onslaught against the anti-Christ.[133] This led some to suggest a philo-semitic element in Brightman's thought. As Crome points out, however, Bellarmine's interpretation of Revelation—which posited the future reign of a Jewish anti-Christ—was not exactly critiqued, but rather *co-opted* and *inverted* by Brightman.[134] Whereas Bellarmine contended that a Jewish anti-Christ would rule from Jerusalem and would attack the Church of Rome, Brightman contended that a *righteous* Jewish ruler would occupy Jerusalem and participate in the assault on Rome. In different terms, therefore, both Brightman and Bellarmine identify the figure of the Jew as irreducibly anterior: one as righteous, eschatological avenger, the other as anti-Christian, eschatological avenger.

Philip Almond identifies another issue with Katz's appraisal, highlighting the complex 'mix of philo-semitic and anti-judaic elements' in Brightman's work.[135] Brightman lays great stress on the total depravity of the Jews, commensurately accentuating the claim that the restoration of the Jews would be an act of divine mercy, rather than a reward. Brightman laid equal emphasis on the distinction between *future* Jews—transformed by the miraculous, providential power of their conversion—and the *present* Jews. He wrote that those who 'thrust upon God the ancient ceremonies,' were not truly Jews but rather 'the Synagogue of Sathan' of Revelation 2:9. The

130. Weemes, *Four Degenerate Sons*, 370.

131. Weemes, *Four Degenerate Sons*, 307.

132. Weemes, *Four Degenerate Sons*, 321–22; Brightman, *Commentary on Canticles*, 1060.

133. Brightman, *Revelation of the Apocalypse*, 492–597.

134. Crome, 'Proper and Naturall Meaning of the Prophets,' 738–39.

135. Almond, 'Thomas Brightman,' 5.

restoration of 'the Jews' to Jerusalem, he maintained, would certainly not signal a return to 'ceremonial religion'. He identified Revelation 21:22 ('I saw no temple in the city') as a prediction of the ultimate abolition of Jewish ceremonial worship. 'Let the Iewes heare,' Brightman declares, 'and neither let them expect a renewed temple.'[136] In fact, according to Brightman, the new religion practiced by the converted Jews would be *anti*typical of ceremonial Judaism:

> Their excellent forme and beauty could not be better painted out, then by the opposite deformity of that old and degenerate *Synagogue*.[137]

Especially in this Judeocentric, eschatological context—therefore—Judaism itself is counterposed to true, apostolic religion.

It is true that Brightman tempered many of the demonizing tropes that surrounded Jews and Judaism.[138] Furthermore, he envisioned (indeed he 'dreamed of') an eschatological future in which the Jews would be allotted their own homeland.[139] As such, it is tempting to draw a link between his thought and the practices of Judaizing millenarians like Thomas Tillam and Thomas Totney. There are compelling reasons to suggest that such a reduction is—to use Andrew Crome's word—'impossible.'[140] Brightman's eschatological expectations for the Jews can only be very loosely translated into a form of philo-semitism. Brightman did not believe that the restoration of the Jews was a mark of their righteousness, but rather that it would be an act of superlative, divine mercy. Secondly, Brightman's eschatology served to *reinforce* the distinctiveness of the Jews and therefore cannot be seen as a facilitator of Jewish-Christian osmosis. Thirdly, Brightman's hope for the Jewish people was based solely on an ethnic conception of the Jews. Whilst he believed that the Jews would retain their separateness, he absolutely refuted the notion that the Jewish ceremonial law would be maintained or renovated. 'These things,' he wrote, 'are eternally buried, not worne out by time, but utterly abolished by Christ.'[141] In fact, he situated the ceremonial religion of Jews (and Catholics) as *anti*typical to the true religion that would be practiced by the converted Jews in Jerusalem.

---

136. Brightman, *Revelation of the Apocalypse*, 51, 96, 440, 212, 696.

137. Brightman, *Commentary on Canticles*, 1070.

138. This is acknowledged, with significant caveats, by Crome. See Crome, 'Proper and Naturall Meaning of the Prophets,' 730n.

139. Brightman, *Commentary on Canticles*, 1060.

140. Crome, 'Proper and Naturall Meaning of the Prophets,' 735.

141. Brightman, *Commentary on the Canticles*, 1060.

Early seventeenth-century Judeocentric, eschatological thought, therefore, served to *enhance*, rather than decreasing, the otherness of 'the Jew'
and of Judaism. It also shifted the figure of 'the Jew' into an allegorical space.
It could not have formed the basis for a kind of mimetic philo-semitism,
therefore. But it did help to create a more profound point of contact between
Jews and English Reformed Protestants. Thomas Luxon has suggested that
Reformed Protestant soteriology led to the allegorization of the self.[142] The
typological reading of the Hebrew Bible described the patriarchs, the sacrifices of the Temple, and ceremonial law as both signified and signifier.
Meanwhile, supersessionary thought 'denied the Jews a place in the present.'[143]
But the denial of coevalness to Jews by Christians mirrored the denial of coevalness to the believer by the doctrine of Grace. Christ's sacrifice, in Paul's
terms, was understood as an event that both occurred historically *and* pre-
figured typologically the experience of crucifixion within the heart of each
believer. In the Puritan era, the Godly professor described him or herself as
both a being and an allegory, prefiguring the true selfhood that had been
allotted them before creation: the identity of the elect saint. As such, the
experience of Godly piety—and the separation it provided—functioned as
an allegory for the separation of the sheep from the goats, of the elect from
the mass of the reprobate. In rebooting the Judeocentric components of
Christian eschatology, Brightman reminded the English Protestant that the
Jews occupied much the same space, trapped in the amber of time since the
moment of Christ's last breath, awaiting defossilization, awaiting a new existence that lay 'beyond the telic horizon' of the millennium.[144] Immersed in
predestinarian soteriology, the Godly saw themselves diplopically, both as
fleshly beings and as members of a timeless and eternal elect: 'fulfilled in the
concrete future but . . . at all times present.'[145] For some, the tension of this
dichotomy proved too taut and they turned to soteriological systems—such
as Familism, antinomianism or the more imputative elements of Behmenist occultism—which rendered the allegorically represented future self, the
elect saint. For others, behavioral components and doctrinal innovations
also served to allay this anxiety.

In this experience of 'lived allegory', the Godly occupied the space that
Augustine had allotted the Jews: inside and outside of time, at the *same* time.
The Jews and the elect, as simultaneously (and both) signified and signifier

142. Luxon, *Literal Figures*; 'Not I, but Christ', 899–937.

143. Holmberg, *Jews in the Early Modern English Imagination*, 44; Biddick, *Typological Imaginary*, 23.

144. Luxon, *Literal Figures*, 34–77 (quotation at 43).

145. Auerbach, 'Figura', 54.

'point to one another and both point to something in the future.'[146] This point of contact, as Barbara Lewalski has shown, was reflected in the ways in which Puritans understood their own acts of piety. Since they no longer saw works as being 'conduits of special grace' but rather as 'signs,' they shared in the allegorical experience of the Jews: 'both alike depending on signs which will be fulfilled at the end of time.'[147] It is to the Puritan understanding of the Law that we turn next.

JUDAIZING AND THE LAW

The Godly read the Bible differently to their predecessors. This holds true for the ethical content of the Bible inasmuch as it does for the prophetic content. The Godly believed Biblical laws to be the sole source of moral guidance available to Christians. Moral guidance could no longer be found in 'the church' and nor could it be found in 'reason.'[148] 'Without a Bible,' Perry Miller wrote, 'Puritan piety would have confronted chaos.'[149] As such the Godly had a more direct and unmediated relationship with the laws of the Old and New Testaments. This has led some to claim that Judaizing represented simply an over-exuberant form of Puritan scripturalism.[150]

There are three key elements commonly attributed to Puritan Biblicism: the literalist ethic, the edificatory reading of Biblical literature, and the primitivist impulse. Each of these attitudes within Puritanism appears to have weakened, rather than reinforcing, the argument for the observation of ceremonial law.

The literal turn in Biblical hermeneutics is often cited as a hallmark of Reformed Protestant thought. Literalists like John Weemes and William Whitaker rejected scholastic hermeneutics—particularly the practice of *quadriga* which dominated medieval exegesis—arguing that there was 'but one literall sense' of the scripture.[151] At the same time, these exegetes were

146. Auerbach, 'Figura,' 55.

147. Lewalski, *Protestant Poetics*, 126.

148. John Morgan has shown that many Puritans actually treated learning with respect, treated 'schools as seminaries' and that they wrestled with the issue of hubris and the corruption of human reason. Nonetheless, at least rhetorically, many Puritans repudiated the value of learning in the pursuit of truth and certainly of institutions of learning. This is demonstrably true of the key figures with whom this book is concerned (Morgan, *Godly Learning*, 185).

149. Miller, *New England Mind*, 1:19.

150. Goldish, 'Battle for "True" Jewish Christianity,' 153; Ball, *Seventh-Day Men*, 292–310; Smith, 'Christian Judaizers in Early Stuart England,' 125–33, esp. 130–31.

151. MacCallum, 'Milton and the Figurative Interpretation of the Bible,' 397–415.

influenced by Calvin's departure from Luther, in his attempt to rehabilitate the Law as a valid and important aspect of divine revelation. Calvin claimed that the ceremonial law represented a corollary of the Decalogue.[152] As such, the Fathers were not unfit for the Gospel (as the supersessionist right had contended) but rather they *received* the Gospel, in a shadow form, mediated through the ceremonial Law. Thus—for Calvinists—the binary distinction between the Law and the Gospel, which lay at the heart of Lutheran theology, was problematized. At the heart of Calvin's claims for the 'third use,' therefore, was the belief that elements of the Law were edifying.

The tendency to read the Law as an edifying text originated in the work of renaissance humanists like Desiderius Erasmus and, filtered through the writing of Heinrich Bullinger and Thomas Cranmer, it eventually became a staple of English Reformed Protestantism.[153] Throughout the early Stuart period, the notion that the Bible contained within it edifying guidance for living the Christian life prevailed. Henry Scudder cautioned his reader to 'carry in your head a *Catalogue* or *Table* of the principal duties, and vices, required, and forbidden in each Commandment.'[154] Richard Bernard advised that the Godly professor should take 'awful regard to all Gods Commandments,' whilst Thomas Taylor claimed that 'our apparell, our houses, our recreations must all be undertaken and used, *first,* by the warrant of the word.'[155] It was precisely this tendency that infuriated the peers and the critics of the Godly. Richard Hooker implored his precisianist interlocutors 'not to exact at our hands for every action the knowledge of some place of Scripture.'[156] Judaizing, Bryan W. Ball claims, simply represented an extension of this position.[157] Since the Biblical Laws *revealed* the Gospel, literal interpretation of the ceremonial Law was validated. As such, these phenomena demonstrated that over-zealous interpretation of the New Testament could lead to over-zealous interpretation of the Old Testament also.[158]

This hermeneutic position was augmented, according to Bozeman, by a desire amongst the Godly to 'live ancient lives.' Bozeman claims that the principle impetus for Puritan practical divinity was a desire to return to the 'purity' of the historical, apostolic Church, as described in Acts.[159] It is on

---

152. Elliot, 'Calvin and the Ceremonial Law of Moses,' 275–93.

153. Knott, *Sword of the Spirit,* 16–28.

154. Scudder, *Christians Daily Walke,* 31–33.

155. Bernard, *Weekes Worke,* 14; Taylor, *Circumspect Walking,* 203.

156. Hooker, *Works of Mr. Richard Hooker,* 40.

157. Ball, *Seventh-Day Men,* 292–310.

158. Ball *Seventh-Day Men,* 273, 301.

159. Bozeman, *To Live Ancient Lives,* 13–51.

this basis that Matt Goldish has attributed the emergence of 'syncretistic Jewish Christianity'—including the Traskite movement and the thought of Thomas Totney—to a 'widespread desire to be identified with ancient Jewish Christians.'[160] Robert Smith, in a similar vein, has identified Traskism as the product of 'a desire to return to the simple modes of prayer and worship which characterized early Christianity.'[161]

There are significant unacknowledged caveats to each of these claims. Firstly, the term 'literalism' as it was used by early-modern, Protestant exegetes is decidedly slippery. Weemes, whilst arguing that there 'is but one literall sense' of the scriptures, defined 'the literall' as 'that which the words bear eyther properly or figuratively.' Furthermore, one single passage could, for Weemes, have a 'compound' meaning, combining the two.[162] Amongst the population, meanwhile, even the Godly laity expressed doubts about the plausibility of an *historical* interpretation of the Old Testament.[163] For this reason, Kevin Killeen has written that the nomenclature of literalism 'tells us less than it may seem to.' *Sola Scriptura*, Killeen writes, 'did not imply the Bible's insularity as much as its primacy.'[164]

In order to determine the true or literal meaning of the scripture, the Godly reader practiced the *analogia fidei*. This strategy originated in the work of Augustine and reached full efflorescence in the writing of Godly apologetes like William Perkins. As Donald McKim has demonstrated, Perkin's variation on the *analogia* was informed by Ramist logic. The Ramist approach allowed Godly exegetes like Perkins, Ames, Chaderton and others to interpret the entirety of scripture in light of key, kerygmatic truths.[165] Perkins defined this approach as 'a certain abridgement or summe of the scriptures collected out of the most manifest and familiar places.'[166] Use of the *analogia fidei* had profound and practical implications for the ways in which the Godly treated scripture. Thomas Cartwright, for example, did not seek to 'obey' the whole Bible. He boiled it down to four 'general rules of scripture' including: 'not to offend any . . . that all be done in order and comeliness . . . that all be done to edifying . . . that they be done to the glory

160. Goldish 'Battle for "True" Jewish-Christianity,' 153.

161. Smith, 'Christian Judaizers in Early Stuart England,' 131.

162. Weemes, *Exercitations Divine*, 177–179; *Christian Synagogue*, 223.

163. Gibbons, *Questions and Disputations*, 168.

164. Killeen, *Biblical Scholarship, Science, and Politics*, 66–67.

165. McKim, *Ramism in William Perkins Theology*, 51–119; McKim, 'Function of Ramism in Perkins's Theology,' 503–17; Crome, *Restoration of the Jews*, 45–49.

166. Perkins, *Arte of Prophecying*, 32.

of God.'[167] A similar mentality informed the publication and distribution of the *Souldier's Pocket Bible*, carried by the soldiers of the New Model Army, which contained within it only sixteen pages and one hundred and fifty verses. George Herbert saw this 'crumbling' of scripture as the greatest folly of the Godly during this period.[168]

Stanley Fish has pointed out the limitations of the *analogia* in developing consensual ethical norms. 'Whenever you find something that doesn't say what it is supposed to say,' he writes, '[you can] decide that it doesn't mean what it says and then make it say what it's supposed to say.'[169] This epistemic fragility is evident in the earliest iterations of the practice. Augustine wrote that 'in the consideration of figurative expressions, a rule such as this will serve: that what is read should be subjected to diligent scrutiny until an interpretation contributing to the reign of charity is produced.'[170] Transplanted in the soil of early-modern Protestantism, this method was wedded to the pneumatological reading of scripture. The Word, Luther claimed, was quite distinct from 'the Letter.' When Cartwright asserted that his readers should 'have the Word of God go before (them) in all actions,' he did not mean that they should be literally obedient to the letter of the Biblical Laws, but rather that they should be guided in their reading of the Letter of the law by the Spirit.[171] This approach facilitated 'private' and idiosyncratic understandings of the meaning of scripture and of the Law itself, each of which could be identified as 'literall.' Reformed Protestants in England in the seventeenth century asserted their ability to read the scripture and to deduce meaning—independently of earthly authority, scholarship or even reason—as a denotation of their Godliness. Puritan preference for the Word preached over the word read has led Arnold Hunt to propose the controversial claim that Puritans *could* legitimately be considered '*anti*-scripturalist.'[172] This was certainly the assumption of some of their contemporaries.[173] At any rate, it is demonstrably the case that the Godly readers were—to use De Certeau's terms—'travellers, poachers and nomads' who proved the truth of the preacher's words by identifying his citations in the Bible. Only in this, more limited, sense was the Puritan experience of the scriptures

---

167. Cartwright, *Replye to an Answere*, 27.

168. Herbert, *Priest to the Temple*, 27.

169. Fish, *Self-Consuming Artifacts*, 22.

170. Augustine, *On Christian Doctrine*, 93.

171. Cartwright, *Second Replie*, 61.

172. Hunt, *Art of Hearing*, 31 (emphasis added).

173. Vaughan, *Plaine and Perfect Method*, 32.

unmediated.[174] Traske, Tillam and Totney all—at various points—indicated that they believed the Bible only to be intelligible, in the truest sense, in the hands of the Godly and under the influence of the Spirit.[175] This tendency, as Nicholas McDowell and David Como have pointed out, led inevitably to a 'splintering' of meaning and—eventually—to the anti-legalist modes of Puritan divinity, of which John Traske was a principle figure.[176]

Nor can a distinct causal link be drawn from a general ethic of 'obedience' and the edificatory reading of scripture to Judaizing. In fact, in the English context, many Godly apologetes accentuated, rather than reducing, the distinction between the ceremonial, judicial and moral law. The expediency of this distinction was *increased* for those who were more amenable to the renovation of judicial law. Aquinas had written that, while the judicial injunctions may be considered dead, the ceremonial law was 'not only dead but deadly.'[177] This perspective was reiterated by Calvin and was referred to in the Westminster Confession.[178] Samuel Mather claimed that 'to talk of literal Sacrifices under the Gospel, is to dig *Moses* out of his Grave, and to deny Jesus Christ.'[179] Focus on and *reverence* for the ceremonial Law—in what it *signified*—precisely correlated to the rejection of its *use*. This dissociation was particularly pressing in the context of the association of Popish ceremonies and carnal ritualism.[180] If ceremonies are to be read—as Calvin contended—as typologies of the Christian covenant, then they necessarily represent the antitype of the latter. The former is annihilated by the latter. As such, observation of the former functioned as a *denial* of the latter.[181] Observing ceremonial law, therefore, was not seen as an extreme or 'hotter' or 'militant' tendency of Biblicism or legalism. It was seen as *a rejection of obedience*. Thomas Tillam, for example, was not accused of legalism or of carnality by his peers, but rather of disobedience and *anti*-Scripturalism.[182] Those who were committed to certain aspects of the ceremonial law, by definition, were disobedient to the Law of the Gospel. The claim that obedience

174. DeCerteau, *Practice of Everyday Life*, 175; Green, *Print and Protestantism*, 130.

175. Pagitt, *Heresiography*, 190; Tillam, *Temple of Lively Stones*, 55; Tany, *Theauraujohn his Theous Ori Apokolipikal*, 25–29.

176. McDowell, 'Ghost in the Marble,' 176–92; Como, *Blown by the Spirit*, 439–40.

177. Aquinas, *Summa Theologica* II-I.104.3.

178. Calvin, *Institutes of the Christian Religion* 2.7.17; *Humble Advice of the Assembly of Divines*, 30–33.

179. Mather, *Figures or Types of the Old Testament*, 350.

180. Glaser, *Judaism without Jews*, 76; Abbot, *Reasons Which Dr. Hill Hath Brought*, 57.

181. Lewalski, *Protestant Poetics*, 111.

182. Weld, *Mr. Tillam's Account Examined*, 18.

to the different forms of the Law lay on a spectrum, therefore, is a significant over-simplification. Attachment to the ceremonial Law was not seen as a heightened form of obedience. It was seen as *dis*obedience.

Similarly, there are significant caveats to the contention that Judaizing represented a form of over-exuberant 'primitivism.' 'Primitivists' often agitated for the reintroduction of elements of the judicial Law. But even the most 'extreme' exemplars of Puritan primitivism objected on ethical grounds to the renovation of ceremonial law. Bozeman identified Henry Barrow as the initiator of a 'radical Puritan Biblicism.'[183] Barrow sought to reintroduce wholesale the Mosaic 'judicials.' He protested the right of the church to execute those guilty of capital crimes such as 'idolatrie, disobedience to parents, incest, adulterie.' Nonetheless, Barrow asserted that avowal of the ceremonial law was not simply a matter of adiaphora, but that it constituted an act of *dis*obedience. 'If we observe or are brought into the bondage of such feasts and daies,' he wrote, 'we turne from Christ.'[184] Godly primitivists like Barrow, sought a return to the condition of the apostolic Church. But the apostolic Church was notable, for Barrow, in its valiant rejection of ceremonies. For Barrow, true Christians had a responsibility to throw off the ceremonialism of Romish custom and, in doing so, to relive the repudiation of ceremonialism that the first disciples prototypified. As such, the renovation of ceremonies held no place whatever in the model of primitivism exemplified by Barrow and his peers.

JUDAIZING AND ISRAEL

On the November 10, 1644, with the Royalists reeling from defeat at Newbury, Barten Holyday prayed for the people of England:

O let not our Israel become Jewish![185]

The claim that Jacobethan England sought to supplant Israel as the 'chosen nation' originated in the work of William Haller and William Lamont. For Haller, it was the publication and dissemination of Foxe's *Book of Martyrs* that solidified this notion in the consciousness of the average English Protestant.[186] As such, Haller drew Foxe as the 'ancestor of the apocalyptic nationalism of the seventeenth century.'[187] It is certainly the case that England

183. Bozeman, *To Live Ancient Lives*, 166–67.

184. Barrow, *Brief Discoverie of the False Church*, 77, 217.

185. Holyday, *Against Disloyalty Fower Sermons*, 128.

186. Haller, *Foxe's Book of Martyrs*, 19; Lamont, *Godly Rule*, 23.

187. Olsen, *John Foxe and the Elizabethan Church*, 36.

was allegorically linked with 'Sion' in much of the formal rhetoric of the day. The carefully crafted personae of the Protestant monarchs of this period invited comparison between the English monarchy and the rulers of Biblical Israel. Elizabeth was crowned as a new Deborah, James as a new Solomon.[188] The persecution of Judeocentric millenarians like Henry Finch and William Gouge, meanwhile, has been attributed to the challenge they posed to 'the King's fantasy of being ruler over an Israelite England.'[189] This fantasy was pursued in James's project to rebuild the Temple at Ludgate Hill, and was reflected in Laud's sermon at the opening of Parliament in 1625.[190] The semiotic association of St. Paul's with the Temple even led some to suggest that Cromwell was intending to donate it to the Jews upon their readmission.[191]

It is also the case that the use of the typology of Israel continued unabated with the dawn of the Commonwealth. Where James was Solomon, Cromwell was Moses.[192] Henry Scudder and Francis Cheynell identified themselves with the Biblical prophets, warning Israel against impropriety, wantonness, idolatry and impiety. Scudder called on Parliament to be both 'Moses and Phineasses.'[193] The notion of the 'covenant' had been a mainstay of the Godly mode of devotion from the Elizabethan era onwards, and both successes and reversals were interpreted in light of this providential relationship.[194] The notion of a covenantal relationship between God and the Protestant people came to the fore in the English Civil War with the miraculous victories at Wakefield and Wetherby.[195] Meanwhile, the Fifth-Monarchist John Rogers sought to persuade Cromwell that 'the Laws of God [be] made *Republick* Laws in these latter dayes.'[196] With this in mind, a number of scholars have claimed that the Judaizing tendency within Puritanism represented an intuitive shift for the Reformed Protestant zealot of the revolutionary period. Since Protestant England was the inheritor of Israel, it may seem intuitive that Protestant England should adopt the ceremonies of Israel.

188. Hoak, 'Tudor Deborah?,' 73–88; Doelman, *King James and the Religious Culture of England*, 73–100; Aylmer, *Harborowe for Trewe and Faithful Subjects*, O4v.

189. Guibbory, *Christian Identity, Jews, and Israel*, 45.

190. Laud, *Seven Sermons*, 95–145.

191. Crowley, *Visions and Prophecies of Ezekiel Grebner*, 63.

192. Guibbory, *Christian Identity, Jews, and Israel*, 33–40; Dawbeny, *Historie and Policie Reviewed*, a4r.

193. Scudder, *Gods Warning to England*, a3r.

194. Field, *Godly Exhortation*, c1v.

195. Fairfax, *Fuller Relation of that Miraculous Victory*, 1–5.

196. Rogers, *To His Highnesse Lord Generall Cromwell*, br.

This too, though, is a slightly limited analysis. The fundamental claim that English Protestants believed England to be an 'elect nation,' has been criticized by Katherine Frith, Richard Cogley, Richard Bauckham and Viggo Olsen.[197] Certainly the notion that this trope existed earlier than 1640 in anything more than an ambiguous form is incorrect.[198] In his recent work on English national identity, Andrew Crome has demonstrated that the English-Israel trope, which retained its currency up to the twentieth century, actually facilitated—rather than compromised—the continued othering of the Jewish people. There is no indication, according to Crome, that those who vaunted England as a 'second Israel,' understood this to mean that a 'one-to-one replacement of Israel,' had taken place. England was not identified as *the* elect nation, according to Crome, but rather as *a* chosen nation. The separation of England and Israel—through the processes of allosemitism—served to bolster the claim that God worked through nations in order to bring about His providential plan. As such, whilst it remains true that the topos of Israel was widely used to denote chosenness—of the nation or of the church—it is (as the quotation from Holyday demonstrates) problematic to draw too close an identification between the topos of Israel and the topos of Jewry.[199] The allegorical association of England and Israel was not an innovation of the English Godly of the Jacobethan period. The concept of covenantal nationalism was replicated, as Bozeman demonstrated, in numerous settings across Protestant Europe.[200] Even when the English did invoke the language of national election, their imagery was often borrowed from non-English sources.[201] In England, admiration for the Biblical polity of Israel was evident across the denominational gamut, including amongst the *enemies* of the Godly. The Caroline divines—Laud, Cosin, Taylor—all claimed legitimacy for their ecclesiastical and liturgical innovations on the basis of Old Testament precedence.[202] And long *before* the development of the Foxean narrative of English exceptionalism, England had been tropologically linked with Israel. In the sixteenth century, Henry VIII was lauded as a new David. In the thirteenth, Henry III ordered

197. Collinson, 'John Foxe and National Consciousness,' 10; Firth, *Apocalyptic Tradition in Reformation Britain*, 108; Cogley, 'Fall of the Ottoman Empire,' 304–32; Bauckham, *Tudor Apocalypse*, 70–88; Olsen, *John Foxe and the Elizabethan Church*, 36–47.

198. Bozeman, *To Live Ancient Lives*, 89n.

199. Crome, 'English National Identity,' 49–50, 298.

200. Bozeman, *Precisianist Strain*, 25.

201. Kumar, *Making of English National Identity*, 109.

202. Guibbory, *Christian Identity, Jews, and Israel*, 58–74.

a throne carved in the image of King Solomon's.[203] In the *sixth* century, the chronicler Gildas associated England with the polity of Israel.[204] Collinson points out that England's identification with Israel, and the identification of her monarchs with Hebrew monarchs, never placed her in jeopardy of being associated with Jews or Judaizing. In fact, anti-Jewish violence and prejudice increased during the medieval era. Israel—in short—inhabited a place in the English popular imagination that was quite distinct from the ceremonial religion of the Jews.

If England in some sense was Israel, then Israel was *not* Jewish. This remarkable claim had germinated in the soil of a thousand years of super-sessionary thought. Christian discourse had positioned the Biblical topos of Israel, not only as distinctive from, but *antithetical* to Judaism. For Rosemary Ruether the development of this discourse was necessary for the definition of Christianity. 'The *Adversos* literature,' she writes, 'was not created to convert Jews, or to attack Jews, but to affirm the identity of Christianity.'[205] This process, starting with Justin Martyr and recurring thematically in the work of Augustine and Cyprian and Gregory of Nyssa, was central to what Ruether called 'the negation of the Jews' in the early Church.[206] As the church adopted the position of 'new Israel' in the dispensatory analysis of the Church Fathers, it supplanted the 'old Israel' of the Hebrew Bible. As such, the topos of the 'old Israel' of 'the Jews' was framed as the antithesis of the 'new Israel.' The fulcrum of this distinction was carnality. While Israel was 'spiritual,' 'the Jews' were carnal.

In England, the topos of Israel was certainly adopted to denote providential favor for the King and his subjects. It would also be adopted in similar terms to denote the covenantal relationship that God had with a particular Church or people. But usually this allegorical adoption of the topos of Israel went hand-in-hand with the assertion of power and grandeur. England was associated with Israel 'in her flourishing under Solomon and as she was imagined in her glorious future restoration.'[207] In each case, the need to disassociate this 'new Israel' with 'Jewishness' became more pressing, not less.[208] William Prynne contended that England-Israel's providential

203. Rodwell, *Coronation Chair and Stone of Scone*, 35.

204. Scheil, *Footsteps of Israel*, 143–47.

205. Ruether, *Faith and Fratricide*, 181.

206. Ruether, *Faith and Fratricide*, 117–81.

207. Guibbory, *Christian Identity, Jews, and Israel*, 47.

208. Shapiro, *Shakespeare and the Jews*, 40, 43, 189–193; Achinstein, 'John Foxe and the Jews,' 86–116; Bartels, *Spectacles of Strangeness*, 82–109.

favor necessitated the rejection and desolation of the Jews.[209] 'Israel's' success was identified in direct contrast with the pauperized condition of the Jews. 'With the Jews rejected,' Crome writes 'Englishness could be defined by alterity.'[210] Whilst the figure of Israel was identified with 'her flourishing under Solomon,' the figure of 'the Jew' was typically rendered as the reverse. Prynne described Jews as 'the saddest spectacles of divine justice and humane misery.'[211] The association of the Jews with 'alterity' bled into English Reformed Protestant hermeneutics. It informed the image of the Jews that appeared in the very opening lines of the first commentary on the first chapter of Genesis in the Geneva Bible. The examples of the patriarchs, it reads, show that God's people 'stand not in the multitude but in the poore and despised, in the small flocke.' This image formed a bridge, between the self-image of the Godly and the understanding of the topos of 'the Jew' in early modern England. It was this image, and *not* the 'glory of Israel,' that we find in the writings of Tillam, Totney and Traske.

Throughout the early-modern period, the denunciation of Judaizing and of Jews remained ubiquitous, including amongst the ranks of those who vaunted the association of England and Sion. The identification of the Godly with Israel *demanded* scrutiny of (and the supplanting of) the Jews. Foxe himself, who stands at the center of Haller's analysis of national election, was trenchantly anti-Jewish and even *stressed* the continuity of his appraisal of Judaism with that of the medieval church. The 'plague' of anti-Judaic violence which marked the medieval period, he wrote, was 'not undeserved.'[212] For Foxe, the 'existence of Judaism [was a] blasphemy,' a caveat to the entirety of Christian soteriology.[213]

Even those Laudians who sought Hebraic precedence as a legitimation for ancient customs balked at what they saw as Judaizing innovation. Lancelot Andrewes, as an apologist for the Jacobean regime, advocated for the maintenance of episcopal structures and certain ceremonies, on the basis that 'we should fetch our pattern from the Jews.'[214] In the meantime, Andrewes offered one of the most public denunciations of Judaizing, in his examination of John Traske. Judaizing, Andrewes claimed, 'hath ever been holden a foul act.' In resurrecting the ceremonies of the Jews, Traske

209. Prynne, *Short Demurrer to the Jewes*, 1–8.

210. Crome, 'English National Identity,' 298.

211. Prynne, *Short Demurrer*, 1.

212. Foxe, *Actes and Monuments*, 235.

213. Achinstein, 'John Foxe and the Jews,' 116.

214. Andrewes, *Summarie View of the Government*, 23.

had made himself 'anathema Deo et Christo.'[215] This was not hypocrisy on Andrewes's part. Observing those things that were shadows of the incarnation was quite different from mimicking the Jews in matters of indifference. Whether or not the latter was dead, he knew that the former was deadly.

Christians have turned to the topos of Israel throughout the history of the church. Richard Hooker saw, in Davidic Israel, the model for a 'church coterminous with the nation.'[216] James Stuart saw a model for divinely ordained kingship. The Godly, meanwhile, saw the concept of chosenness and election—embodied in the Jews—as antithetical to these models.

A great tension existed at the heart of the English Reformed Protestant experience and its fulcrum was the single but seemingly, internally contradictory concept of Israel.

In his interrogation of John Rogers, Stephen Gardiner made the claim that nothing could be proven by scripture, without interpretation, 'for the Scripture is dead.' John Rogers replied: 'No. The scripture is alive.'[217]

The pneumatological reading of scripture allowed for the emergence of distinctive, private, self-authenticating and irreducible forms of the Word. The meaning of Israel—for English Protestants—formed their broader theological outlook. But it was also formed by their ways of reading the Bible. Those who read the Biblical, historical narratives through an 'Anglican,' or conformist lens, saw the model and type of the Church of England in Israel. This approach required the 'negation of the Jews' in English culture and the desolation of Jewish ceremonies.[218] Elements within the Godly hemisphere, however, saw quite a different image of Israel, and one which more closely enmeshed Israel and Jewishness.

JEWISH-CHRISTIANITY AND JUDAIZING

The very notion of a mimetic, philo-semitic relationship between Jews and Christians in the seventeenth century rests on the presupposition that Judaism and Christianity are irreducibly separate entities. The original Jewish-Christian 'schism' has been revisited by a number of scholars in recent decades. In the middle of the twentieth century, James Parkes and Marcel Simon propogated the notion that a 'parting of ways' originated in the first century as the result of socio-political conflicts that emerged

215. Andrewes, 'Speech Delivered in the Star-Chamber,' 84.

216. Guibbory, Christian Identity, Jews, and Israel, 63.

217. Foxe, Actes and Monuments, 1486.

218. Ruether, Faith and Fratricide, 117.

between Christian and non-Christian groups.[219] More and more, however, scholars have challenged the notion that such an event took place. A growing number of historians of the early Church now claim that Christianity and Judaism were not considered discrete confessions, but rather 'varied entities with loose structures,' until 'centuries into the Christian story.'[220] The making of distinction between Judaism and Christianity, they argue, was a novelty of 'separatists' like Ignatius, Gregory of Nyssa and Justin Martyr.

John Howard Yoder problematized the presupposition that the Christian and Jewish traditions were irreducibly distinctive entities, not only in the first but also in the seventeenth century. He identified a range of sensibilities and tendencies within Christianity as part of a latent, Jewish mode of divinity.[221] In this respect, Yoder shares a critical disposition with Daniel Boyarin, who claims that 'the category of Jews/Christians constitutes a family in which any one sub-group might share features with any other.' Attempts to 'defuzzify' these categories, he writes, should be considered heresiological.[222] The cleavage between Jews and Christians, Boyarin believes, was not an historical reality, but a construct of 'separatist' ideologues.[223]

Yoder argued that, rather than marking a departure, or a supersession of the Jewish tradition, Jesus' ministry 'prolonged the critical stance which previous centuries of Jewish experience had already rehearsed.'[224] The apostolic Church provided a manifestation of precisely that 'distinctive moral commitment,' which the Biblical polity of Israel *itself* manifested.[225] From this same lineage of 'dissent and descent' the 'radical' Reform movements of the sixteenth and seventeenth centuries emerged. For Yoder, therefore, seventeenth-century radicalism was *itself* a 'Jewish' phenomenon. 'Free Church' Protestants gravitated towards, and assembled their Christianity out of, those elements of the Gospels that were most profoundly Jewish. Different aspects of Godly culture in the seventeenth century, on this reading, lay along a spectrum of Jewishness, one end of which was populated by figures like Curtyn, Jackson, Totney and Tillam. Their actions were an expression of Protestantism, in short, not mimicry of Judaism.

---

219. Parkes, *Conflict of the Church and Synagogue*, 71–93; Simon, *Verus Israel*, 433.

220. Carleton Paget, *Jews, Christians, and Jewish Christians in Antiquity*, 1–37; Reed and Becker, 'Introduction,' 1–35; Boyarin, 'Rethinking Jewish Christianity,' 7–36.

221. Yoder, 'Jewishness of the Free Church Vision,' 105–20.

222. Boyarin, *Border Lines*, 22.

223. Carleton Paget, *Jews, Christians, and Jewish Christians*, 4.

224. Yoder, 'Jesus the Jewish Pacifist,' 71.

225. Yoder, 'Jesus the Jewish Pacifist,' 78.

Yoder identified three aspects of Protestantism's Jewish inheritance. Firstly, he saw the radical movements as continuing a 'peace tradition' of Judaism. Secondly, he saw the separatist tradition as mirroring the Jewish 'acceptance of exile.' Thirdly, he saw the anticlericalism of 'free church' movements as an inheritance of Jewish-Christianity.[226] All three of these facets lead, essentially, to a kind of ethical singularity, a determination that the maintenance of strong, impermeable boundaries between the Godly in-group and the majoritarian out-group has intrinsic value. In ethical terms, this equates to—what John Coolidge has called—the idiographic turn in Protestant thought.[227] At the heart of each of these tendencies is a concern for the 'particularity' and historicity of God's people, the requirement to remain apart from 'the nations.'

Yoder's 'peace tradition' is exemplified in the prophetic texts of the Hebrew Bible. It is found in 'the abandonment of kingship,' in Jeremiah, Ezra and Nehemiah. The prophetic tradition itself stands for 'the rejection that Israel should be . . . like other nations.'[228] Rejection of kingship also stands for the rejection of coercive violence and therefore a rejection of 'power' in its worldly iteration. The rejection of conventional discourses of power, and the rejection of conventional binaries of worldly 'strength' and 'weakness' in the Jewish tradition is, for Yoder, mirrored in the teachings of the Beatitudes and in the 'resolutely out-of-power' politics of the apostolic Church. 'Only the Jew Jesus,' Yoder writes, 'could make of accepting powerlessness not only a viable compromise but an identity.'[229] According to Yoder, the rejection of 'the world' and the condition of rejection *by* 'the world,' extoled by Jesus in the Farewell Discourses of John 17, echo the instruction of Ezra 6:21. Even those texts in the Gospels that seem to avow *anti*-Judaic tendencies can be read as 'Jewish' according to Yoder's typology. In Acts 7, for example, Stephen lambasts the High Priest for being 'stiff-necked,' and 'uncircumcised in heart and ears.' This criticism, like John's, seems not to be confined to Stephen's judges alone, but to their predecessors and antecedents:

> You do always resist the Holy Ghost! As your fathers did, so do you do! Which of the prophets have your fathers not persecuted? They have slain those who foretold the coming of the Just One. Of Him you are the betrayers and murderers. (Acts 7:51)

---

226. Yoder, 'Jewishness of the Free Church Vision,' 105–19.

227. Coolidge, *Pauline Renaissance in England*, 11–27.

228. Yoder, 'Jesus the Jewish Pacifist,' 82–85.

229. Yoder, 'Jewishness of the Free Church Vision,' 112–13; 'Jesus the Jewish Pacifist,' 75.

Acts 7 provided some of the basis for the *Adversos Judaeos* calumnies. However, there are other nuances in the text. Here again, we find prophetic, Jewish voice railing against earthly authorities. Stephen here represents the 'value' of Jewishness, the prophetic exilic voice, resolutely out-of-power. The religious authorities, as conformists and collaborators, are the real *heathens*. This sense is redolent in the language used by Stephen. He accuses the authorities of being 'uncircumcised.' Stephen's allegation here is not that the Abrahamic covenant has been abrogated and supplanted by the Christian, but rather that the authorities *themselves* have abrogated the Abrahamic covenant. Those 'Churches' of the sixteenth and seventeenth centuries that developed traditions and discourses that rejected and resisted the conventional binaries of worldly power were, for Yoder, the latter day incarnations of this profoundly 'Jewish' Christianity.

This commitment to live 'resolutely out of power' leads, in practical terms, to an 'acceptance of exile.' The belief that disempowerment, vassalage and even bondage did not denote reprobation but rather providential favor, is as evident in the writing of William Bradford, Richard Baxter and John Foxe as it is in Isaiah. The literature of exile and bondage that we find in the apocalyptic writings of Daniel, the prophetic texts of Isaiah, and the Priestly interpolations of the Holiness Code, represent a mode of ethical defiance of domination, of resistance—though not *rejection*—which is equally resonant with the work of sixteenth- and seventeenth-century Reformed Protestants.

Yoder identifies a common heritage of anticlericalism, extending from the prophetic tradition, the exilic redactions of the Torah, through the establishment of the apostolic Church, the Reforms of the sixteenth- and seventeenth-century radicals and up to the present day in the form of 'free churches.' This tradition is interrupted only by the ecclesiastical Constantinianism of the Roman Catholic Church and Churches of the Magisterial Reformation. Both the true, 'free' church and the Jewish religion are reliant solely on scriptural revelation for truth.[230] No intermediary organ has any role in such a tradition. The reignition of anti-clericalism which characterized the 'radical' Reformation of the sixteenth and seventeenth centuries, was, therefore, a re-Judaization of Christianity:

> The issues raised by John Hus and Peter Cheltschitsky, Michael Sattler and Pilgram Marpeck were transpositions of the old Jewish identity agenda, now restated as an intra-Christian critique.[231]

230. Yoder, *To Hear the Word*, 6–7.

231. Yoder, 'Jewishness of the Free Church Vision,' 107; 'Constantinian Sources,' 136–38.

Their concerns were 'rooted Jewishly.' Yoder designates this tendency as another facet of ethical powerlessness. He identifies a tendency in the Jewish-Christian tradition which rejects 'coercive epistemologies' of all kinds, encompassing both hegemonic metanarratives and totalizing, 'out-there, absolutes.' Truth is discernible only through faith. This epistemological vantage necessarily positions the faithful individual 'out of power.'[232] The *akedah* provides the most dramatic account of such an epistemology: Abraham is called to abandon all reason, abandon all conventional, ethical reference points and thereby to follow God. Job is called upon to abandon the rationalism of Eliphaz the Temanite (Job 4:22). This rejection of reason as the 'left hand' of fidelity is resonant with the experience of the apostolic Christians, asked to remain faithful to the Messiah in the aftermath of His humiliation and death on Calvary. This central ideological theme of the early church is typified by Christ's rebuke of Doubting Thomas. A further example emerges from the free churches and their abandonment of sacramental worship and conventional epistemological structures in the development of their soteriology, choosing instead to gaze into the vertiginous abyss of divine fiat.[233] 'Free Church' Protestants of the seventeenth century remained within the Jewish tradition of remaining 'resolutely out of power' and within 'the identity of powerlessness,' not only in the political sense but also in the epistemological, in relation to the divine.

In each of these aspects of 'Jewish-Christianity,' Yoder identifies the recurring theme of 'particularity.' The global domination of Christianity and the identification of Christianity with power, authority and hegemony was not, for the radical reformers (nor for Yoder), a fulfilment of Christianity, nor a providential vindication of the Christian message, but rather a betrayal. In order to ensure the success of their movement, Yoder argues, early Christian 'separatists,' 'reconceived the Christian message so as to make it credible or palatable to the authorities of Gentile culture . . . by sloughing off the dimensions of Jewish particularity.'[234] This 'loss of Jewishness' led to 'the faith [becoming] an ahistorical moral monotheism, with no particular peoplehood and no defences against acculturation, no ability to discern the line between mission and syncretism.' In Coolidge's terms, the loss of Jewishness represented an erosion of the idiographic in deference to the nomothetic.[235] According to Yoder's schema, the loss of particularity, the loss of Jewishness and the establishment in its place of 'ahistorical moral monotheism,' was

232. Yoder, 'On Not Being Ashamed of the Gospel,' 290.

233. Lake, *Boxmaker's Revenge*, 35.

234. Yoder, 'Jewishness of the Free Church Vision,' 107.

235. Coolidge, *Pauline Renaissance*, 16–20.

ultimately the basis for the 'Great Apostasy,' the 'Constantinian Church.' The Jewish aspects of Christianity lay in the understanding of faith as a 'distinctive moral commitment.' As Yoder writes:

> With its Jewishness, Christianity lost its understanding of Torah as grace and privilege, replacing it with morality as requirement for salvation.[236]

This, too, has profound implications for our reading of Puritanism. The ethics of Puritanism was informed by, what Coolidge called, an idiographic rather than a nomothetic world-view: a focus on the historical and the legal, rather than the general and natural.[237] This represents an inversion of the Popkinian account of the Judaizers. For Popkin, philo-semitic and Judaizing millenarianism was the midwife of the nomothetic turn in Western morality. Conversely, Yoder's identification of idiographic ethics as fundamentally 'Jewish' as opposed to 'Constantinian,' offers a distinctive but complementary component to the pejorative label of Judaizing, as it was used in early-modern England.

This aspect of Judaizing—a focus on the idiographic rather than the nomothetic aspects of religion—also informs Yoder's notion of Jewish-Christianity as 'historical.' For Yoder, the 'historical' is intrinsically different from the 'religious.' Religion is

> that which sanctifies and celebrates life as it is, things as they are, the personal cycle of life from birth to death and the annual cycle of the sun and the culture from spring to winter. Against this understanding of 'religion,' the category of 'history' represents the morally meaningful particular processes, which may not go in a straight line but at least go somewhere; they are non-cyclical, stable, repetitive.[238]

Yoder's analysis posits a profound point of contact between the religious sensibilities of the earliest Christians and those of the Puritans. As such, it provides the basis for an analysis of the relationship between the Godly and Jewish ceremony which goes beyond admiration and mimesis. Before interrogating this relationship further, however, it is important to examine precisely what we mean by the word 'Puritan.'

---

236. Yoder, 'Jewishness of the Free Church Vision,' 107.
237. Coolidge, *Pauline Renaissance*, 16–20.
238. Yoder, 'Jewishness of the Free Church Vision,' 108.

WHAT IS THE PURITAN?

The problem of how to define Puritanism is as old as Puritanism itself. As early as 1631, one commentator declared the term 'ambiguous' and 'fallacious.'[239] The intervening centuries have seen the waxing and waning of Whig, Marxist and revisionist interpretations. Each have included variously defined iterations of Puritanism in their own meta-narratives.[240] Whigs, like Babington MacCauley, identified Puritanism as a staging post in the inexorable march of progress towards consensual democracy. The period leading up to the crisis of the 1642 was characterized as one of conflict between dissenting, Puritan Parliamentarians and the autocratic regime of Charles I. As a result of this confrontation, MacCauley suggested, large swathes of the population joined the fight to overturn Stuart tyranny and to usher in a new period of enlightened, tolerant rule. Puritans, in other words, were a political vanguard, the shock troops of English parliamentary democracy.[241] Revisionists took aim at this interpretation in the 1960s. Far from representing an 'escalating conflict over constitutional principles,' they characterized the period leading up to the rise of Laudianism in the late 1620s as one of 'relative ideological homogeneity, consistency and stability.'[242]

For materialists like Christopher Hill and A. L. Morton, the rise of Puritanism was an episode within a secular eschatology of class struggle.[243] According to this model, the Puritans were the vanguard of a new capitalist, bourgeois class who sought—by means of armed struggle—to overthrow the domination of feudal power as represented by the government of Charles Stuart. In place of feudal order, Puritans asserted a new, heavily-disciplinarian, bourgeois morality. Hill, in his later work, developed a secondary narrative that better accommodated the putative phenomenon of 'radical Puritanism.' He suggested that groups like the Levellers and Diggers—who exhibited the anti-authoritarianism of the mainline Puritans but not their pietism—were part of a long continuum of revolutionary populism starting with the Lollards and continuing in various guises up to the era of the Civil War.[244] But the central assertion that Puritanism was essentially a bourgeois political movement, emerging from the 'middling sort,' has

239. Widdowes, *Schismaticall Puritan*, A3r.

240. A rehearsal of the debate about the definition of Puritanism can be found in Lake, 'Defining Puritanism,' 3–29.

241. Macaulay, *History of England*, 219–22.

242. Como, *Blown by the Spirit*, 10–11.

243. Hill, *Puritanism and Revolution*, 121; *Society and Puritanism*, 1–13; Morton, *World of the Ranters*, 14.

244. Hill, *World Turned Upside Down*, 1–14.

been questioned. Kevin Wrightson, in a revision of his study of the village of Terling, conceded that Puritanism was far from a 'middle-class, capitalist' ideology. Rather, it was a 'religious movement with potentially universal appeal.'[245] This claim has been corroborated by a number of scholars, not least Margaret Spufford whose extensive research demonstrated that Puritanism was 'a grass-roots phenomenon amongst the very humble.'[246]

In the latter half of the twentieth century, a wave of revisionism carried away these developmentalist readings of the rise of Puritanism. Peter White, Richard Greaves, and James Sears McGee all proposed that Puritanism be understood as fundamentally a religious, rather than a political or socio-economic phenomenon.[247] On this basis, John Morrill famously claimed that the English Civil War should be understood as 'the last of the wars of religion' rather than 'the first European revolution.'[248] In service to this model, Puritanism, as a religious movement, was often essentialized as analogous to Calvinism. As such, Puritans were identified by a 'shopping list' of doctrinal positions, the most central of which was the doctrine of predestination.[249]

Nicholas Tyacke repudiated the assertion that Puritanism was basically Calvinism thirty years ago. In his seminal work, *Anti-Calvinists: the Rise of English Arminianism*, he demonstrated that—far from being a distinguishing characteristic—Calvinism was the default, consensual position of the ecclesiastical hierarchy from the time of the Elizabethan settlement up to the publication of Richard Montagu's *New Gagg for an Old Goose*.[250] Susan Hardman Moore noted that Whitgift, tormenter of the Godly in Elizabethan England, took the side of the Calvinists against Peter Baro in 1581. This, Hardman Moore suggests, is evidence of a 'broad acceptance of Reformed Theology.'[251] Until the appointment of Laud, George Abbot had been Archbishop of Canterbury and his rule was characterized by a staunch defence of Calvinist orthodoxy in the face of the threat from Arminianism, which was gathering momentum in the United Provinces.

The evident doctrinal discontinuity within the Godly party creates further problems for the definition of Puritanism as a religious sect. Whilst

245. Wrighton, 'Terling Revisited,' 208.

246. Spufford, *Contrasting Communities*, 351.

247. Greaves, *Society and Religion in Elizabethan England*; McGee, *Godly Man in Stuart England*; White, *Predestination, Policy, and Polemic*, i-ix.

248. Morrill, 'Religious Context of the English Civil War,' 155–78.

249. Durston, 'Introduction,' 7.

250. Tyacke, *Anti-Calvinists*; Wallace, *Puritans and Predestination*, 1–110.

251. Hardman Moore, 'Reformed Theology and Puritanism,' 203. See also Knott, *Sword of the Spirit*, 4.

many prominent Puritans avowed a supralapsarian model of predestination, many others held the infralapsarian view. John Preston proposed that the atonement was hypothetically universal, whilst William Perkins asserted that the atoning power of the crucifixion was limited.[252] In the early Stuart period, David Como has made the case that elements within the Puritan milieu held anti-legalist views whilst others maintained the 'precise' piety of disciplinary religion.[253] As the Godly party was riddled with division, so the soul of the individual Godly professor was often in conflict.[254] The Godly were often as unsure about the function of their devotional practices as the historians who have studied them. In Joseph Salmon's A Rout the author defended the claim that orthodoxy was mutable, that right worship was chimerical and that the notion of the 'Church' was cloaked in mystery:

> [God's power] comes forth and offers itself in a diversity of appearance, and still (by a divine progress in the affairs of the earth) moves from one power to another, from one dispensation to another, from one party to another.[255]

Some have addressed the apparently nebulous nature of Puritan definition—and self-definition—by classifying Puritans simply as the more *serious*, the more engaged, the 'hotter' Protestants. Collinson defined the Elizabethan Puritans as the shock troops of Reform Protestantism, the 'militant tendency.'[256] More recently, however, Judith Maltby and others have taken issue with this representation, arguing that to portray the early Stuart Puritans as an elite — more committed, more pious, more dedicated to reform even — is to take them too much at their word. The Godly, Maltby argues, made self-validating claims about their own righteousness and about the irreligion of their non-Godly peers. But Puritanism did not 'have a monopoly on all that could be considered successful in the Church of England.' Many English Protestants in the early seventeenth century took to prayerbook piety with as much zeal as the Puritans exhibited in their own worship.[257]

On the basis of this 'problem of definition,' it is understandable that sceptics like C. H. George, Nicholas Tyacke, Colin Davis and Alec Ryrie have sought to minimize or even retire the concept of 'Puritanism' altogether.

252. Kendall, 'Puritan Modification of Calvin's Theology,' 205.

253. Como, *Blown by the Spirit*, 439.

254. Nuttall, *Holy Spirit in Puritan Faith and Experience*, 105.

255. Salmon, *Rout*, 1.

256. Collinson, *Richard Bancroft and Elizabethan Anti-Puritanism*, 1.

257. Maltby, *Prayer-Book and People*, 9–10.

Davis accused his colleagues—most directly Christopher Hill—of using the term 'indiscriminately.'[258] C. H. George claimed that those things usually attributed to Puritanism easily fit within what he called 'the Protestant Mind.'[259] Nicholas Tyacke questioned the extent to which Puritanism could be seen as a coherent category, since the term was used to describe radically different phenomena at different points in history.[260] Alec Ryrie's recent work has also attempted to offer a more holistic understanding of Protestantism, minimizing the differences within a British 'Protestant mainstream.'[261]

In spite of its chimerical nature, it is clear that early Stuart Puritanism was real. It might not have been organized around clear, achievable political goals—before or after the Revolution itself—but it was a recognizable, functional, identification. The fact that the Godly were easily identified by each other and were identified by others attests to this fact. The Puritan diarist Robert Woodford claimed that he could identify whether or not a perfect stranger, encountered on the road, was a fellow professor or not.[262] Nehemiah Wallington, meanwhile, claimed to have had the converse experience:

> How common and often have I been mocked and called round-head in as reprochfull a maner as they can and saying you that preach in a tub by those that know me not nor never see me.[263]

Rather than considering the phenomenon as a movement *per se*—with stated goals, characteristics, *modi operandi*—some scholars have sought to describe the Puritan 'character,' Puritan 'culture' or the Puritan 'identity' in the early Stuart context. Peter Lake has advanced a vision of an ideologically expansive Puritan community, holding some doctrines in common, but encountering frequent disagreement. The Puritan world was characterized by 'debates and altercations between a variety of different schools of thought . . . advanced by persons accepted as in some sense members of the godly community.'[264] Kevin Sharpe has also repudiated efforts at defining Puritanism doctrinally, suggesting that religious practice—especially in the early-modern context—was laden with all kinds of meanings, identities and political significances, the profundity of which an awareness of doctrinal

258. Davis, *Fear, Myth, and History*, 17.

259. George, *Protestant Mind of the English Reformation*, 1–8.

260. Tyacke, 'Puritanism, Arminianism, and Counter-Revolution,' 119–43.

261. Ryrie, *Being Protestant in Reformation*.

262. Woodford, *Diary of Robert Woodford*, 170, 278, 342.

263. Wallington, *Notebooks of Nehemiah Wallington*, 169.

264. Lake, 'Puritanism, Familism, and Heresy,' 95–96.

niceties can scarcely fathom.[265] These are perennial issues for students of religion. Rarely do taxonomical accounts of a religion manage to embrace the full gamut of people who identify as members of a religious community. In defining the parameters of religious groups, it is not sufficient to identify 'what-they-did.' We must consider what 'what-they-did' *meant* (or *means*). Puritanism should not—in this sense—be defined by its 'customs, usages, traditions, habit clusters' but rather by its 'plans, recipes, rules, instructions for determining behaviour.'[266]

Peter Lake both 'confirmed' and 'destabilized' the concept of Puritanism in recent scholarship.[267] He has argued *against* the 'hard-edged' or 'shopping list,' taxonomical style of definition and *for* a 'fuzzy' yet 'phenomenological' approach, through which 'the social entity of the Godly or Puritan community is defined in terms of the social fact of godly insiderhood.' In an article written in 1985, Lake made the following definitive claim about Puritanism:

> The whole thrust of the puritan conception of true religion and the community of the Godly was towards the division of existing communities and groups between the godly and the ungodly.[268]

Puritanism was not static but fluid, not homogeneous but diverse. It was defined from without and within on the basis of its members being 'different from most people.' It is best identified, therefore, not by its discrete characteristics—whether confessional, political or economic—but rather by the dynamics which led to the emergence of the array of characteristics that have—at various points—been ascribed to 'Puritans.' As such, we should endeavor to define Puritanism by what 'Puritans saw in each other.'[269] In order to achieve this, it is imperative to rely less on empirical, detached, taxonomies and more on accounts of 'mutual recognition of those who did indeed perceive one another' to be members of one group or another. In this statement, Peter Lake points towards a truth, central to contemporary social-psychological thought: that identities are formed not spontaneously or autonomously but rather by a process of dialogue and interaction between the subject and their peers.[270]

265. Sharpe, *Remapping Early Modern England*, 12.

266. Geertz, *Interpretation of Cultures*, 363, 44.

267. Hessayon, *Gold Tried in the Fire*, 9.

268. Lake, 'William Bradshaw,' 570–589.

269. Spurr, *English Puritanism 1603–1689*, 7–8.

270. Lake, 'Anti-Puritanism,' 80–97.

Puritanism originated as a label, attributed to the godly by their enemies. As such the phenomenon of 'Puritanism' itself, and the practices of Puritan divinity, cannot be understood in isolation from the attitudes of those who sought to identify, classify and stigmatize Puritanism. Rather, as Christopher Durston writes, it must be understood as *one* component of 'a set of fluid, dynamic, polarities,' or, as Collinson writes 'not [as] a thing definable in itself but only one half of a stressful relationship.'[271] Without this insight, accounts of Puritanism and its various epiphenomena cannot be properly understood:

> Natural historians of Puritanism will find that what matters is not what people were in themselves but what they were doing *to* each other and saying *about* each other and *against* each other.[272]

Puritanism was moulded by anti-Puritanism, and anti-Puritanism was molded by Puritanism. These two cultural phenomena became, to use Peter Lake's phrase 'evil twins.' Thus, the 'basic polarities,' and 'binary opposites' of these didymic, social, phenomena emerged.[273] For anti-Puritanism to exist, it obviously required Puritanism. But the reverse was also true. Without the opprobrium of the world, Puritans could not themselves be clearly defined. In Collinson's words, Puritanism 'was a religious tendency which was defined by its difference from the religion of "most people."' For Collinson, Puritanism was not necessarily ecclesiologically divisive. But where the Godly maintained ecclesiological unity, their separateness from the massed reprobate was enacted in a variety of quotidian behaviors.[274] Only by being different from 'most people' could Puritan goodness be clearly seen. Early-modern commentators appear to have agreed, one writing that 'when I consider Puritans, and compare them with their common notorious adversaries, then their goodnesse seemes most evident to me.'[275]

For Puritans, this social reality had a deep religious significance. The Godly, as proponents of experimental predestinarianism, were deeply concerned with discovering the evidence for the distinction between the elect and the reprobate. John Brinsley fervently prayed: 'Hasten that glorious day, when the difference shall appeare betwene us thy subjects, and those who serue thee not.'[276] Analysing the meaning of Judaizing in the eyes of the

---

271. Collinson, *Birthpangs of Protestant England*, 143; Durston, 'Introduction,' 3.

272. Collinson, 'Godly Preachers and Zealous Magistrates,' 9.

273. Lake, 'Anti-Puritanism,' 96.

274. Collinson, *Puritan Character*, 16.

275. Ley, *Discourse Concerning Puritans*, 53.

276. Brinsley, *Second Part of the True Watch*, 10.

enemies of the Godly *and* the Godly allows us to 'follow their distinctions, appreciate their beliefs, see things their way,' to come closer to the evasive, 'native point of view.'[277] This does not mean, however, that we should simply transcribe the stated claims that these figures make about themselves. Rather, it enjoins scholars to look at the signs and symbols, the 'systems of shared meaning' that make up communication, to not only describe what people *said* but 'to understand what people *meant* by doing and saying things.'[278] Kevin Sharpe describes the duty of an historian 'to pay attention to the representations that contemporaries presented of and to themselves.'[279] Each representation was a choice that 'could provoke dissatisfaction, alienation, and most importantly divisive identification.'[280] Symbols and symbolic modes of communication are not timeless. They require rediscovery. The world the Puritans inhabited was just as laden with symbolic meaning as any other society. The topos of Judaism was just as laden with symbolic meaning as any other topos. If Puritanism was the religion of being 'different from most people,' then this model should form the basis of any analysis of Puritan culture, not least the culture of Judaizing Puritanism. Puritanism, in other words, should be primarily treated as a phenomenon concerned with the quality of 'singularity.' This, necessarily, is a quality which is defined both from without and from within.

PURITANISM AND DANGER

If it is the case that 'Puritans' are best defined as 'different from most people,' then this indicates a profound affinity between Puritanism and elements within Judaism. The claim that Judaism values a 'distinctive moral commitment,' which exists in 'history' rather than on a 'moral' plain, points to a wider concern within the Jewish religious corpora with notions of separation and purity. This tendency was identified in the work of Mary Douglas and has been explored and refined in more recent scholarship. Douglas's central claim was that the notion of holiness, in the Hebrew Bible, referred to 'unity, integrity, and perfection.'[281] She rejected previous claims that ritual purity functioned as a primitive mode of 'medical materialism.'[282] Impurity, she

---

277. Skinner, *Visions of Politics*, 3:1.

278. Cambers, *Godly Reading*, 14.

279. Sharpe, *Remapping Early Modern England*, 3.

280. Webster, 'Early Stuart Puritanism,' 54.

281. Douglas, *Purity and Danger*, 55.

282. Douglas, *Purity and Danger*, 30.

claims, refers only to 'matter out of place.'[283] As such, the separation of meats and other practices, points to an irreducible concern for separation itself.

These claims were developed in the writing of Julia Kristeva in the 1980s. Kristeva inaugurated the concept of abjection. The Biblical concept of purity, she claimed, functioned to ritualise the disgust (primarily misogynistic) of the other. This perspective, specifically in relation to the Biblical iteration of purity, has been challenged in recent years by Jonathan Klawans and latterly by Daniel Weiss.[284] Klawans points out that the Biblical concept of 'purity' is best bifurcated into more accurate concepts of 'ritual purity' and 'moral purity.' Neither, necessarily, provoke sentiments of abjection: while the former is *contagious* it is not, necessarily, valuational; while the latter is negatively valued, it is not contagious. Ritually unclean things are not necessarily 'bad.' Genesis 7 specifically notes that 'unclean animals' are *rescued* from obliteration. As such, feelings of disgust are not necessarily linked to 'purity.' Klawans's and Weiss's analysis provides a more nuanced understanding of the significance of purity in the Jewish context. Concern for sacrality, they claim is not necessarily a valuational desire to eliminate filth. Rather, it rests on a necessity of separating things 'pure' and things 'impure.' If this is the case, then we can further claim that the presence of the impure is *essential* for the practice of separation. Furthermore, we can assert that the *act* of separation is the intrinsic good.

The trope of impurity has (at least) an analogous relationship with the notion of cultural miscegenation. The Ezra-Nehemiah texts, which provide the basis for much of our understanding of the polity of Israel in the early Second Temple period, are characterized by concern for the holiness of Israel as a body politic. The policy of rejecting inter-marriage with the nations in these texts points to a general concern with maintaining 'separation' in the cultural as well as the ritual sphere. The act of separation functions as an ethical foundation for an ethnic polity; the 'mixed multitude' *become* the 'priestly nation.' This concern with miscegenation characterized the texts that emerged from the condition of exile in the Babylonian period. Throughout the early diasporic period and into the medieval era, these concerns were revised, renewed and revisited.[285]

This refinement of the notion of purity has significant implications for the study of Jewish rituals as renovated by seventeenth-century English Puritans. While figures like Traske, Tillam and Totney did not see the rituals

---

283. Douglas, *Purity and Danger*, 36, 41, 165.

284. Klawans, *Impurity and Sin*, 17, 23–25; Weiss, 'Impurity without Repression,' 205–21.

285. Lachter, 'Israel as a Holy People in Medieval Kabbalah,' 137–59.

they participated in as 'valuational,' they saw intrinsic value in the act of separation that the rituals demonstrated. As Weiss points out, these themes do not necessarily entail a need to eliminate or eradicate otherness. Impurity is not necessarily something that must be 'expelled' or 'repressed' but rather something that can be 'lived alongside.' One of Kristeva's most significant contributions is to demonstrate that—in order for the separation of pure and impure to be maintained—the impure is as vital as the pure. This also holds for the religion of 'being different from most people.'[286] The religious identity of the Godly was only functional in the presence of the religion of its 'evil twin.' In this respect, they shared a bifurcated notion of purity with their Jewish antecedents. If it is the case that the rituals and ceremonies associated with the Judaizing Puritans were *intrinsically* and *circumstantially* associated with the notion of separation, the next question must be: in what conditions does the concern for demonstrable separation come to the fore?

POWERLESSNESS AS AN IDENTITY

'Accepting powerlessness was not just a compromise,' wrote John Howard Yoder of the early, free Church movements 'but an identity.'[287] The 'identity of powerlessness' was a significant component of the experience of many of the Godly, as it was for many of the early Christians and for many of the Jews of the Second Temple period.[288] In the task of studying Puritanism as an identity, a number of scholars have proposed the adoption of the tools used by social-psychologists, whose specialism is the study of the emergence of identity. In part this is an acknowledgement that social-psychology and social-identity theory have offered clear and analysable explanatory structures for the formation of political, religious and cultural movements following the decline of materialist and modernization models. Patrick Collinson lamented that 'the social-psychological circumstances' which facilitated the

---

286. Collinson, 'Godly Preachers and Zealous Magistrates,' 9.

287. Yoder, 'Jewishness of the Free Church Vision,' 112–13.

288. Spraggon, 'Puritan Iconoclasm,' 18; Walsham, 'Happiness of Suffering,' 56–58; Cambers, *Godly Reading*, 13–14, 22. This is not to say that all Puritans sought to *be* powerless, but rather that they often sought to associate themselves with cultural *topoi* of powerlessness. Clearly, many of those who identified as Godly saw ways of validating the pursuit of earthly power, not least the engineers of the Cromwellian commonwealth. Taking power in the context of the Civil War was perceived as a duty, not just an act of Knoxean resistance but a 'crusade' (see George, 'War and Peace in the Puritan Tradition'). Nonetheless, even the language of Holy War situated the Godly combatant in a powerless mode. 'Less of man and more of God,' was a repeated refrain in Godly explanations for victories in the Civil War (see Rowley, 'From Fratricide to Revival').

rise of Puritanism 'have so far been neglected by historians.'[289] Margaret Spufford stressed the importance of 'anxiety' in the emergence of dissent.[290] Bozeman argued that the disciplinary aspect of seventeenth-century Puritanism could—in part—be explained as the product of a 'variety of psychic discomforts' which 'accompanied social change.'[291] Peter Lake, meanwhile, has made the assertion that elements of Protestant culture served 'to express, contain and control the anxieties and tensions at the very center of the experience and outlook of English Protestants.'[292] As such, cultural components functioned as 'psychological anchors' in 'a world seemingly menaced with destabilizing domestic changes.'[293] Alexandra Walsham called 'covenant divinity' a response to the 'psychological need for assurance.'[294] These scholars agree, in short, that some aspects of 'voluntary religion' came to fruition in order to allay societally and soteriologically precipitated anxieties. We even find the Godly themselves discussing their condition in terms that presaged key concepts of social-psychology and social-identity theory. Godly practices were edifying in that they encouraged 'Christian society' and 'sweet consent.' Ezekiel Culverwell, encouraging his readers to engage in extemporary, collective prayer, confessed that 'when by some sweet conference my affection is enlarged to God's saints ... [I have] a taste of the happiness to come.'[295]

Several scholars of the period have identified the 'siege mentality' or the 'holy huddle' aspect of Puritan piety as a strategy for reducing 'anxiety.'[296] Diane Willen writes that the condition of Puritan 'anxiety' could only be alleviated by 'spiritual reciprocity.' Puritan piety, Willen writes, 'created a strong need among individual believers for spiritual support and sustenance from one another.'[297] David Leverenz argues that Puritan expression was best described as a combination of the 'private language of agonized doubt and the public language of militant submission.'[298] Walsham, meanwhile, notes that Puritans found the 'experience of persecution' to be 'immensely

---

289. Collinson, *Puritan Character*, 21.

290. Spufford, *Contrasting Communities*, 350.

291. Bozeman, *Precisianist Strain*, 51.

292. Lake, 'Anti-Popery,' 80.

293. Stone, *Anatomy of Revolution Revisited*, 119.

294. Walsham, *Providence in Early Modern England*, 305.

295. Culverwell, *Time Well Spent in Sacred Meditations*, 209.

296. Collinson, 'Godly Preachers and Zealous Magistrates,' 7; Webster, 'Early Stuart Puritanism,' 61.

297. Willen, 'Communion of the Saints,' 40.

298. Leverenz, *Language of Puritan Feeling*, 14.

empowering.'[299] Furthermore, Walsham argues that the experience of being 'the objects of verbal mockery and civil ostracism' was in some sense 'psychologically affirming.' In the interests of pursuing this psychological affirmation, she claims, the Godly tended towards the 'cultivation of crises.'[300] Dwight Bozeman makes a similar claim regarding the entitativity of Godly communities and its relation to assurance:

> By redefining relationships, by valuing the comradeship and exclusiveness brought by membership in an intensive subculture, they provided a new basis for interpersonal trust and community.[301]

This preoccupation with singularity was precipitated by a deep desire to *see* the difference between the eternally decreed elect and the eternally decreed reprobate, between God's subjects, and those who served him not.[302]

Mary Douglas suggested that the need to symbolise boundaries of separation through ritual came to the fore when the boundaries of the group were under pressure.[303] It could be argued, similarly, that the perceived permeability of the boundary between the 'Godly' and the 'ungodly,' which the decline of sacramentalism created, facilitated the need to perform acts that facilitated 'resistance' on the part of the Godly. Resistance can be defined as any action that demonstrates a 'refusal to accept the ideas, actions or positions' of the majority.[304] For many, resistance functions not only as a form of 'criticism,' as Hill would have it, but as a mode of identity. Opposition to cultural norms or majoritarian values, for such groups, forms the *basis* for self-concept. Behavior and attitudes, therefore, are shaped by dialogue between the majority and the minority. Oppositional or resistance identities rely on the shifting attitudes of the majority in order to define their *own* attitudes and behaviors. Shibboleths and ethnic markers are in a constant condition of flux and adaptation. In the work of Manuel Castells, American Fundamentalist Christianity, Wahabi Islam and Hindu nationalism are all identified as the creatures of resistance-identity. Castells also notes the prevalence of resistance identities in the gay community, aligned with efforts to secure gay rights.[305] In each of these cases, groups attempt to assert

---

299. Walsham, *Charitable Hatred,* 212.

300. Walsham, 'Happiness of Suffering,' 58, 56.

301. Bozeman, *Precisianist Strain,* 59.

302. Brinsley, *Second Part of the True Watch,* 60.

303. Douglas, *Purity and Danger,* 153–57.

304. Walraven and Abbink, 'Rethinking Resistance in African History,' 8.

305. Castells, *Power of Identity,* 7–15.

the narratives of their own identities by adopting and accentuating those particular characteristics that are perceived to be most unpalatable to the majority. Resistance, therefore, should be understood in this context as the adoption of behaviors that specifically subvert societal norms and binaries in order to designate the otherness, outsiderliness, distinctiveness or 'singularity' of the actor or group of actors. As several scholars have noted, this tendency was the impetus behind much Puritan devotional innovation.[306]

What are the conditions within which resistance identities tend to emerge? There are several critical vantage points on this question. The insights of those social-psychologists associated with Social-Identity theory are particularly applicable to the study of the 'holy huddle' mentality.[307] In the 1970s, Henri Tajfel and John Turner developed the central concepts of the Social-Identity approach. Tajfel in particular was incentivized by his experience of ethnic separation and the violent fixation of ethnic purity which he had experienced first hand in Nazi occupied Poland. Tajfel and Turner demonstrated that identity-formation *is* a dialogical process. 'In-groups' develop identities by comparing and contrasting themselves with 'out-groups.'[308] The goal in this process is to secure positive-distinctiveness: the sense that 'we' are better than 'them,' and hence that 'I' am better than 'him.' When this social comparison renders unsatisfying results, groups are able to change their collective behaviors in a consensual way. At times, this process causes groups to change their identities to mollify societal discourses or to conform to societal norms. Tajfel refers to this as 'passing.'[309] At other times, groups of individuals can behave in ways that flout, dispute, renegotiate or antagonise societal norms. When the latter is the case, the outcome appears as 'resistance identity.'

Central to the formation and maintenance of social identity is the 'salience,' or 'entitativity,' of a group: the sense that one's group is a coherent entity.[310] At varying times and by varying degrees, individuals require greater or lesser entitativity. Individuals who are regarded as successful

306. Collinson, *Richard Bancroft and Elizabethan Anti-Puritanism*, 218; *This England*, 51; 'Beginnings of English Sabbatarianism,' 207–21; Todd, *Christian Humanism and the Puritan Social Order*, 13; Sprunger, 'English and Dutch Sabbatarianism,' 24–28.

307. Collinson, 'Godly Preachers and Zealous Magistrates,' 7; 'Shearmen's Tree and the Preacher,' 219.

308. Tajfel, *Differentiation Between Social Groups*; *Human Groups and Social Categories*; 'Social Psychology of Intergroup Relations,' 1–39; 'Cognitive Aspects of Prejudice,' 79–97; 'Experiments in Intergroup Discrimination,' 96–102; Turner, 'Social Categorization and the Self-concept,' 2, 77–122; 'Social Identification and Psychological Group Formation,' 2, 518–38; Turner et al, *Rediscovering the Social Group*; Campbell, 'Common Fate,' 202–4.

309. Tajfel, *Human Groups and Social Categories*, 278–80.

310. Campbell, 'Common Fate,' 202–4.

by the standards of societal norms, for example, require lower entitativity since their self-worth as individuals is less predicated on the success of their group. At certain times, entitativity becomes vital. Michael Hogg has demonstrated that the need for entitativity becomes heightened at times of personal uncertainty. At times of uncertainty, an individual requires the straightforward narratives and intelligible relationships that highly entitative groups can provide. Often, during times of uncertainty, entitativity is secured through the adoption or accentuation of behaviors and identities that are considered deviant or extreme. By engaging in deviant or extreme behaviors, groups can strengthen the membranes between the in-group and the out-group, forming a kind of 'resistance identity,' and thereby safeguarding the coherence and continuity of the group.[311]

The experience of many Reformed Protestants in Stuart England was one of soteriological uncertainty. Reformed Protestants and their peers were exposed to the idea that assurance of salvation was valuable and indeed necessary, but they were also cautioned that it was nearly impossible to attain. No sources of authority—the church, the academy, even 'the Letter' of scripture—could guarantee assurance. The epistemic pillars of soteriology, as Leif Dixon writes, were demolished.[312] In the context of the revolutionary conflict, this epistemology formed the basis of a peculiarly Puritan concept of liberty. 'No man or sort of men can presume of an unerring spirit, since there remains the possibility of error,' wrote William Walwyn. 'Men are not to compel each other that he who is in error may be the constrainer of he who is in truth.'[313] This process provided the basis for a renewed focus on separation—both ritual and social—amongst the Godly of Stuart England. The rituals that Traske, Tillam and Totney renovated in their devotional practices functioned as marks of separation both intrinsically and circumstantially. As such, the soteriological aspects of Reformed Protestantism, rather than the Biblicist aspects, provided the stimulus for the rise of Judaizing.

This approach should not be read as a psychological 'reduction' of religious convictions. Nor should the claim that resistance and concern for singularity was central to Godly divinity be read as a delegitimization. On the contrary. As Lake and Stephens write:

> The tensions and animosities that the godly stirred up in their contemporaries and that their contemporaries stirred up in

---

311. Hogg, 'Uncertainty-identity Theory,' 69–126; Hogg et al., 'Uncertainty, Entitativity, and Group Identification,' 135–42.

312. Dixon, *Practical Predestinarians in England*, 91.

313. Walwyn, *Compassionate Samaritane Unbinding the Conscience*, 11.

them, were central to their sense of themselves and indeed to some of their intensely felt spiritual and even devotional experiences.[314]

Reading Puritanism as functional identity, defined by 'singularity,' by a need to maintain the boundaries that separated a 'peculiar people' from the unregenerate mass, allows us to describe, with a *greater* degree of understanding, the behaviors of these figures. The intention, here, is to provide a 'thick' account of Judaizing: one that takes into account not just *what* these figures did or said but also what it *meant*, both to their peers and to themselves.

ORDER OF CHAPTERS

We shall proceed as follows. The opening two chapters of this book are concerned with the gestation of the Judaizing phenomenon. The first chapter offers an account of the dissemination of soteriological uncertainty in the period following the Protestant Reformation. This led to a process of Godly identity-formation, whereby significant numbers of Reformed Protestants developed religious practices that functioned to separate them, passively, from the majority *and* to symbolise that separation. At the same time, Godly professors expressed their attachment to an 'ethic of singularity.'

The second chapter explores the ways in which Judaizing functioned as a locus of resistance. Both intrinsically and circumstantially, I contend, Jewish rituals functioned as 'divisive identifications,' endowed with the power to render the participant separate from the majority. The ways in which these practices functioned as markers of separation between the pure and the impure has been extensively explored in the work of Douglas, Klawans, Weiss and others. But, in a complementary sense, they also functioned as markers of separation in the context of a culture which, for various philo-semitic and anti-semitic reasons, associated the Jew with irreducible 'otherness.'

The third chapter concerns the figure of John Traske. Traske is a much storied figure, and his career has been used a reference point for the origins of the observance of the Seventh-Day Sabbath in the Protestant sphere. Aside from the Saturday Sabbath, Traske and his followers also embraced the Levitical dietary laws and the celebration of the Passover. At least one of his followers was circumcised by a *mohel* in Amsterdam. Traske's career appears to be marked with a great contradiction. His writings assert a commitment to an anti-legal form of soteriology. But his practices demonstrated a commitment to Jewish rituals. The literature produced by Traske does not

---

314. Lake and Stephens, *Scandal and Religious Identity*, 357.

refer openly to any of these practices. However, it does attest to a keen and fulsome embrace of the ethic of singularity. Traske wrote at great length about the need to maintain small, close-knit, impenetrable circles of true Christians. This commitment to 'separation' and singularity, I argue, was the impetus for Traske's anti-legal tendencies as well as his Judaizing tendencies.

The fourth chapter concerns Thomas Totney. Totney was a soldier in Cromwell's army. After a transformative conversion experience, he took on a prophetic role. He wrote extensively on the subject of Christian liberty during the period of the interregnum. In the later years of the interregnum, he adopted a new identity: that of a 'Jew of the tribe of Reuben.' Arguing that he was indeed a Jew—and in fact the King of seven nations—Totney proclaimed himself above and immune to the persecutions of the Cromwellian government. He demonstrated the seriousness of his conviction by becoming circumcised. Totney's thought has been represented as a model of 'symbolic criticism' of political oppression. This chapter contends that Totney's interest was more in 'separation'—of the oppressed from the oppressor but also of the Godly from the profane world—than in the political concept of liberty.

The fifth chapter concerns Thomas Tillam and his followers. Tillam, like Traske was a confessional wanderer, embracing a wide range of different liturgical and ecclesiological beliefs during the period of the interregnum. A common theme of Tillam's work is his determination to belong to a small, distinctive congregation, not to become immersed in the rabble of the reprobate. Towards the tail-end of the interregnum, Tillam devised a mode of worship that he believed would consummate his vision of a small, obedient, remnant. It involved the reintroduction of a number of practices—Levitical dietary observance, the celebration of the Seventh Day Sabbath, the growing of beards and even circumcision—through which Tillam and his followers demonstrated their singularity.

In these wider discussions of Puritan culture and its interaction with Jewishness, and in the closer examination of these three illustrative figures, I want to demonstrate that admiration was *not* the impetus for Judaizing in early modern England. In concluding, I argue that Judaizers did not seek to take on the glories of Israel, but rather the hardships and pariah-hood of the Jews. I believe that this is evident from the descriptions that these figures, themselves, offer of Godliness, Jews and Judaizing. Moreover, I want to point to the many ways in which oppositional self-definition and resistance can give rise to complex and meaningful religious identities. Thirdly, I want to propose that soteriological uncertainty, elicited by the rise of Reformed Protestant devotion, provided a stimulus for the centrifugal forces within Puritanism in early modern England.

CHAPTER 1

Singularity and Puritanism

IN ARTHUR DENT's *A Plaine Man's Pathway to Heaven*, two interlocutors—
Theologus and Asunetus—engage in a discussion about how one should
attain assurance of one's salvation. Asunetus—the 'cold Christian', described
by Theologus as 'a very ignorant man'—gives 'an old fashioned and silly',
account of assurance:

> If a man say his Lords praier, his Ten Commandements, keepe
> them, say no body no harme, nor doe no body no harme, and
> doe as he would be done to, have a good faith to God-ward, and
> be a man of Gods beliefe, no doubt he shall be saved.[1]

His assumption is denounced by Theologus, Dent's prolocutor:

> Alas, you have bewraied your great ignorance. For you imag-
> ine, a man may be saved, without the word: which is a grosse
> errour.[2]

'Ignorance', Christopher Haigh wrote of this encounter, 'was bliss.'[3] The
fictional conversation between Theologus and Asunetus represented the
very real encounter between the 'popular pelagian' soteriology of the pre-
Reformation era and the soteriological outlook of the Godly in early Stuart
England. Attaining assurance of one's salvation for the former was a relatively straightforward matter involving: 'avoidance of extraordinary sin, regular
church attendance and the discharge of everyday social duties.'[4] But with
the epiphany of Reformed Protestantism, the matter of attaining assurance

1. Haigh, *Plain Man's Pathway*, 59; Dent, *Plaine Man's Pathway*, 25.
2. Dent, *Plaine Man's Pathway*, 25–26.
3. Haigh, *Plain Man's Pathway*, 59.
4. Lake, *Antichrist's Lewd Hat*, 180.

became both more pressing and more problematic. Reformed Protestant soteriology placed strict limitations on the atonement. John Norden wrote that 'since the beginning of the church God hath bin farre the least part of the world.' Perhaps even more discomfortingly, God was with the 'least part of each congregation.'[5] Calvinist soteriology stressed the irresistible, unconditional, absolute nature of the divine decree of predestination and the strict, binary and irreducible distinction between the elect and the reprobate. 'Can there be greater antipathy,' asked Joseph Bentham, 'than betwixt God's saints and Satan's slaves? God's darlings and Satan's dross?'[6] Meanwhile, the array of works-based, 'semi-Pelagian,' practices which promised a warrant of salvation was washed away with the tide.

This chapter explores the process by which assurance became problematized in early modern, Protestant England, going on to explain how different sections of English society—in the decades leading up to the Civil War and during the period of the interregnum—sought to mitigate the uncertainties aroused by the dissemination of Reformed Protestant soteriology. Many Protestants found assurance in familiar places: participation in officially mandated acts of worship and membership of the church-by-law-established. Others, however—in particular those who would be identified as 'Puritans'—found new and elaborate ways of pursuing assurance. For many, the development of strong relational bonds between themselves and their Godly peers provided the best 'warrant' for their own salvation.[7] Using various strategies, groups and individuals sought to strengthen these bonds, through greater and greater accentuation of the difference between themselves and their 'ungodly' neighbors. This was a dialogical process, in which the so-called 'ungodly' were actively participant. It therefore resulted in the construction of a Godly identity that was molded (in part) by the slanders, libels and stereotypes the ungodly used to describe the Godly.

This narrative has three discrete stages: the period in which 'traditional religion' offered some guarantee of assurance, the period in which traditional religion was dismantled and the period in which new structures of assurance were established by the Godly community. Starting in the fifteenth century and moving through the development and dissemination of Protestant thought in Europe, the first section demonstrates how the sacramental structures within pre-Reformation Christianity, that had offered assurance of salvation, were gradually stripped away. This process was facilitated in England by the return of the Marian exiles. The generations that

---

5. Norden, *Mirror for the Multitude*, 38–39.

6. Bentham, *Saints Societie*, 6.

7. Dent, *Plaine Man's Pathway*, 239.

returned and which were taught by returnees were pickled in the 'severe supralapsarianism' of Zanchius, Ursinus and Beza.[8] We then turn to the 'credal predestinarians' who emerged in the context of the Calvinist consensus, seeking to reconcile continued obedience to the church, adherence to the *via media* and avowal of Reformed Protestant soteriology.

Their counterparts—according to R. T. Kendall—were the 'experimental predestinarians' whose role in English history developed through the period of the decline of the Tudor dynasty and the rise of the Stuarts, eventually reaching a crescendo with the crisis of Laudianism, the Civil War and the Interregnum.[9] Throughout this era, members of the latter group sought to create greater and greater distinction between themselves and their ungodly neighbors in the hope of establishing 'singular' Godly identities. This process was characterized by an intellectual tendency to argue using 'binary opposition, inversion and argument from contraries.'[10]

This chapter will demonstrate that Reformed Protestantism carried within it the germ of a desire for separation, for clear demarcations between the Godly and the unregenerate, a desire that was consummated in behaviors that *exhibited* this distinction. Critics of the Godly and ultimately the Godly themselves would refer to this tendency as 'singularity.' But the majoritarian practice of labelling and expelling trends functioned as a didymic counterpoint to the Godly association of expulsion and marginality with Godliness.[11]

'NO MAN CAN BE ASSURED'

The fifteenth-century morality play *The Somonyng of Everyman* traces the journey of Everyman who, abandoned by his comrades—'Kindred, Cousin and Goods'—is accompanied by 'Good Deeds' as he travels towards his salvation. Good Deeds is too weak to support Everyman on his journey, but is

---

8. Como, 'Puritans, Predestination,' 67.

9. Kendall, *Calvin and English Calvinism*, viii. Leif Dixon has taken issue with Kendall's typology of 'experimental' and 'credal' predestinarianism. Dixon's concern is that the former is too often used to denote a Weberian concept of the despairing Puritan (see Dixon, *Practical Predestinarians*, 209–53). For the interests of this discussion, this terminology is to be used only to describe those who sought to discover assurance, and as such incorporates those who were successful as well as those who were unsuccessful in this endeavor.

10. Lake, 'Anti-Popery,' 72–107 (quotation at 73).

11. Lake, 'Anti-Popery,' 74.

revived by a visit to Confession. Completing his journey, Everyman climbs into his grave, content, contrite and confident that his salvation is assured.[12]

From the era of the Pelagian controversy onwards, the doctrine of predestination had formed a plank of Christian orthodoxy. But the medieval period saw the rise of the concept of 'infused righteousness' and the waning of the influence of Augustinian soteriology.[13] The seeming paradox presented by the juxtaposition of sacramental worship and the predestination of souls was resolved, primarily, by claiming that sacramental efficacy worked *ex opere operandum*. Medieval homiletics rarely referred to predestination.[14] Those, like the Lollards, who *did* avow predestinarian ideas were ostracized and persecuted.[15] Regardless of the complexities of the Thomist soteriology which validated sacramental worship, most ordinary Christians believed that the pathway to heaven was one of good works, regular confession of sins, participation in sacraments and other, extra-ecclesial devotional practices.[16] Within the popular sphere the sacraments were imputed with supernatural powers to redeem and to heal.[17] Some believed that to be buried in a scapular guaranteed safe passage to paradise.[18] Devotions to particular saints, pilgrimages and relics all offered a voluntarist map of salvation for ordinary believers. Meanwhile, the varied practices associated with the remission of the sins of the souls in purgatory (including the sale of indulgences) remained popular into the sixteenth century.[19]

Sin, when committed, was absolved through auricular confession. The ability to seek absolution for sins and reconcile with God, offered an understanding of life as a journey through 'the penitential terrain.'[20] Confession and absolution were often compared, metaphorically, with medical procedures. *Jacob's Well*, a pastoral manual of the fifteenth century, described the

12. *Everyman, a Morality Play*, 116.

13. Aquinas, *Summa Theologica* I.23.5; Levering, 'Aquinas on Romans 8,' 197; Davies, *Thomas Aquinas's Summa Theologiae*, 88–91; Ginther, *Westminster Handbook to Medieval Theology*, 153.

14. Lynch, *Medieval Church*, 286; Vauchez, *Laity in the Middle Ages*, 12, 23–25, 119–29.

15. Thomson, *Later Lollards*, 238; Rex, *Lollards*, 54–88.

16. McGrath, *Iustitia Dei*, 117–28.

17. Thomas, *Religion and the Decline of Magic*, 45–48, 118–19, 214; Watkins, *History and the Supernatural*, 36, 95–96.

18. Thomas, *Religion and the Decline of Magic*, 32.

19. Brown, *Popular Piety in Late Medieval England*, 90–94; Kamerick, *Popular Piety and Art*; Tyerman, *England and the Crusades*, 354.

20. Meens, *Penance in Medieval Europe*, 120–39, 163; Starr-LeBeau, 'Lay Piety and Community Identity,' 395–419.

surgical procedure of confession: the 'deed flesch' of 'hard obstynacye' being cut with a 'scharp corryzie,' by the confessor.[21]

These facets of late medieval, plebeian soteriology were swept away with the tide of Reformed Theology in the sixteenth and seventeenth century. The reformers repudiated the 'semi-Pelagianism' of the unreformed Church and affirmed what they believed to be the most fidelitous reading of Augustine: that man could not ascertain on the basis of his actions or his relationship with the sacraments the nature of his soteriological condition.[22] Luther wrote to Erasmus of Rotterdam in 1524, denouncing the hubris of sacramentalism and cautioning that man 'must despair of himself' if he is to be sufficiently humbled before God.[23] The utility of the sacraments, Calvin wrote, was only a correlative of faith. With or without the sacraments, the invisible Church of the Saints would persevere.[24]

The resurgence of Augustinian soteriology and the stigmatization of 'semi-Pelagianism' precipitated an excarnation of ritual across Protestant Europe.[25] The church, which had once been visible, was now invisible. The monasteries which had once populated the landscape disappeared. The ceremonies which had embodied the message of salvation, were denounced as carnal and were banned. The priesthood that had guaranteed the efficacy of the sacrament of confession was stripped of its sacerdotal role. The sacraments themselves, efficacious components of salvation for so many ordinary Christians, were stripped of their soteriological potency and became no more than symbols of an inner, working faith. In short, the structures that Asunetus looked to, to warrant his salvation, were dismantled.

Auricular confession, envisioned in *The Somonynge of Everyman* as the elixir that strengthened Christians on their journey through the penitential terrain, was disparaged since it required sacerdotal intermediarity in the relationship between God and Christian. Calvin called it a 'frivolous absurdity,' a perversion of the apostolic tradition described in James 5:16.[26] Where confessional practices were retained, in the Lutheran hemisphere, they functioned as 'an avenue of priestly instruction and consolation . . . not

21. Langum, 'Discerning Skin,' 141–61.

22. Luther, 'Disputation for Clarifying the Power and Efficacy of Indulgences,' 13–47.

23. Luther, 'On the Bondage of the Will,' 178.

24. Calvin, *Institutes of the Christian Religion* 4.15.22.

25. Taylor, *Secular Age*, 614–15.

26. Calvin, *Institutes of the Christian Religion* 3.40.6.

in terms of guilt and punishment in the afterlife but on earth and in terms of concrete modes of behaviour.'[27]

A second generation of Reformed Protestant thinkers pursued Calvin's premises toward ever more challenging conclusions. Theodor Beza called auricular confession an insult to the oblation made by Christ.[28] He wrote that the sacramental systems of the Eucharist and Extreme Unction (insofar as they were freighted with soteriological significance) represented the nadir of 'Romish,' superstition.[29] Claiming that it was impossible to attain assurance of salvation and election from participation in collective worship, he furthermore affirmed that participation in any form of sacramental worship could *theoretically* offer evidence of reprobation. Touching on the Eucharist, in particular, he claimed that the sacrament, when celebrated collectively, *could* serve as an act of devotion or it *could* serve as an act of idolatry. After all, individuals celebrating the Eucharist could not expect to discern the intentions of their fellow congregants, nor the celebrant.[30] Beza and Zanchius promulgated a form of predestinarianism that placed even greater emphasis on the sovereignty of God. The doctrine of supralapsarianism, asserted that the double, binding decree of predestination had taken place *before* the decree of the Fall, rather than as a result of it. This doctrine placed even greater emphasis on the impotence of human agency in the matter of salvation, claiming as it did that the Fall had no bearing on God's decision to damn and elect. It also served to further entrench the difference between the elect and the reprobate.[31]

In the era of Protestant confessionalization and the rise of Bucanus, Beza, Ursinus and Zanchius, the planks of soteriological certainty—which the sacramental model of the medieval Church had guaranteed—were torn away. The Heidelberg Reformers coined the reflexive mode of ethics by which the Godly were required to look, not to the Word, but to their own consciences for the repository of assurance.[32] It was this tendency that would inform the deeply reflexive approach to ethics, typical of the Godly in the Stuart period. These figures, through the intercession of Foxe, Knox,

27. Karant-Nunn, *Reformation of Ritual*, 98.

28. Beza, *Master Bezaes Sermons*, 424.

29. Beza, *Christian Faith*, 143–56.

30. Beza, *Christian Faith*, 158.

31. White, *Predestination, Policy, and Polemic*, 9, 16.

32. Kendall, *Calvin and English Calvinists*, 33; Cefalu, *Moral Identity in Early Modern English Literature*, 30–31.

Perkins and Hill, helped to form the devotional and—ultimately—social landscape of England in the proceeding century.[33]

THE ENGLISH CAREER OF THE DOCTRINE

The gestation of English Reformed Protestantism during this period was an idiosyncratic one, and it bore forth an idiosyncratic Church. It was a process characterized, predominantly, by fitfulness. Predestinarian thought had been a component of the Lollard heresy as early as the fourteenth century. Lollard texts from the fifteenth century presaged the Reformation concept of the 'invisible church.'[34] Lollardry had been crushed by Henry VII.[35] The constructed memory of Lollardry and 'the great abjuration' would form part of Protestant mythology and hagiography for successive generations.[36] Henry VIII's reign, and the break with Rome, seemed to offer a window of opportunity for those scholars and churchmen who were sympathetic to Continental Reform. Tyndale, Coverdale, Joye and many others published declarations of confessional predestinarianism.[37] This, however, was not to be a period of fruition for Reformed Protestantism in England. Henry's theological views were unmoved by the Calvinist apologetes and several were persecuted for their heterodoxy.[38] Edward VI's reign marked the dawn of English Reformed Protestantism as a national project. Cranmer was installed as Archbishop of Canterbury. Martin Bucer, Peter Vermigli and Jan Laski moved to England and took up positions of influence. Myles Coverdale returned from Antwerp and was given the position of chaplain to the King.[39] Once again, hope was short-lived. Upon her accession, Mary I attempted to reverse the progress of Reform, exiling and executing Protestant opinion-formers.[40] Many Protestant luminaries fled to continental Europe, where the ideas of Beza and Calvin, Bucanus, Zanchius and Ursinus fermented in

---

33. Collinson, *Elizabethan Puritan Movement*, 1–43.

34. 'Duty of the Priesthood,' 115.

35. Rex, *Lollards*, 110–25.

36. Foxe, *Actes and Monuments*, 818; Bedford, *Luthers Predecessours*, 26; Young, *Breviary of the Later Persecutions*, 51.

37. Tyndale, *Obedience of a Christian Man*; Coverdale, *Certain Most Godly*; Joye, *Compendyouse Somme*; Joye, *Defence of the Mariage of Preistes*.

38. Rex, 'Religion of Henry VIII,' 1–32; Ryrie, *Gospels and Henry VIII*, 95; Scarisbrick, *Henry VIII*, 409.

39. Macculloch, *Thomas Cranmer*, 9–12; Loach, *Edward VI*, 116–35; Williams, *Late Tudors*, 60–86.

40. Danner, *Pilgrimage to Puritanism*, 111; Eveden, *Religion and the Book in Early Modern England*, 87.

the humidity of persecution.[41] Those Reformed Protestants who weathered the storms of Mary's reign returned to establish a 'fully-reformed,' church in Elizabethan England.[42] Their travails were not successful. However, through writing and preaching they disseminated a new, predestinarian soteriology. The literature that emerged from this era laid the foundations for a peculiarly English form of predestinarian soteriology with a particular emphasis on the 'reflexive' ethic and on an 'identity of powerlessness' whereby Godliness was associated with marginality and weakness.[43] It would provide the intellectual ballast for the Godly movements of the proceeding generations. A notable characteristic of English predestinarian thought was the zealous dismantling of epistemic structures of certainty. 'If a want-to-be saint put too much store in their reason, their senses, or the pull of tradition,' wrote Leif Dixon of this period, 'he was unlikely to be touched by the Spirit.'[44]

The most notable text to emerge from this milieu was *The Actes and Monuments of these Latter and Perillous Days, Touching Matters of the Church*, compiled by John Foxe and John Bale during their years of exile in Basle. In Basle, Foxe and Bale worked as translators and proof-readers in the workshop of Johannes Oporinus. Foxe later described their living conditions as 'total poverty.'[45] Bale and Foxe's family were accommodated in the Clarakloster, a dissolved convent, which had previously housed a community of Poor Clares. The civic authorities had reserved the building as a refugee camp for English exiles. It was rented to the English in 1557 at a rate of 24 pounds per annum. Alongside the Foxe family, the Clarakloster housed Sir Anthony Denny and his family, and Sir Francis Knollys's. Surviving floorplans of the Clarakloster show that the sleeping quarters were little more than dormitories.[46] The text that Bale and Foxe produced stressed the virtue of heroic endurance and drew a constellatory map of the troubled progress of Protestant thought, confounding the claim that Protestant misfortune denoted providential condemnation.[47] Foxe stressed that one *could not know* if one was elect simply by one's earthly condition or experience. The 'true

---

41. Garrett, *Marian Exiles.*

42. Collinson, *Archbishop Grindal,* 23–67; *Elizabethan Puritan Movement,* 33–36; Macculloch, *Tudor Church Militant,* 183–91; Pettegree, *Marian Protestantism,* 1–7, 86–117.

43. Cefalu, *Moral Identity in Early Modern English Literature,* 31; Yoder, 'Jewishness of the Free Church Vision,' 112–13; 'Jesus the Jewish Pacifist,' 75.

44. Dixon, *Practical Predestinarians,* 112.

45. Eveden, *Religion and the Book in Early Modern England,* 55–75, 102–35 (quotation at 72).

46. Garrett, *Marian Exiles,* 55–57.

47. Olsen, *John Foxe,* 51–101; Christianson, *Reformers and Babylon,* 39–45.

church,' he wrote, was not discernible to human sense or reason.[48] It was only discernible to those who were participant in it, and this only through revelation, by grace of God.[49] Foxe stressed that those characteristics which might lead one to believe a group to be reprobate and punished, often in fact denoted beatification. In Foxe's system, the success of the 'Romish,' church as a political institution, its very longevity, was evidence of its reprobation rather than its election. The Church of Rome had not been persecuted and was thus no Church of Christ.[50] Meanwhile, a long and arduous history of marginalization and persecution, marked out the Protestant Church as the true Church.[51] The concatenation of historical oppressions and persecutions contributed to the character of English predestinarianism. The Marian exiles returned to take up the reins of the newly restored, reformed Church of England with a distinctive—amongst other European Reformed movements—attachment to the notion that the true church was marked by suffering, exile and rejection at the hands of 'the World.'[52]

Throughout the years which followed the Elizabethan settlement and the return of the Marian exiles, 'moderate Puritans' sought to build—as Collinson puts it—a 'church within a church': a Godly, spiritual, Church using the carnal, Laodicean Church as its vehicle.[53] Whilst they conceded defeat on the foundation of a Presbyterian model of church governance, they nonetheless hoped to secure concessions from Elizabeth's government on issues like vestments, extra-ecclesial conventicles and the like.[54] However, even fraternal criticism of the established church was greeted with suspicion, antagonism and derision. John Field and Thomas Wilcox presented an 'Admonition to Parliament,' suggesting adjustments to the 'unperfect,' prayerbook and the Settlement in general.[55] They were imprisoned. Thomas Sampson and Laurence Humphrey petitioned the Queen to exempt conscientious pastors from wearing the vestments prescribed by the Book of Common Prayer.[56] They were deprived. Thomas Cartwright made several sermons on the subject of the Acts of the Apostles, advocating a

---

48. Foxe, *Actes and Monuments*, 18.

49. Foxe, *Actes and Monuments*, 32.

50. Foxe, *Actes and Monuments*, 4.

51. Foxe, *Actes and Monuments*, 18.

52. White, *Predestination, Policy, and Polemic*, 110, 158.

53. Collinson, 'John Field and Elizabethan Puritanism,' 335–71 (quotation at 369).

54. Collinson, *Elizabethan Puritan Movement*, 93–98, 101–21.

55. Collinson, 'Aspects of Popular Protestantism,' 52.

56. Collinson, 'Aspects of Popular Protestantism,' 11.

return to Apostolic systems of discipline.[57] He was hounded by Whitgift, then Dean of Lincoln. The Conventicle Act was established in order to root out small, extra-ecclesial communities of the Godly. At St. Paul's Cross, Richard Bancroft mocked, slandered and maligned the 'certain men,' whilst Richard Hatton denounced them as Genevans, a treacherous fifth column from the floor of the House of Commons.[58] These events contributed to a sense of unease amongst some sections of society who felt—as Bozeman has it—that the English Reformation 'had been arrested at an immature stage.'[59] It also led to a shift in emphasis amongst the Godly. From the early Stuart period they began to engage in a process of social reification, of Godly identity formation.

'WISDOM IS FOLLY'

Exhortations to epistemological negativity, to the *abandonment* of certainty characterized the Ur-texts of Reformed Protestant soteriology. Girolamo Zanchi's *Doctrine of Absolute Predestination* evoked an experience of epistemic lawlessness, of disorientation:

> In a state of unregeneracy, our wisdom is folly, our strength weakness, our righteousness nothing worth.[60]

Zanchius labels this experience 'self-despair.' He identifies it as a great boon to the righteous believer in that

> it tends to inspire us with true humility of soul, and to lay us, as impotent dust and ashes, at the feet of sovereign Omnipotence.[61]

These sentiments were echoed by the English reformers of the early seventeenth century. This period—in the aftermath of the failures of successive projects to promote further reform of the Church—has been characterized as one of increased Protestant pietism. Bozeman defined this new, Puritan divinity as 'more introspective, more troubled by issues of certitude, more laden with ritual.'[62] The Puritans turned their attentions from society to the self. Exercises in casuistry were introduced in order to replace the practice of

---

57. Collinson, 'Aspects of Popular Protestantism,' 67–81.

58. Bancroft, *Sermon Preached at Paules Crosse*, 72; Hartley, *Proceedings in the Parliament of Elizabeth the First*, 2:414–24.

59. Bozeman, *To Live Ancient Lives*, 7–9.

60. Zanchius, *Doctrine of Absolute Predestination*, 35.

61. Zanchius, *Doctrine of Absolute Predestination*, 28.

62. Bozeman, *Precisianist Strain*, 67.

auricular confession. But the evidence demonstrates that 'none of these were sufficient substitute for the old sacrament.'[63] Even William Perkins lamented the decline of the sacrament as a method for unburdening the conscience.[64]

One element of this process, was a boom in the publication of devotional Protestant texts, targeted at a wider, more plebeian readership.[65] These texts encouraged their readers to avoid any form of Pelagianism and to throw themselves on the mercy of God both soteriologically and (more broadly) epistemologically. The leading lights of the genre were Nicholas Byfield, Arthur Dent and William Perkins. Aimed at the 'ignorant and vulgar sort,' Dent's *Plaine Man's Pathway to Heaven* offered to show 'wherein every man may cleerely see, whether he shall be saved or damned.'[66] Dent's project was to dismantle the semi-articulate, 'popular pelagianism' of rustic piety, thereby laying the groundwork for the inculcation of 'proper Protestantism.'[67] In several passages of dialogue between the Godly 'Theologus' and 'Asunetus' his 'ignorant,' neighbor, expressions of 'simple,' popular piety are dismissed as either incorrect or dangerous. Theologus delights in dismantling the homespun, intuitive ethics of his interlocutor. When Asunetus complains about the hypocrisy of his precise neighbors, Theologus replies that the outward actions of the Godly are subsumed into their election, so that to the naked eye they may appear immoral, when in fact their justification is intact: 'Full little doe you know what they feele . . . for the worke of the Spirit in the hearts of the elect is very secret, and altogether hid from the world.'[68]

Perkins was 'Puritan pietism's greatest publicist.'[69] Like Foxe and Bale, Perkins warned against any claims of ecclesiastical monopoly on salvation.[70] Whilst he reconciled himself to the establishment of a national church as a practical expediency (in order to facilitate the building of a 'church within a church'), he saw no great distinction between the hubris of the church of Rome (in claiming soteriological prerogative) and any other church. All churches, other than the invisible Church, were made up of regenerate and unregenerate. As such, they were 'built on sand,' and would not

63. Collinson, 'Shepherds, Sheep-Dogs, and Hirelings,' 215.

64. Perkins, *Of the Calling of the Ministerie*, 28.

65. Zaret, *Origins of Democratic Culture*, 152–58; Collinson et al., 'Religious Publishing in England,' 29–67.

66. Dent, *Plaine Man's Pathway*, a1r.

67. Dent, *Plaine Man's Pathway*, 1, 3; Lake, *Antichrist's Lewd Hat*, 180; Haigh, *Plain Man's Pathway*, 59.

68. Dent, *Plaine Man's Pathway*, 25.

69. Bozeman, *Precisianist Strain*, 68.

70. Foxe, *Actes and Monuments*, 16.

last. No longer could membership of such congregations be relied on as sources of assurance.[71]

Perkins's theology undermined the trustworthiness of human experience as a medium of ethical action or of salvation altogether. Perkins believed that human reason and experience was impeded in its pursuit of assurance of salvation, not only by its own weakness, but also by the obtrusion of the forces of evil. The universe was fluid, deceptive and inscrutable to human reason. There was a 'naturall Distemper in the minde of man.'[72] Perkins ecclesiology, epistemology and soteriology placed man in a condition of helplessness in the hand of the Almighty. Man, 'whose knowledge since the Fall is mingled with much ignorance,' is ill-equipped to understand the world in which he exists.[73] Dixon has written that William Perkins 'demolished every conceivable basis for making truth claims.' Neither 'tradition,' nor 'churches,' nor 'princes,' nor 'human reason,' nor 'senses,' nor 'common sense morality' could offer any help to the Godly professor.[74]

In the abandonment of the body in favor of a more cerebral form of religious devotion, Charles Taylor has argued, Calvinism laid the groundwork for modern secularism.[75] In the writings of Dent and Byfield and Perkins, we find another vista of excarnation: the stripping away of the epistemic flesh of traditional soteriology. This impulse can be traced back through Luther's writings—his concept of the 'theology of Glory'—and further still to St. Paul's dictum: 'If there is knowledge, it will be set aside when what is perfect comes' (1 Cor 13:10).[76] In the English context, the active dismantlement of epistemic structures became a centerpiece of popular, Reformed Protestant divinity. And whilst the mechanics of salvation, as it had been understood for centuries, were being dismantled, the onus of soteriological responsibility was atomized. In place of the sacramental traditions of the pre-Reformation church, some English Protestants—particularly those of a more 'experimental' bent—sought new and ever more complex strategies for attaining assurance of their own salvations.

---

71. Perkins, *Godlie and Learned Exposition*, 5.

72. Perkins, *Discourse of the Damned Art of Witchcraft* 4v.

73. Perkins, *Discourse of the Damned Art of Witchcraft*, 21.

74. Dixon, *Practical Predestinarians*, 91, 101.

75. Taylor, *Secular Age*, 614–15.

76. Luther, 'Heidelberg Disputation,' 67–121.

THE PLAIN MAN'S PATHWAY

But were ordinary, early-modern, English Protestants *really* immersed in Reformed Protestant soteriological thought to the extent that it affected the way they thought, the way they behaved? Can we really say that these ideas fathomed the unconscious of a nation? Or at least of a significant, and diverse demographic of a nation?

Whiggish readers of the events of the English Reformation, such as A. G. Dickens, hailed it as a kind of national transformation, which swept away the corruptions of late medieval Catholicism and laid the groundwork for the construction of a new, democratic, enlightened nation.[77] But in the decades that followed the publication of Dickens's *The English Reformation*, a succession of revisionist historians argued against the idea that Protestantism took root in England with quite the tenacity that Dickens' had suggested. These scholars—Christopher Haigh, Jack Scarisbrick and (more equivocally) Eamonn Duffy—made the claim that thinking about predestination was a niche activity which occupied only the highly literate few. Haigh characterized the genesis of English Protestantism as 'the premature birth, and difficult labour, of a sickly child.'[78] He contended that Reformed Protestantism—with its intellectual rigour, its unforgiving soteriological formulations and its emphasis on the written word—was a beast ill-suited to the habitat of early-modern England, in areas of which 90 percent of the population were illiterate.[79] Haigh argued that the majority of English Christians were attached to the old rituals of the pre-Reformation church, and were generally hostile—though compliant—to Protestant thought, liturgy, and ecclesiology. All in all, Haigh characterized the Tudor period as one of 'blundering reformation,' which introduced a form of worship 'most did not understand, or want and which nobody knew was here to stay.' Haigh also suggests that religious heterodoxy, at least during the Tudor period was anomalous rather than widespread, thereby debunking wholesale the notion of a *Gemeindereformation* on English soil.[80] This description was corroborated by John Scarisbrick in his book *The Reformation and the English People*.[81] Scarisbrick claimed that reading and preaching—rather than ritual—were the central media through which Calvinist ideas were communicated to the general population. Bibliocentrism, for

77. Dickens, *English Reformation*.

78. Haigh, 'English Reformation,' 449–59; *English Reformations*, 14, 28; Scarisbrick, *Reformation and the English People*; Duffy, *Stripping of the Altars*.

79. Hughes, *Causes of the English Civil War*, 63.

80. Haigh, 'Premature Birth,' 451.

81. Scarisbrick, *Reformation and the English People*, 135.

Haigh and Scarisbrick, made the task of Protestant evangelism 'immense.' This—coupled with the 'laggardly' nature of Protestant preachers—meant that meaningful, Reformed, Protestant enlightenment was dead on arrival.[82] John Morrill argued that real engagement with Reformed Protestantism remained within the preserve of a few, and that Calvinism, up until the mid-seventeenth century was 'exclusionary' and 'elitist.'[83] Eamonn Duffy broadly adhered to this account whilst conceding that most English people eventually developed a kind of Protestant partisanship, believing: 'the Pope to be Antichrist, the Mass a mummery.'[84]

In more recent times this view has fallen out of favor. Calvinism, according to Nicholas Tyacke, was in fact the dominant force within the English pulpit until the emergence of Laudianism and English Calvinist thought was itself 'rooted in the theology of Grace.'[85] Christopher Marsh has identified key flaws in the methodology of Haigh's study, claiming that his selection of sources gave a distorted image of the nature of Protestantism in the sixteenth century in England. In reality, Marsh argues, the majority of the population of England in the late sixteenth century were broadly acquiescent to changes in the modes of worship whilst the reformist programme was 'less objectionable to commonplace Christians' than Haigh implied. Whilst they may not have been fully engaged with the theological gravitas of the changes, to the degree that the Godly were, they may well have found them 'not repulsive.'[86] We might think of Tom Kernan's expression of admiration for the vernacular liturgy at Paddy Dignam's funeral.[87] Margaret Spufford's research has suggested that poor and disadvantaged people engaged with written sources more frequently than Haigh and the revisionists had presumed. 'Even the humblest members, the very poor, women and those in physical isolation,' she writes, 'thought very deeply on religious matters and were often profoundly influenced by them.'[88] Nor does it appear that Protestant clergy 'watered down' the intellectual rigor of their message. At the funeral of Robert Bolton, Nicholas Estwick claimed that Bolton 'prepared nothing for his people but what might have served a very learned auditory.'[89] The research of Margo Todd shows that preachers engaged their

82. Haigh, 'Puritan Evangelism in the Reign of Elizabeth,' 30–58.

83. Morrill, 'Church in England,' 89–114.

84. Duffy, *Stripping of the Altars*, 593.

85. Tyacke, 'Puritanism, Arminianism, and Counter-Revolution,' 53–71.

86. Marsh, *Popular Religion in Sixteenth-Century England*, 200.

87. Joyce, *Ulysses*, 101.

88. Spufford, *World of Rural Dissenters; Contrasting Communities*, 343.

89. Estwick, *Mr. Bolton's Last and Learned Work*, 9.

congregations in discussions of Calvin and Beza, and also of untranslated Greek and Latin texts.[90]

Arnold Hunt asserts that 'predestination was a common topic of discussion in the pulpit' in pre-Laudian *and* Laudian England.[91] From the Elizabethan period onwards, Puritans were identified—at least by their peers—with a greater degree of engagement with the doctrine of predestination. This was the opinion of Richard Bancroft who complained that the Godly 'laid all their religion upon predestination.'[92] Hunt has shown how early modern congregations were trained—through the use of manuals and handbooks—to endure the most challenging homilies. Manuals advised auditors how best to listen and absorb the messages of the sermon, but also offered practical advice on how to avoid becoming distracted or even falling asleep. In order to better digest and internalise the message, auditors were taught to memorise and repeat sections of the sermon upon their return home from church.[93] David Leverenz writes that 'congregations sat for up to two hours listening to God's familiar instructions repeated in the familiar format.'[94] Leif Dixon has also shown that many thorough and important texts produced on the subject of predestination during this period were 'quick to read and cheap to buy.'[95] The suggestion that discussion of predestination belonged 'solely to the realm of academic theology and rarely filtered down into popular preaching' is—on this evidence—'fundamentally mistaken.'[96]

Nonetheless, some revisionist scholars maintain that exposure to the doctrine did not suffice to effect change. The doctrine itself was intrinsically so unappealing, they argue, 'that the majority of Englishmen responded [to it] with indifference and hostility.'[97] Calvinism, some have asserted was too cerebral, too cold to have mass appeal.[98] This, too, appears to have been a canard. Godly preachers were encouraged to deliver homilies which conformed to a process of 'affective identification,' by 'stirring up emotion . . . to communicate it to others.'[99] Puritan homiletics engaged the heart as much as it did the head. Godly ministers 'warmed the hearts' of their congregants.

---

90. Todd, *Culture of Protestantism in Early Modern Scotland*, 51.

91. Hunt, *Art of Hearing*, 17, 356.

92. Barlow, *Summe and Substance of the Conference*, 29.

93. Hunt, *Art of Hearing*, 71–74.

94. Leverenz, *Language of Puritan Feeling*, 142.

95. Dixon, *Practical Predestinarians*, 8, 253–302.

96. Hunt, *Art of Hearing*, 17.

97. Walsham, *Providence in Early Modern England*, 3.

98. Haigh, 'Church of England, the Catholics, and the People,' 195–219.

99. Hunt, *Art of Hearing*, 84.

They made 'the very hairs of their heads to stand up.'[100] Walsham argues that certain patterns of belief created the conditions for an eased transition from 'popular Pelagianism' to 'proper Protestantism.' Despite the disharmonies that existed between 'elite' and 'street' culture, epistemic structures—like providentialism—created 'cultural cement,' 'ligatures' that bound English Protestants together.[101] Reformed Protestant polemicists used familiar cultural tropes, 'sublimating and mutating ancient tendencies' in order to communicate new ideas around predestination. Meanwhile, cheap print and organs of popular culture produced by Puritan writers allowed 'novel priorities to be interweaved with inherited formulae,' the better to sugar the pill of predestinarian ideas.[102]

Predestinarian thought precipitated a major, far-reaching cultural shift in England. It not only reached, but also engaged a very substantial proportion of the population, turning 'popular pelagians' into 'proper Protestants' along the way.[103] This shift brought with it significant cultural and psychological changes.

'DOING AS OTHERS DO'

How, then, did ordinary Christians assuage the uncertainties arising from the dismantlement of ancient systems of soteriological assurance? Many English men and women, during the period of the Calvinist consensus, and through the period of the Laudian crisis and the interregnum, sought assurance of salvation from the source that had always provided it: membership of the established church, and participation in consensual worship. A significant majority of confessing Protestants chose to attend services in their local churches throughout this period.[104]

The assiduous policing of the boundaries of moderate religion which had begun with the Elizabethan settlement, continued into the Stuart era. As Ethan Shagan's research has demonstrated, a fixation with 'moderation' dominated the culture of ecclesiastical and political leadership during this period.[105] The 'inexorable interweaving of spiritual deviance and political sedition' beginning with the Act of Supremacy, continuing through Hatton's

---

100. Todd, *Culture of Protestantism*, 52.

101. Walsham, *Providence in Early Modern England*, 248.

102. Lake, 'Popular Form, Puritan Content?,' 313–35.

103. Haigh, *Plain Man's Pathway*, 65.

104. Maltby, *Prayerbook and People*, 2, 181–224; Spufford, 'Can We Count the Godly,' 428–38.

105. Shagan, *Rule of Moderation*, 111–49; Walsham, *Charitable Hatred*, 207–28.

denunciations of Rome and Geneva in Parliament, 'the nastiness of the 90s' and the Marprelate scandal, Harsnet's attacks on (both Jesuit and Puritan) exorcism, and reaching its denouement in the personal rule of Charles I, all served to construct a model of moderation and extremism.[106] Lake claims that the rise of Arminianism in the 1620s can be explained partly as an inoculation against the apparently dangerously destabilizing demotic and antinomian tendencies that were believed to be inherent to the doctrine of predestination. Laudians, for a season, reinstated ceremony and ritual at the heart of English Protestant devotion, supplanting the sermon, and tamping down on what they saw as a seditious and socially divisive doctrine.[107] In a more immediate sense, strategies employed in the early Stuart period— most prominently the 1622 Declaration of Preachers—neutered the political clout of the early Puritan grandees, sending the movement underground.[108] Walsham has demonstrated that, during this period, religious policy be- came more oriented towards behavioral expressions of fidelity—church at- tendance for example—than intellectual expressions of fidelity. This process was initiated, in part, by the Act of Uniformity of 1559 and the Religion Act of 1592. In other words, from the Elizabethan period onwards, social- identity became gradually more enmeshed with soteriological identity in the maintenance of a moderate middle ground.[109] Puritanism and Popery— 'Scylla and Charybdis'—were tarred with the brush of 'enthusiasm.'[110] This served the purpose of defining—indeed *constructing*—insiderliness and outsiderliness in Protestant England. As different modes of worship moved in and out of favor, so the parameters of (what was perceived as) Godly dissent shifted.[111]

There are strong arguments for ascribing this moderating tendency to political and social conditions.[112] But concern for ecclesiastical consensus and moderation was not only fed by a desire for political stability. Maltby's research has demonstrated that a great many Protestants were devotedly and piously committed to prayer-book worship throughout this period. When

---

106. Walsham, *Charitable Hatred*, 51; Hartley, *Proceedings in the Parliament of Elizabeth I*, 2:414–24; Collinson, *Elizabethan Puritan Movement*, 404–5; 'Ecclesiastical Vitriol,' 154; Brownslow, *Shakespeare, Harsnet, and the Devils of Denham*, 21–48.

107. Lake, 'Anti-Popery,' 86; Parry, *Glory, Laud, and Honour*, 20–21; Reynolds, *Godly Reformers*, 126.

108. Webster, 'Early Stuart Puritanism,' 50.

109. Walsham, *Charitable Hatred*, 59–61.

110. Lake, 'Anti-Puritanism,' 94; Brautigam, 'Prelates and Politics,' 51

111. Walsham, *Charitable Hatred*, 26.

112. Bozeman, *Precisianist Strain*, 41; Sharpe, *Crime in Early Modern England*.

their ministers failed to conform, they informed on them.[113] Affinity and adherence to the *via media* was particularly prevalent amongst those who could be loosely associated with—what R. T. Kendall would call—credal predestinarians.[114] Since the decree of predestination was mysterious, and since no-one could tell who was of the elect and who was not, it was seen by many as futile to engage in the process of seeking assurance. Similarly, it was considered presumptuous to 'sectarize', to exclude any professing Christian from collective worship. The consequence of the visible Church, thus, was limited and the consequence of the invisible church was extended. This 'Whitgiftian fatalism', was embraced by many in the period of the Calvinist consensus.[115] Conforming membership of the established church, for those of a credal predestinarian orientation, remained the most straightforward method of self-assurance. For these, as Marsh writes, 'doing as others do was a religious principle in itself.'[116]

But while 'doing as others do' provided assurance for many Protestants, being 'different from most people' offered assurance for others.[117] In the twilight of the Elizabethan period, new devotional fault-lines were drawn within the Calvinist consensus. Although many elected to worship alongside each other and—when it came to soteriology—to treat that of which they could not speak with silence, others demanded that sides be chosen. The latter became seen by their peers and neighbors as bothersome and contrarian, and they were labelled and derided as the 'precise sort' or as Puritans. At times they would be labelled as Jews or Judaizers. They believed that the distinctions between the Godly and the ungodly were clear, distinct and investigable, not only in the Book of Life, but in the marketplace, the pew and the tavern. Moreover, they saw it as a component of their Christian duty to seek out and sojourn with their fellow professors, to the exclusion of the majority, the 'mass of the reprobate'. In the sense that they were perceived as desiring to be 'different' from their peers, the Godly were labelled as 'singular'.[118] Those who chose sides, and who sequestered themselves from the mass, were of the Godly. Those who lingered in the liminal sphere of credal predestinarianism and conformity were, to use Stephen Marshall's terms, 'neuter', 'Meroz'.[119] Many of these professors—holding that

113. Maltby, *Prayer Book and People*; 'By This Book', 115–37.

114. Lake, 'Calvinism and the English Church', 32–76.

115. Lake, 'Calvinism and the English Church', 41–43.

116. Marsh, *Popular Religion in Sixteenth-Century England*, 203.

117. Collinson, 'Godly Preachers and Zealous Magistrates', 9.

118. Edwards, *Antapologia*, 209; Reeve, *God's Plea for Nineveh*, 72.

119. Marshall, *Meroz Curse*, A1r–B1r.

singularity and distinctiveness was a designation of Godliness—*responded negatively* to the call for conformity, compromise and consensus. Indeed, many of their devotional practices, their ideas, their innovations and their identities functioned as evocations of this refusal.

'THE CURE OF THE FEAR OF DEATH'

A text appeared in 1614 bearing the title *The Cure of the Fear of Death*. It was written by Nicholas Byfield. Its subtitle prescribed a tonic:

> Assurance is an admirable medicine to kill this feare, and to speake distinctly, wee should get the assurance first of Gods favour, and our owne calling and election.[120]

Assurance, if it could be attained, was a mark of election. Meanwhile, *failure* to attain assurance of salvation—and therefore 'feare of death'—was an indication of 'weake faith.' 'Weake faith' was an indication of reprobation. Godly preachers, in their sermons, facilitated this 'oscillation between anxiety and assurance.'[121] If God loved His saints, they argued, then He would surely not allow them to live in uncertainty. He would offer them assurance of their salvation. Thus we find the development—during the early Stuart period—of a form of inverted Pelagianism, a scion of the reflexive ethics of the Heidelberg reformers: one's actions could not lead to the attainment salvation, but they may lead to the attainment of assurance that one had *been* saved. Each of these strategies functioned to place the Godly professor in a *passive* position in relation to the discovery of the warrant of assurance.

In the early Stuart period, experimental forms of predestinarianism became the preoccupation of a Godly minority of English Protestants.[122] The journals of Reformed Protestant professors of this period offer privileged access to their 'insides.' 'Meticulously detailed' journal-keeping was characteristic of the reflexive moral scrutiny that was central to the Puritan

---

120. Byfield, *Cure for the Fear of Death*, 180.

121. Lake, *Boxmaker's Revenge*, 35.

122. Leif Dixon has cautioned against the notion that Predestinarianism necessarily elicited feelings of anxiety. On the contrary, he has argued that, for many, the doctrine was couched in terms that rendered it 'comfortable' or even 'comforting.' But this was true only to the extent that Godly professors were able to develop effective strategies for mitigating the anxieties inherent to predestinarian thought. Dixon allows that it would be 'foolish' to deny that 'ministers called their listeners to oscillate between presumption and despair in a way that brought them back—again and again—to the question of whether or not they were saved . . . particularly within Puritan theological culture' (Dixon, *Practical Predestinarians*, 11).

experience.[123] Accounts of the inner lives of Dionys Fitzherbert, Mary Chester, Anna Trapnel, Richard Rogers, Ralph Josselin, Nehemiah Wallington, William Leonard and Samuel Ward share certain, striking characteristics.[124] The experience of these—and many—English Reformed Protestants, shaped by the stoicism of Perkins, Byfield, Dent and others, was characterized by a never-ending, ouroboric quest for 'assurance.'[125] The Puritan experience, as evidenced in these journals, was one of 'relentless self-observation of personal sinfulness.'[126]

Godly primers of this period promised to equip their readers for the task of 'fetching the warrant of salvation from within.'[127] Byfield's *The Signes*, which identified 'sixteen infallible signs' that one was elect, ran to five editions.[128] His *Marrow of the Oracles of God* collated:

> Treatise gathered out of the Scriptures, *signes* of Gods own making, by which men may try their estate, how by the help of those signes men may settle their *assurance*.[129]

The Godly were not to give undue account to ethical conduct, prayerfulness or 'security' itself in their quest for assurance.[130] Readers were warned that demonstrative moralism could bleed into arrogance or worse, hypocrisy. Robert Bolton's St. Paul's Cross sermon, published in 1625 with the title *A Discourse on the State of True Happiness*, promised to guide its readers to a state of clear and lucid assurance.[131] But his description of hypocrisy muddied the waters considerably. Bolton conceded that a 'hypocrite,' may demonstrate some of the moral qualities usually associated with righteousness. For instance, he may be 'endewed with understanding and knowledge in the word of God.' He may 'see clearly by the Law of God the grieuous intollerablenesse of his sinnes.' He may 'bee amazed and terrified with fearefull

123. Leverenz, *Language of Puritan Feeling*, 13.

124. Seaver, *Wallington's World*, 16–19; Hodgkin, *Women, Madness, and Sin*, 17–19; Mack, *Visionary Women*, 90–106.

125. For the 'stoicism' of Perkins, Dent, and others, see Balfour, *English Epicures and Stoics*, 112–45.

126. Ryrie, *Being Protestant in Reformation Britain*, 44–49; Leverenz, *Language of Puritan Feeling*, 13–14.

127. Dent, *Plaine Man's Pathway*, 259; Zaret, *Origins of Democracy*, 158; Stowe, *Practice of Piety*.

128. Byfield, *Signes*, 1; Ryrie, *Being Protestant*, 39.

129. Byfield, *Marrow of the Oracles of God*, 4.

130. Ryrie, *Being Protestant*, 23–24, 62–63; Beeke, *Assurance of Faith*.

131. Bolton, *Discourse on the State of True Happiness*, 1.

horror, and remorse of conscience for his sinnes.'[132] Puritan preachers warned their flocks against the perils of apathy and hubris in the quest for salvation.[133] William Pinke warned that a 'deadly slumber' had overtaken almost the entire Christian people.[134] Richard Capel, meanwhile, described security as a form of decay, of 'rust.'[135] All of these texts cautioned against any act, in pursuit of assurance, that smacked too much of voluntarism, and thus of Pelagianism.

Puritan despair is a much-discussed topic in scholarship of this period.[136] It is certainly true that the image of the sober, poe-faced Puritan is a stereotype, but it is also true that Puritan manuals and sermons of this period attributed great value to the sensation of sadness and sorrow. Byfield saw it as a duty of the Christian 'to conceive true *mourning* and *sorrow* for sinnes.'[137] Tears and weeping as passively experienced evidence of 'sorrow for sinnes' could, therefore, offer assurance. Henry Greenwood's *Treatise on the Great and General Day of Judgement* offered advice on how to prove, when confronted by Satan, that one was of the elect. Greenwood ventriloquized the justified sinner's soul in dialogue with the accuser, Sathan:

> Sathan: Shewe me Gods seale for that, or els thou art mine.
> Soule: I can weepe for sinne, and I hate sinne in my selfe and others.[138]

Gilbert Primrose thanked God for the 'gifts' of mourning—weeping, tearing clothes, plucking hair—since they gave real evidence of a remorseful soul.[139] John Andrewes warned that 'it will cost him many a prayer and many a teare before he can be certayne or sure to have pardon for his sinnes.'[140] Thomas Playfere wrote that 'salty teares,' were 'the onely drink which Christ will drinke with us.'[141] Anne Trapnel recalled a time in her life when 'if I had not shed some tears in a sermon, I then went home full

---

132. Bolton, *Discourse*, 35–36.

133. Ryrie, *Gospels and Henry VIII*, 22–25.

134. Pinke, *Triall of a Christians Sincere Love*, 68.

135. Capel, *Tentations*, 81.

136. Stanchiewski, *Persecutory Imagination*; Schmidt, *Melancholy and the Care of the Soul*; Seaver, *Wallington's World*, 15–26; Snyder, 'Left Hand of God,' 18–59.

137. Byfield, *Marrow of the Oracles*, 24.

138. Greenwood, *Treatise of the Great and Generall Daye of Judgement*, f2r.

139. Primrose, *Christian Mans Teares and Christs Comforts*, 63–64.

140. Andrewes, *Andrewes Repentance*, 5.

141. Playfere, *Hearts Delight*, 26.

of horror, concluding myself to be that stony ground Christ spake of in the parable of the sower."[142]

Many of the Godly attested to having experiences of 'conversion.' According to Dwight Bozeman—with the influence of pietistic Puritans like Knewstub and Gifford—conversion became, during this period, 'the standard locus for theological discussion.'[143] Many descriptions of conversion are mystical in character.[144] The unspeakable nature of conversion served to accentuate the passivity of the Godly in relation to assurance. As such, conversion experiences represented the antithesis to Pelagianism. They represented the most radical iteration of the Protestant conviction that God chose an elect and rendered them, by Grace, irresistibly, unconditionally and perpetually as saints.

The accounts of Wallington, Dionys Fitzherbert, Joan Barrington and Anna Trapnel all attest to a real and deep-seated anxiety, which accompanied belief that the elect were discernible. This anxiety centered on the problem of how to attain tangible proof that one was of that number, without resorting to Pelagian voluntarism.[145] This could only be attained by *passively* affecting the conditions of saintliness. In a sermon made at St. Paul's Cross on January 17, 1619, Stephen Dennison warned his auditors that it was almost impossible to discern the difference between the Godly and the ungodly. The reprobate too—he told them—may feel effects very similar to those of sanctification. They too may 'attain a kind of desire after the word' and may 'have a kind of persuasion of God's favour to them.'[146] And yet, Denison also preached that 'such is the sweetnesse of full assurance, that whosoeuer hath it, he would not part with it againe for anie pleasure.'[147] Exposure to predestinarian soteriology led, in many cases, to feelings of uncertainty about the afterlife. At the heart of the ideological project of Reformed Protestantism, therefore, was a paradox and a conflict: the active repudiation of soteriological certainty and a strong incentive to pursue it. Lake contends that this combination of messages—the mysterious, excarnated nature of election and the *necessity* of obtaining assurance of election—made it 'ever more urgent for the true child of God to be able to distinguish between his

142. Trapnel, *Legacy for a Saint*, 2.

143. Bozeman, *Precisianist Strain*, 93.

144. Shea, *Spiritual Autobiography in Early America*, 119–24; Dever, *Richard Sibbes*, 121–25; Stoever, *Faire and Easie Way to Heaven*, 61–63.

145. Seaver, *Wallington's World*, 16–19; Hodgkin, *Women, Madness, and Sin*, 17–19; Mack, *Visionary Women*, 90–106; Willen, 'Communion of the Saints,' 19–41; Ryrie, *Being Protestant*, 195–99.

146. Denison, *New Creature*, 67.

147. Denison, *Exposition upon the First Chapter*, 91.

and her own spiritual estate and that of the reprobate.'[148] For many of the Godly, this distinction was best known by the company that they kept.

'SWEET CONSENT'

By 1618, the Godly had tried for a generation to affect the direction of the Church-by-law-established, and they had failed. Presbyterianism as a political project 'died' in 1604 at Hampton Court.[149] In the early Stuart period they began a process of 'turning inward.' Assurance could not be found in the certainty that one belonged to a beatified, Protestant polity (of the kind that some had experienced in Geneva). England, but halfly reformed, was a reprobate nation. The greatest assurance of one's own election could be found in the knowledge that one was of the small, embattled, Godly remnant. Willen writes that the Godly were beset with a sense of anxiety, which could only be allayed by a sense of camaraderie between fellow professors *and* in the rejection of one's ungodly foes. Puritan identity was built on the desire to attain assurance through the medium of 'sweet consent,' itself built on the 'spiritual reciprocity' that emerged from a mutually authenticating 'identity of powerlessness.'[150]

'Nothing giveth more sensible evidence of conversion,' wrote Henry Scudder, 'than Christian society.'[151] This belief was acted out in the scandalous fall of John Barker, vicar of Pitchley, who was found guilty of adultery and infanticide in July 1637. Meeting with his Godly peers in anticipation of his execution, Barker asked them whether they believed he would attain salvation. When they replied in the affirmative, he declared himself assured that he would see them in heaven. The evidence attained by his sense of fellowship with the Godly out-weighed the evidence of his crimes. 'It was through his reintegration into the community of the godly,' Lake writes 'and through the dynamic interaction between the ministers' good opinion of him and his affection for them that Barker achieved a sense that he was indeed going to heaven from the gallows.'[152] The Godly perceived themselves as bound together by a common, social and soteriological identity. These bonds traversed barriers of class and of distance.[153] In the sense of Godly

---

148. Lake, *Boxmaker's Revenge*, 21.

149. Como, *Blown by the Spirit*, 29.

150. Willen, 'Communion of the Saints,' 19–41; Yoder, 'Jewishness of the Free Church Vision,' 112–13.

151. Scudder, *Christian's Daily Walk*, 243.

152. Lake, *Scandal and Religious Identity*, 72.

153. Clarke, *Lives of Sundry Eminent Persons*, 4; Fulbrook, *Piety and Politics*, 37–40;

solidarity, they found a 'spiritual reciprocity' which allayed the incumbent anxieties of Reformed Protestant soteriology.[154]

The importance of maintaining fellowship and consensus—a Godly culture—led to the development of particular and homogeneous cultural practices: fasting, sermon-gadding, conventicling. Broadly, these practices have been referred to as 'voluntary religious' observation or 'Puritan practical divinity.' Collinson notes a lack of significant local variation in Godly culture, debunking the link between Puritanism and individuality. Far from encouraging social atomization, Puritan divinity encouraged a 'programmed corporateness,' which accentuated a consensual sense of the 'tightly knit community amongst the greater mass of the reprobate.'[155] This was an ideological and eschatological concern, but it was also a localized and practical and revealed concern. The Godly needed to be able to identify one another in the 'corrupt mass present in the church.'[156] They were, as Robert Woodford and Nehemiah Wallington attested, easily identifiable to themselves and others. They dressed and even conversed in ways that distinguished themselves from their peers.[157]

The peers of the Godly recognized the slightest of behaviors as expressions of 'singularity.' Collinson has drawn attention to the character of 'shee-Puritan' in John Earle's *Microcosmographie*. The 'Shee-Puritan' is described as being 'much in the turning up of her eye and turning down the leaf in her book, when she hears named chapter and verse.'[158] Thirty years later William Doyle held a feast where a 'rascal' impersonated a Puritan, holding up his hands and 'lifting his eyes.'[159] While the opinions of the Godly were 'singular,' their 'life and conversation were no less.' The Godly exhibited their difference from others in 'voices, faces, gestures, motions, salutations,' and so on.[160] These dramaturgical acts served as 'rituals of sociability,' usually performed in public, and they marked the Godly as members of the justified minority.[161] Such miniscule actions may seem trivial, but they were the building blocks of a shared identity and as such served to promote Godly

---

Stone, 'Bourgeois Revolution,' 44–54; Wrightson 'Terling Revisited,' 208.

154. Lake, *Boxmaker's Revenge*, 21.

155. Collinson, *Religion of Protestants*, 251; *Godly People*, 548; Morgan, *Godly Learning*, 308.

156. Milton, 'Religion and Community,' 70.

157. Parker, *Discourse Concerning Puritans*, 58.

158. Earle, *Microcosmographie*, H6r; Collinson, *Puritan Character*, 6.

159. Thurloe, *Collection of the State Papers of John Thurloe*, 5:371.

160. Crouch, *Posthuma Christiana*, 153.

161. Webster, *Godly Clergy*, 60; Cambers, *Godly Reading*, 159–212.

kinship. In this sense they served a valuable function for those who sought the assurance guaranteed by 'Christian society.'[162] Bentham, in his advice to the Godly on how to pray, cautioned that it was important to do so in assembly since: 'such prayers manifest our mutuall communion, and are an effectuall meanes of mutuall edification, stirring up the zeale, and in-flaming the affections of each other.' The gaze of the ungodly outsider was a vital part of this process of identity formation. The Godly were advised to pray in ways which demonstrated their continuity. They should pray, he cautioned, 'in unanimous uniformity in regard of our outward carriage and gesture' and without 'diversity of gestures which causeth distractions, and hindereth devotion.'[163]

Participating in these rituals allowed the Godly access to a Pentecostal sense of spiritual synergy: 'they kindle one another,' wrote John Cotton 'and the breath of Christians is like bellows.'[164]

Separation from the world and the physical sequestration of the Godly functioned as one component of the Godly concern for Christian society. In the act of 'godly conference' the Godly were advised to be 'separated from the world and the societie of profane men.'[165] 'The critical criterion,' wrote Collinson, 'of being a "Christian indeed" was to gather with others of the same persuasion in self-selective, exclusive company.'[166] This, for some, was the sum value of the atonement. John Knewstub, in his St. Paul's Cross ser-mon, preached that 'Christ Jesus gave him self for us, to purge us, that we might be a peculiar people unto him selfe.'[167]

In the sixteenth century, some took the radical step of removing alto-gether—first from the Church of England and latterly from England itself. 'Brownism' was unusual, however. It occurred 'rarely, even exceptionally, and in response to particular circumstances.'[168] Those who chose to 'sepa-rate within' rather than 'separating out of' the church, as Lake and Collinson have noted, were left more 'exposed,' more imperilled by the threat of being immersed into the mass of the reprobate.[169] For these, physical separation from the 'wicked world' took more quotidian—but nonetheless more so-cially creative—forms. Stephen Denison cautioned his congregation that

---

162. Morgan, *Godly Learning*, 308; Thomas, 'Introduction,' 1–15.

163. Bentham, *Christian Conflict*, 264.

164. Cotton, *Christ the Fountain of Life*, 148.

165. Rollock, *Lectures*, 395.

166. Collinson, 'Godly Preachers and Zealous Magistrates,' 8.

167. Knewstub, *Confutation of Monstrous and Horrible Heresies*, S2r.

168. Collinson, 'Godly Preachers and Zealous Magistrates,' 9.

169. Collinson, *Character*, 32; Lake, 'William Bradshaw,' 570–89.

they should avoid socializing with the reprobate, or even 'liking them, grieving for them or applauding them.'[170] 'Sorting out company' as such, was an act of piety.[171] The better to facilitate Godly separation, worship often took place in the home. 'If he might have no other Church,' Philip Henry said 'yet he had a Church in his House.' The development of the practice of closet prayer—the 'secret duty'—around this time attests to a fetishization of privacy, separation and sequestration in matters of devotion. 'Apostasy' the saying went 'begins at the closet door.'[172]

Bozeman, therefore, is right to identify Puritanism by a functional definition: 'a hunger for purity.'[173] But for the Godly, passively eliciting separation from the ungodly was far more favorable than actively separating. The passive mode in matters of assurance -seeking was safely immured from semi-Pelagianism. It savored more of providence to be rejected than to reject. In this vein, any number of Godly practices functioned both to increase Godly 'consent' and to alienate the onlooking unregenerate. These 'divisive identifications' were 'used by the Godly in order to distinguish themselves from the alien and lacklustre majority.'[174] Often, Godly behaviors were openly intended to alienate. Robert Bolton, avowedly averse to active separation, suggested that the task of a Godly preacher was to deliver a message so challenging and distasteful that it would estrange the majority, thereby separating the wheat from the chaff, Israel from Meroz.[175] The Godly also espoused an 'ethic of social shunning.'[176] Taverns, festivals and card games drew the opprobrium of the Godly. The observation of Christmas festivities and maypoles were disparaged. Stephen Denison, meanwhile, enjoined his flock to scowl at 'wicked men.'[177]

Acts of Godly 'voluntary religion' sometimes took the form of violent repudiations of ungodliness. Idolatry was a central concern of 'all Calvinist resistance theories' of this period. Concern about idolatry was a 'red blinking light,' which served to identify Calvinists in contradistinction to their peers.[178] Iconoclasm occurred periodically from the period of the Reformation onward. However, as Collinson has pointed out, the different

170. Denison cited in Lake, *Boxmaker's Revenge*, 46.

171. Collinson, *Puritan Character*, 32.

172. Matthew, *Account of the Life and Death of Mr. Philip Henry*, 75.

173. Bozeman, *Precisianist Strain*, 3.

174. Webster, 'Early Stuart Puritanism,' 48–66; Cambers, *Godly Reading*, 14.

175. Bolton, *Instructions for a Right*, 370.

176. Collinson, *Puritan Character*, 31.

177. Denison cited in Lake, *Boxmaker's Revenge*, 47.

178. Eire, *War Against the Idols*, 308

outpourings of iconoclastic—and iconophobic—fervor, had different characters. Collinson identified two main periods in the story of early modern iconoclasm in England: the first, from 1550 to 1580, constituting an assault on representations of heterodoxy in art; the second, from 1580 to 1660, constituting a broader, Puritan assault on mimetic art in general.[179] Whilst it is probably the case—as Tessa Watt has indicated—that Collinson's claims about Puritan iconophobia are overstated, these practices certainly accelerated in the period leading up to the Civil War.[180] Spraggon and Aston have both drawn the link between the explosion of iconoclasm during this period and the re-politicization of religious art—the 'holiness of beauty'—during the ascendancy of Archbishop Laud. These activities were 'widely resisted' and resulted in 'miserable failure', despite the zeal with which a small minority heeded the call.[181]

Destroying images became a violent evocation of the singularity of the Godly, a ritual for demonstrating distinctiveness between themselves and their neighbors, a 'central sacrament of reform'.[182] John Morrill puzzled about the inability of the Godly to involve the wider population in these activities given that earlier iconoclastic campaigns had deployed strategies to mitigate the antipathy of the population.[183] However, as Spraggon points out, it seems likely that the Godly were at best careless of the approbation of their peers, or even that they *desired* their antipathy, given that they believed themselves to be 'a minority who were anyway sure of the reprobate state of the common majority'.[184]

But even apparently non-confrontational practices formed 'passive critiques' of the ungodly. The most 'innocent rituals of sociability were divisive', in that they 'raised the question' of the respective piety of the devotee and his observer.[185] The 'concomitants' of sermon-gadding, for example, were just as important as the practice itself: being seen carrying the Bible under one's arm, even singing psalms on the road from village to village.[186] The practice of gadding to sermons was perceived, at least by the peers of the Godly, as predominantly an act of identity formation. John Earle wrote

---

179. Collinson, *Birthpangs of Protestant England*, 117.

180. Watt, *Cheap Print*, 131–40.

181. Morrill, 'Church in England', 90; Dowsing, *Journal of William Dowsing*.

182. Cressy, 'Different Kinds of Speaking', 19–43.

183. Morrill, 'Church in England' 90.

184. Spraggon, 'Puritan Iconoclasm in England', 18.

185. Webster, *Godly Clergy*, 74.

186. Collinson, 'Puritanism as Popular Religious Culture', 48.

that the Puritan would 'pilgrimage five miles' to listen to a 'silenc'd minister' even if there was a perfectly good sermon to be heard in her home parish.[187]

Even the act of prayer provided a forum for the Godly to exhibit both their difference from the majority and their cohesiveness and entitativity. Prayer-book worship was regarded by the Godly of the Stuart period with suspicion.[188] But the Puritans were not averse to creating their own, distinctive patterns of prayer. Members of Godly congregations were initiated into new prayer styles which served as shibboleths but also as a medium for collective, exclusive worship. Patrick Collinson observed that the Broadmead Baptist congregation in Bristol, 'grew by degrees out of the practice of repetition.'[189] At Broadmead, the Godly adopted the practice of 'repeating their notes to one another, whetting it on their hearts,' thus creating synergetic and *exclusive* liturgical structures. Robert Rollock wrote that the purpose of meeting as groups of Godly Christians was to 'handle secret and hid mysteries of salvation.'[190] On this basis, Bremer has drawn comparisons with the gnostic elements of the early church.[191]

VERY FIT TO BE DESPISED

The aim of antagonizing and alienating the 'lackluster majority' was successful.[192] By 1619, Stephen Denison could define 'the Godly' as 'those who are evil spoken of in every place.'[193] The Godly were perceived as 'singular': self-righteous, judgemental and—essentially—antagonistic to their peers. Not for nothing did Walter Curle claim that 'a Puritan is one who loves God and hates his neighbour.'[194] The early Stuart period saw a revival of the accusation of Puritanism. 'We call you *Puritanes,*' says Protestant, in Oliver Ormerod's *The Picture of a Puritane*, 'not because you are purer than other men are, but because you *think* yourselves to be purer than others.'[195] And

187. Earle, *Microcosmographie*, H6r.

188. Ainsworth, *Apologie or Defence of Brownists*, 69; Sprunger, *Dutch Puritanism*, 132; Bremer, *Lay Empowerment*, 32; Collinson, *Richard Bancroft and Elizabethan Anti-Puritanism*, 131; Maltby, 'Suffering and Surviving,' 163.

189. Collinson, 'English Conventicle,' 158–60.

190. Rollock, *Lectures*, 395.

191. Bremer, *Lay Empowerment*, 5.

192. Cambers, *Godly Reading*, 14.

193. Denison, *New Creature*, 44.

194. Manningham, *Diary of John Manningham*, 219.

195. Ormerod, *Picture of a Puritane*, O3r.

the Godly got the message. It was 'a detested odious name,' according to Henry Parker, a 'hell invented nick name' according to Stephen Denison.[196]

The Godly 'made use of opposed models of the social order to shape and maintain their view of themselves.'[197] This tendency was part of a broader cultural practice of defining things oppositionally, 'dichotomizing,' arguing from contraries and creating inversions.[198] The oppositional nature of discourse during this period facilitated a form of resistance based on the strategic inversion of these firm, manichean binaries. The appropriation of the skimmington—in which participants switched roles of gender and class—as a form of protest began to increase.[199] It was also the era in which anxiety about the contingency of moral structures was heightened by the inversionary rhetorical practice of 'paradiastole.' Vices could be reframed as virtues, whilst the virtuous could be besmirched as 'precise' or 'singular' or joyless.[200]

These oscillations were also at play in the hearts of the Godly. Richard Baxter saw his father being scorned by the revellers on the village green. From that point he was 'fully convinc'd' that 'Godly people are the best and those that despised them and lived in sin and pleasure were a malignant unhappy sort of people.'[201] In each instance, binaries of male/female, weak/strong, good/bad, are inverted. By turning the world upside down, in this way, practitioners could create an 'imaginative breathing space,' an encounter with the realization that 'categories of order and hierarchy are less than completely inevitable.'[202]

Critical inversions pepper the soteriological and ecclesiological writings of the Godly in the first decades of the seventeenth century. Earthly power was fleeting. Experiences of poverty, marginalization, persecution were redrawn and inverted as indications of sanctity; learnedness as unlearnedness and vice versa. John Fry claimed that 'the pleasure of God in all ages was to confound the wise by his poor, despicable instruments.'[203] The Godly accentuated their own weakness, hopelessness, helplessness— 'the powerlessness and passivity of slaves.' This was done partly in order to

196. Parker, Discours Concerning Puritans, 53; Denison, New Creature, 44.

197. Lake, Boxmaker's Revenge, 47.

198. Lake, 'Anti-Popery,' 72–75; Hunter, 'Problem of "Atheism,"' 135–57; Leverenz, Language of Puritan Feeling, 27.

199. Underdown, Revel, Riot, and Rebellion, 103.

200. Skinner, 'Paradiastole,' 149–67.

201. Baxter, Reliquiæ Baxterianæ, 3.

202. Scott, Domination and the Arts of Resistance, 168.

203. Fry, Clergy in their Colours, 3.

emphasize their dependence on grace. But it also served to mark out the gulf between themselves and their peers, rendering the vituperations of 'Satan's slaves' toothless.[204]

Richard Bauman writes that the refusal by the Quakers in the early seventeenth century to use conventional pronouns and greetings provoked anathema in the wider society. In fact, he suggests that the practice was so alien that 'some observers, when they first encountered the unconventional Quaker style could only conclude that the Quakers were deranged.'[205] These quotidian practices were partly acts of religious devotion.[206] But they also functioned as 'weapons of the weak,' identifications whereby the Godly demarcated themselves as distinctive—even mad—in the eyes of their peers.[207] More often than not the Godly rejected the conventional valuation of 'learnedness.' This attitude was articulated as an elevation of revelatory knowledge over 'book knowledge,' of the theology of the cross over the theology of glory.[208] Calvin's dictum that 'the sun shines upon all to whom the Gospel is proclaimed, but with no effect on the blind,' echoed through the work of English Calvinists.[209] William Whittaker asserted that 'scripture cannot be proven by scripture . . . but all Christ's sheep know his role.'[210] Thomas Godwin admonished that 'there comes a light of the Spirit beyond the light of reason.'[211] In Gifford's *Countrie Divinitie*, Atheos is warned by Zelotes not to take for granted the superiority of those who have acquired more formal education:

> It is not learning alone whiche must judge of sound preaching, for there be manie learned men which cannot judge well, as also there be manie unlearned, which are verie well able to discerne, all lieth in this point: the doctrine is of God, and not of men, and therefore those doe feele it, and judge rightly whether they be learned or unlearned, whom God doth inwardly teach with his spirite.[212]

204. Coffey, *Exodus and Liberation*, 37.

205. Baumann, *Let Your Words Be Few*, 50.

206. Goffman, *Presentation of the Self in Everyday Life*.

207. Scott, *Weapons of the Weak*, 37–41.

208. Luther, 'Heidelberg Disputation,' 43.

209. Calvin, *Institutes of the Christian Religion* 3.2.34; Bremer, *Lay Empowerment*, 21.

210. Bremer, *Lay Empowerment*, 17.

211. Goodwin, *Works of Thomas Goodwin*, 7:65fc.

212. Gifford, *Briefe Discourse on Countrie Divinitie*, 11.

George Fox announced that the Lord had 'opened unto me that being bred at Oxford and Cambridge was not enough to fit and qualify men to be ministers of God.' John Jewel conceded that 'oftentimes the unlearned seeth things that the learned cannot see.'[213] William Dell, meanwhile, argued that 'the thrones of the beast . . . are the universities,' and that 'the reading of authors comes from want of the spirit.'[214] The emphasis placed by Puritan thought-leaders on the 'plain-style' in writing and preaching corresponded with the association of rhetoric and 'verbal facility' with the 'manipulative strategies of evil.'[215] Partly due to this ethical anti-intellectualism, Richard Hooker despaired that Puritans 'disgraced reason.'[216] Put into practice, these epistemological claims could lead to disturbing exchanges. The young antinomian tailor, Richard Lane, engaged the bishops of the High Commission in scriptural disputation when he was arraigned before them in 1631.[217] Isaac Penington, writing about the recruitment of the first Quakers described them as 'young country lads, of no deep understanding or ready expression, very fit to be despised every where by the wisdom of man, and only to be owned in the power of that life wherein they came forth!'[218] Mark Bell points out that none of the signatories of the Baptist Confession of 1646 had any theological training.[219] It is no wonder that early Stuart governments were concerned about the potential of Calvinism to 'stir up the lower orders by giving them a spurious interest in matters above and beyond them.'[220]

The first generation of Puritans may have returned from exile with stated aims and goals. But Stuart Puritanism was not a party, not a sect, not a 'shopping list' of behaviors. It was a culture, constructed 'out of a variety of discursive materials by a number of different groups and individuals.'[221] The Godly 'made use of opposed models of the social order to shape and maintain their view of themselves.'[222] This tendency was part of a broader cultural practice of defining things oppositionally, 'dichotomizing,' arguing

213. Jewel, *Replie to M. Hardinge*, 532.

214. Fox, *Journal of George Fox*, 5; Dell, *Tryal of Spirits*, 43.

215. Knott, *Sword of the Spirit*, 4.

216. Hooker, *Of the Lawes*, 139.

217. Gardiner, *Reports of Cases*, 189–92.

218. Penington, *Many Deep Considerations*, 3

219. Bell, 'Freedom to Form,' 189.

220. Lake, 'Anti-Popery,' 85.

221. Lake, 'Anti-Puritanism,' 86–87.

222. Lake, *Boxmaker's Revenge*, 47.

from contraries and creating inversions.[223] It was born, at least in part, out of the deeply antagonistic and binary understanding of the world that lay at the heart of the Reformed Protestant project. 'The Puritan,' it was said 'accounted his whole life . . . a warfare,' a 'continual battle.'[224] He saw himself as fundamentally and diametrically opposed to 'the world.' How 'the world' was constructed depended from group to group, individual to individual. But for each, there existed a 'basic polarity, a binary opposition, around which they arranged their view' of it.[225] For Stephen Denison, the Christian was—by definition—the man despised by the world for his Godliness.[226]

It was therefore necessary for 'the Godly to watch the ungodly hating [them],' to understand how and why they hated them, and to interact with the ungodly in this process in order to maintain the structures of exclusion and inclusion upon which the salience of their identity depended.[227] More than anything, the Godly desired 'confirmation [of] their status as a persecuted minority.'[228] 'It was a sign of the truth of their religion,' Cambers writes, 'that they were persecuted.'[229] Lake writes that 'the Godly could use the . . . ungodly and their rooted hostility to the saints as a confirmation and prop for their own righteousness,' most obviously since 'the obloquy of the mob was ever the lot of the saints.'[230] Collinson writes that 'the experience of oppression, real or imagined, provided necessary evidence of election.' Of course, at times, the Godly party were 'on top.' During the reign of Edward VI and during the interregnum, Godly men wielded power. Nonetheless, in their writings, they still found it impossible to forego the identity of powerlessness. 'Highly motivated Protestants needed an antagonist,' Collinson wrote. 'Not to have been in an adversarial position would have been a cause of inner discomfort.'[231] In an essay entitled 'the Happiness of Suffering,' Walsham writes that:

> The self inflicted separation of puritans from the unregener-
> ate was the means by which they fed their addiction to regular

223. Lake, 'Anti-Popery,' 72–75; Hunter, 'Problem of "Atheism,"' 135–57; Leverenz, *Language of Puritan Feeling*, 27.

224. Gerree, *Character of an old English Puritan*, 6; Knott, *Sword of the Spirit*, 7.

225. Lake, 'Charitable Christian Hatred,' 154.

226. Dennison, *Monument or Tombe Stone*, 65.

227. Lake and Stephens, *Scandal and Religious Identity*, 113.

228. Cambers, *Godly Reading*, 13.

229. Cambers, *Godly Reading*, 22.

230. Lake and Stephens, *Scandal and Religious Identity*, 123.

231. Collinson, 'Cohabitation of the Faithful with the Unfaithful,' 56.

doses of affliction. . . . When the godly had no real antagonists, they found it necessary to invent them.[232]

Recognizing that the process of Godly identity formation was so closely dependent on the discourse of anti-Puritanism helps to resolve a key problem with the study of Puritanism: the question of whether Puritanism the thing or Puritanism the name came first. Davis's analysis of the historiography of Ranterism established the precedent of avoiding reliance on antipathetic sources in making claims about the religious landscape of seventeenth-century England.[233] Mary Adkins made a similar claim in a study of the play A Knacke to Know a Knave in which she argued that the origin of the stage-Puritan had its roots in Medieval satires of the clergy, rather than in any ethnographic observation of Reformed Protestants.[234] Patrick Collinson pursued this claim, leading to the radical conclusion that the Puritans 'only existed by virtue of being perceived to exist, mostly by their enemies but eventually to themselves and to each other.'[235] Collinson suggests, on this basis, that the representation of the Godly in the literature of this period, are the shadows on the wall of a Platonic cave.[236]

Perhaps, however, the interaction between the shadow and the thing is more symbiotic. Peter Lake, in response to Collinson, made the claim that the distinction between the 'stage Puritan' and the 'Puritan'—and the chronology that situated the former before the latter—was not necessarily as clear as Collinson and Adkins presumed. 'What we are looking at,' Lake wrote, 'is a constant series of interactions and exchanges.'[237] Ann Hughes, building on this claim, encouraged historians to move towards a 'post-structural' approach to defining Puritanism, 'blurring the boundary between the represented and the real.' Historians, Hughes argues, should be cautious of unravelling types and ideals from objective 'reality' as Davis sought to.[238] Stereotypes and real people are not discrete entities. They interact with each other, the one moulding the other, in particular when—socially or ideologically or imaginatively—a society is divided into stark, manichean binaries (i.e., elect and reprobate, godly and ungodly). This, as Hughes demonstrated in her study of Thomas Edwards's Gangraena, was as

---

232. Walsham, 'Happiness of Suffering,' 58.

233. Davis, Fear, Myth, and History, 1–17.

234. Adkins, 'Genesis of Dramatic Satire,' 81–95.

235. Collinson, 'Theatre Constructs Puritanism,' 158.

236. Collinson, Puritan Character, 8.

237. Lake, 'Anti-Puritanism,' 86–87.

238. Hughes, Gangraena, 10–11.

true in the early-modern world as it is today.[239] As Lake and Stephens noted, in their study of the experience of the Godly community in Broughton: 'Puritan—both name and thing—was not merely a product of anti-Puritan stereotyping, but also a positive process of self-fashioning.'[240]

Attempting clear distinctions between the polemical representations of Godliness and the phenomenon itself, or the representation of Judaizing and the phenomenon itself, therefore, is somewhat fruitless. The Godly sought to capture, redirect and reconfigure the rhetoric of anti-Puritanism in innumerable, complex, quotidian interactions. The most obvious example can be found in the usage of the word 'Puritan' itself. As Peter Lake has it, 'the term Puritan came to be internalized and appropriated by the Godly,' a designation of separateness, constructed by the ungodly, but put to work by the Godly.[241] The 'Puritans' adopted the name as a designation of singularity, an 'insult they were proud to own.' Judge Yelverton, sitting on the assizes at Durham in 1629, asserted that 'he had been always accounted a Puritan, and he thanked God for it; and that so he would die,' whilst Owen Felltham described acquaintances of his who 'rejoiced in the name Puritan.'[242] Baxter called the term 'a word of scorn in wicked mens mouths, against all that truly feared God,' whilst Fawcet said that 'with that staffe, the prophane world beates all that are better than themselves.'[243] In fact, Stephen Denison argued that the key distinction between the godly and the reprobate lay in the tenor with which they used—or abused—the word Puritan. In their analysis of the lectures of Joseph Bentham, Isaac Stephens and Peter Lake note that 'the definition and ownership of the word Puritan is central to nearly all of them.'[244] The same process of reappropriation took place with the charge of 'singularity.' Richard Baxter lamented that the Godly were accused of humourless singularity in the mouths of ungodly men, but Jeremiah Burroughs refused to acknowledge the pejorative mood of the term. 'Singularity is cast upon God's servants as their disgrace,' he wrote, 'but certainly it is their glory . . . their separation is a wonderful separation.'[245]

239. Hughes, *Gangraena*, 11.

240. Lake and Stephens, *Scandal and Identity*, 99.

241. Lake, 'Anti-Puritanism,' 86.

242. Seaver, 'Puritan Preachers and their Patrons,' 131; Calendar of State Papers Domestic, 19/7/1629; Felltham, *Resolves*, 6.

243. Baxter, *Church Told of Mr. Bagshaw's Scandals*, 28; Fawcet, *Seasonable Sermon*, 24.

244. Lake and Stephens, *Scandal and Identity*, 98.

245. Burroughs, *Excellency of a Gracious Spirit*, 151; Baxter, *Non-conformity without Controversie*, 38.

Robert Sanderson, preaching at Whitehall in 1632, warned that 'the enmity of the wicked is not an undoubted mark either of truth or goodness.'[246] Sanderson noted that the parameters of wickedness were understood by the Godly as value-laden, subjective constructs and were therefore malleable. 'Through wretched uncharitableness,' he warned 'we are apt to stretch the title of the wicked further than we ought.'[247] In their devotional practices, the Godly called to mind the distinction between themselves and their peers. Without the gaze of the wicked, the Godly identity could not exist. Moreover, the categories of wickedness and goodness became more and more dependent on their use by both sides in this dialogical discourse.

SOTERIOLOGY AND SOCIAL IDENTITY

The originators of social-identity theory, Jonathan Turner and Henri Tajfel, offered a theoretical framework for understanding identity and its relation to the group. Tajfel and Turner demonstrated that identity-formation is a dialogical process, which takes place on the level of inter-group comparison. 'In-groups,' develop identities by comparing and contrasting themselves with 'out-groups.' The goal in this process is to secure positive-distinctiveness—the sense that 'we' are better than 'them,' and hence that 'I' am better than 'him.'

The estimation of the groups to which an individual belongs has a profound effect on the self-estimation of the individual himself. The research conducted by Tajfel and Turner, during the 1970s, formed the basis of Social-Identity theory.[248] Tajfel's thought, in particular, was shaped by his experiences as a survivor of the Nazi Holocaust and of social fragmentation during the 1960s.[249] He sought to offer a coherent narrative that would help to explain the seemingly inescapable cycle of chauvinism, rivalry, intolerance and conflict, which dogs human society.[250] Tajfel believed that the answer could be found in the way in which individuals adopted social-identities. He outlined his theory in the opening chapters of *Differentiation between Social Groups*.[251] Tajfel's central hypothesis was that social-identity is formed and determined by a constant process of cognitive identification

---

246. Sanderson, *Sermons*, 2:61.

247. Sanderson, *Sermons*, 2:59.

248. Tajfel, *Human Groups and Social Categories* 1–13; 'Social Psychology of Inter-group Relations,' 1–39.

249. Tajfel, 'Cognitive Aspects of Prejudice,' 79–97.

250. Tajfel, 'Experiments in Intergroup Discrimination,' 96–102.

251. Tajfel, *Differentiation Between Social Groups*, 1–22.

and evaluation: the individual's sense that he or she is a member of a group and the subsequent comparison between his or her own group (the in-group) and other groups (the out-group).[252] The parameters of all groups, therefore, are defined through a comparative and dialogical process between the in-group and the out-group. Tajfel believed that the emotional response of the individual to this evaluation process (whether it rendered positive or negative conclusions) determined the individual group-members' behaviors and attitudes.[253]

John Turner's work on the theory of Social-Categorization deepened and clarified some aspects of Tajfel's thought. Turner argued that the process of social-identity formation relied on the development of membranes between groups.[254] Whereas Tajfel was concerned to find the root of inter-group conflict, Turner was interested in the ways in which groups acquired 'salience' (the sense that one is a member of a coherent group) and thus, entitativity. Turner sought to find an explanation for 'how individuals are able to act as a group at all.' The fundamental condition for group salience is the prevalent sense amongst group members that 'the degree to which the subjectively perceived differences between them are less than the differences between them and other people.' When salience is established, group-membership becomes internalized.[255] At this point, the conditions are established under which group-membership 'becomes cognitively prepotent in self-perception to act as the immediate influence on perception and behaviour.' Seen as a whole, groups in which members experience salience are more entitative. In other words, they are 'perceived to be cohesive, interconnected, similar, interactive and sharing common goals.'[256] This analysis suggests that variance in the degree of entitativity can affect the behavior and attitudes of the group-member. Often, a process of 'out-group homogenization' proves strategically valuable in the pursuit of entitativity and salience. Members of salient groups often perceive non-members as alike, not recognizing difference between members of the majority out-group. Through these processes, groups seek two goals: 'difference' from other groups and positive self-identification.[257]

252. Turner, 'Towards a Cognitive Redefinition of the Social Group,' 15–41.

253. Tajfel, *Differentiation Between Social Groups*, 39; Tajfel, 'Social-Identity and Intergroup Behavior,' 67–71.

254. Turner, 'Social Categorization and Self-concept,' 77–122; 'Social Identification,' 518–538.

255. Turner et al., *Rediscovering the Social Group*, 42, 51, 48.

256. Campbell, 'Common Fate,' 202–4.

257. Halsam et al., 'Social Identity, Self-categorization,' 182–222; 'Social Categorization and Group Homogeneity,' 139–60.

This self-conceptualization as 'different' and 'good' is conventionally referred to as 'positive distinctiveness.' Positive-distinctiveness can therefore be achieved via a logic which the group *itself* defines and determines *creatively*. Tajfel saw examples and evidence of socially-creative action everywhere during the 1960s, 1970s and 1980s. The most cited example is the 'Black is Beautiful,' movement in the United States, during the second half of the twentieth century. For Tajfel, the movement to *celebrate* those aspects of their experience and identity which had previously been *derogated* opened new vistas of opportunity for young African-Americans. Not only could they create an impermeable, salient and entitative group-identity, they themselves could determine the values against which that group was evaluated (both by themselves and by out-group members):

> The beauty of blackness, the African hair-do, the African cultural past and traditions which serve to illustrate the phenomenon. . . . At the same time, the old attempts to be a little more like the other people are proudly rejected: no more straightening of hair for beautiful black girls or using of various procedures for lightening the skin.[258]

Preserved, enhanced, re-evaluated. It is the second of these words which encapsulates the 'creative' aspect of social-identity. By rejecting the prevalent criteria for evaluation, groups free themselves to develop new and meaningful attitudes and behaviors which emphasize a new, free identity.

In certain conditions the need for group-entitativity is heightened. At these times there is an increased impetus for groups to develop more impermeable boundaries and accentuate those aspects of the group that are more distinctive, or even resistant. This reality was first noted by Tajfel, and formed a key component of Turner's theoretical framework.[259] Different scholars have, subsequently, attempted to identify stimuli for this 'accentuation' process. Michael Hogg has posited a link between feelings of uncertainty and (in his typology) 'Extremist Behaviours.'[260] He describes uncertainty as a sensation or a feeling which demands the attention of individual and requires the individual to perform certain actions in order to allay or resolve it.[261]

258. Tajfel, *Human Groups and Social Categories*, 339.

259. Tajfel, *Human Groups and Social Categories*, 276; Turner, 'Social Categorization and the Self-concept,' 77–122.

260. Hogg, *Extremism and the Psychology of Uncertainty*; 'From Uncertainty to Extremism,' 338–42; 'Uncertainty-identity Theory,' 69–126; Hogg et al, 'Uncertainty, Entitativity, and Group Identification,' 135–42.

261. Hogg et al., 'Religion in the Face of Uncertainty,' 73.

One way of allaying uncertainty is to build entitativity within social groups. Groups which offer low entitativity fail to resolve uncertainty.[262] Entitative groups, meanwhile, provide group-members with a useful conceptual armoury: coherent narratives, camaraderie, context. In times of uncertainty, these assets become more highly prized and are (consciously or unconsciously) sought after.[263] Thus, individuals experiencing uncertainty tend to seek high-entitativity groups. In order for groups to maintain this high-level of entitativity, groups *must* maintain 'impermeable membranes,' and 'sharp boundaries,' between themselves and the majoritarian out-group. Because of this, the urgency of need for entitativity within groups can, in times of great uncertainty, lead to 'extremist' behaviors:

> People may zealously cling to all-embracing ideologies and world views, engage in aggressive or disruptive behaviors aimed at protecting or promoting their world view, and identify as true believers with rigidly structured social groups or categories that are ethnocentric and intolerant of dissent and diversity.[264]

This description shares striking characteristics with the descriptions of the 'Puritan character' offered by Patrick Collinson and others. Such 'extremist' or resistant behaviors serve to accentuate the difference between the in-group and the out-group. But in the Godly context they served a much grander function.

Through this process of adopting, accentuating and evaluating extreme behaviors, in-group members can create insular, impermeable groups, which, in turn, allay anxieties about the uncertainty of the present and the future. As Hogg puts it:

> Because group prototypes are shared ('we' agree 'we' are like this, 'they' are like that) thus one's worldview and self-concept are validated. Social categorization renders one's own and others' behavior predictable and allows one to avoid harm, plan effective action, and know how one should feel and behave.[265]

From this theoretical perspective it is easy to see how resistant identities emerge. The individual feels uncertain about his or her role in the majoritarian culture; the sharp boundaries offered by extremist groups provide the sanctuary of entitativity; the assails of criticism from the out-group majority become impotent in changing the individual's perspective and, since the

---

262. Hogg et al., 'Religion in the Face of Uncertainty,' 74.
263. Hogg, 'Uncertainty-Identity Theory,' 69.
264. Hogg et al., 'Uncertainty and the Roots of Extremism,' 8.
265. Hogg, 'Uncertainty-Identity Theory,' 439.

attraction of the group is its separateness from the majority, they serve only to heighten the zeal of the individual for the group. Criticism and abuse serve only to pour petrol on the flames.

Working within the context of social-identity theory, Hogg offers several illustrative accounts of uncertainty-identity at work. He suggests that the 'collapse of the order that Roman rule provided, and the attendant uncertainties that this engendered, lent momentum to a wave of religious fanaticism, and the spawning of a plethora of religious movements that demanded extreme ideological commitment from their adherents.' He notes that:

> the Great Depression of the 1930s witnessed a global rise of national-political extremism, sliding into fascism, communism, and nationalism.

Finally, he draws a parallel between the uncertainty induced by technological advancement and the Damocletian threat of nuclear war, and the surge in counter-cultural movements in the West in the 1960s:

> The 1960s and early 1970s saw a period of rapid technological, sociocultural, and normative change that raised uncertainty about America's future. The USA was swept by unprecedented race riots and antiwar demonstrations, and many young people were drawn to extreme countercultural movements, religious cults, and radical political organizations that may well be characterized as "extreme."[266]

In short, in times of desperate uncertainty, individuals often gravitate towards highly-entitative (and by extension highly 'unusual') groups. Often, the means of securing that entitativity can be extreme or resistant behavior. The preconditions for the development of this extremism-inducing uncertainty are manifold. Hogg proposes a number. He suggests sources of uncertainty ranging from the familial to the political to the economic:

> People can feel uncertain about many things: their perceptions, beliefs, attitudes, values, relationships, and careers; their future and their place in the world; and even more fundamentally about their very self and identity. The origins of uncertainty can reside in self-reflection, interpersonal relationships, group and intergroup dynamics, or widespread events in the larger society or global community.[267]

266. Hogg et al., 'Uncertainty and the Roots of Extremism,' 409.
267. Hogg et al., 'Uncertainty and the Roots of Extremism,' 411.

As we have seen, the Godly of the seventeenth century contended with a different kind of uncertainty, precipitated by the excarnation of traditional forms of soteriological assurance. Lake's claim that 'the tensions and animosities that the godly stirred up in their contemporaries, were central to their sense of themselves,' therefore conforms to the central themes of social-identity theory.[268] The need to maintain a sense that the Godly were different to their peers, as such, was central to their sense that they were of the elect. It was, therefore, neither a superficial nor a trivial concern, but was, rather, the center of their religious experience.

CONCLUSION

'None make more Puritans,' wrote Francis Rogers in 1630, 'than they that most speake against them.'[269] This 'dialectical spiral' was the center of 'Godliness' in seventeenth-century England.[270] Puritanism, the religious sensibility defined by Collinson as being 'different from most people,' was formed in a continuous series of interactions between the Godly and those they perceived to be their enemies.[271]

But this was not informed, as Hill claimed, by a concern to *criticize*, to *transform* their society. The development of Godly, practical divinity served to separate, to divide the Godly from their peers, to render them singular. Whilst their claims may have been valuational, they *also* attributed intrinsic value to the act of separation itself. Whenever the Godly did have an opportunity to collectively change society, they inevitably turned towards more and more microscopic acts of sectarianism, of auto-differentiation. No phenomenon in English history has demonstrated a greater tendency towards 'splintering into numerous competing factions.'[272] No movement has ever been so contrary, so singular, so 'oppositional, agitatory and so frequently in conflict.'[273] Puritans appeared doomed to 'endless . . . internal feuds against one another.'[274] This tendency led to a process whereby Puritanism itself 'fragmented into smaller and smaller units.'[275] Christianity moved from the

268. Lake and Stephens, *Scandal and Identity*, 357.

269. Rogers, *Visitation Sermon*, C3r.

270. Durston, 'Puritan Ethos,' 9.

271. Collinson, 'Godly Preachers and Zealous Magistrates,' 9.

272. Como, *Blown by the Spirit*, 13.

273. Collinson, 'Sects and the Evolution of Puritanism,' 147–66.

274. Morrill, 'Puritan Revolution,' 84.

275. Lamont, 'Two National Churches,' 335; Collinson, *Cranmer to Sancroft*, 129–45

uniform to the milliform in a handful of generations.[276] The 1640s saw the number of sectarian congregations grow from ten to eighty in the space of two years, the number of pamphlets published annually grow from the tens to the thousands, and the end of the Presbyterian consensus with the publication of the *Apologeticall Nation*.[277]

'I take it to be impossible,' one Puritan wrote 'to have true peace with God and not wars with men.'[278] If ethical singularity and the desire for distinctiveness was central to their worldview, if the Puritan—indeed— 'accounted his whole life a warfare,' the factious nature of Puritanism must be understood not as a 'circumstantial' aspect of the Godly identity, but rather its foundation.[279]

Even those who have cautioned against defining Calvinism as intrinsically sectarian have conceded that in the context of the early seventeenth century, the Godly were 'circumstantially' so.[280] As Como and others have shown, the paradoxes at play within early seventeenth-century Puritan divinity carried within them a 'centrifugal force,' a germ of conflict, indeed of entropy.[281] Calvinist soteriology, and the dog-whistle toward ethical singularity—rather than 'the efflorescence of an autochthonous folk irreligion'— was that germ.[282] It was the bosom of Reformed Protestantism—of 'practical divinity and theology'—that rendered 'the vast array of social and religious radicalisms' that emerged in this period. 'Sectarianism,' as Como writes 'emerged not from a separate, marginal tradition of plebeian heterodoxy but from the very center of the culture of puritanism.'[283]

Hughes notes the intimate connection between the centrifugal nature of Puritanism and the radical shifts that had taken place in the plebeian, cultural understanding of the nature of salvation. The Godly were 'troublemakers,' she wrote 'because they could not be presumptuous about their own salvation.'[284] The process by which the Godly effected this separation depended on an interaction between the Godly and their peers. The assertion of singularity *requires* a concept of consensus. Moreover, the assertion

---

276. Grindal, *Remains of Edmund Grindal*, 471.

277. Coffey, *Persecution and Toleration*, 142.

278. Slack, 'Public Conscience of Henry Sherfield,' 151.

279. Durston, 'Puritan Ethos,' 3; Gerree, *Character of an Old English Puritane*, 6.

280. Collinson, *From Cranmer to Sancroft*, xiv.

281. Como, *Blown by the Spirit*, 13, 28, 439; Brachlow, 'John Smyth and the Ghost of Anabaptism,' 297.

282. McDowell, *English Radical Imagination*, 11.

283. Como, *Blown by the Spirit*, 13, 28, 439.

284. Hughes, *Causes of the English Civil War*, 105.

of singularity *requires* a consensually constructed ideal of deviance. These interactions had a religious quality which complemented the doctrinal claims of Calvinist Predestinarianism: shifting the categories of 'elect' and 'reprobate' into the social sphere. 'Protestant Religion had two sides,' wrote Peter Lake, 'firstly the objective realm of doctrinal truth, and secondly the subjective religious experience undergone by the godly in their internalization of those truths.'[285] Through these interactions, therefore, Puritans and anti-Puritans both participated in the process of creating 'idealized types and dichotomies' which were 'crucial to the self-image of the Godly.'[286]

Separation became the central, discursive concern of Godly men and women. The primary locus for this discourse lay in the separation of the Godly from the ungodly. But this process, itself, was mediated through innumerable symbolic and ceremonial practices. As the next chapter will demonstrate, this concern for separation and the enactment of this concern in ritual was also at the heart of the topos of Judaism in early modern England.

285. Lake, *Moderate Puritans and the Elizabethan Church*, 155.
286. Lake, *Boxmaker's Revenge*, 47.

CHAPTER 2

Judaizing and Singularity

IN 1555, POPE PAUL IV issued a bull entitled *Cum nimis absurdum*. The Bull urged Christians to be more muscular in their condemnation of Judaism. It carried some legal injunctions. The Pope ordered that all Jews should be forced to wear a hat 'that they might be identified everywhere as Jews.'[1] Fifty years after this edict was issued, a text written by the Rabbinic scholar David HaLevi Segal made a similar point. He urged all Jews to wear the kippah in order that 'those who follow God might be distinguished from those who do not.' Segal saw the uncovering of the head in public as a contravention of *hukkot hagoyim*.[2]

In early modern England, the confluence of a broad range of cultural factors led to the representation of the Jew as paradigmatically 'other.' As Bauman demonstrates, this tendency to 'other' the Jew was not a novelty of this period. Nor, he writes, was this 'otherness' intrinsically pejorative. Both the philo-semitic elements (so prominent in David Katz's account of the period) and the anti-Judaic elements (prominent in James Shapiro's accounts) contributed to this process. The identification of 'the Jew' and of Judaism as the counterpoint of Christianity, of Englishness and of decency placed Judaism at the center of the consciousness of English men and women in the matter of their own and the collective, confessional identity. 'Royalists and republicans, high churchmen and radical sectarians, women and men, royalty, gentry and the middling sort,' Achsah Guibbory writes, 'looked to the Jews to define, confirm or legitimate their identity.'[3] So, as William Prynne walked to Westminster on 6 December 1648, he encountered in a

---

1. Paul IV, 'Cum nimis absurdum,' 294.
2. Grossman, 'Kippah Comes to America,' 130.
3. Guibbory, *Christian Identity, Jews, and Israel*, 14.

short period of time several different kinds of people—soldiers, politicians and artisans—all defining themselves by alterity in relation to the Jews.[4] But at the same time, a more positive sense of the irreducible otherness of the Jews arose from the pages of the Biblical accounts, read through the lens of a Puritan ethic of singularity.

A decade ago, Kevin Sharpe admonished historians of this period to 'pay attention to the representations that contemporaries presented of (and to) themselves.'[5] In no area is this more pressing than in the study of early-modern Judaizers. The picture of the Jew and of Judaism which sat in the consciousness of English men and women was extremely complex. In order to understand what was *meant* by Judaizing therefore, it is vital to understand what was *meant* by Judaism.

SINGULARITY AND THE LAW

When a seventeenth-century Godly professor turned to the first page of the first book of the Geneva Bible, he would have been greeted with a description of the patriarchal Jews:

> this church dependeth not on the estimation and nobilitie of the world: and also by the fewnesse of them which have at all times worshipped him purely according to his word, that it standeth not in the multitude but in the poore and despised, in the small flocke and little number, that man in his wisedom might be confounded and the name of God evermore praised.[6]

This was the lens through which the Godly read the books of the Law in early modern England. Within the texts of Genesis, Exodus, Leviticus and Deuteronomy they found the story of a 'smalle flocke,' 'little in number,' seeking to affirm their righteousness in spite of their 'fewnesse.' This was not a perversion. Reading the Hebrew Bible through this lens allowed the Godly to perceive a literature of singularity and resistance that already existed in the texts themselves.[7]

4. Prynne, *Short Demurrer*, a3r.

5. Sharpe, *Remapping Early Modern England*, 3.

6. *Bible and the Holy Scripture*, a1r.

7. Grabbe, *Leviticus*, 49–60; Houston, *Purity and Monotheism*; Weinfeld, *Deuteronomy and the Deuteronomic School*. For critical reflections on the holiness motif in the Priestly source—specifically Leviticus—see Haran, 'Holiness Code,' 9:318–21; Hurowitz, 'P-Understanding the Priestly Source,' 30–37; Milgrom, 'Leviticus 17–22'; 'Priestly ("P") Source,' 454–61; Schwartz, 'Leviticus,' 203–80; Sun 'Holiness Code,' 254–57; Klawans, *Impurity and Sin in Ancient Judaism*, 17–25.

Two radicals are used to denote separation in the Hebrew Bible: בדל and קדש. Both of these words are used periodically throughout the books of the Law to identify the separation of the sacred from the common. They are particularly prevalent in those texts which emerged from the experience of exile. In various forms these words are also used to articulate the separation of Israel from the nations. The phrase 'I am the Lord your God, who has separated (הִבְדַּלְתִּי) you from the peoples,' recurs throughout the Levitical laws (Lev 20:24). It is also used to describe ethical action of individuals to maintain their own purity. Ezra describes the Passover, celebrated after the return from Babylon, 'by every one who had joined them and separated (הַנִּבְדָּל) himself from the uncleanness of the peoples of the land.' Nehemiah repeats this formulation to describe the people who renewed the covenant after the return from exile. Here, separation from the heathen is read as directly correlative to orthodoxy. Separation is also used to describe the status of the Levitical priesthood *within* the community of Israel. In Deuteronomy, it is recorded that 'the Lord set apart (הִבְדִּיל) the tribe of Levi to carry the ark of the covenant of the Lord to stand before the Lord' (Deut 10:8). Addressing the rebellious Levites, Moses asks 'is it too small a thing for you that the God of Israel has separated you (הִבְדִּיל־כִּי) from the congregation of Israel, to bring you near to himself' (Num 16:9). The Ark itself is kept behind a curtain and is therefore 'separate' (וְהִבְדִּילָה) from the people (Exod 26:33). In this mood, 'separation' from the majority is directly correlative to 'closeness to God.' The root בדל is not, however, only used positively in the Hebrew Bible. In Deuteronomy 29, the penalty for apostasy is described: 'and the Lord will separate him (וְהִבְדִּילוֹ) from all the tribes of Israel for calamity' (Deut 29:21). In Ezra the word הַנִּבְדָּל is used to describe the honorable conduct of those exiles who had maintained Israel's ethnic cohesion, but is later used to describe the penalty for not attending collective worship after the deliverance from Babylon. Anyone who failed to comply with the proclamation would be punished: 'all his property should be forfeited, and he himself separated (יִבָּדֵל) from the congregation of the exiles' (Ezra 10:8). Isaiah ventriloquizes the foreigner who frets that he may be counted unworthy of election: 'The Lord will surely separate (יַבְדִּילֵנִי) me from his people' (Isa 56:3).

The root קדוש is equally multi-valent. At Sinai, Moses is told to draw a boundary around the mountain to protect its sanctity ('אֶת־הָהָר, וְקִדַּשְׁתּוֹ'). In Genesis 2, God ordains the Sabbath as a day of rest and worship, separating it from the working week. The text reads 'God blessed the seventh day and made it holy (וַיְבָרֶךְ אֱלֹהִים אֶת־יוֹם הַשְּׁבִיעִי, וַיְקַדֵּשׁ אֹתוֹ).' In these settings, קדש denotes holy and precious to God. Elsewhere, however, the word is used with profoundly negative connotations. An edict from Deuteronomy

23 reads: 'There shall be no *qedesha* (קְדֵשָׁה) of the daughters of Israel' (Isa 56:3). Another mention of the *qedesha* appears in in Job 36 and is here associated with uncleanliness and impurity. Hosea laments that 'the men themselves go aside with prostitutes and sacrifice with the *qedeshot* (הַקְּדֵשׁוֹת)' (Hos 4:14).

In her initial work on Leviticus, Mary Douglas emphasized the significance of 'wholeness . . . unity, integrity, and perfection' when describing ritual purity in the Biblical context.[8] Elements which threatened the coherence of a category with mixture and miscegenation were eradicated. This concept was developed in Kristeva's concept of abjection. Kristeva claims that the Biblical categories of 'impurity' emerged from a desire to eliminate and expel that which 'undermines the clean and proper and makes it filthy.'[9] Weiss, following Klawans, questions the notion that ritual impurity was valuational category. The ritual does not concern elimination of the 'negative,' but rather a fruitful act of separation.[10] If this is the case, then ritual impurity is a necessary component of existence, a corollary of divinely mandated acts—most obviously reproduction. As such, that which is ritually impure must remain separate from that which is ritually pure. But nonetheless it must *exist*. Indeed, without that which is ritually impure, the category of ritual purity ceases to contain meaning. Klawans places the *imitatio dei* at the heart of the sacrificial Holiness Code. Participation in sacrificial worship required separation of the devotee from those aspects of human existence most alien to the Godhead: sex and death.[11] At other times—of course—the Israelites were enjoined to come into contact with sex and death. As such, the heart of ritual worship—and the principle responsibility of the priesthood—was not to eliminate that which was valuationally negative, but rather 'the separation between the sacred and the profane.' Within the category of the profane, are those entities which are themselves *tahor* or impure. These entities represent mixture, confusion or anomaly: 'blurred frontiers.'[12] In performing these duties of separation, the ancient Israelites created, what Klawans calls, 'a productive expression of religious ideals.'[13]

Those foods—most notably swine—which failed to conform clearly to carefully defined categories were removed from the diet. But the separation

8. Douglas, *Purity and Danger*, 54–55. Douglas moderated this position substantially in *Leviticus as Literature*.

9. Kristeva, *Powers of Horror*, 3.

10. Klawans, *Impurity and Sin*, 23–25; Weiss, 'Impurity without Repression,' 205–21.

11. Klawans, *Purity, Sacrifice, and the Temple*, 49–74, esp. 58.

12. Schmidt, *How the Temple Thinks*, 90–95.

13. Klawans, *Purity, Sacrifice, and the Temple*, 73.

of foods in Jewish life regularly functioned as a reflection of Israel itself, due to forces within and without of her control. In the Hellenistic period, pork became a 'uniquely abhorred substance.'[14] Kraemer contends that this is due to the fact that, during this period, observant Jews would have had regular opportunities to watch non-Jewish neighbors consuming pork. As such, pork was 'viewed more and more as the food of the other.'[15] Moreover, the *non*-consumption of pork became a stick with which the heathen beat the Jews. In the Roman context, the non-consumption of pork came to be a defining characteristic of Jewish otherness.[16] The midrashic reading of Leviticus 18 included the claim that the non-consumption of pork was *specifically* a practice which the gentiles objected to. The same passage enjoined Jews not to 'do as they do in the land of Egypt' (Lev 18:3).

And the otherness of the Jew was just as entangled with the practice of abstaining from pork in the early-modern world. The financial successes of the Jews in medieval England was attributed by Fuller to their saving money by not buying pork.[17] Meanwhile, those who looked for the conversion of the Jews recalled the strategy of Antiochus, who 'forced the *Iews* to eat Swines flesh, to forsake their Circumcision, and to adore his Gods.'[18] The fact that 'in America they eat no swine's flesh,' was evidence for Thomas Thorowgood that the 'people lost in the world' were to be found amongst the indigenous people of the new world.[19]

The practice of circumcision and its link with the covenant probably emerged during the period of the Babylonian captivity. Whilst circumcision had been a 'culturally expansive' practice in West Semitic cultures, it became associated primarily with Israel during the Second Temple period. As such, circumcision became the pre-eminent ethnic marker, 'a fruitful cut' by which the 'Jewish social body became differentiated from the body of other cultures.'[20] The distinctiveness of circumcision as an ethnic marker was particularly heightened during the reign of Hadrian when the practice was banned and stigmatized.[21] So it would remain up to the early modern period. Intermittently, in the times and places when the sociological context for the initial requirement of circumcision was revived or recalled—that is

14. Kraemer, *Jewish Eating and Identity*, 30.

15. Kraemer, *Jewish Eating and Identity*, 33.

16. Rosenblum, *Food and Identity in Early Rabbinic Judaism*.

17. Fuller, *Church-History of Britain*, 13:85.

18. J. J., *Resurrection of Dead Bones*, 87.

19. Thorowgood, *Digitus Dei*, 7.

20. Hendel, *Remembering Abraham*, 21.

21. Cohen, *Beginnings of Jewishness*, 47.

in the condition of exile with the concomitant threat of miscegenation—the significance of circumcision was redoubled. Even Menasseh ben Israel was moved to refer to it as 'the strange act.'[22]

The observation of the Sabbath represented another 'productive expression' of the separation of the Israelites. In the condition of exile, the locus of ritual separation shifted from the Temple to the quotidian practices of daily life. Daniel Smith, Claus Westermann, Yaira Amit and John Van Seters have all argued that the significance of the Sabbath was augmented by the destruction of the Temple and the suspension of sacrificial worship.[23] Amit has claimed that the creation story of Genesis 1 emerged from a redaction of the Holiness School. Amit claims that the establishment of the Sabbath as described in this text was 'an effective technique of separation.' In the observation of the Sabbath, the Israelites were 'cut off' from the 'rhythm of the environment' and were 'connected to a new understanding of . . . Divine time.' For Amit, the establishment of these new ways of separating and 'preserving Israelite society' was necessitated by the absence of the Temple. The observation of the Sabbath provided a way to 'establish a sanctified realm within an impure environment.'[24] As such, it functioned as a form of resistance, separating the devotee from 'the world.' To use the terminology we find in the letter of Aristeas, the law was a 'wall.'[25] A similar understanding of ethics would emerge in the writings of seventeenth-century Judaizers. In other words, the presence of these practices in the devotional life of Judaizing Godly professors like Tillam, Totney and Traske represented something more profound than mimesis.

JUDAISM AND SINGULARITY IN THE BIBLICAL APOCALYPTIC LITERATURE

These concerns for passive separation by resistance—and in particular the association of Israel with 'divine time'—also lie at the heart of early Jewish apocalyptic literature. The authors of Daniel and Enoch drew upon the exilic experiences of previous generations in order to make sense of their own experiences during the period of Seleucid domination. In the early 1990s, Rainer Albertz identified a connection between apocalyptic prophecy and resistance. By describing a 'complex of eschatological ideas' and envisioning

22. Israel, *Hope of Israel,* 71.

23. Smith, *Religion of the Landless*; VanSeters, *Law Book for the Diaspora,* 160–61; Westermann, *Isaiah 40–66,* 309–10.

24. Amit, *Hidden Polemics in the Biblical Narrative,* 239.

25. Aristeas, *Aristeas to Philocrates,* 156–57.

a 'total end of world history,' these authors 'preserved the religion of Israel from succumbing to Hellenistic pressure.'[26]

The suggestion that apocalyptic thought and apocalyptic chronology served to shore up the boundaries between a Godly in-group and an ungodly outgroup has been revisited in recent years by Anathea Portier-Young. In resisting the attempts by hegemonic forces to assimilate Jewish culture and religion, the authors of apocalyptic literature engaged in a cultural struggle, engaging with and disrupting the 'everyday metaphors of power.'[27] Portier-Young suggests that the apocalypses of Daniel and Enoch exemplify a number of strategies that served to undermine the authority of the secular rulers of the day—who sought to 'de-create' Jewish identity. Apocalyptic writers, she claims, established 'critical inversions,' reversing the conventional binaries of 'the hegemonic construction of reality' in order to 'create the possibility for resistance to hegemony . . . wherein categories are retained but the hierarchy of values or assignment of value is turned upside down.' They also 'turn to history to reveal the contingency of present reality.'[28]

In the book of Daniel, the use of apocalyptic time served as a mode of resistance, rendering contingent the structures of earthly power. This tendency is both explicit and implicit in the text. In chapter 7, Daniel has a vision of the fourth Kingdom:

> It will be different from all the other kingdoms and will devour the whole earth, trampling it down and crushing it. The ten horns are ten kings who will come from this kingdom. After them another king will arise, different from the earlier ones; he will subdue three kings. He will speak against the Most High and oppress his holy people and try to change the set times and the laws. The holy people will be delivered into his hands for a time, times and half a time.

For the authors of this text, the measuring of time, and the observation of 'God time,' provided the field of conflict between the Godly and 'the world.' This text informed a raft of millenarian theories in the early Stuart period.

For Portier-Young, the maintenance of clear, distinct boundaries between the sacred minority and the dominant, ungodly majority was both a political and a religious concern. The assertion of apocalyptic time at once demonstrated the temporal limits of earthly power, acting as a form of discursive resistance, and promised the fulfilment and the unveiling of a future condition in which the fortunes of the minority are reversed. In the latter

26. Albertz, *History of Israelite Religion*, 564.

27. Mitchell, 'Everyday Metaphors of Power,' 545–77.

28. Portier-Young, *Apocalypse Against Empire*, 202–17, 14, 13.

instance, the use of apocalyptic time located the author in an allegorical space, suspended between the future and the past and immune to the conditional, historical realities of the present. When Godly readers—and particularly those like Thomas Totney and Thomas Tillam who were engaged in a millenarian, political struggle—turned to these texts, they found within them profound resonances, shared convictions, shared concerns. Both the Godly, who believed themselves to be 'elect,' and the authors of Daniel, 'depended upon signs which will be fulfilled at the end of time.'[29]

ALLOSEMITISM AND THE EARLY CHURCH

The term 'allosemitism' was most clearly defined by Zygmunt Bauman in an essay written in 1998. The neologism itself was coined originally by Artur Sandauer. Bauman writes that philo-Semitic and anti-Semitic Christians, alike, share a common commitment to the 'othering' of 'the Jew.' Bauman cites the example of Friedrich Rühs who, observing the process of Jewish de-ghettoization in early nineteenth-century Germany, expressed relief that Jewish people would always be distinctive, inimitable and distinguishable. Rühs 'could not bear the idea of the Jew melting inconspicuously into the crowd,' Bauman writes: 'Jews were different and their difference mattered.'[30] The origins of this tendency, to portray the Jew as irreducibly other, began in the earliest period of Christianity. During the period which followed the destruction of the Second Temple, radical reformulations of Judaism emerged from Christian, Jewish and Jewish Christian spheres. Each of these developments contributed to a physical and discursive separation of Judaism from Christianity.

The attitude of allosemitism is identifiable in the earliest Christian documents. The Johannine complaints concerning 'the Jews' and St. Paul's discussion of carnal circumcision were read by early Christian apologetes as expressions of supersessionism.[31] Traditionally conceived, Paul's epistle to the Romans represents a rejection of the binding nature of the ceremonial law and a derogation of the function of circumcision. Supersessionist tradition identifies these texts as proof of the abrogation of the old, carnal covenant, of the Law and of the chosenness of the Jews.

During the period in which the 'whatness' of Christianity was defined, a number of apologetes contributed to the canon of, what has subsequently

---

29. Lewalski, *Protestant Poetics*, 126.

30. Bauman, 'Allosemitism,' 143–56.

31. Bieringer et al., 'Wrestling with Johannine Anti-Judaism,' 3–41.

become known as, *Adversus Iudaeos* literature.[32] The claim that Judaism and Jews themselves were 'carnal' was articulated in Justin Martyr's *Dialogue with Trypho*. The promise of salvation did not, Justin claimed, belong to the 'carnal seed' of Abraham, but rather to his 'spiritual seed.' Additional texts served to demonstrate that Israel's covenant was not only *superseded* but that it was intrinsically *inferior* to the spiritual. Moreover, Israel herself was characterized as irredeemably carnal, a tendency which necessitated the carnality of the old covenant.[33] The story of the Golden Calf was used as evidence of this (Acts 7:37). Given that Jewish religion was intrinsically carnal, and given that God had abandoned His covenant with the Jewish people, Christian apologists were required to explain the continued existence of observant Jews in the early Christian era. The troubling perpetuation of Jewry was addressed by Augustine. The Jews, he contended, were the *scrinaria*, bearers of the truth to which they could not themselves attest.[34] They were 'vessels of wrath' of the kind mentioned by Paul in his letter to the Romans, walking testimonies to the wages of sin.[35] As such, the figure of the Jew was frozen in time, fossilized in the act of deicide. Jews existed as 'biohermeneutic and biopolitical figures,' walking reminders of divine vengefulness.[36] Denied coevalness, the Jews were located in an atemporal, allegorical space. For Bauman, this period marked the beginning of the association of Judaism and ambivalence. Anti-Judaism, for Bauman, was a form of proteaphobia, an anxiety elicited by the troublingly mixed nature of the Jew. The Jew was both blessed and cursed, empirical and symbolic. The protean nature of the Jew stood in counterpart to the pure, untarnished ideal of Christendom. Each of these claims centered on the otherness of the Jews, not only as different, as anterior but as anti*thetical* to their Christian cousins. As Ruether, claims, the 'negation of Judaism' was a crucial stage in the development of the Christian identity in late antiquity. Judaism—and in particular the 'carnal' image of Judaism—was constructed as a productive antithesis to early Christianity. This process was replicated and mirrored in the proceeding centuries. Early modern scholars referred back to the texts of the *Adversus Iudaeos* canon in attempts to 'other' the Jews and Judaizers of their own period.[37]

---

32. Ruether, *Faith and Fratricide*, 117–23.

33. Mach, 'Justin Martyr's *Dialogus cum Tryphone Iudaeo*,' 27–85.

34. Cohen, *Living Letters of the Law*, 36; Augustine, 'Reply to Faustus the Manichaean,' 128.

35. Fredriksen, *Augustine and the Jews*, 177–79.

36. Nirneberg, 'Politics of Love and its Enemies,' 508.

37. Warren, *Jews Sabbath Antiquated*, 220.

But the separation of Judaism during the period of late antiquity was not a one-way street. The 'maximalist' account of the emergence of rabbinic Judaism suggests that this phenomenon was catalysed by the interaction with anti-Jewish, Christian texts.[38] Knohl shows how, during the second Temple period, the Pharisees emerged as the successors of the Holiness School, promoting an ethos which broadened the concept of 'holiness' beyond the sacrificial cult. Holiness in this context does not necessarily imply 'moral,' but rather 'ritual' separation. Whilst the authors of the Priestly Torah maintained 'holiness' within the temple and the priesthood, the Holiness School 'burst the walls of the sanctuary.' It was this tradition that would form the cultural basis for the development of Pharisaism.[39] The Pharisees did not seek to supplant the priesthood, but rather to apply the holiness of the priesthood to the entire people of Israel. This project became even more urgent in the context of diaspora. As part of this process, rabbinic scholars engaged in a process of critical inversion. Drawing upon the negative appraisal of Judaism as described in the Hellenistic literature of the period, early rabbinic thinkers sought out and inhabited the pejorative space as an assertion of the distinctiveness and separateness of Israel from the heathen of the land. Rabbinic literature from the proto-Rabbinical period records an explosion of apparently 'carnal' beliefs and devotional practices. Rabbinic writers actively protested that the first man was embodied, in opposition to Hellenic contemporaries. Rabbinic scholars described the human person as an animated body. Rabbinic scholars avowed that the patriarchs observed Mosaic ritual laws.[40] The period during which Talmudic thought developed and during which the most 'carnal' aspects of Jewish divinity began to develop coincided with a sustained period of Jewish minority experience. During this time, as Boyarin notes, 'rabbinic Judaism was substantially differentiated in its representations of discourses of the body and sexuality from Greek speaking Jewish formations.'[41] On this basis, Boyarin has contended that the earliest rabbinic traditions emerged from a desire to meet the anti-Judaic critiques of 'carnal Israel' with an inversion of this critique, an *embrace* of carnality. 'Proto-rabbinate Jews,' writes Boyarin, 'seem to have strongly resisted dualistic notions. ... This resistance was at least in part owing to cultural politics.'[42] Boyarin suggests that midrash represented an embrace of a carnal reading of the scriptures in the face of this very charge

38. Boyarin, *Dying for God*.

39. Knohl, *Divine Symphony*, 67; *Sanctuary of Silence*, 223–25.

40. Boyarin, *Carnal Israel*, 33.

41. Boyarin, *Carnal Israel*, 5.

42. Boyarin, *Carnal Israel*, 6.

from the Patristic authors. 'Midrash,' claims Boyarin 'refuses that dualism, eschewing the inner-outer, visible-invisible, body-soul dichotomies of allegorical reading.' Rabbinic scholars 'insisted on the essentiality of corporeality and sexuality' in the face of a prevailing ethos of self-abnegation in Pauline Christianity and Hellenic Judaism.[43] 'The division between Christianity and Judaism,' Peter Brown writes, 'was sharpest in this.'[44] Ruether, meanwhile, describes the Talmudic literature of this period as 'less of a direct argument with Christians than a defensive affirmation of Judaism.'[45] Rabbinic Judaism and early Christianity therefore, supervened upon one another.

On August 21, 1646, an advertisement appeared in a London newspaper. It read:

> The Body of the Antient Lawes, both Civill and Ecclesiasticall of the Jews called Mischnaioth is printed and perfected this week at Amsterdam. A work much desired for its utility, never before published with the points.[46]

The printing of rabbinic literature in early modern Europe—and the work of Hebraists like Jacob Buxtorf—brought about new and wider exposure of rabbinic thought to non-Jewish audiences.[47] The Talmud became emblematic of the distinctiveness of Jewishness from Christianity in the eyes of Christians as well as Jews. The 'sharp' distinction of carnality became heightened in the context of a Protestant culture that placed even more accent on the distinction between the carnal and the spiritual. The Talmud moved closer to the center of the devotional life of European Jewry. With the emergence of the practice of *pilpul*, the Talmud became even more internalized as a component of European Jewish identity.[48] Leon of Modena marvelled at the assiduousness of ordinary Jews in maintaining Talmudic observation.[49] The 'hypertrophic' significance of Talmud for European Jews drew the criticism of their Christian peers, and became a point of distinction for Christian apologetes between the polity of Israel and the 'pharasaical,' ceremonial religion of rabbinic Judaism. The Talmud became

---

43. Boyarin, *Carnal Israel*, 7, 35.

44. Brown, 'Person and Group,' 253–67.

45. Ruether, *Faith and Fratricide*, 169. It is worth noting that this process of auto-differentiation was not wholly immediately successful. This has been amply demonstrated in Fredriksen, *Jesus of Nazareth, King of the Jews*, 94–106.

46. *Perfect Occurrences of Both Houses of Parliament and Martiall Affairs*, no. 34.

47. Burnett, *From Christian Hebraism to Jewish Studies*; Heller, 'Earliest Printings of the Talmud,' 61–78.

48. Berkovitz, 'Rabbinic Culture,' 349–78.

49. Carlebach, 'Status of the Talmud,' 87–89.

JUDAIZING AND SINGULARITY   109

a symbol of Jewish carnality. If the Gospel was 'light,' John Paget believed, then the Talmud was 'utter darkness.'[50] It was burnt in the streets.[51] Talmud, a thousand years after its initial incarnation, once again became a fulcrum for sharp, discursive distinctions between Christians and Jews.

ALLOSEMITISM IN ENGLISH CULTURE

In 1583, Phillip Stubbes retold the story of the Jew of Tewkesbury:

> So it chaunced that a certaine Iewe . . . by greate casualtie fell into a Privie upon one of their Sabbaoth daies, and the people endeuouryng to helpe hym forthe, he forbad them to labor about hym upon the Sabbaoth daie, chosing to dye in that filthie stincking place, (as by morning he was dead) then to breake the Lordes Sabbaoth.[52]

This myth was first recorded four-hundred years earlier but had remained canonical throughout the period of the expulsion.[53] It provides a crystallization of the central themes of anti-Judaic bias in medieval and early-modern England. The Jew, in his bondage to the carnal Law, is humiliated, destroyed and—most pertinently—rendered untouchable for his Christian peers. Carnality, legalism, humiliation and otherness are inextricably intertwined.

Before the expulsion, the English were more allosemitic than the people of any other country in Europe. Jews, during the medieval period, were monitored and excluded from participation in feudal life.[54] In graphic art, in literature and in every aspect of culture, Jews were portrayed as anterior, debased and deviant.[55] The figure of the male Jew was often located in a liminal space between genders, subject to lactation and to menstruation.[56] Demonstrations of Christian piety were often complemented by acts of anti-Judaic violence or slander. Anti-Judaic mythology often took the form of

50. Paget, *Arrow Against the Separation of the Brownistes*, 26, 287.

51. Burnett, 'Regulation of Hebrew Printing in Germany,' 348; Carlebach, 'Status of the Talmud,' 87–89.

52. Stubbes, *Anatomie of Abuses*, M8v.

53. Bale, *Jew in the Medieval Book*, 23–55; Bale, 'Framing Antisemitic Exempla,' 19–47.

54. Skinner, *Jews in Medieval Britain*, 2; Despres, 'Cultic Anti-Judaism and Chaucer's Litel Clergeon,' 413–27; Stacey, 'Anti-Semitism and the Medieval English State,' 166.

55. Lipton, *Images of Intolerance*, 25.

56. Katz, 'Shylock's Gender,' 44–48.

an inversion: Christian iconography or tradition was inverted, satirized or contorted into grotesque and scandalous forms. Blood libels, host-desecration libels, and other myths identified Jewish ritual as the shadow-form of Christian worship.[57]

But even after the expulsion and into the early-modern period, the othering of the Jew retained a central role in English life. As James Shapiro has demonstrated, the anterior figure of the Jew remained a staple of Jacobean culture. Most famously in Marlowe's *The Jew of Malta*, but also in *The Tragicall Raigne of Selimus*, *Jack Drum's Entertainment* and *The Travels of Three English Brothers*, the familiar tropes of Jewish villainy were rehearsed. Jews 'went about poisoning wells.'[58] The claim that Jews 'crucified children' remained feasible.[59] Jewish pleasure was correlative to Christian suffering: 'we smile when Christian's moan' says Marlowe's Barabbas.[60] Travel literature of this period perpetuated myths that presented Jews as alien, exotic and utterly other. Their worship was filled with roaring and chaos. Their skin was black and peculiar.[61] Their nostrils flared.[62] Even self-appointed ethnographers of European Jewry took as the basis for their descriptions of Jewish life the old, familiar, medieval slanders against Jewry, filling new skins with old, anti-Judaic wine.[63] Prynne's objections to readmission were based on the deeply entrenched impression that Jews were interlopers, 'murmuring, mutinous, rebellious, seditious against Governor, King and Priest.'[64]

Various explanations could be offered for the prevalence of anti-Judaic sentiment in English culture. Some have argued that it represented an oedipal contest for the prize of elect nationhood, some that it represents the cultural valence of supersessionist theology.[65] In recent years Robert Stacey, Miri Rubin, Geraldine Heng and Anthony Bale have pointed to the identification of the Jew as antitype in the generation of English national identity in the medieval period.[66] The framing of Englishness as the antithesis of Juda-

---

57. Bale, *Jew in the Medieval Book*, 23–55; Rubin, *Gentile Tales*; Heng, 'Jews, Saracens, "Black Men," Tartars,' 249–55; Feselstein, *Anti-Semitic Stereotypes*; Dundes, *Blood Libel Legend*.

58. Marlowe, *Jew of Malta* 2.3.179.

59. Marlowe, *Jew of Malta* 3.4.49–50.

60. Marlowe, *Jew of Malta* 2.3.170–73.

61. Munster, *Messias of the Christians and the Jewes*, 2.

62. Daborne, *Christian Turn'd Turk*, C4r.

63. Shapiro, *Shakespeare and the Jews*, 102.

64. Prynne, *Short Demurrer*, 79.

65. Loewenstein, *Christians and the Jews*; Ruether, *Faith and Fratricide*, 1–23.

66. Rubin, 'Identities' 408–12; Bale, *Jew in the Medieval Book*, 130–35; Rubin, *Gentile Tales*, 25–28; Heng, 'Jews, Saracens, "Black Men," Tartars,' 249–55.

ism recurred periodically throughout English history. In the period leading up to the expulsion of the Jews in 1290, anti-Judaic discourse and violence served in turn as cultural mechanisms, which incubated the nascent, national identity. The figure of the king, as the totemic figure of the nation, was often placed in contrast with images of Jews. The rood-screen at St. Peter and St. Paul in Eye, Suffolk bears the images of English kings (Henry VI and Edward the Confessor) along with the image of martyred William of Norwich tacitly positioning 'the Jews,' in the anterior. This polarity was dramatized in the events surrounding the coronation of Richard I. Notable Jews attending the coronation were set upon by an angry mob.[67] This event would linger in the consciousness of John Foxe and later of William Prynne. Especially at moments of heightened anxiety surrounding the stability and cohesion of the nation, myths which offered accounts of English, Christian victories over Judaism were mobilized in order to inculcate solidarity and unity. Ranulf Higden's *Polychronicon* book-ends an account of the Barons' War (which constituted an existential threat to the cohesion of a relatively young nation) with seemingly extraneous anti-Judaic anecdotes.[68] This rhetorical stratagem was intended as a warning of the perennial fragility of the Christian state.[69]

In the early modern era, just as in the medieval era, the antitype of the Jew was mobilized in the task of crafting a national identity. An additional layer of Bauman's analysis of allosemitism posits that the topos of the Jew was identifiable—in Christian discourse—with 'radical ambivalence.' As such, anti-Judaic hatred is properly understood not as a form of heterophobia, but rather as a form of proteophobia; not fear of 'the unfamiliar,' but rather the fear of 'something or someone that does not fit the structure of the orderly world, does not fall easily into established categories, emits contradictory signals and . . . blurs the borderlines.' Stigmatization of 'blurry' Jews, therefore, served in turn to sharpen the definition of the image of Englishness. In England, this tendency reasserted itself during sustained periods of uncertainty about national and ecclesiastical unity. Prynne rehearsed the stories of the threat of Jewish otherness that had been told generations earlier by Higden.[70] Samantha Zacher claims that the 'Jewish other,' formed the 'mythological ground' for the development of English national identity at the dawn of modernity.[71] Rosenblatt links 'fear and loathing of Jews' in

67. Bale, *Jew in the Medieval Book*, 132, 26.

68. Higden, *Prolicionycion*.

69. Bale, 'Framing Antisemitic Exempla,' 19–47.

70. Prynne, *Short Demurrer*, 8.

71. Zacher, 'Judaism and National Identity,' 375.

the seventeenth century with 'the confused struggles among the English ... to develop a religious and national identity.'[72] The absence of 'real-life' Jews did little to undermine the success of this cultural strategy. 'England,' Shapiro writes 'was defined by its having purged itself of the Jews.' As such, 'English character was defined by its need to exclude Jewishness.'[73] By extension, renewed awareness of 'real-life Jews' brought with it renewed anxiety about 'cultural and personal miscegenation.'[74] The vicious response to the proposal of readmission from figures like William Prynne has been identified by Shapiro as a sign of the anxiety felt by Englishmen and women about the frailty of the nation in the aftermath of the English Revolution. This fear seeped into the cultural consciousness. Some feared that Judaism was infectious, a form of leprosy.[75] Ralph Josselin had nightmares that Thurloe himself would 'turn Jew.'[76] In other ways, the boundaries between Jewishness and Christianity were blurred, problematized and deliberated over. The question of whether Jews could easily be identified became fraught. James Howell reported that the Habasines were 'Christians from the girdle upwards, and Jews downward.'[77] The suggestion that Jewish immorality brought about somatic changes remained on the table, further demonstrating the anxiety that was abroad about the distinctiveness of the Jew from the Christian.[78]

Most of all, commentators of this period feared the slippage that existed between Jewish and Christian ritual and devotional practice. This informed the perennial use of the charge of Judaizing as a rhetorical designation of doctrinal error and heterodoxy.[79] If Jews did not exist, it is tempting to claim, it would have been necessary for early-modern Englishmen and women to invent them. In a time of crisis of national identity—the period leading up to the Civil War—they did precisely that. It is to the charge of Judaizing that we turn next.

---

72. Rosenblatt, 'John Selden's *De Jure Naturalis*,' 103.

73. Shapiro, *Shakespeare and the Jews*, 7

74. Shapiro, *Shakespeare and the Jews*, 8.

75. Collier, *Brief Answer to Some of the Objections*, 12.

76. Josselin, *Diary of Ralph Josselin*, 337.

77. Howell, *Instructions for Forreine Travel*, 154.

78. Daborn, *Christian Turned Turk*, c4r. For a broader discussion on early-modern conceptions of ethnicity in relation to morality and humor, see Wilson, 'English Mettle,' 133–34.

79. Glaser, *Judaism without Jews*, 54–63.

THE CHARGE OF JUDAIZING

Thomas Coryat was surprised, when he arrived in Venice, to find Jews who were 'goodly and proper men.' Living in a society within which the figure of the Jew had taken on mythic proportions, Coryat understood the word Jew to denote 'a *weather beaten warp-faced* fellow, sometimes a phrenticke and lunaticke person, sometimes one discontented.'[80] 'The Jew' was an outsider: odd-looking, contrary and mad. In early-modern England, Glassman notes, 'an entire people were made a derogatory term in the English language.'[81] In this context, therefore, the topos of Judaism developed an additional association with sedition and deviance. In a variety of different settings, the singularity of 'the Jew' was co-opted as a pejorative term in order to marginalize a rival religious or political claim. Thomas Netter had accused the Lollards of being 'Judaizers.'[82] In the sixteenth and seventeenth centuries this term was adopted by the antagonists of the Godly in their attempts to enforce conformity. They stigmatized the Godly, and thereby provided for them a sphere within which the Godly could exhibit their own, devotional, 'singularity.'

In travel journals of this period, the Jew is portrayed as misguided but nonetheless assiduous in his commitment to the Law. The Law, as such, provided an obstacle to commerce, to progress and to reason. John Taylor expressed a grudging admiration for the misguided but, nonetheless, unimpeachably dedicated Jews:

> When Christians dare Gods Sabboth to abuse,
> They make themselues a scorne to Turkes and Iewes:
> You stealing *Barabasses* beastly Race,
> Rob God of glory, and your selues of Grace.
> Thinke on the supreame Iudge who all things tries,
> When Iewes in Iudgement shall against you rise.
> Their feigned trueth, with feruent Zeale they show.[83]

Routinely, in this period, identification was drawn between the Jews— as extremists, zealous for the carnal law—and the Godly. At times, this identification was brazen. In Robert Davenport's *A New Trick to Cheat the Devil*, Davenport describes a Puritan as:

---

80. Coryat, *Coryats Crudities*, 232.
81. Glassman, *Anti-Semitic Stereotypes without Jews*, 72.
82. Groeneveld, 'Mourning, Heresy, and Ressurection,' 16.
83. Taylor, *Three Weekes*, b4r.

> One that will eat no pork. Doth use to shut his shop on Sat-
> urdays, And open them on Sundays: A Jewish Christian and a
> Christian Jew.[84]

At other times, the identification was more muted but nonetheless insidious. Godly conventicles were referred to as 'sinagogues.'[85] Godly professors were labelled as 'rabbis.'[86] Acts of 'divisive identification,' by which the Godly identified themselves as other, were met with the accusation of being 'Jewish.'

The portrayal of Puritanism, and in particular the Judaizing figure of 'Zeal-of-the-Land Busy,' in *Bartholomew Fair* has been examined by Jeanette Fereira Ross, Eliane Glaser, Patrick Collinson and Nicholas McDowell.[87] Busy is portrayed as a zealot, an extremist, an enemy of fun, a killjoy. In his own words, he is:

> One that rejoiceth in his affliction, and siteth here to prophes the
> destruction of fairs and Maygames, wakes and Whitsun-ales,
> and doth sigh and groan for the reformation of these abuses.[88]

Busy makes regular reference to his sense of separateness and deviation from worldly society:

> The lion may roar, but he cannot bite. I am glad to be thus sepa-
> rated from the heathen of the land and put apart in the stocks
> for the holy cause.[89]

Like the woman who was arrested for hooting at the bishop of London in the late sixteenth century, and who, throughout her ordeal, 'praysed the Lorde for that He had made hir worthy to soffer persecution for ryghtwysnes,' Busy saw the humiliation of the stocks as a mark of 'separation' and thus a benediction.[90]

Zeal-of-the-Land himself professes concern about the association of his own community with Judaism. In order to dispel the similarity, he attempts to negate the comparison by ostentatiously indulging in 'swine's flesh':

84. Davenport, *Pleasant and Witty Comedy*, f4v.

85. Sacristan, *Whetstone of Reproofe*, 431; Cleveland, *Revived Poems*, 71.

86. Heath, *Clarastella*, 8.

87. Ferreira-Ross, 'Religion and the Law,' 348–63; Collinson, 'Ben Johnson's *Bartholomew Fair*,' 157–69.

88. Jonson, *Bartholomew Fair* 4.6.87.

89. Jonson, *Bartholomew Fair* 4.6.83.

90. Stowe, 'Stowe's Memoranda,' 140.

Indeed, I will eat exceedingly, and prophesy; there may be good use made of it, too, now I think on't: by the publike eating of swine's flesh, to profess our hate and loathing of Judaisme, whereof the brethren stand taxed. I will therefore eat, yea, I will eat exceedingly.[91]

Jonson's audience would have recognized the tropological interaction between the extremism and carnality of the Jews and the extremism and carnality of the Godly. But it is also telling that 'Rabbi' Busy here explores the process of the development of his own pious practices *in light of* the way in which these practices will be apprehended by his peers. In this respect, the figure of Zeal-of-the-Land Busy reflects the problem of Puritan identity that Fereira, Collinson and—latterly—Glaser have all debated. Zeal-of-the-Land is a stereotype. But as Ann Hughes has demonstrated, the distinction between the stereotype of the Puritan and the real thing was not a straightforward one. Stereotypes, as Hughes writes, 'interact in a complex way with stigmatized groups' self-images in processes of identity formation.'[92] The question of whether Puritan-Judaizer 'the thing' or Puritan-Judaizer 'the name' came first is recognized as frought by Jonson and, indeed, by Zeal-of-the-Land himself.[93] In the play, Zeal-of-the-Land's character is created by a series of interactions between the Godly and the ungodly. The same was true of the interaction between Jonson and his Godly peers.

CRANKISHNESS, SEPARATION, AND THE SABBATH

The centerpiece of Godly 'Judaizing' in the discourse of seventeenth-century England was sabbatarianism. Sabbatarianism offers perhaps the clearest picture of the distinctiveness of Puritan divinity, not only in relation to English Protestantism but also in relation to the other Reformed Protestant movements of continental Europe. Popkin called it 'a crankish kind of reform.' He meant that it appeared to have no point of correspondence with the ethos of the continental Reform project.[94] 'The English attitude,' Katz writes, 'was radically different from that which prevailed on the continent.'[95] Calvin ostentatiously played bowls on the Sabbath, while Luther famously declared

91. Jonson, *Bartholomew Fair* 1.6.95.

92. Hughes, *Gangraena*, 10–11.

93. Collinson, 'Theatre Constructs Puritanism,' 158; Ferreira-Ross, 'Religion and the Law,' 45–66; Glaser, *Judaism without Jews*, 33; Adkins, 'Genesis of Dramatic Satire,' 81–95.

94. Popkin, *Jewish Christians and Christian Jews*, 7.

95. Katz, 'Jewish Sabbath and Christian Sunday,' 119.

that 'if Sunday were anywhere made holy merely for the day's sake or its observance set on a Jewish foundation, then I order you to walk on it, to ride on it, to dance on it.'[96] Puritans, on the other hand, zealously exhibited their veneration of the Sabbath day.[97] Katz identifies this phenomenon as an offshoot of Puritan Biblicism. 'The explanation for English Sabbatarianism,' he writes 'must in the first instance be sought in light of the Puritan emphasis on a direct understanding of the word of God as it appears in the Bible.'[98]

Certainly, however, Sabbatarianism was understood by the peers of the Godly as denoting something *apart* from Biblicist obedience. Sabbatarianism was rather understood as a designation of deviance and dissent. The flash-points of conflict between the Godly and their neighbors often centered on issues relating to Sabbath observation.[99] The most obvious of these related to the playing of Sports. The playing of Sports became a politicized issue in Jacobean England because Sabbatarianism was understood to be demonstrative of a refusal to conform to the traditional patterns of rural life. This in itself was understood as an act of non-conformity which threatened the cohesion of the Kingdom. Sabbath festivities were identified explicitly by the authorities as a means of generating social solidarity and cohesive social-identities. On November 5, 1633, Bishop Piers of Bath and Wells wrote to Archbishop Laud detailing the extent to which Feasts of Dedication were observed in his see. Piers reported that seventy-two of his ministers had defended the celebration of the feasts on the basis that they should be maintained:

> For the civilizing of the people, for their lawful recreations, for composing differences by meeting of friends, for increase of love and amity as being feasts of charity.[100]

In refusing to participate in them, therefore, the Godly were disruptive of this process.

That the Sabbath offers an intrinsic demarcation of holiness—of the devotee as well as the practice—was recognized by Bozeman who called it 'a showpiece of a repertoire of means for ethical amendment and self-control.'[101] The English people recalled the role of the Jews themselves as interrupters, uneasy presences in economic and social life. The tenacity of myths like that

96. Katz, 'Jewish Sabbath and Christian Sunday,' 121.
97. Parker, *English Sabbath*, 139–61.
98. Katz, *God's Last Words*, 62.
99. Watt, *Cheap Print and Popular Piety*, 325.
100. Prynne, *Canterburies Doome*, 142.
101. Bozeman, *Precisianist Strain*, 113.

of the Jew of Tewkesbury, which itself located Sabbatarianism, deviance and extremism in juxtaposition with Judaism, attests to this. The Sabbath was one of an armoury of practices that firmly designated the Jews as 'other.' It was on this basis, not *just* on the basis of the similarity of the doctrinal claims of the Sabbatarians to Judaism, that they were designated Judaizers. 'Judaizing' represented a rupture in social life and it was described as such by the critics of Sabbatarianism. For Bishop Morton, Sabbatarianism was a sinister undermining of clerical and secular authority. He ordered that 'all such kinds of people as are said to encline to Judaisme' be 'observed.'[102] William Cotton also assimilated Sabbatarianism with an overall spirit of anti-authoritarianism:

> Every day complaints are made by ministers who are railed on and shrewdly beaten by lewd persons; in one place a minister was made to kiss the bare hinder parts of a man. Jewism also aboundeth, twenty factions in one city; many conventicles held in gardens and fields and sermons preached at midnight; few or none come to church, but they will follow rattle headed preachers from town to town.[103]

Peter Heylyn saw the practice of Sabbatarianism as far more than simply a matter of doctrinal difference. He suggested that it was evidence of 'the declining period of the church.'[104] The Sabbath was disturbing, uncanny. In the words of Thomas Fuller, the Godly were 'conjuring up the ghosts of long dead Judaisme,' which were 'walking, frighting people with their terrible apparitions.'[105]

But the association of Sabbatarianism with dissent and disruption was not a contingent association. The Sabbath, from its inception and in every instance of its observation *necessarily* represents an interruption of life, commerce, and normality. The Sabbath cut off its observer from 'natural time.'[106] The power of the Sabbath to subvert earthly authority was recognized by Romme and Depuis when they devised the Revolutionary Calendar. It was also recognized by James and Charles Stuart in their attempts to enforce conformity on the English Church. It was championed as a mark of resistance by Judas Maccabeus in the struggle against Seleucid domination. Daniel 7 visioned the changing of times and days as a struggle between

102. Tait, 'Declaration of Sports for Lancashire,' 561–68.

103. *Calendar of the Manuscript of the Marquis of Salisbury*, 10:450–51.

104. Heylyn, *History of the Sabbath*, 129.

105. Fuller, *Infants Advocate of Circumcision*, 81; Fuller, *Church-History of Britain*, 17:76.

106. Amit, *Hidden Polemics in the Biblical Narrative*, 239.

the saints and the beast. Whatever else, these acts functioned as a mark of resistance, of self-differentiation. By observing the Sabbath—and by refusing to observe saints' days—the Godly were not only exhibiting their own piety, they were putting their bodies upon the gears and the wheels of the communal life, creating an 'assault on the existing order.'[107]

CONCLUSION

'All things are in pairs,' reads Ecclesiasticus, 'each the opposite of the other, but nothing the Lord made is incomplete. Everything completes the goodness of something' (Sir 42:24–25). The observation of the Sabbath is incomplete without the observation of days of labor. The recognition of the sacred is impossible without the recognition of the profane. The identification of early Christians was impossible without 'the Jews.' The identification of the Godly in early modern England was incomplete without the presence of the ungodly. Much ink has been spilt in recent decades over the responsibility of relying on pejorative terms in order to develop a clear picture of religious practices during the seventeenth century. Christopher Hill relied on figures like Thomas Edwards and Ephraim Pagett and their descriptions of the devotional practices of Godly professors. Colin Davis, on the other hand, lamented this practice and claimed that it was akin to 'relying on Horatio Bottomley or Joseph McCarthy for sound, objective depictions of the social realities of their day.'[108] Ann Hughes, however, has argued that representations should not be unravelled from reality. In order to understand phenomena like Puritanism, or antinomianism or Judaizing, it is important to 'take polemical classifications seriously.'[109] The distinction between the signified and the signifier, the stereotype and the stereotyped is often unclear. The attempt to differentiate between the point at which the labelling of the Godly as Judaizers was descriptive and the point at which it was pejorative is not straightforward. The Godly exhibited many of those characteristics that their counterparts regarded as Judaizing. The ungodly stigmatized those behaviors as Judaizing. But these factors *cannot* be isolated or described in isolation. The stigmatization of the Godly as Judaizing is an essential component of the story of the emergence of Judaizing itself. Judaizing stereotype and Judaizer represent the 'two sides of a stressful relationship.' The figures to whom we turn next—John Traske, Thomas Tillam, and Thomas Totney— occupied *and* shaped the space created by this relationship.

107. Moltmann, 'Liberation of the Future,' 8.

108. Davis, *Fear, Myth, and History*, 126.

109. Hughes, *Gangraena*, 11.

CHAPTER 3

'A Jewish Faccion'

Anti-Legalism, Judaizing, and the Traskites

ON THE FOURTEENTH OF September, 1618, John Chamberlain wrote to his brother-in-law Dudley Carleton, reporting:

> There is one Trask or Thrask who was first a Puritan and now is become a Jewish Christian, observing the Sabbath on Saturday and abstaining from swine's flesh.

Chamberlain was struck by the large numbers of followers that Traske had managed to attract in a relatively short time.[1] Amongst this number only a few names survive. A young lawyer named John Pecke.[2] A tailor named Hamlet Jackson and his associate Christopher Sands.[3] A school-teacher named Dorothy Coome (whom Traske would marry).[4] A Sussex land-owner named Return Hebdon.[5] The vacillating figure of Mary Chester, who converted to and from Traskism more than once.[6]

Traske had been on trial before the Star Chamber three months before Chamberlain wrote to Carleton, charged with 'haveing a fantasticall opynion of himselfe, with ambicion to bee the Father of a Jewish faccion.'[7]

1. National Archives, SP 14/96, f. 34–35.
2. Bland, *Guide to Early Printed Books and Manuscripts*, 198.
3. Pagitt, *Heresiography*, 180.
4. Pagitt, *Heresiography*, 209–10.
5. Hebdon, *Guide to the Godly*, a2r; Pagitt, *Heresiography*, 192.
6. Pagitt, *Heresiography*, 194–95; National Archives, SP 16/261 f. 307.
7. Greene, 'Trask in the Star-Chamber,' 8.

Traske's trial threw a spotlight on a congregation of English Protestants who had begun to adopt so many Jewish ceremonies—including the observation of the Saturday Sabbath, dietary laws and even Passover seders—that Lancelot Andrewes was prepared to label them as Jews. 'It is a good work to *make a Jew a Christian*,' Andrewes proclaimed 'but to *make Christian* men *Jews*, hath ever been holden a foul act.'[8] Traske was tortured and imprisoned. A record of his ordeal in the Fleet prison was left by one Alexander Harris, the warden.[9] His forehead was branded with the letter 'J.'[10] He was imprisoned for a year before recanting.[11] His followers—including his wife Dorothy—were also imprisoned and at least two of them remained in prison until their deaths.[12] Some others, including Jackson and Sands fled to Amsterdam, where they sought out a *mohel* in order to be circumcised.[13] Mary Chester told her story to the anonymous 'T. S.' who offered an account of the whole story of the Traskites to be reproduced in Ephraim Pagitt's *Heresiography*.

Traske's adoption of Jewish ceremonies is particularly surprising, given that he appears to have assimilated elements of both anti-legalist Calvinism and precisianist Puritanism. These tendencies, ordinarily, are understood to have formed opposite ends of the Calvinist spectrum. This has provided a conundrum for several historians, calling into question the meaning of antinomianism in this period, as well as the meaning of Judaizing. This chapter follows the career of John Traske—the proto-typical 'Jewish-Christian' of this era. It will demonstrate the interaction at the heart of Traske's thought between the desire to 'separate', the assertion of anti-legalist perfectibilism and the renovation of aspects of ceremonial law.

David S. Katz describes Traske as the prototypical Saturday Sabbatarian. Ball has taken issue with this, however, suggesting that this is an imprecise description of Traske. Traske appears to have gone further than other Sabbatarians and perhaps for this reason 'Traskism' is listed as a separate heresy from 'Sabbatarianism' in Pagitt's *Heresiography*.[14] Katz identifies the genealogy of Traskism with renewed academic interest in the Hebrew tongue. He writes that 'when Hebrew became a subject of study in the universities, and the focus of attention among philosophers, it was clear that the

8. Andrewes, 'Speech Delivered in the Star-Chamber,' 84.

9. Harris, *Œconomy of the Fleete*, 48.

10. Greene, 'Trask in the Star-Chamber,' 11.

11. Traske, *Treatise of Libertie from Judaisme* 1r-A3v.

12. Pagitt, *Heresiography*, 196–97.

13. For other accounts of Traske's career, see Como, *Blown by the Spirit*, 138–76; Katz, *Philo-Semitism*, 18–34.

14. Ball, *Seventh Day Men*, 48; Pagitt, *Heresiography*, a3r.

discussion would soon turn to the Jews themselves.'[15] As Protestant Hebraists rediscovered Jewish works of philosophy and jurisprudence, they developed a 'very positive' impression of 'the Jews.' This positivity filtered through society, preparing the conditions for the readmission of the Jews in the 1650s. This 'philo-semitism' also helped form the basis of John Traske's ideology.[16] However, feelings of positivity towards the Jews seldom stretched to the ceremonies of Judaism. On the contrary, the most progressive 'philo-semites' of this period, looked forward to the abolition of Jewish ceremonies—vestiges of superstition, associated with Catholicism—the better to facilitate greater interaction between Jews and Christians.[17] Philo-semites of the period preferred the chimerical figure of 'Caraism'—a kind of enlightened, de-ceremonialized, de-sacerdotalized, 'rational reformed' Protestant ideal of Judaism—over the problematic 'Pharaism' of the Rabbinic tradition.[18]

Raphael Patai associated Traskism with Biblical literalism or 'overenthusiasm.' He wrote that Traske was 'impressed by the laws and the warnings contained in [the Bible].'[19] Glassman calls Traske 'a very zealous Puritan,' whilst Philips attributes Traske's Judaizing to his 'extreme Puritanism.'[20] Parker's suggestion that Traske's thought 'stemmed from a fixation on Levitical laws,' is somewhat causally redundant.[21] Bryan Ball acknowledges that Traske's actions were *perceived* as 'savouring too strongly of anarchy and sedition.' But he stops short of drawing a connection between the seditious quality of Judaizing and its potential attraction (on that basis) for Traskites. Ball argues instead that Traske's activities were an indication of his 'legalism.'[22] Offering 'Biblicism' as an holistic explanation for Judaizing ceremonialism is somewhat problematic. The Bible was central to the development of the Judaizing tendency. But the fact that the Traskites took things from the Biblical texts that their peers, predecessors and descendants (even the *most* scripturalist) did *not* demands closer inspection. *How* did the Traskites read these texts in ways that were different to previous generations, and *why* did they approach these texts in these ways?

---

15. Katz, *Jews in the History of England*, 112.

16. Katz, *Jews in the History of England*, 112.

17. Selden, *Table Talk*, 166; John Dury, 'Epistolic All Discourse,' in Thorowgood, *Digitus Dei*, C2r, 2v, 3r.

18. Popkin, *Third Force*, 365; Marana, *Letters Writ by a Turkish Spy*, 5:104; Dury, 'Epistolicall Discourse,' C2r–3r.

19. Patai, *Myth of the Jewish Race*, 81.

20. Glassman, *Anti-Semitic Stereotypes*, 78; Phillips, 'Early Stuart Judaizing Sect,' 65.

21. Parker, *English Sabbath*, 162.

22. Ball, *English Connection*, 139; Ball, *Seventh Day Men*, 53.

In the case of the Traskites, the Biblicist account is especially prob-lematic. Some of their ceremonial practices appear to have originated in immediate rather than mediate revelation.[23] Meanwhile, Traske and Jackson were seen by their peers as prophetic figures, with the ability to interpret the Law autonomously. 'The light of the Law was more fully revealed to him,' Jackson believed 'than to any since the apostles.'[24] Traske, in this respect, played a role not dissimilar to that of H. N. to the Familist community.[25] He believed that God's will was revealed to him, not via the scripture solely, but also via dreams.[26] Nor did Traske's peers see him as a stringent observer of deontological, ceremonial law. On the contrary, he was described as a restless innovator, prone to 'dangerous novelty and notable giddiness,' to 'coyne at his pleasure weekly doctrines; defending them with such peremp-tory pride of judgment, as if he had receaved cleare and certaine revelations therof.'[27] Traske himself contended that faithfulness to the Word was, itself, insufficient evidence of Godliness.[28] Biblicism was a component of Traskism. But it cannot be identified as the *explanatory endpoint* of Traskism.

Mark Robert Bell pursues the claim that the imminence of the apoca-lypse induced further association with Biblical Israel and that this associa-tion led to mimicry of Jewish ritual practice.[29] Bell, in this respect, echoes the earliest critics of Traskism who drew a connection between Judaizing and more treasonous elements of Henry Finch's Judeocentric eschatology. Judeocentric eschatology certainly cannot be discounted from the analysis of Traskism. It was a new and rapidly disseminated tradition during pre-cisely this period. Nonetheless, there are scant references to Judeocentric eschatological themes in Traske's writing. Moreover, admiration for the Jews in the eschatological setting cannot easily be linked with the revival of Jew-ish ceremonies. Indeed, Andrew Crome has called this link 'impossible,' on the basis of the 'firm divisions' between Christianity and Judaism implicit in the Judeocentric eschatological mode. Far from perforating the boundaries between Jews and Christians, the eschatological innovations of Brightman and Finch and others actually served to *shore up* the distinctiveness of the

23. Pagitt, *Heresiography*, 190.

24. Pagitt, *Heresiography*, 191.

25. An English Familist defended the precedence given to H. N.'s writings in 1570 by arguing that the *Evangelium Regni* was not superior to the Gospels but rather was functionally the same revelation, 'concordable, and uniforme testimonye' with the Gos-pels (Wilkinson, *Confutation of Certain Articles*, B1r).

26. Harris, *Œconomy of the Fleet*, 49.

27. Falconer, *Brief Refutation*, 18.

28. Traske, *Pearle for a Prince*, 9.

29. Bell, *Apocalypse How?*, 214.

Jews, maintaining that the Jews would *remain* a distinctive polity beyond the eschatological event of their conversion.[30] Moreover, one of Brightman's central concerns was the eschatological *abolition* of Jewish ceremonies.[31] There is no intuitive leap, in short, that can be made from Judeocentric apocalypticism to Judaizing ceremonialism.

Nor can these accounts offer an adequate explanation of the complex combination of ceremonialism and anti-legalism in Traske's thought. This element is certainly lacking from Ball's description of Traske as a 'legalist,' or Philips's appraisal of Traskism as 'extreme Puritanism.' Where scholars *have* referred to Traske's anti-legalism, many have—at best—relied upon a false chronology, hypothesizing a '180 degree turn in Traske's thought' around the year 1618. At worst, scholars have used the *apparent* contradictions in Traske's thought as evidence that he was 'a drifter of no fixed intellectual abode.'[32]

In this respect, the recent scholarship of David Como has been corrective. Como sees elements of antinomianism in Traskite literature from before, during and after the scandal of 1618. Como claims that Traske's later writings were influenced by the 'imputative antinomianism' of John Eaton: 'the father of seventeenth-century English antinomianism.'[33] But even in his earliest writings Traske appears to occasionally 'veer off into antinomian excess.'[34] Como suggests that this earlier iteration of Traskite antinomianism was influenced by Familist thought. The thesis that Traske personally embodied the 'antinomian backlash' to precisianist pietism does not fit with the chronology. Rather than seeing Traske's antinomianism as representing a reaction against a previously avowed precisianist strain, Como uses Traske's career as a template for the claim that Puritanism was neither 'radical nor inherently conservative.'[35] Como is clear that there is no necessary discontinuity between these two elements—antilegal and ceremonial—in Traske's thought. The Traskite belief that 'freedom from the law meant obedience to

30. Crome, 'Proper and Naturall Meaning,' 734–36.

31. Brightman, *Commentary on the Canticles*, 1060.

32. Como, 'Kingdom of Christ,' 64.

33. Como, *Blown by the Spirit*, 40; Hessayon has taken issue with Como's definition of antinomianism and the taxonomy of 'imputative' and 'perfectibilist' antinomianism, arguing that the former threatens to broaden the parameters of the term beyond the bounds of coherence. Regardless of the terminology, it is clear that Traske embraced some elements that were recogniseably anti-legal in character. The point of contact between Traske's 'antinomianism' and his 'legalism'—I will argue—lie in the common theme of separation which intertwines both strands of Puritanism (Hessayon, *Gold Tried in the Fire*, 10).

34. Como, 'Kingdom of Traske,' 75.

35. Como, 'Kingdom of Traske,' 81.

the law,' for Como, 'explains why Traske's early theology accomodated both antinomian and legalistic elements.'[36] The Traskites had attained a degree of perfection of which legal ceremonies were only the symptom. 'Perfect obedience to the Mosaic Law,' denoted 'heavenly perfection in this life.'[37] In other words, Traskism represented the apogee of the Heidelbergean, reflexive ethic.

As such, Como does not differentiate between ceremonialism and other forms of biblicism or obedience. Perfection went hand-in-hand, for the Traskites, with ceremonialism. But for Como, ceremonialism still represented—in some sense—a form of pietism: a 'typically Puritan attitude ... pushed to perfectionist extremes,' a form of 'moralism,' and 'extreme Puritanism.'[38] Como's claim, that Traske's followers were 'primitivists' who were enjoined 'to perfectly obey the Law of God,' occludes the *intrinsic* values of the ceremonies that Traske enjoined upon his followers. For almost all of Traske's contemporaries, his ceremonialism would have been perceived as an act of *dis*obedience. Moreover, the Traskites themselves *understood* and even *declared* that their observation of the Law constituted a privileging of one Biblical injunction *over* another. Hamlet Jackson claimed that he *preferred* to be obedient to the Torah than to the New Testament.[39] They did not, therefore consider ceremonialism to be an assertion of 'perfect obedience.' And, whilst his analysis draws closer to the claim that Traske's primary concern was the social reification of a Godly remnant, with impermeable boundaries between the visible elect and the visible reprobate, Como does not pursue the many and complex ways in which *both* anti-legalism *and* Judaizing ceremonialism conformed to this same function. Ceremonialism is, according to this reading, a surprising appendage, one Como himself confesses to finding 'most curious.'[40] Como reaches the unhappy conclusion that Traske's attachment to ceremonies as a designation of perfection was simply a 'distinctively godly misunderstanding' of Familism.[41]

Nicholas McDowell has pointed out that the Traskite controversy coincided with the identification of Puritans with Jews in popular culture. He argues that this coincidence offers an insight into the strategy employed by the state in trying John Traske before the Star Chamber. This unusual decision, McDowell argues, suggests that the state was eager to draw

36. Como, 'Kingdom of Traske,' 76.

37. Como, 'Kingdom of Traske,' 75.

38. Como, 'Kingdom of Traske,' 80.

39. Pagitt, *Heresiography*, 191.

40. Como, 'Kingdom of Traske,' 71.

41. Como, 'Kingdom of Traske,' 80.

connections between Puritanism, Judaism and sedition in the popular imagination. The Traskite scandal, therefore, was a piece of political theatre, a 'public spectacle of state discipline.'[42] Whereas Como reads the 'threat posed by Traskism' as being Traske's own 'hubristic rhetoric and posturing,' for McDowell the threat was more closely associated with the Judaizing elements of the Traskite message.[43] Certainly Francis Bacon's appraisal of the movement closely juxtaposed 'danger' with 'Judaizing.'[44] Meanwhile, the prejudices and anxieties that informed the public response to the Traskites were being played out at the Hope Theatre, only three miles from the Palace of Westminster. Ben Jonson's *Bartholomew Fair*, with the archetypal Judaizing stage-Puritan 'Zeal-of-the-Land Busy,' was drawing crowds. McDowell suggests that the hysteria which surrounded the Traskite phenomenon was a bi-product of a broader anxiety relating to the association of Judaism and Puritanism: 'the Jewish bogeyman behind the mask of Puritan sedition.'[45]

McDowell's insights are extremely valuable and highlight an aspect of Traskism that Ball gestures towards but does not fully explain. Absent from McDowell's analysis, though, is the claim that the same tensions which informed the reception of the Traskite phenomenon, should also be factored into our interpretation of the Traskite phenomenon *itself*. Traske and his followers, in exhibiting Judaizing behaviors, were as participant in the process of negotiation between conformity and dissent, separation and resistance, as those who drew attention to them. Lake's appraisal of the stigmatization of Judaizing Puritans by Ben Jonson highlights the complex interplay between the formation of anti-Puritan stereotypes and the formation of the very Puritan identity that the stereotypes were intended to satirise.[46] Jonson himself was aware of the ways in which the image that the ungodly had of the Godly served to inform the image that the Godly had of themselves. When Zeal-of-the-Land Busy speaks to the audience, he does not only speak of what he intends to do, but of what he intends for others to *think* about what he is doing.[47]

This is also implicit in Traske's work and in his behavior. Pagitt, reflecting on the Traskites expressed amazement at the apparent desire of Traske's devotees to 'excommunicate themselves.' The Traskites 'wilfully separate and

42. McDowell, 'Stigmatizing of Puritans as Jews,' 349.

43. McDowell, 'Stigmatizing of Puritans as Jews,' 354.

44. Bacon, 'Speech to the Judges,' 13:315.

45. McDowell, 'Stigmatizing of Puritans as Jews,' 363.

46. Lake, *Boxmaker's Revenge*, 47.

47. Jonson, *Bartholomew Fair* 1.6.95.

condemn themselves,' he wrote, 'yea, how fearless they are.'[48] This chapter will focus on an additional, underlying theme in Traske's writing—one that correlates with the Familist influences that Como identifies: the theme of separation. Ball refers to the 'division of men' as 'a key element in [Traske's] work.'[49] This concern was as central to the thought of the originators and advocates of Jewish ceremonies within the Jewish sphere as it was the originators and advocates of Jewish ceremonies within the Traskite sphere.

The insights of Collinson, Lake and Hughes in recent years have helped scholars to understand these complex interactions whereby the stigmatization and stereotyping of one group helps, in fact, to consolidate or even generate notions of identity within that group.[50] Bringing together Como's analysis of Traskism as a component part in the broader picture of 'radicalism,' McDowell's analysis of the *use* of the topos of Judaism as a medium for exploring conformity and dissent and a thicker understanding of the *meaning* of the topos of Judaism allows us to see a wider picture of Traskism which accommodates both his anti-legalism and his ceremonialism under a broader canopy of ethical singularity and resistance. We start, however, by considering some context for the emergence of the Traskite movement.

PURITANISM, SEPARATION, AND JOHN TRASKE

Traske was born in East Coker in the mid-1580s. The early years of his life saw out the end of the Tudor era. He was born at a point in English history when the aspirations of the Puritan party who had returned from exile with the expectation that they would establish a fully-reformed Church *of* England, had been finally disappointed.[51] His youth and young-manhood coincided with the period of the decline of the influence of the Bancroftian anti-Puritans and rise of *detentistes* like George Abbot. As the Godly had given up hope of effecting real ecclesiastical, political change, they had—to use Peter Marshall's phrase—'turned inwards,' seeking to bring about a reformation of manners in their own communities.[52] This led to significant attitudinal changes in communities across England which in turn led to regular, periodic intervals of 'moral panic.' In small towns across the South of England—particularly in those where Godly reformers had

---

48. Pagitt, *Heresiography*, 179.

49. Ball, *Seventh Day Men*, 52.

50. Lake and Stephens, *Scandal and Identity*, 99; Hughes, *Gangraena*, 10–11; Lake, *Boxmaker's Revenge*, 47.

51. Durston, 'Puritan Ethos,' 4.

52. Marshall, *Reformation England*, 135.

managed to attain a degree of political clout—conflict between the Godly and the ungodly occasionally combusted.[53] The Godly, began the process of a 'double internalization,' separating themselves through quotidian acts of 'divisive identification' from their peers, the better to establish a salient Godly identity, 'a holy huddle.'[54] Fasting, sermon-gadding, sabbatarianism and various other practices functioned, during this period, to consolidate the sense of an entitative, Godly identity, both within communities and in the nation more broadly.[55] This period persisted from the time of Bancroft's death in 1611 until the mid-1620s when fissures began to emerge in the Calvinist consensus as a result of the rise of Arminianism.

How, where and when was John Traske exposed to—and engaged in— these questions and controversies? East Coker in the early years of Traske's life was a turbulent parish. The incumbent minister on Traske's birth was John Gold. Gold was briefly deprived as a result of his failing to subscribe to the Articles of Religion. When he died, in 1618, Gold was replaced by William Buckland. Buckland, according to Margaret Stieg, was an 'exceptionally difficult personality.'[56] He was presented twice and was initially excommunicated for refusing to read prayers over the bodies of the deceased.[57] He was also involved in a case before the Star Chamber which centered around whether the teacher Francis Wood could teach in the chapel of ease. Buckland alledged that there was a conspiracy against him personally. He claimed that his religious convictions had irritated Wood, the constable and others, who did not like that he 'preached agaynst popery and popish opinions.'[58] Stieg notes that deprivation at the behest of the local population was an extreme and unusual step.[59] The record of Buckland's ministry casts light on a 'contrasting community' clearly divided along 'godly' and 'ungodly' lines.

In 1611 Traske was ordained. His peers feared that his character was unsuited to ministry.[60] Whilst serving as curate of Brimpton, he was

53. Underdown, *Revel, Riot, and Rebellion*, 51–58.

54. Collinson, 'Religious Satire,' 150–71.

55. Collinson, 'Puritanism as Popular Religious Culture,' 32–57.

56. Fincham, *Prelate as Pastor*, 210; Stieg, *Laud's Laboratory*, 262.

57. Somerset Records Office, D/D/Ca, 204, 3/10/1617 (Stieg, *Laud's Laboratory*, 280).

58. National Archives, STAC 8/49/8, 30/4/1614 (Stieg, *Laud's Laboratory*, 280).

59. Stieg, *Laud's Laboratory*, 262.

60. Fuller, *Church History of Britain*, 17:77; Historical Manuscripts Commission, 'City of Exeter,' in *Report On the Records of the City of Exeter*, 95–96 (Como, *Blown by the Spirit*, 145).

suspended for refusing to wear a square cap.[61] Some time during this period, Traske was imprisoned for 'opinions.'[62] Perhaps for this reason Samuel Ward, the ecclesiastical examiner, actively campaigned to bar him from ordination.[63] Nevertheless, he was given the cure of Chilton Cantelo in Somerset.[64] The vicar at Chilton was William Knowles.[65] Traske was suspended in 1613 for unlicensed preaching. This tendency would prove to be characteristic as his career progressed. Sometime in the summer of 1613, he took up a position as chaplain to John Drake of Axminster in Devonshire.[66] His appointment to this chaplaincy coincided with the appointment of William Knowles to the vicarage of Axminster.[67] If Knowles was an ally of Traske's at this stage, by 1616 he was apparently able to concede the 'fanciful' nature of Traske's beliefs.[68]

As J. B. Whitely has shown, Axminster would soon become the seat of an emergent Baptist community. Nearby Loughwood was the site of a clandestine Baptist meeting place from the reign of Charles I onwards. This particular community was notable for its disciplinary tendency and was riven by a number of controversies in the early decades of the movement.[69] Traske remained at Ashe for the duration of 1613, occasionally preaching at Honiton, but by the beginning of the following year he was back on the road. He would never have a secure pension or cure again.[70] In 1614, he left Somerset and travelled to Chettisham, near Ely. There, he was accused of unlicensed preaching.[71] Ely was also a theatre of Godly conflict. Chettisham's rector Nicholas Bonnington, was suspended by Whitgift at the end of the sixteenth century.[72] Chettisham was the birthplace of at least one Mayflower passenger: Elizabeth Barker who married Edward Winslow at Leiden in 1618. Littleport, Traske's second port-of-call, was a slightly larger village. In the 1650s, the villagers of Littleport contributed a not inconsiderable three

61. Somerset Records Office, D/D/Ca 140, f. 379, 5/9/1605 (Stieg, *Laud's Laboratory*, 270).

62. Norris, *New Gospel*, 7.

63. Fuller, *Church History of Britain*, 17:76.

64. Como, 'Kingdom of Traske,' 305.

65. Stieg, *Laud's Laboratory*, 193.

66. Cassidy, 'Episcopate of William Cotton,' 87.

67. Davidson, *History of Axminster Church*, 43.

68. HMC, 'City of Exeter,' 95–96.

69. Whitely, 'Loughwood Baptists,' 288–94.

70. Cassidy, 'Episcopate of William Cotton,' 87.

71. Cambridge University Library, Ely Diocesan Records B/2/35, fs. 3r, 62r, 76–77, 82r, 113–14, 190r (Parker, *English Sabbath*, 162).

72. Brook, *Lives of the Puritans*, 46.

pounds for the maintenance of persecuted Protestants in the Piedmont valleys.[73] At around the same time, Littleport became an intellectual battlefield, contested by the Baptists and the Quakers after Ezekiel and Samuel
Cater—who had been Baptist elders—defected to the Society of Friends.
This defection was heralded by the visit of James Parnell, who recalled being
harangued by Baptists during a meeting in an orchard in Littleport.[74]

In the early summer of 1614, Traske was allowed to preach in the parish church there. Littleport had been without a vicar for the duration of
1613. Matthew Helie had died at Christmas in 1612, and his replacement,
Salomon Lacy, did not arrive until 1617. At Traske's trial, most of his accused auditors were residents of Littleport. Traske's third conventicle took
place in December, in Ely, at the house of one Nicholas Massey.[75] Massey's
family were originally from the North. His father, also Nicholas, had moved
from Cheshire to Ely in order to procure some of the profits of the dissolu-
tion of the monasteries. Also in attendance was 'J. Orwell.' In 1620, 'John
Orwell, gentleman of Ely,' bought the old 'Hospital,' and its grounds in Ely.[76]
Orwell was on a list of those who were to be called as character witnesses for
Sir Simon Steward in 1626.[77] 'John Orwell' was registered as 'a gentleman of
Ely,' on a passenger list of a ship travelling from Yarmouth to Amsterdam in
1637. His intention, according to the examination, was to 'sarve under the
stattes.' This denoted a desire to fight for the Prince of Orange and the Dutch
Republic against Catholic, Imperial Spain.[78]

Between 1614 and 1615, Traske appears to have had no fixed abode.
He had acquired a reputation for being a 'notoriously schismaticall preacher
and factious.'[79] Returning to Somerset, he was arrested for conventicling at
the house of Thomas Millerd in Shepton Mallet and also for preaching in
nearby Batcombe during 1614. He was periodically arrested for itineracy, in
Somerset, and latterly in Middlesex.[80] In 1615 he arrived in London. It was

---

73. *Distinct and Faithful Accompt*, 13.

74. Parnell, *Watcher*, 49.

75. Cambridge University Library, Ely Diocesan Records, B/2/35 f. 3, 76.

76. Cobbett, 'Hospitals,' 104.

77. Dasent et al., *Acts of the Privy Council of England*, 41:29.

78. Jewson, 'Transcript of Three Registers of Passengers,' 28.

79. Somerset Records Office, D/D/Ca 189, f. 150. 22/11/1614 (Como, *Blown by the Spirit*, 145); Somerset Records Office, D/D/Ca 189, f. 183–184 20/12/1614 (Steig, *Laud's Laboratory*, 252).

80. Somerset Records Office, D/D/Ca 189, f. 150; Somerset Records Office, D/D/Ca 189 f. 183–84 20/12/1614; Hardy, *Calendar to the Sessions Records, Middlesex Sessions Records, New Series*, 3:107.

during this period that Traske penned three texts: *Christ's Kingdom Discovered*, *Heaven's Joy* and *A Pearle For A Prince*.

ANTILEGALISM, SEPARATION, AND JOHN TRASKE

The Godly party was not itself entirely cohesive in the years of Traske's intellectual maturation. Antinomian groups began to emerge during this period under the banner of a radically, ultra-Pauline soteriology. Conflict developed between adherents to this new mode of Reformed Protestantism and the more precisianist, 'Puritan' caucus. The latter were aware that the association of antinomianism with predestinarianism could scupper the Godly project and they were proven to be correct within the decade.[81] In Suffolk and (eventually) London, John Eaton established a significant movement which asserted the guiltlessness of the elect. In Lancashire and North Yorkshire, a form of antinomianism that would later become known as Grindletonianism gathered momentum.[82] Antinomian texts, like the *Theologia Germanica* and the anonymous manuscript separate simply known as '*Antinomus Anonymous*,' were circulated.[83] The Wiltshire rector Tobias Crisp began preaching a form of anti-legalism that skirted close to what would later be called 'Ranterism.'[84] The elect were sanctified and assured of their salvation, these antinomians argued. As such, they were immune to the guilt of sin.[85] This position departed, theoretically, from mainline Puritan soteriology which asserted that the sin of the elect remained as a stain, absolved only by the grace of God. Part of the novelty of Calvinist antinomianism was that it accentuated the distinction between the Godly and the majoritarian reprobate. The decree of election was even more linked

81. Lake, 'Puritans, Antinomians, and the Laudians,' 684–715.

82. Hill, *World Turned Upside Down*, 81–84; Como, *Blown by the Spirit*, 40–45.

83. Bozeman, *Precisianist Strain*, 186, 197, 200.

84. Bozeman, *Precisianist Strain*, 183–211; Como, *Blown by the Spirit*, 41–49.

85. Como draws a distinction between 'imputative' and 'perfectionist' antinomianism, the former accounting for those who believed that Christ's sacrifice expunged the guilt of sin for believers in the eyes of God and the latter claiming that the Godly are perfected in *this* life. Hessayon has objected that this casts too broad a net when it comes to the definition of antinomianism. However, as Caughey has pointed out, the former position was identified as 'radical' by their contemporaries in that it threatened to allow 'justification' to 'swallow up sanctification' further delimiting the importance of good works. See Hessayon, *Gold Tried in the Fire*, 10; Caughey, 'Anti-Christs and Rumours of Anti-Christs,' 114–16. Moreover, the fact that the slur of antinomianism was so frequently used to beat the Godly (in successive generations) made it an extremely charged accusation (Barlow, *Summe and Substance*, 29–30; Como and Lake, 'Puritans, Antinomians, and the Laudians,' 684–715).

with the lived experience of the Godly. Whilst mainline Calvinists believed that elect and reprobate shared in the guilt of Adam, anti-legalist Calvinists denied even this kinship.

The drift towards a more antinomian mode of Reformed Protestantism amongst a minority of Calvinists during this period has been explained by Dwight Bozeman as a reaction against the precisianist strain.[86] David Como, however, argues that the impetus for both the precisianist and antinomian tendencies emerged from the same source. For Como, Puritanism was not a religious tradition that could be categorized as either 'disciplinary or radical' but rather a *sensibility* that gave rise to both 'orderly and self-consciously orthodox' and 'theologically, socially and politically deviant' modes of piety. The disciplinary character of the precisianist Godly and the antinomian efflorescence of the Grindletonians and the Eatonists, therefore, both took root in the same theological soil.[87]

Traske's later writings bear the hallmarks of an Eatonist mode of soteriology. On this basis, several scholars have affirmed that Traske was a fixture of the antinomian scene during the reign of Charles I. But it is *also* evident that *elements* of Traske's later anti-legalism can be found in his earlier writings. In the first accounts of Traske's time in London he is described, primarily, as an antinomian, whose doctrines included the claim that 're- pentance was not only begun, but also finished, before justifying faith' and that 'none that were justifyed did commit sinne.'[88] Como claims that Traske was associated in some way with the remnants of the Familist movement in Cambridgeshire during the period immediately preceding his publication spree in 1615. A number of those who came to hear Traske preach—Como has demonstrated—were associated or related to figures within the Familist movement. Moreover, Como notes that it would seem coincidental that Traske should move from Somerset to Ely, unless he had some connection in the area.[89] As such, Como claims that it was this Familist influence that accounts for Traske's early—and otherwise apparently spontaneous—adoption of antinomianism.

Christopher Marsh's study of Familism exposed the weaknesses at the heart of Christopher Hill's 'radical continuity' narrative.[90] Marsh showed that the Familists were decidedly *not* late-blooming Lollards. Nor were they provocateurs of social or political activism. Nor, in fact, could they be

86. Bozeman, *Precisianist Strain*, 3–9.

87. Como, *Blown by the Spirit*, 439

88. Norris, *New Gospel*, 7.

89. Como, *Blown by the Spirit*, 170.

90. Hill, 'Norman Yoke,' 11–67.

associated with any particular element of the class struggle of the period, since their membership bisected economic strata.[91] The devotional practices and theological claims of the Family of Love were based on the thought of Heinrich Niclaes. Niclaes's writings—pseudonymously published in England under the name 'H. N.'—were cherished by his followers. His soteriology offered a heterodox doctrine of justification. The elect would be transformed, he claimed, by the process of sanctification into a condition of 'new humanity.' In this transformed condition, the 'family member' was 'Godded with God.'[92] As part of this process, their relationships with other Family members was also transformed. Familists shared in an blissful state, referred to in Familist literature as 'the Love.'[93] The sensibilities of the Familists led to them being labelled as 'singular' by their critics.[94] The Traskite Return Hebdon would later use this formulation when describing the 'common communion.'[95] Familism originated in the Low Countries, but was brought to England—and in particular to East Anglia—by the Dutch carpenter and mystic Christopher Vitell.[96] A striking characteristic of the Family of Love in the English context was its nicodemism. Their gatherings were secretive and their scepticism of the facility of any form of outward ceremonies allowed them to disappear into the landscape of conformist worship without compromising on their beliefs: supra-formalist rather than anti-formalist in their ecclesiology.[97] 'They had little wish to be studied,' writes Marsh.[98] At Ely, Como suggests, John Traske interacted with what remained of the Familist movement.[99] Acheson has suggested that the already 'introverted' tendency at the heart of Niclaes's message was 'reinforced' by the 'geographical isolation' of the isle of Ely.[100] It is perhaps due to this isolation that Familism persisted in Ely after it appears to have evaporated in England more broadly. It seems that the Familists of Ely had a strong sense of their own chosenness, 'reinforced' and 'sustained' by their own experiences of isolation. These themes also form the heart of Traske's writings

91. Marsh, *Family of Love in English Society*, 5.

92. *Supplication of the Family of Love*, 17.

93. Dietz-Moss, *Godded with God*, 26–27; Marsh, 'Gracelesse, and Audacious Companie?,' 191–208.

94. Rogers, *Answere Unto a Wicked and Infamous Libel*, a7r.

95. Hebdon, *Guide to the Godly*, 32, 49, 51, 54.

96. Martin, 'Christopher Vittell,' 15–22.

97. Caricchio, 'Giles Calvert and the Radical Experience,' 82–84.

98. Marsh, *Family of Love*, 6.

99. Como, *Blown by the Spirit*, 170.

100. Acheson, *Radical Puritans in England*, 16.

during the flurry of publications in 1615 and 1616. This is not to say that Traske was a card-carrying Familist. Familism as a confessional grouping had evaporated by this stage. But 'dabbling' in Familism remained a habitual tendency amongst religious radicals of this period, perhaps most notably John Etherington.[101]

In a number of plays of this period (including Middleton's *Family of Love*, but also Chapman's *Gyles Goosecap*, and Carter's *The Schismatick Stigmatized*) the stage-Familist occupied a space which—in some senses—was antithetical to the figure of the stage-Puritan: libertinist, amoral, antinomian. The presentation of Familists in the theatre was certainly not ethnographic. It was rather 'scurrilous, scandalous and sexy.'[102] But the dydymic, anterior figures of the 'Familist' and the 'Judaizer' *did* serve a function. They formed a helix of dissent and deviance which intertwined in the cultural process of rendering religious insiderliness and outsiderliness in early Stuart England.[103]

In 1631, John Eachard, a prominent Eatonist, referred to John Traske in a list of fellow faithful laborers.[104] Traske is also mentioned alongside Eaton and Shaw as one of the progenitors of English Antinomianism in John Sedgwick's *Anatomie of Antinomianism* in 1644.[105] At the very latest, by the early years of Charles I's reign, Traske was an antinomian. Each variation of antinomianism had its idiosyncrasies, but there existed some common themes. Generally, the antinomians of this period were concerned to sweep away—what they perceived to be—the gloomy, moralistic preaching of the mainline, precisianist, Puritan clergy. In addition, they situated themselves further towards the anti-formalist end of the spectrum of Protestant divinity than most mainline Puritans. Most importantly, however, the antinomians pursued a form of soteriology which widened immeasurably the gulf between the elect and the reprobate and which further enmeshed the lived experience of Godliness with the soteriological identity. The Godly were completely assured, they argued, in this life. They were transformed (sometimes meta-physiognomically) into a new form of humanity.[106] At the same time, this process of transformation was rendered utterly inscrutable to the ungodly observer. Eaton avowed the belief that God could see no sin in the elect and that the elect were 'sanctified by inherent righteousness.' At the

---

101. Marsh, *Family of Love*, 8; Tyacke, *English Revolution*, 71.

102. *Family of Love*; Chapman, *Gyles Goosecap Knight*, d3r; Carter, *Schismatick Stigmatized*, 15.

103. Poole, *Radical Religion From Shakespeare to Milton*, 76–79.

104. Como, *Blown by the Spirit*, 60.

105. Sedgewick, *Antinomianism Anatomized*, 1.

106. Falconer, *Briefe Refutation*, 7.

same time, Eaton suggested that the elect were privy to a special revelation of their own assurance, and that God:

> shewes how a man may know in his owne heart, and how hee himself and others may discern, that he is justified, absolved before God from all fault and blame, and freed from all sinne, guilt and punishment.[107]

Paul Cefalu has noted the strongly Johannine strains in antinomian literature of this period. Cefalu writes that the Johannine tradition, and 'particularly the dualistic orientation of John's Gospel and First epistle,' were a 'foundational influence' on seventeenth-century dissenting literature. Cefalu points specifically to the writings of Hendrik Niclaes as a fountainhead of this Johanine strand. Whilst the followers of Niclaes were secretive, camouflaged and nicodemist, their literature was replete with the language of separation: 'insiders from outsiders.'[108] Niclaes saw separation as a dialogical process, centring around passivity and resistance, whereby the ungodly rejected the godly and vice versa. 'That they likewise turn away from us,' he wrote, 'so turn you then also away from them, and let them hardelie depart from you.'[109] Separation and divinity were never far apart in Niclaes's writing. 'God is,' he wrote 'one, alone, separated from all.'[110] In the English context, the writing of John Eaton, John Everard, John Traske and Return Hebdon, also show a concern for 'light/dark dualism.'[111]

The ultra-Pauline soteriology of Eatonism appears *antithetical* to the Judaizing 'legalism' that Traske and his followers were known for. Even in the Familist context, however, we find small indications of a Judaizing tendency. The Familist text written by Elidad was published in England with Hebrew characters on the frontispiece.[112] There is some suggestion that leaders within the Familist community were referred to as 'Rabbi.'[113] On an underlying level, both represent different iterations of the same fundamental concern: that of singularity and separation. Como has pointed out that there were often extremely close ideological and behavioral correlatives between the two, such that situating the latter as a *repudiation* of the former is illegitimate. Nor is it legitimate to identify Puritanism specifically with its

---

107. Eaton, *Honey-combe*, 311.

108. Cefalu, *Johannine Renaissance*, 225.

109. Niclaes, *Dicta HN*, 39.

110. Ainsworth, *Epistle Sent Unto Two Daughters*, 41.

111. Cefalu, *Johannine Renaissance*, 230–34; Hebdon, *Guide to the Godly*, 11, 14.

112. Elidad, *Good and Fruitfull Exhortation*, a1r.

113. Jones, *Arte and Science*, 92.

pietist, disciplinary element.[114] For Como, Traske represents the principle occupant of this liminal space between the precisianist and the antinomian wings of English Reformed Protestantism.

THE FORM AND THE POWER OF GODLINESSE

Traske and his followers believed that humanity was strictly, clearly and irreducibly divided into elect and reprobate. In line with the experimental predestinarians of the period, they believed that this binate distinction was mirrored in human society. Return Hebdon, a later incarcerated member of Traske's community, had a vision of the division of humanity 'into two sorts, the one terrene, humain, and . . . the other coelestical, divine, and baptized under the annointing and authority of the only true God.'[115]

Many, perhaps the majority, of the Puritans of this period, held views that were comparable to this. The divisions that existed within the Calvinist consensus were not founded on differences of soteriological doctrine, they were founded on differences of opinion about what to *do* with this information. For some, membership of the Church-by-law-established, itself provided adequate assurance that one would be numbered amongst the 'baptized.' For others (the 'Whitgiftian fatalists'), the question of salvation was cloaked in mystery to the extent that it resisted any scrutiny.[116] For others still, assurance could be found in the establishment of separated, exclusively Godly, communities of faith.

The Traskite reception of predestinarian thought was problematized somewhat by their profound ecclesiological scepticism. Like Perkins before and Stephen Denison after, Traske stressed the distinction between those who 'haue the forme, and those as haue also the power of godlinesse.'[117] As such, he refused to acknowledge that any Church of man's design could hope to establish truly Godly concert. Any such endeavor, whether it be undertaken by the architects of an Erastian, national Church or of a wee, free, separatist congregation, was nothing more than hubris. This ecclesiological scepticism was informed, at least in part, by Traske's antipathy to precisianist Puritan clergy. In *A Pearle for a Prince*, Traske expressed a derision of Puritan ministers that was typical of early Stuart antinomian writing. They were hypocrites, he wrote: 'reformers of others and most irreformed

---

114. Como, *Blown by the Spirit*, 438–439.

115. Hebdon, *Guide to the Godly*, 60.

116. Lake, *Anglicans and Puritans?*, 128, 244.

117. Traske, *Power of Preaching*, a2v; Denison, *New Creature*, 67.

themselves.'[118] As Como writes, Traske was clearly disaffected both 'with the Church of England and with the puritan wing of the Church.'[119]

This led Traske towards a soteriology that was clearly—at least in part—informed by anti-legalist traditions. Knowledge of one's election could not be attained from membership of any church—established or separated. Rather: 'the only way to know that wee are in Christ is by the knowledge that yourselves are in Christ.'[120] In the condition of justifying faith, in fact, the Godly were not only assured of their own salvation. True believers, Traske claimed, were free from the guilt of sin and shared in the 'mind of Christ.'[121] As such, Traske's soteriology presented the Godly as irreducibly, unconditionally and mysteriously perfected.

Secondly, Traske firmly asserted that the concept of the Kingdom of God referred not to an eschatological or spiritual condition, but rather to the lived experience of the Godly in their condition as the assured and sanctified elect. He unpacked this claim in his third publication, Heaven's Joy. For Traske, the concept of the Kingdom of God referred not to a heavenly, spiritual afterlife, nor to an eschatological future, but rather to the lived experience of the Godly in the condition of justifying faith.[122]

Thirdly, Traske developed a particularly innovative interpretation of the meaning of 'repentance.' For Traske the condition of repentance was not abstract. It referred to a transitional period between the condition of unregeneracy and the condition of faith. The Traskites observation of 'Repentance' involved a number of flagellatory ordeals which were noted by their contemporaries. His followers were adjured to wear sackcloth, to fast, to renounce sexual activity. T. S. describes how the followers of John Traske 'pulled downe their bodies,' hoping thus to 'get into the third estate of justified saints.' Traske told his followers that the painful task of repentance was akin to 'the travel of a woman,' or 'the taking out of the heart from within the body.'[123] Traske himself acknowledged the struggle that repentance represented. Nonetheless, the attainment of assurance it offered was worth the ordeal. 'What if it fill your hearts with sorrow, your head with care, your eyes with teares, your chambers with complaints,' he promised, 'you shall finde a recompence even here: yea, and a full reward hereafter.'[124] This provides

---

118. Traske, Pearle for a Prince, 6.

119. Como, Blown by the Spirit, 159.

120. Traske, Christs Kingdome Discovered, 41.

121. Traske, Heaven's Joy, 69, 70.

122. Traske, Christs Kingdome Discovered, 6–10.

123. Pagitt, Heresiography, 184.

124. Traske, Heaven's Joy, 158.

a striking example of the 'unacknowledged league' between the practices of Puritan divinity—based on the Heidelbergean 'reflex'—and the Pelagian 'tenor,' which they disparaged in others.[125] The period of 'repentance' Traske prescribed, of course, did not hold a promise of grace as a *reward*. Nonetheless, the Godly professor who experienced the hardships it denoted could, reflexively, discover in his or her own experiences evidence and assurance of salvation, and—ultimately—'unspeakable comfort.'[126]

THE ASSURANCE OF ACCEPTATION

Traske, then, was even more epistemologically rudderless in the quest for assurance than his Godly peers. The Godly were guaranteed in this life, through the guarantee of grace, but the nature of this guarantee was highly mysterious. No man could know through his own efforts, the destiny of his immortal soul.[127] God's choice of who to elect was beyond the reach of reason. The figure that Traske most frequently compared himself to was Job. Like Job, he accepted the unknowability of God's will. He refused the council of latter-day Temanites. Knowledge of God's will did not come from human volition or investigation, he wrote. It was 'laid up . . . for the Righteous' by the Lord. Even the apostles themselves were blind to the Kingdom of God as it was described to them, before their Pentecostal conversion.[128] This epistemological vacuum appears to have aroused feelings of profound unhappiness and anxiety in Traske, just as it would his contemporaries Nehemiah Wallington, Joan Barrington and Dionys Fitzherbert.[129] He was beset with temptations and torments. 'The Creatures are at enmitie with me,' he wrote. 'The sunne, moone and stares in theyr courses . . . the very stones of the field were at oddes with me.'[130] Like Job, he was 'at much disquiet . . . as the troubled Sea that cannot rest.'[131] Job too was forced to confront the horror of divine fiat. Pagitt noted that those who gravitated towards Traske were 'troubled in [their] minds,' by the difficulty of ascertaining assurance.[132] One of Traske's followers, Mary Chester, would describe her own anxiety:

125. Bozeman, *Precisianist Strain*, 4.

126. Traske, *Heaven's Joy*, 75; Walsham, 'Happiness of Suffering,' 56.

127. Traske, *Christs Kingdome Discovered*, 67.

128. Traske, *Christs Kingdome Discovered*, 47.

129. Seaver, *Wallington's World*, 16–19; Hodgkin, *Women, Madness, and Sin*, 17–19; Mack, *Visionary Women*, 90–106; Willen, 'Communion of the Saints,' 19–41.

130. Traske, *Heaven's Joy*, 149.

131. Traske, *Heaven's Joy*, 10.

132. Pagitt, *Heresiography*, 185.

'having many things that did trouble my Mind, insomuch as I was never at any Quiet Day or Night, and at last affrighted and greviously tormented.' Chester proclaimed, meanwhile, that she 'desire[d] nothing more, nor so much, as the assurance of acceptance with God.'[133] Traske identified the experience of assurance as a cure for this anxiety. Those who are 'justified by faith' were given 'peace: such rest as cannot be expressed' he wrote.[134] In the aftermath of his arrest, his recantation and his re-emergence in the antinomian milieu, Traske wrote a short text entitled *The True Gospel Vindicated*. In it, he promised to extend this peace to all those 'sad souls' who were seeking 'assurance of faith.'[135]

Traske's own ecclesiological scepticism was part of the stimulus for these feelings of uncertainty. Como refers to Traske's 'indifference to ecclesiology.'[136] This is, perhaps, a little too soft a term. Traske was anxious about the diversity of ecclesiological positions and the competing claims of separatists and conformists in the period of Abbot's ascendancy. 'I heare one cry out for want of discipline; others for Order,' he wrote. 'One saith Here is Christ; another There is Christ.' For Traske, as for Bolton, the success of one faction or another was not necessarily a providential sign of the righteousness of their cause. 'Christ hath made it a marke of a seducing spirit to drawe desciples after him,' he wrote.[137] Those, like Traske, who avowed a belief in the visibility and distinctiveness of the saints, but who nonetheless refused to align themselves with confessional separation, were even more exposed than their contemporaries who chose the path of so-called 'Brownism.' They were faced with the difficult task of 'separating within' the Church, separating without separating.[138] But for Traske, passively accepting the role of the saint was safer than pursuing it, since it savored less of Pelagianism. Often, the only way in which this task was achievable was through a form of passive, auto-anathematization, inviting the 'obloquy of the mob,' rather than actively asserting one's own distinctiveness from it, in short by engaging in euphemistic acts of resistance.[139]

In various ways, Traske was afflicted with uncertainty. He saw the Godly life as one of a quest for the warrant of election, but described it as an epistemological chimera. He knew that the Godly were required to seek out

133. Pagitt, *Heresiography*, 194.

134. Traske, *Heaven's Joy*, 11.

135. Traske, *True Gospel Vindicated*, A3r.

136. Como, *Blown by the Spirit*, 168.

137. Traske, *Christ's Kingdome Discovered*, 42; Bolton, *Discourse*, 35–36.

138. Collinson, *Puritan Character*, 32.

139. Lake and Stephens, *Scandal and Religious Identity*, 123.

society with the people of God, but he was unconvinced by the ecclesiological formulations of both the established church and the separatists. Caught between these twin poles, Traske found himself in limbo. In response, he gravitated towards a system of self-authenticating assurance, based not on the mandate of any established church, nor on obedience to the Law, but rather on the 'ethical singularity' that could be found in the mutual assurance of a 'holy huddle' of Godly fellows.[140]

UNSPEAKABLE COMFORT AMONGST THE SAINTS IN LIGHT

The writings Traske produced in the years leading up to his arrest in 1618 emphasized the association of assurance and 'Christian society.' It was Christian society, after all, that brought with it the 'Peace' of assurance following the agony of unregeneracy and repentance.[141] He produced a text entitled *Heaven's Joy*, which described the blissful assurance he attained from the synergetic relationship he shared with his Godly peers. The saints, like Aquila and Priscilla, 'watch over one another, *exhorting one another, and provoking to love, and to good works*.'[142] They are 'one anothers keepers.' These texts come close to the Familist mode of expression.[143] Traske spoke of the 'unspeakable comfort' he experienced 'amongst the saints in light.'[144] This phrase exhibits both Traske's identification of assurance with Godly singularity, but also the ineffable, 'unspeakable,' irreducible nature of the experience of justification.

Traske believed that those who had experienced sanctification were not only newly aware of their own election, but were also made aware of the 'warrant' of their peers.[145] 'Get assurance that thou art thyself in Christ,' he wrote, 'and when this is done, I doubt not to say thou shalt know others also.'[146] In this form, Traske's claim was not dissimilar to the antinomian views of later figures. John Saltmarsh, for example, claimed that 'spiritual men are revealed to each other, and have as ful assurance of each other in

---

140. Collinson, 'Shearmen's Tree,' 219.

141. Traske, *Heaven's Joy*, 11.

142. Traske, *Heaven's Joy*, 79.

143. An earlier Familist text, translated by Christopher Vitell, encouraged its readers to 'daylie exhort one-another to the same Concorde and Peace and like-wise suffer or forbeare one-another in the Love' (Elidad, *Good and Fruitfull Exhortation*, a8r).

144. Traske, *Heaven's Joy*, 75.

145. Dent, *Plaine Man's Pathway*, 239.

146. Traske, *Christ's Kingdome Discovered*, 41.

Spirit and in Truth as *men* know *men* by the *voice, features, complexions, statures* of the outward man.'[147] Falconer noted that Traske had 'become famous abroad' for being able, 'by physiognomy, to make certain guesses whether particular persons shall be damned or saved.'[148] This is corroborated by Kellet, who wrote that the Traskites 'bragged they would know the saved from the damned by their looks.'[149] William Sclater, writing in the midst of the Traskite scandal in 1618, also attested to this trope in Traske's teaching and derided him for it.[150] The association of the Traskites with this heterodox opinion persevered for several decades. In 1658, four decades having passed since Traske's trial, Richard Baxter rebuked his congregation for being judgemental, using Traske as an exemplar. 'Are you able to search and know the heart?' he asked. 'Can you discern sincerity by an infallible judgment? I know none but Mr. *Trask* that pretended to it.'[151]

Traske believed in a *physically* transformative process of regeneration, but one that was only perceptible to the elect themselves. In this regard, a comparison may be drawn between the career of Traske and his near contemporary William Franklin. Franklin, like Traske, avowed coherently Calvinist views regarding the eternal decree of election but took the claims of spiritual regeneration to refer to the body. Like Traske, Franklin was not content with an allegorical understanding his own sanctification.[152] The idea that the elect and the reprobate were only 'notionally'—rather than physically, literally, somatically—distinguished was not sufficiently assuring. It failed to offer a tangible distinction between the elect and the reprobate, of the kind that John Brinsley had so fervently prayed for.[153] The saints, Traske assured his readers, shared in a familiarity with countless other of the Godly, 'though we never saw them face to face.'[154] But at the same time, he claimed there was special, 'excellent benefit' to be attained in physical communion with other members of the Godly 'face to face.'[155] Traske, in short, presented himself as a 'saint-seeing, saint-making, saint.'[156]

---

147. Saltmarsh, *Sparkles of Glory*, 142.

148. Falconer, *Briefe Refutation*, 7.

149. Kellet, *Tricoenium Christi*, 74.

150. Sclater, *Exposition upon Thessalonians*, 17.

151. Baxter, *Certain Disputations of Right to Sacraments*, 36.

152. Luxon 'Not I, but Christ,' 899–937.

153. Brinsley, *Second Part of the True Watch*, 60.

154. Traske, *Heaven's Joy*, 72.

155. Traske, *Heaven's Joy*, 73.

156. Sclater, *Exposition upon Thessalonians*, 31.

The profound assurance that came with strong bonds of solidarity, and the inscrutability of this mutually-authenticating claim of election provided the basis for the Traskite mode of divinity. In an immediate sense, it affected their decision to establish a community of goods. Traskites practiced a form of communism which found biblical precedent in Acts 4.[157] They were much derided for it by their peers including William Sclater.[158] In the writing of Return Hebdon, the close association of Christian communism and assurance is clearly drawn. 'If any have the good of this world,' he wrote, they 'communicate in love to him that hath need.' Pointing to the precedent of Ananias, described in Acts 5, Hebdon suggested that those who reneged on the contract of common goods would risk providential death, 'at the hand of the invisible God.'[159]

Traske acknowledged the psychological utility of these practices, emphasizing the value of establishing immutable bonds of Godly society for the purpose of facilitating assurance. Only this, it appears, could offer the Godly dependable resource in the task of seeking out the warrant of their own salvation. All identities depend, for their salience, on the coherence of the group members and on their collective difference from the 'out-group.'[160] Inviting the obloquy of the mob, therefore, attained a spiritual and soteriological significance for figures like Traske and Hebdon.

THE GENERALL SEPARATION

Traske was equally critical of Separatism, as of Anglicanism. Neither, he argued, could offer a vision of a true Church. The Church was 'not *bounded* within any *Nation,* or *limitted* unto any *one People* or *Kingdom.* So that no man can say it is in this *Company,* and *no where else.*'[161] The true Church was unveiled, not by the machinations of man, but by revelation alone. Nonetheless, in the early stages of his career, Traske sought to establish a community that was clearly distinctive from the wider, wicked world. This was not untypical of Puritans of this period. As Lake, Walsham and Collinson have all pointed out, those who 'separated within' the Church were called upon to create cultural rather than physical barriers between themselves and their peers.[162] For many, this involved the development of 'divisive identifica-

157. Pagitt, *Heresiography*, 185.

158. Sclater, *Exposition upon Thessalonians*, 31.

159. Hebdon, *Guide to the Godly*, 32.

160. Tajfel, *Differentiation Between Social Groups*, 96.

161. Traske, *Christ's Kingdom Discovered*, 28.

162. Collinson, *Puritan Character*, 32; Lake, 'William Bradshaw,' 570–89.

tions': practices that actively accentuated the distinctiveness of the Godly from their peers.[163]

Whilst Traske emphasized the continuity and solidarity shared by the Godly, he also placed significant emphasis on the auto-differentiation of the Godly from the wicked world. Traske saw the task of the Godly minister as the separation of the wheat from the chaff, facilitating 'the generall separation between Pagans and Christians . . . betweene Idolaters and true worshippers.'[164] This ethos informed his claims about the value of a period of 'repentance.'[165] Thomas Totney would draw on the imagery of a 'cuppeling' of creation as described in Revelation 3.[166] Traske referred to the image of the 'off-scouring' of the world, described in 1 Corinthians.[167] Hebdon, meanwhile, wrote of the 'great opposition of Christians.'[168] Like Denison, Traske stressed the urgency of discerning the difference between the professor who is merely 'outwardly reformed' and he who is truly justified. Traske characterizes the former as the moderate: one who, professing his own fidelity, 'censures all that are not so forward, of Profanenesse, and all that are more forward, of singularitie.'[169] Clearly, Traske envisioned himself as a member of the latter category, as one besmirched by hypocritical Puritans as 'singular.' He would later identify the 'desire of singularitie' as a pitfall of Godly piety.[170]

Traske's promise that the Godly 'had all the saints in the world as their friends,' was intended to counterpoise the fact that the Godly could expect to be 'friendless.'[171] That the Godly 'live but where they have little fellowship' was offset by the fact that 'they enjoy the helpe of the effectual fervent prayers of all the saints.'[172] The condition of the godly professors, for Traske, was one of marginalization, suffering and abuse at the hands of the wicked world. The ungodly 'oppresse them, draw them before judgement seates, mock them, rent their garments from them, withdraw from them all succor and do scarce account them worthy of the licking of their

---

163. Webster, 'Early Stuart Puritanism,' 48–66.

164. Traske, Power of Preaching, A2v.

165. Traske, Heaven's Joy, 54–55; Traske, Christ's Kingdom Discovered, 15.

166. Tany, My Edict Royal, 4.

167. Traske, Heaven's Joy, 136.

168. Hebdon, Guide to the Godly, 60.

169. Traske, Pearle for a Prince, 10.

170. Traske, Treatise of Libertie from Libertie, 36.

171. Traske, Pearle for a Prince, 33.

172. Traske, Heaven's Joy, 73.

dogges.'[173] Return Hebdon, meanwhile, described himself as a second Antipas (Rev 2).[174] Like many such groups, the Traskites looked forward to an apocalyptic future in which the justice of God's creation would be unveiled, wherein 'the saints will judge the world,' rather than the other way around.[175] In this discourse, the Godly were situated on a different chronological plain from their peers and neighbors and as such, they shared in the constructed non-coevalness of the Jews.

THE PEOPLE OF LEAST ESTEEME

From the earliest stages of his ministry, Traske criticized those who sought to marginalize the weak and the poor. In *A Pearle for a Prince* he lamented the tendency amongst magistrates to 'favour some for their riches, oppressing others that are but of mean estate.' In this practice, Traske wrote, they 'differ from God, and do manifestly discover themselues not yet to be his.' Traske railed against those ministers of the word who 'scorne the weake, and despise the poore.'[176] Moreover, Traske attached a particular spiritual value to the condition of poverty. 'The people of least esteeme were Christ's chief followers,' he notes.[177] Later in the century, with the rise of the Levellers, the Diggers and other groups, egalitarianism became more central to the culture of Puritanism.[178] In 1615, however, Traske's position was more unusual. Calvin saw the structure of society, with its systemic, economic inequalities as providential and heuristic, offering the scope for the wealthy to perform acts of charity. He wrote that poverty itself could be formative of faith. Many scholars have pointed to the, foreseen or unforeseen, sociological consequences of Calvinist predestinarianism, where it served to legitimize and even ordain social and economic disparities.[179] English Reformed Protestantism was no different. Robert Crowley's verse articulated this worldview:

> Fyrste walke in thy vocation
> And do not seke thy lotte to change;
> For through wicked ambition

173. Traske, *Heaven's Joy*, 107.

174. Pagitt, *Heresiography*, 190.

175. Traske, *Pearle for a Prince*, 37.

176. Traske, *Pearle for a Prince*, 5.

177. Traske, *Pearle for a Prince*, 6.

178. Foxley, *Levellers*, 2, 13, 94, 153.

179. Zafirovski, *Protestant Ethic and the Spirit of Authoritarianism*, 55–66.

Many mens fortune hath ben straynge.[180]

Traske's belief that the poor had a particularly privileged relationship with God, therefore, constituted a rebuttal of contemporary, widely assented norms.

In a similar way, Traske vehemently asserted the privilege of revealed wisdom above learnedness. This tendency would become a central theme of later literature—particularly within the Quaker milieu—and many within the broader 'radical Puritan' sphere avowed an ethic of humility and un-learnedness.[181] 'The ground wher Faith is sowen,' Traske wrote, 'is an hum-bled soule, a wounded spirit or rent heart.' Those who were chosen were not typically 'glorious' but rather ones who had 'feared and trembled and felt their soule sick with sinne.'[182] Meanwhile, Traske was scornful of those who believed that having 'a little swimming knowledge in the brain' was suffi-cient evidence of their spiritual superiority.[183] He dismissed the arguments of his critics as the product of 'carnal reason,' which itself 'cannot reach the truth.'[184] 'Leane not over much to thine own judgement,' he cautioned. The mind of the believer should be like an adder, not deaf to the charmer, but ready to surrender autonomy to the divine will.[185] True 'wisdom' Traske claimed 'God hath revealed to us by his Spirit.'[186] Such wisdom 'eye hath not seen, nor eare heard.'[187]

In Hebdon's work this inversion of worldly values was rehearsed. 'He which is most poore and humble in the flesh,' Hebdon wrote, 'is endued with most authority in the spirit of holinesse.'[188] Hebdon also saw the casti-gations endured by the Traskites as evidence of the formation of the Godly in the hands of the Almighty. He described the hardships he had endured as like the beatings endured by a student at the hands of a schoolmaster:

> The Child is the Christian, the book is to learn Christ, the rod are men in authority, the Schoolmaster is the Law, or the heav-enly Father.[189]

180. Crowley, *Voyce of the Laste Trumpet*, a2r.

181. Gardiner, *Reports of Cases in the Star Chamber*, 189–92.

182. Traske, *Pearle for a Prince*, 10.

183. Traske, *Pearle for a Prince*, 15.

184. Traske, *Pearle for a Prince*, 18.

185. Traske, *Treatise of Libertie from Iudaisme*, 36.

186. Traske, *Heaven's Joy*, 70.

187. Traske, *Heaven's Joy*, 5.

188. Hebdon, *Guide for the Godly*, 21.

189. Hebdon, *Guide for the Godly*, 20.

If hardship was evidence of Godliness, then it was tacitly incumbent upon the Godly to seek out hardships.

CULTIVATED CRISES

Traskites exhibited their distinctiveness to—and from—their peers by avowing views that critically inverted cultural norms. The actions of Traskites, moreover, 'demonstrated a refusal to accept the ideas, actions or positions' of the majority.[190] Traskites consciously represented Traskism as antithetical to both the Church of England and mainline Puritanism. The same attitude informed a variety of behaviors that led to the anathematization of the Traskites by their peers. In performing these actions, Traskites were able to 'cultivate crises', to identify themselves as members of a persecuted, Godly remnant, whilst at the same time avoiding the hubris Traske had identified at the heart of the Separatist movement.[191]

The dereliction of courtesy represented one such effort at auto-anathematization. In the mid-sixteenth century, refusal to remove one's hat was identified as a mode of religious deviance.[192] In the seventeenth century, the Quakers popularized the practice of 'plain speech', the refusal to use 'honorific and deferential' terms.[193] As Bauman has explained, the use of plain speech by Quakers was seen as a way of 'taking up the cross'. By employing 'rhetorical impoliteness', the Friends risked 'violence, marginalization, and hostility'. But Bauman recognized that this could be seen as a virtue for the Godly rather than simply an unfortunate bi-product, having a 'strongly reinforcing effect on individual faith and group solidarity'.[194]

It appears that Traske was a fore-runner of this tendency. Around 1615, he began a one-sided correspondence with King James I. The letters touched on matters of doctrine: Traske urged the King to be more forthright in his condemnation of 'Rome and the Iesuites'. By his own account, Traske referred to the King as 'thou'.[195] William Pecke, a young lawyer who acted as emissary to Whitehall for Traske, recalled Traske's attitude on the subject. Pecke had complained that

---

190. Walraven and Abbink, 'Rethinking Resistance', 8.

191. Walsham, 'Happiness of Suffering', 56; Collinson, *Puritan Character*, 124.

192. Bauman, *Let Your Words be Few*, 43.

193. Bauman, *Let Your Words be Few*, 47.

194. Bauman, *Let Your Words be Few*, 51–52. See also Walsham, *Charitable Christian Hatred*, 144; Davies, *Quakers in English Society*, 49.

195. Traske, *True Gospel Vindicated*, a7r.

> The author dealeth with the Kinge in so familiar a manner, us-
> ing the words Thee and Thy. He [Traske] said he would alter
> them but thereupon sat in a muse a pretty while, and in the end
> answered, surely I will not alter them, claiming that the Kinge
> would take no offence at it, because it was the manner of speech
> which was used to God himself.[196]

Apparently, the King was infuriated by Traske's 'presumptuousness.'[197] Nonetheless, the practice was maintained. Later, T. S. noted in a marginal comment that Dorothy Traske 'ever in discoursing used thee and thou as Quakers do.'[198] Perhaps the most notable aspect of Pecke's report is the fact that Traske *considered* his behavior and, moreover, that he actively consid- ered the way in which his behavior would be apprehended by his interlocu- tor (in this instance the King).

The mode of worship most associated with the Traskites—by their peers—was also exclusionary. They appear to have refused rote recitation in favor of extemporary, charismatic prayer. Traske himself was said to have prayed 'not by the book' but rather 'as he thought fit.'[199] The exclusionary nature of this practice, forming a barrier to participation to those who are not immediately inspired, was recognized by Traske's own auditors. One claimed that 'what prayers he used we cannot learn.'[200]

In London, the Traskites would develop yet more demonstratively anti-social modes of worship. T. S. describes how Traske was wont to preach 'in the field and in the city,' at such a pitch that 'he would pierce the heavens.'[201] Fuller described the 'loudness of [Traske's] stentorian voice.'[202] John Falconer writes that the followers of Traske, too, were in the habit of praying with 'roaringes, and such loud out-cries.'[203] Even from his prison cell, Traske continued to disturb the neighbors. He 'did read allowed' and 'preached in his chamber to be heard of prisoners.'[204] David Como asserts that these activities 'created a heightened, almost electric, sense of God among them.'[205] It seems likely that for 'a minority who were anyway sure of

---

196. 'Examination of John Pecke,' 198.

197. Greene, 'Trask in the Star-Chamber, 1619,' 11.

198. Pagitt, *Heresiography*, 196.

199. Cambridge University Library, *Ely Diocesan Records*, B/2/35 3r.

200. Cambridge University Library, *Ely Diocesan Records*, B/2/35 76v.

201. Pagitt, *Heresiography*, 184.

202. Fuller, *Church-History of Britain*, 17:76.

203. Falconer, *Briefe Refutation*, 7.

204. Harris, *Œconomy of the Fleete*, 48.

205. Como, *Blown by the Spirit*, 148.

the reprobate state of the common majority,' the condemnation and disapproval of one's neighbors *would* offer a 'heightened sense of God among them.'[206] Loudness of prayer was often described as a facet of anti-Christian or deviant worship. Later in the century, Richard Baxter would caution his Godly peers against the tendency to 'bawling fervency which the hearers may discern to be but histrionical and affected.'[207] It was a rod that was variously used to beat Catholics and Jews in polemical writing of this period.[208] Conforming to this mode of worship, therefore, provided the Traskites with a divisive form of identification.

At times, the desire to situate themselves beyond the Pale of a reprobate world encouraged the Godly to embrace or even accentuate hardships. As Walsham writes, suffering 'helped to bring the regenerate to an awareness that they numbered among the tiny remnant.'[209] In the interests of 'cultivating crisis' the Godly were prone to 'penitential sorrow and symbolic suffering.'[210] The Traskites were perhaps unsurpassed in this. They 'ate and drank' whilst weeping and 'trembling,' wrote Pagitt.[211] Sclater described the 'sighes, grones, strong cryes and teares,' that accompanied Traskite divinity.[212] The period of 'repentance' Traske prescribed for his followers constituted an eye-catching example of constructive providentialism: submitting oneself to suffering, on the basis that the saints are known to be victims of suffering. The 'travel' they experienced was commensurate to the benediction they would enjoy.[213] This tendency dogged the story of the Traskites until the very end of their story. Traske himself was tortured in painful and humiliating ways, described in the record of the trial:

> And then the said Traske to bee whipped from the prison of
> the Fleete to the Pallace of Westminster with a paper on his
> head inscribed with theise wordes, For writing presumptuous
> lettres to the Kinge, wherein hee much slandered his Maiesty,
> And for slanderinge the proceedinges of the lord Bishopps of
> the high Commission, And for maintayneinge Jewish opynions,
> And then to bee sett on the Pillory and to haue one of his eares

---

206. Spraggon, 'Puritan Iconoclasm in England,' 18.

207. Baxter, *Christian Directory*, 208.

208. Fox, *Looking-Glass for the Jews*, 63; Naogeorg, *Popish Kingdome*, b2r; Evelyn, *Diary of John Evelyn*, 52; Lightfoot, 'Preface,' b1r.

209. Walsham, 'Happiness of Suffering,' 54.

210. Walsham, 'Happiness of Suffering,' 59.

211. Pagitt, *Heresiography*, 185.

212. Sclater, *Exposition upon Thessalonians*, 29.

213. Pagitt, *Heresiography*, 184.

nayled to the Pillory, and after hee hath stood there some con-
venient tyme, to bee burnte in the forehead with the lettre J in
token that hee broached Jewish opynions, And alsoe that the
said Traske shall alsoe bee whipped from the Fleete into Cheep-
eside with the like paper on his head and bee sett in the Pillory
and have his other Eare nayled thereunto.[214]

Traske found the experience of imprisonment extremely difficult. On
first arriving he wrote two letters, one to the King and a second to the Lord
Chancellor. He begged and threatened his warden to deliver the letters. The
Warden apparently went to the court to deliver the message to the King and
the Lord Chancellor. When he arrived at court, he was angrily reprimanded
by the Archbishop of Canterbury for allowing Traske access to writing materials.[215] Harris describes the arduous process of searching Traske's room
in order to find his writing materials. It appears that Traske had bribed,
or convinced, his jailer to warn him of any approaching room-searches.
When this corruption was discovered, the Warden went to search Traske's
room personally:

> Searching around [the Warden] found his Penns, Inck, and pa-
> per . . . and searching Thraske's cloathes (which he did much
> withstand) the Warden found betweene the outside and lyne-
> ing of his hose a paper booke in which he traduced the King's
> Majesty and the State, his lettres to the Archbishop . . . with his
> dreams and interpretations, his repasts, fastings, disputes, con-
> verting of fellow prisoners.[216]

Privation of freedom was only one part of the ordeal experienced by prisoners in the Fleet, where conditions were so 'frightful,' that the prisoners there
revolted in July 1619.[217] The prison was located downwind from the Fleet
Ditch, which was an open sewer. Francis Bacon wrote that 'the most pernicious infection next to the plague is the smell of the jail; when prisoners
have been long and close and nastily kept in.'[218] The worst conditions were
apparently in the 'Boulton's Ward,' where prisoners were left to starve.[219]

Despite their treatment, the Traskite prisoners remained remarkably
resilient. Return Hebdon withstood the privations of prison until his death.

214. Greene, 'Trask in the Star-Chamber,' 11.

215. Harris, Œconomy of the Fleete, 48.

216. Harris, Œconomy of the Fleete, 48.

217. Harris, Œconomy of the Fleete, xi; Lake, Anti-Christ's Lewd Hat, 189–90.

218. Bacon, Sylva Sylvarum, 246.

219. National Archives, SP 14/110, f. 2.

Dorothy Traske committed herself to a lifestyle of ascetic self-abnegation. T. S.'s letter relates that, when she was in prison, she refused to eat anything other than bread and water.[220] There was a degree of choice in the matter of this suffering. Traske secured his release by confessing and renouncing his previous convictions. This makes Hebdon and Dorothy Traske's stoicism all the more remarkable. According to the letter from T. S. relating her death, she would not 'petition (neither suffer others) for her liberty.'[221] Indeed, Dorothy Traske was *allowed* to leave the prison, and yet she chose not to. Her reason for this was that she 'conceived yt God (who knowes what is best for her) hath caused Authority to put her in this place.' It was with consternation that her peers noted that she not only *separated* herself, but rather *excommunicated* herself, seeking, in her activities and in her beliefs, to differentiate herself from the majority. When she died, she asked to be buried in a field, rather than in a churchyard.[222] In being buried beyond the boundaries of communal burial land, she shared the condition of the heretic. But she also shared in the condition of Protestant virtuosi like John Clarke, John Awcocke, James Trevisam, George King, Thomas Leys and John Wade.[223] Indeed, she also shared in the condition of Sarah (Gen 23).

Traske and his followers' attempts to situate themselves at odds with the wider community were successful. In fact Sclater considered 'oddnesse' to be Traske's principle concern.[224] Their 'disquieting' antics led to irritation and hostility from their neighbors.[225] But more concerning, for his peers, was Traske's active sectarianism. Within a short period of his having arrived in London, Traske had cultivated a reputation as a schismatic. T. S. asserts that Traske's reputation, in this early period, was for 'making divisions in the Church about *London*.'[226] Like Robert Bolton, Traske would later recount that the fomentation of division between the elect and the ungodly was his *intention*.[227]

Ben Jonson's *Bartholomew Fair* premiered at the Hope Theatre on Bankside on October 31, 1614. As Collinson has shown, the message of the play was directed, in some sense, at the likes of Traske. Traske may have critiqued the kind of precisianism that Jonson was satirizing, but

---

220. Pagitt, *Heresiography*, 210.
221. Pagitt, *Heresiography*, 212.
222. Pagitt, *Heresiography*, 197, 213.
223. Foxe, *Actes and Monuments*, 830, 1561, 1665, 1689.
224. Sclater, *Exposition upon Thessalonians*, 31.
225. Falconer, *Briefe Refutation*, 7; Pagitt, *Heresiography*, 184
226. Norris, *New Gospel*, 7.
227. Traske, *Power of Preaching*, a2v.

underneath their doctrinal differences, Traske and Busy had more in common than Judaizing. Both were concerned with exhibiting the distinctiveness of themselves from their peers, of the 'darlings' from the 'dross.' Both were concerned, in this vein, to antagonize and precipitate the antagonism of their peers. Both were aware of the sanctifying, obloquial gaze of the reprobate other. For early modern English Protestants, the image of the divisive, extremist, interloping alien instantly called to mind the topos of the Jew. Jonson explored this complex cultural interaction in his drama. Traske explored this interaction in his own devotional life.

'OBSTINATE AS JEWS'

Describing the condition of the imprisoned Traskites, Edward Kellet remarked: 'They all were as obstinate as the Iewes, laughing at imprisonment, and punishment.'[228] In this brief comment, the Traskite identity was entangled with the concept of 'the Jew.' For Kellet, however, this was not solely a matter of doctrine or ritual practice. Rather, the Traskites had become 'Jewish' in character. For Coryat, writing a few years earlier, being 'like a Jew' implied being seditious, alien and mad.[229] It did not *just* imply being ceremonialist or legalist. The Traskites were 'like Jews,' because they refused to recognise or to be corralled by authority. By 'laughing at imprisonment,' the Traskites were associated with the 'extremism' of the Jews, prepared to sacrifice their own comfort or even their own lives for the sake of a misguided and carnal religious dogma. In this sense, the mockery of the Traskites echoed the mockery of the Jew of Tewkesbury. 'Judaism' was communicated by the Traskites and understood by Kellet as a mark of eccentricity and extremism, of difference, of separation, of resistance.

Return Hebdon's references to the Jews offer an insight into the *meaning* of Jewishness and Judaism for the Traskites. Hebdon avows a preferential option for the afflicted. 'Over the poore afflicted people,' he wrote, 'is the protection of the most high.' For Hebdon, the Jews were the group that best conform to this model. 'The Jews,' he wrote, were 'the people who are hated and afflicted of all other people . . . for their creator.'[230] It was this model of the Jews that informed the adoption of 'Judaizing' practices in Traskite writing. The Jews, in short, were 'the people of least esteem.'

Traskite Judaizing can be traced back to several years before Kellet made his assessment. We have evidence of Traske's more unorthodox

228. Kellet, *Tricoenium Christi*, 74.
229. Coryat, *Coryats Crudities*, 232.
230. Hebdon, *Guide to the Godly*, 80

notions about the comparative validity of Christian and Jewish rituals from the very first records of his arrival in London. T. S. notes that Traske taught 'observation of the Lords day, after a Iudaicall manner, neither to kindle fires nor to dresse meates.'[231] Meanwhile, John Falconer described Traske as a 'Puritan minister who is lately growne half a Jew.'[232] Falconer mentions that Traske held 'singular opinions concerning the old Sabbath.'[233] The word 'singularity' represented disparagement for the Catholic Falconer, but praise for Traske.

THE LIGHT OF THE SABBATH

When Christopher Sands and Hamlet Jackson met with representatives of the Jewish community in Amsterdam in 1620, they found that some were disconcerted by the Traskite innovations. 'They told them that the Sabbath was only given to the Israelites and not to the nations,' recounts T. S., 'and that it was a sign betwixt God and the children of Israel.'[234]

Falconer identified Traske's observation of the 'old Sabbath' as a form of resistance, an action that denoted 'singularity' and 'separation.' Observation of the seventh-day was probably without precedent at this point, although in the coming decades a Seventh-Day Baptist congregation would emerge under the stewardship of Peter Chamberlen.[235] Even Seventh-Day Baptists, however, venerated the Seventh-Day as 'the Lord's day.'[236] The claim was often made that 'there [could] be no Sabbath without Christ.'[237] Levitical, legal observation of the Sabbath, as practiced by Traske and his followers, was at odds with the wider principle of Puritan Sabbatarianism as Pagitt and latterly Bryan Ball both noted.[238] One fellow traveller complained that Judaizing brought disrepute upon the Sabbatarian project since 'to introduce some of the Mosaical ceremonies,' would 'occasion slanders upon others.'[239]

Both Katz and Nicholas McDowell have drawn a connection between the Book of Sports controversy, which erupted in the years before Traske's

---

231. Norris, *New Gospel*, 7.

232. Falconer, *Briefe Refutation*, 1.

233. Falconer, *Briefe Refutation*, 1, 26, 33, 42–43.

234. Pagitt, *Heresiography*, 180.

235. For a thorough description of the emergence of the Seventh-Day Sabbath in England, see Ball, *English Connection*, 1–22; *Seventh-Day Men*, 1–30.

236. Stennett, *Royal Law Contended For*, 28.

237. *Moralitie of the Fourth Commandment*, 103–4.

238. Ball, *Seventh Day Men*, 48; Pagitt, *Heresiography*, a3r.

239. Bampfield, *Enquiry Whether the Lord Jesus Christ Made the World*, 3.

arrest, and the Traskite scandal itself. Katz suggests that Traske accrued a degree of infamy, largely on the coat-tails of the controversy.[240] McDowell, too, focuses on the response to Traske's thought, rather than the substance of Traskism. He implies that Traske was a scape-goat, a living *reductio ad absurdum*, hauled before the courts as a piece of political theatre designed to chasten the 'hotter' Puritans who were 'tending to Judaism.'[241] Sabbatarianism was certainly a point of contention between the King and his Puritan subjects. But Traske, *too*, was aware of this controversy and was aware of the very live stigma attached to the idea of Judaizing at that point.

From the bibliocentric analysis of Phillips or Glassman or Ball, one might expect Traske's move towards Seventh-Day Sabbatarianism to have been catalyzed by zealous attention to the *mediate* revelation of scripture. Quite the opposite is true. Traske appears to have been drawn to the practice of Seventh-Day Sabbatarianism as an *innovation*. According to T. S., Hamlet Jackson had a vision:

> Travelling the country on a Saturday, he saw a shining light about him, which struck him with amazement. . . . And thereupon he concluded that the light of the Law was more fully discovered to him, than to any since the Apostles. And it was thought, that the two witnesses which he interpreted to be the Law and the Prophets, yea in a manner the whole letter of the Scriptures lying dead, from the Apostles daies to our times, were now revived and stood up on their feet.[242]

This claim would later be corroborated, in part, by Traske himself.[243]

Kenneth Parker observes that Jackson's revelation appears to be an inversion of Paul's Damascene *metanoia*.[244] T. S. would later assert that Hamlet Jackson prayed for the bars of his cell, in the New Prison in Maiden Lane, to give way. Again, this begs comparison with St. Paul and the account of his manumission in Acts 16.[245] The Traskites represented, in the popular imagination, a tergiversation, a reversal of the Christian supersession which extended more broadly than a simple matter of doctrine. Sabbatarianism was, during this period, seen as a designation of sedition. The Sabbath had become the battlefield in the struggle between the Godly and conformists. Prophecy—and the destabilizing effect that prophetic claims

---

240. Katz, *Sabbath and Sectarianism*, 12.

241. McDowell, 'Stigmatizing of Puritans as Jews,' 348–63.

242. Pagitt, *Heresiography*, 190.

243. National Archives, SP 16/73, f.96.

244. Parker, *English Sabbath*, 161.

245. Pagitt, *Heresiography*, 197.

had on the epistemic structures of conformist ecclesiology—was also seen as a threat. The combination of these two tendencies in the figure of Traskite Sabbatarianism, therefore, functioned as a mark of the dissenting nature of Traskism. This is nowhere more evident than in the clear comparison made by Ephraim Pagitt between Hamlet Jackson—as a visionary—and William Hacket who, twenty-five years previously, had imagined the Queen's death.[246] This, in one sense, should not be surprising. The *function* of the Sabbath, in its inception and in the various ways it had been used throughout the history of the Jewish-Christian tradition, had always been to mark off the separateness and dissent of the minority.

THE DIFFERENCE OF MEATES

From the earliest days of his time in London, Traske preached doctrines that went further than Sabbath observation. As such, Pagitt considered Traskism and Saturday Sabbatarianism to be discrete phenomena. T. S. notes that Mary Chester was rescued from Traskite folly by William Gouge.[247] Gouge wrote a number of sermons on the phenomenon of 'Jewish-Christians,' which he defined as: 'Those that say that . . . what fish, fowl and beast were once forbidden, are still unlawfull to be eaten.'[248] It is quite possible, given T. S.'s allusion to Gouge in the context of Traske, that Gouge had Traskism in mind here. 'Judaizing' in the matter of diet became a component of Traskite practice as early as 1615. Falconer in his *Briefe Refutation of John Traskes judaical and novel fancyes*, claimed that Traske held 'the Mosaical difference of meates . . . as morall Lawes unrepealed by Christ.' Falconer, mentions that 'many men and women' had subscribed to Traske's conclusions.[249] This claim is supported later by Edward Kellet, who lamented 'dangerously many fell into Iudaisme, and turned *Traskites*.'[250] Chamberlain expressed equal concern in his letter to Carleton the following year. Kellet noted that the Traskites 'would bury in the Dunghill, chines of porke or puddings, or any swines flesh, which their neighboures courteously bestowed upon them.'[251] The refusal of the Traskites to consume pork had become the focus of a ritual humiliation at the hands of their neighbors.

246. Pagitt, *Heresiography*, 190.
247. Norris, *New Gospel*, 7.
248. Gouge, *Progresse of Divine Providence*, 23.
249. Falconer, *Briefe Refutation*, 3.
250. Kellet, *Tricoenium Christi*, 74.
251. Kellet, *Tricoenium Christi*, 74.

When he was awaiting trial, Traske's dietary opinions again served as the focus for stigmatization:

> Hee was not restreyned from any meates untill November last, and then hee was only allowed the Flesh meates in his opynion supposed to bee forbidden.[252]

Before the Star Chamber he was accused of a number of charges, including:

> [teaching] that the lawe of Moses concerneinge the differences of meates forbidden the eateinge of Hogges flesh, Conies, etc.[253]

Harris confirmed that during the period of his residence within the Fleet, Traske conformed to the Levitical dietary restrictions. Harris was at pains to stress that, under his administration, Traske's dietary needs were catered for:

> The Warden delivered that money to him which was Thraske's keeper to provide weekes dyett for Thraske, when he refused the Warden's meat, because porke, connyes, ducks and such like are uncleane meates (as he held opinion) were dressed with it . . . the warden with all affableness found dyett and lodging to Thraske.[254]

For Return Hebdon, as for Traske, the Law was fundamentally bankrupt, rendered arcane by the triumph of the atonement. Obedience to the law held no salvific power. Indeed, Hebdon wrote, teaching moral law to a member of the reprobate 'can no more helpe a man to go the way of immortality, then a natural blind man can direct a man.'[255] However, the Law did have *instrumental* if not *intrinsic* virtue. Hebdon describes the Law using much the same language that Traske would later use to describe preaching: the Law served to *separate* the Godly from the unregenerate. Hebdon acknowledged that the epistle to the Galatians appeared to undermine the morality of circumcision, yet also noted that the text does not *ban* the practice. Hebdon concluded that the salience of the Law lay not in its observation but rather in the *motivation* for its observation. Should a man be obliged to seek circumcision, then the action is morally bankrupt. Equally, however, any man who *refuses* circumcision, for fear of the morality of the world, and 'makes circumcision in the liberty of the Gospel to be a sin,' is equally guilty of 'denying the liberty wherein Christ hath made them free.'[256]

---

252. Greene, 'Trask in the Star-Chamber,' 9.

253. Greene, 'Trask in the Star-Chamber,' 8.

254. Harris, Œconomy of the Fleete, 50.

255. Hebdon, Guide to the Godly, 61.

256. Hebdon, Guide to the Godly, 47–48.

The Laws themselves served only as indicators of man's election or reprobation. And the sign of reprobation is *obedience* to the laws and mores of the world. 'From the opposition of the authority of men and against the authority of God in Christ,' he wrote 'we may see the bondage under men by the Law, and the liberty of the Law in Christ.'[257]

Hebdon avowed the value of the observation of Levitical dietary restrictions. Those who were 'inforced to eat swine's flesh,' he writes, 'justi-fie themselves in defiance of God.' Such people were 'in bondage after the worldly elements of the heathen.'[258] This is broadly in the vein of the anti-Precisianist backlash and the general complaint against 'formalism.' Being enjoined by any person to do any act rendered that act ethically vacuous. The other side of the coin, which Hebdon saw, was that the adoption of practices which *repudiated* heteronomy exhibited Godliness. The fear of men and the fear of God *was* 'the separation' according to Hebdon's think-ing. The 'enmity' of the world (while painful), as such facilitated the 'perfect separation in the Word.[259]

The act of refusing to consume unlawful meats, was understood by the neighbors of the Traskites and by the authorities as a mark of resistance, such that the Traskites were forced to touch and eat forbidden meats as a form of humiliation. But the act of separating meats was an affirmation of the *intrinsic* good of separation. For Douglas, the very inception of the dietary restrictions of Leviticus were a symbolic designation of the importance of 'wholeness.' Ambiguous, anomalous creatures like pigs represented a sym-bolic aberration of these categories of wholeness.[260] Certainly, the initial concern for maintaining separation of foods emerged from a period when 'ethnic markers' were becoming more central to Israelite religion. Food, during this period, became an 'expression of social bonds and boundaries.'[261] The midrashic reading of Leviticus 18 included the claim that the non-con-sumption of pork was *specifically* a practice which the gentiles objected to. Philo wrote that the function of Moses' selection of forbidden meats was to prevent slavishness to the senses amongst the Israelites. As such, he banned the most delicious meats. Whilst the pleasures of the flesh were sufficient for the gentiles, the pleasures of the spirit were stored up for Israel.[262] The non-consumption of pork remained a forum for the reification, stigmatization,

257. Hebdon, *Guide to the Godly*, 47.

258. Hebdon, *Guide to the Godly*, 40.

259. Hebdon, *Guide to the Godly*, 79–88.

260. Douglas, *Purity and Danger*, 30–32.

261. Hendel, *Remembering Abraham*, 22.

262. Termini, 'Philo's Thought,' 120.

and humiliation of Jews down the centuries and right up to the period of Traske's flourishing.[263] This was what Robert Davenport *meant* when he said that a Puritan was 'one that would eat no pork.'[264] It was also what Return Hebdon and Dorothy Traske and John Traske meant by *not eating* pork. In both an intrinsic and a circumstantial sense, the refusal by the Traskites to eat pork constituted a marker of separation.

THE FESTIVALL OBSERVANCES OF AZIMES

Traske and his followers also observed rites associated with the festival of Passover. John Falconer noted that Traske required his followers to celebrate Easter on the '14th of Marche moone.'[265] The celebration of Easter on the fourteenth day of the 'March-moone' (or Nisan) was a practice shared by several groups throughout Christian history, most obviously the Ebionites.[266] Indeed, the Quartodeciman controversy which engaged the Church in the third century, was characterized by anti-Judaic rhetoric. Emperor Constantine, denouncing the practice, deemed it an 'unworthy thing that in the celebration of this most holy feast we should follow the practice of the Jews,' and urged Christians to 'have nothing in common with the mob of Jews.'[267] Traske would have been familiar with the anti-Judaic tenor of the Quartodeciman controversy. The history of the controversy was frequently mobilized in anti-Judaic homiletics of the period. Lancelot Andrewes (who would later speak against Traskism in the Star Chamber) raised the spectre of Quartodecimanism in a sermon preached on Easter Sunday 1618.[268] The arch-heretic Edward Wightman, the last person to be burned at the stake in England, was sentenced to death in April 1612 charged with a range of heresies including Ebionism.[269] In his denunciation of the Traskites, T. S. made several pointed references to the Ebionite heresy.[270] As such, the Traskite adoption of this practice can be understood as a resistant mode of Judaizing on two levels. Firstly, it courted anti-Judaic criticism from Traske's peers.

---

263. Kraemer, *Jewish Eating and Identity*, 30–33; J. J., *Resurrection of Dead Bones*, 87; Thorowgood, *Digitus Dei*, 7.

264. Davenport, *New Tricke to Cheat the Divell*, 48.

265. Falconer, *Briefe Refutation*, 57.

266. Luomanen, *Recovering Jewish-Christian Sects and Gospels*, 17–45.

267. Eusebius, *Life of Constantine*, 178.

268. Andrewes, *Sermon Preached Before His Maiestie at Whitehall*, 25, 37.

269. National Archives, SP 14/68, f. 136.

270. Pagitt, *Heresiography*, 190.

Secondly it aligned the Traskites with a movement which had, historically, been maligned and accused of Judaizing.

It could be claimed that this attempt to reinvigorate the Easter observation of the earliest Christians was a form of 'primitivism.' However, Traske appears to have developed even more concertedly Judaizing practices whilst in prison. Falconer, having interviewed a number of other prisoners in the Fleet in 1619, gathered that Traske 'hath added to his Easter the festiuall observance of Azimes.' Falconer wrote that Traske had been seen by other prisoners 'after the fourteenth of March moone, to eate contrary to their custome at other times, withe unleavened loaves.'[271] Falconer himself draws a clear distinction between primitivism—as exemplified by the celebration of Easter according to the Quartodeciman calculation—and avowed Judaizing as manifest in the celebration of Passover.[272] Of course the question of whether Traske *did* celebrate the Passover in accordance with the stipulations of Exodus 12 is secondary to the fact that he behaved in a manner, which was *perceived to be* an observance of Passover and therefore was *perceived to be* Judaizing.

The celebration of Passover is a celebration of resistance. Israel, in the observation of Passover, enacts the distinction of herself from the Egyptian majority. This act of distinction is the prototypical act of Israel's self-definition, establishing the polity of Israel and differentiating Israel from Egypt. The penalty for failing to differentiate oneself in the Passover narrative is death, the death of the first born. Any Israelite who fails to comply with the injunction against the consumption of yeast at Passover will be cut-off from Israel (Exod 12:15). The verb to 'cut off' (כְּרִית) recurs in a number of texts which describe the reification of the holy polity. In the act of circumcision, the foreskin is 'cut off' (כְּרִית). The covenant, itself, is 'cut' (אֶכְרֹת).

The meaning of Passover as an act of resistance was particularly heightened in the context of Jacobean England. In 1600, William Cotton reported that a Passover had been celebrated in Exeter.[273] The same William Cotton berated John Hazard, sixteen years later, for his association with John Traske.[274] Elsewhere, it was claimed that Francis Russell, the Earl of Bedford, was 'a puritan, and keeps his Passover every Easter.'[275] Undoubtedly, this use of the topos of Passover was an attempt to besmirch and marginalize the Puritan Russell.

271. Falconer, *Briefe Refutation*, 17.

272. Falconer, *Briefe Refutation*, 18.

273. Roberts, *Calendar of the Manuscripts*, 10:450.

274. HMC, 'City of Exeter,' 3 of 10, 95–96.

275. National Archives, SP 12/155, f. 42.

THE TRASKITE EPILOGUE

Hamlet Jackson evaded capture. He and Christopher Sands resurfaced in Amsterdam. According to T. S., both Sands and Jackson sought out the leaders of the Jewish community there with the intention of being converted to Judaism. When they were told that this would only be possible if they submitted to circumcision, Christopher Sands decided against it. He was willing, he said, to observe 'the seven ordinances,' and thereby to remain 'a Gentile saint.' Jackson on the other hand, agreed to undergo the procedure.[276] T. S. told Dorothy Traske that he knew many witnesses who could attest the veracity of this event. In 1632, Theophilus Brabourne's *Defence of that Most Ancient and Sacred Ordinance of God, the Sabbath Day* was published in Amsterdam at the behest of English-speaking 'Jewish-Christians.' It is possible that Hamlet Jackson was involved in this enterprise.[277]

From there, Christopher Sands moved to the North of Ireland. On October 15 1635, nearly two decades after the arrest of John Traske, he was brought before the Court of High Commission and his address was listed as Lyssen in County Tyrone. The proceedings detail that Sands 'had formerly in his answers disclaimed all judaical or heretical opinions, and that in regard of his necessary affairs in Ireland, he be respited till Easter term for his answers, or that they may be taken in Ireland by commission.' His case was referred to the Bishop of Ely, Francis White.[278] Sands was charged before Bishop White with being a Jew and once more declared himself to be 'a National or a Gentile Saint,' that is, an observer of the 'Seven Noahide Precepts.' Mary Chester, having written to Christopher Sands pleading with him to return to the fold of Christianity, herself relapsed into 'Judaisme,' sometime in 1636.[279]

The word resistant itself is polyvalent. Traskite behaviors functioned to 'resist' the immersion of the Godly in the mass of the reprobate. Traskites *also* exhibited a significant degree of resistance—that is to say fortitude and resilience—to the intrigues of earthly power. Several aspects of their writing exemplify a disregard for or disinterest in the punishment they suffered at the hands of the state. Dorothy Traske refused to appeal against her conviction, seeing it as a providential sign. Return Hebdon wrote that, in the face

---

276. Pagitt, *Heresiography*, 180.

277. Brabourne, *Defence*. A number of tracts were published directly to counter the rise of Saturday-Sabbatarianism within the English, Puritan community in Holland, including Walker, *Doctrine of the Sabbath*; Young, *Dies Dominicas*.

278. National Archives, SP 16/324, f. 2; SP 16/261, f. 267.

279. Paggitt, *Heresiography*, 194–95.

of persecution, men of God 'doe not scare but are more bold and confident.'[280] For Edward Kellet, the Traskites were as 'obstinate as Jews.'[281]

The fact of Traske's apostasy makes the resilience of the remaining Traskites even more intriguing. Traske provided the ideological architecture for the movement. In 1620, he published a text distancing himself from his own followers and from his previously held convictions. He described his previous thought as 'errors', and committed to 'neuer separate what God hath joyned, nor joyne what he hath severed.'[282] Precisely the ethic that Traske had instilled in his followers—the anti-rational, singular ethic—provided the ideological apparatus for this resilience. A similar group apparatus was instilled in the Sabbateans a generation later. For Coome and Hebdon, the very irrationality of their convictions in the eyes of the wider society served to convince them of their rectitude. In fact, it emphasized the very special, singular nature of their revelatory knowledge.

CONCLUSION

The decision by Lord Chancellor Bacon to brand John Traske was not without legal precedent. Branding was in use as a punishment for thieves. It was also used to punish blasphemers—James Nayler would later be branded with the letter B on his forehead.[283] The nascent Puritan communities in the New World adopted this practice. In each case, whilst the immediate pain of the ordeal was punishment enough, the more profound punishment was the pariah-hood that branding brought with it. Thieves who were branded were known by their communities to be thieves. Adulterers—like Mary Batcheller—were known to be adulterers.[284] This aspect of the punishment was alluded to by Bacon in his judgement of Traske, with the witticism: 'he that was schismaticus may now be stigmaticus.'[285] The irony of this should not be lost. The punishment allotted to Traske was that he be marked out as a pariah for the remainder of his days. The J, emblazoned on his forehead, designated him as 'Judaizer' and, therefore, 'outsider.' This brutal punishment, it seems, was the consummation of the Traskite desire for 'singularity.' He was not only a practitioner of certain practices, but rather 'a Judaizer', a pariah, rejected by the world. With the branding of his forehead, his

280. Hebdon, *Guide to the Godly*, 101.

281. Kellet, *Tricoenium Christi*, 74.

282. Traske, *Treatise of Libertie from Iudaisme*, 41.

283. Reay, 'Quakerism and Society', 159.

284. McManus, *Law and Liberty in Early New England*, 161.

285. Bourgchier, 'Henry Bourgchier to Dr. James Ussher', 359.

rejection by society became part of his identity, part of his physical being. For Traske, it was both stigma and stigmata.

Como suggests that 'Traske and his associates . . . had little compunction about submitting to what they perceived as the winds of God's spirit, even when it led them directly away from the safe harbours of orthodoxy.'[286] This—at very least—is true. The practices which the Traskites employed, most notably but not exclusively their Judaizing practices, set them at odds with their peers. But the practices they employed also functioned *intrinsically* as modes of separation. Sabbath observation, the separation of meats, the celebration of the Passover are all intrinsically associated with a concern for separation. It may seem incongruous that Traske, associated as he was with anti-legal forms of Protestant divinity and soteriology, would gravitate towards apparently ceremonial modes of worship. However, on closer inspection, we find that all aspects of Traske's divinity—the Johannine overtones of his writing, the Familist overtones of his soteriology, the Judaizing overtones of his ritual practice—speak to an underlying and abiding concern with separation and resistance. 'It is not the signe, but the thing signified,' wrote John Traske. 'Not the shew, but the substance.'[287]

286. Como, *Blown by the Spirit*, 149.
287. Traske, *Pearle for a Prince*, 25.

CHAPTER 4

Thomas Totney, Judaizing, and England's Exodus

IN 1651, IN THE first part of his *Theauraujohn his Theos-ori Apokolipikal*, the prophet Thomas Totney declared: 'I am a Jew, begotten by the Gospel, Circumcised both in flesh and spirit.'[1] From 1649, Totney had believed himself to be prophetically gifted. He had spent the summer of 1650 in the company of William Everard and John Pordage at Bradfield. He took to living in a tent, which he referred to as 'the Tent of Judah.'[2] He was arrested and imprisoned twice for expressing blasphemous opinions along with his comrade and financier Robert Norwood.[3] He wrote to the 'Jews of Amsterdam,' referring to himself as a Jew of the tribe of Reuben.[4] He also referred to himself as the King of Naples, Sicily and Jerusalem.[5] At Christmastide in 1654 he turned on his erstwhile hero, Cromwell. He claimed that Cromwell had been 'cut off' from Israel.[6] He burnt all his possessions including a Bible.[7] He attempted to invade the House of Commons, brandishing a rusty sword, was arrested and held for two months.[8] He returned to preaching from the Tent of Judah at St. George's Hill where he attracted 'multitudes of people' and refused to move until the justices of the peace

---

1. Tany, *Theauraujohn His Theous Ori Apokolipikal*, 9, 28, 42.

2. Many details of the life of Thomas Totney were first identified in Hessayon, *Gold Tried in the Fire*; Tany, *Hear, O Earth*, brs.

3. Norwood, *Case and Trial of Captain Robert Norwood*, 3.

4. Tany, *High News for Hierusalem*, 12.

5. Tany, *ThauRam Tanjah*, brs.

6. Tany, *My Edict Royal*, 5.

7. Tany, *My Edict Royal*, 6.

8. Tany, *My Edict Royal*, 11.

intervened.[9] He attempted a mission to the Jews of Amsterdam (who he believed would be shortly restored) and he surfaced briefly at Brill in the Netherlands. Whilst attempting to return from the Netherlands, he was 'cast a way,' and was never seen again.[10] In the documentation for his daughter's marriage in 1663, he was presumed dead.[11]

All of these actions could be traced to a conversion experience he had in 1649:

> The power fell upon me in my shop, and smote me dumb, then after blinde, and then dead; then I was corded and bound in my bed, and then I received instruction, which afterwards I was forced to put the same into action.[12]

In Damascene fashion, he was given a new name:

> Then I saw the great light shine in me and upon me, saying *The-aurau John* my servant, I have chosen thee my Shepherd, thou art adorned with the jewel of Exceliency.[13]

Before 1649, Totney had been an unremarkable figure. The son of a Lincolnshire farmer.[14] An apprentice fishmonger in London.[15] A congregant of Stephen Denison's at St. Katherine's Creechurch.[16] An inheritor of a farm in Cambridgeshire.[17] A harquebusier in the New Model army.[18] In 1648, he returned to London and opened the same goldsmiths shop on the Strand

---

9. National Archives, SP 25/57, f. 62; *Calendar of State Papers Domestic*, 8:356.

10. Occurences from Foreign Parts no. 50, 20–27, December 1659, 552 (Hessayon, *Gold Tried in the Fire*, 389).

11. Lambeth Palace Library, F/M/I 4, f. 71r (Hessayon, *Gold Tried in the Fire*, 390).

12. Tany, *Theauraujohn His Theous Ori Apokolipikal*, a2v.

13. Tany, *Theaurauiohn High Priest to the Iewes*, 6.

14. Lincolnshire Archives Office, Bishop's Transcripts, South Hykeham; Cambridgeshire Records Office, CCE CW: Will of John Totney of Little Shelford (Probate, 22 December 1638) (Hessayon, *Gold Tried in the Fire*, 29, 79).

15. Guildhall Library, Manuscript 5576/1 f. 64 (Hessayon, *Gold Tried in the Fire*, 31).

16. London Metropolitan Archive, Manuscript 9274, f. 171 (Hessayon, *Gold Tried in the Fire*, 51).

17. Cambridgeshire Records Office, CCE CW: Will of John Totney of Little Shelford (Probate, December 22, 1638) (Hessayon, *Gold Tried in the Fire*, 61).

18. Tany, *Theauraujohn High Priest to the Iewes*, 7; *Nations Right*, 8; Hessayon, *Gold Tried in the Fire*, 80.

where 'the power' would 'fall upon him' a year later.[19] Shortly before his conversion, he was widowed, for the second time.[20]

His activities after his conversion, however, have led many scholars to analyse his significance in light of wider cultural and religious phenomena. Some consider Totney to be yet another philo-semite, 'fascinated with Jews and things Judaic.'[21] Nigel Smith attributes the Judaizing elements of Coppe and Tany's activities to 'a general interest in Jewry,' encouraged by the rise of Judeocentric millenarianism.[22] Luxon contends that Totney was one of a 'flurry' of 'pseudo-Christs' who—like William Franklin—believed that the allegory of election had been consummated and that they had been somatically transformed into prelapsarian, perfect bodies.[23] David Katz counted Totney amongst the 'doers' of the philo-semitic, millenarian milieu. Whilst figures like Jessey and Dury agitated through political channels for the re-admission of the Jews, Katz suggests, Totney was prepared to take matters into his own hands, to 'gather the Jews out of the nations and lead them to the Mount of Olives.'[24] Katz gives Totney more credit than some in acknowledging that his writings highlighted key concerns of the period. However, he takes Totney too much at his word—perhaps—when he characterizes him as 'unlearned' and 'confused.'[25] There are, moreover, clear shortcomings to the unproblematized association of millenarian philo-semitism with the renovation of ceremonial law.

Hessayon takes an alternative approach, tracing much of Totney's doctrinal innovations to literary sources. Hessayon explains the Judaizing elements of Totney's divinity as a manifestation of his Biblicism.[26] However, simply attributing these tendencies to a kind of Biblicism, elides the fact that Totney was extremely interpretative in his relation to scripture and would often deduce meanings that were at odds with the consensual interpretations of his time.[27] And even if we allow that Christopher Fowler's description of Totney and his peers as deniers of the authority of scripture was slanderous, and that those who charged Norwood and Totney with anti-scriptuarian

19. Tany, *Theauraujohn His Theous Ori Apokolipikal*, a2v.

20. London Metropolitan Archive, Manuscript 10,091/17, f. 157; Westminster City Archives, STC/B, mf. 2., 8/6/1648 (Hessayon, *Gold Tried in the Fire*, 34, 72).

21. Luxon, *Literal Figures*, 210.

22. Smith, *Perfection Proclaimed*, 56n.

23. Luxon, *Literal Figures*, 2.

24. Katz, *Philo-Semitism*, 108.

25. Katz, *Philo-Semitism*, 117–19.

26. Hessayon, *Gold Tried in the Fire*, 97, 134, 344.

27. Smith, *Perfection Proclaimed*, 304–5.

heresies were mistaken, it is nonetheless demonstrable that Totney believed the Bible itself to be a problematic document which had been perverted by the Popish conspiracy and which had lost the lustre of its perfect, hiero-glyphic form.[28] He mocked those who 'treasured up names, verses, texts' in order to make doctrinal claims.[29] He actively warned against the idolatry of the Bible and—as an enactment of this—burnt his own.[30]

Nigel Smith has focused particularly on the use of language in Tot-ney's writings. Totney wrote in a highly idiosyncratic way, using snippets of Hebrew, in which (as Hessayon has proved) he had some facility and oc-casionally lapsing into a form of written glossolalia. Smith contends that, for Totney, this form of language created a signification whereby the prophetic visionary attained a mode of communication that transcended rational communication. Totney's creative use of Hebrew provided the substance for this process. The use of Hebrew, by extension, situated Totney in—what Smith calls—'the pose of divinely instituted madness.'[31]

Undoubtedly, concern with 'liberation' from enslavement was a cen-tral theme of Totney's writings. Drawing, in part, on Walzer's insights, Coffey uses Thomas Totney as an exemplar in his depiction of 'England's Exodus.' Totney 'fused Exodus and Apocalypse,' allowing an unveiling of the true, eschatological meaning of the liberation from Egypt. Coffey claims that Totney represented 'the Judaizing tendency in Puritanism taken to an extreme.'[32] For Coffey, therefore, the root of Totney's 'Judaizing' was a fixation on the liberation narrative of Exodus. According to Skinner, the rhetoric of Protestant liberty was provoked by the over-reaching power of the monarchy. According to Morrill, it was provoked by the fear of Laudian innovations and the 'holiness of beauty.'[33] Nonetheless, Totney continued to campaign for 'liberty' long after these spectres had dissolved. Coffey's contention that the origins of the Puritan zeal for liberty were Biblical rather than theoretical, and that—as such—it constituted a kind of 'liberation the-ology' is corrective. Like the Godly, liberation theologians are typically more attentive to an intrinsic, proactive and therefore abstract understanding of liberty, rather than a political, historical and reactive notion. But it leaves

---

28. Tany, *Theauraujohn His Theous Ori Apokolipikal*, 8.

29. Tany, *Second Part*, 51.

30. Tany, *My Edict Royal*, 10.

31. Smith, *Perfection Proclaimed*, 56. For other reflections on the rhetorical use of madness, see Hill, *World Turned Upside Down*, 115.

32. Coffey, 'England's Exodus,' 272.

33. Morrill, 'Religious Context of the English Civil War,' 178.

only partially explained the connection between admiration for the Biblical polity of Israel and the renovation of Jewish ceremonies.

Coffey accounts for the 'concern with slavery and liberation' in the fact that 'Calvinists were close readers of Exodus and Deuteronomy.'[34] Throughout the history of Christianity, and across the world, Christians have expressed admiration for and emulated the Biblical polity of Israel. Indeed—as the scope of both Coffey and Walzer's work demonstrates—there are innumerable examples of Hebreo-centric, liberation theologies. But only in small pockets—most notably in England during the mid-seventeenth century—have Christians renewed the observation of circumcision, sabbatarianism and Levitical dietary laws.

Following Coffey, I want to argue that for Totney freedom was an irreducible good. Totney's commitment to 'freedom' was *pro*active, rather than reactive. But rather than a political liberation from enslavement Totney was primarily concerned with separation from a reprobate society. In fact, Totney's underlying concern, in every aspect of his thought, appeared to be with acts of separation, differentiation and resistance. This, too, was a central concern of the originators of the ceremonies to which Totney was drawn, and which he renovated. For Totney, the appeal of these ceremonies was the guarantee of autonomy, separation and singularity, a demonstration of a 'distinctive moral commitment.' Those same concerns were expressed by the Biblical authors, afflicted as they were by similar anxieties to those that afflicted Totney and his peers. It was these concerns that allowed Totney to rediscover those anxieties in the pages of Exodus and—in the descriptions of the ceremonial laws—a cure for those anxieties.

I argue that the roots of Totney's concern for autonomy and singularity can be found in the anxieties of assurance that were elicited in him by exposure to Reformed Protestant soteriology. Totney was exposed to the deep conflicts and contradictions at the center of Reformed Protestant thought during this period, and the 'deep structural instabilities,' which it formented. By extension, I argue that Totney's self-representation as a 'Jew by seed and by line' functioned as an attempt to render himself as the member of a distinctive, singular group, a 'holy huddle.' In the context of early-modern England, a concomitance of factors led to the rendering of the Jew as 'other.' As such, to exhibit one's identity as the member of a 'poor, embattled remnant,' and thus to construct the architecture of 'symbolic suffering' was easily achieved by self-identification with the Jews.[35] A complimentary experience could also be found in the English iteration of Behmenist thought. Böhme

---

34. Coffey, 'England's Exodus,' 257.
35. Walsham, 'Happiness of Suffering,' 59.

also offered formulations of soteriology and cosmology that posited a fundamental co-mixture of competing and conflicting elements and held out the promise of an eschatological reckoning within which this entanglement of light and dark, good and evil, would be resolved. As such, although radically different in character, a similar concern can be found in the roots of the Biblical texts, in the origins of the ceremonies advocated in those texts, in the Behmenist cosmology and in the experiences of Thomas Totney.

PURITANISM AND SINGULARITY

Between the period of Traske's flourishing and the period of Totney's, radical shifts had taken place in the landscape of English Protestantism. Whereas, under the ascendancy of George Abbot, the Godly had begun the process of developing a Godly identity, whilst sharing the broad theological structures of the established church, in Totney's period, a greater degree of enmity was evident between the Godly and the Church of England. This was principally formented by the emergence of Laudianism—breaking the Calvinist consensus—amongst the leadership of the Church, and growing suspicion of the Protestant credentials of the Crown itself provoked (amongst other things) by the Spanish match. As the work of Como and Lake has demonstrated—the architecture of the phenomenon of intra-Puritan sectarianism and the 'efflorescence of religious polemic,' was already in place in the 1630s and even earlier.[36] During the 1630s, a period when Godly preaching and the political clout of the Puritan party was under direct assault, these dynamics remained 'underground' not least as a result of self-censorship.[37] And yet, by its very nature, the soteriology of Reformed Protestantism, all the while, invited the Godly to engage in clandestine, quotidian and only translucent acts of sectarianism; exhibitions (often muted or euphemistic) of positive-distinctiveness. As such, it was this spirit of 'singularity,' that would lead to the greatest triumph of Puritanism as a political force, and its ultimate collapse as a confessional phenomenon.[38]

The start of Thomas Totney's confessional journey towards Judaizing was in Calvinism. In St. Katharine Cree, Totney was a member of Stephen Denison's congregation.[39] The intricate internal politics of Denison's parish

---

36. Como and Lake, 'Puritans, Antinomians, and the Laudians,' 684–715; Lake, *Boxmaker's Revenge*, 365.

37. Lake, *Boxmaker's Revenge*, 395.

38. Lamont, 'Two National Churches,' 335; Collinson, 'Sects and the Evolution of Puritanism,' 147–66.

39. Guildhall Library, Manuscript 9274, f. 171.

have been explored in the work of Peter Lake. As Lake demonstrates, Denison—in his homiletics—facilitated a constant 'oscillation between anxiety and assurance' in his congregation.[40] Denison's preaching constituted an 'austere statement of Calvinist orthodoxy.' His homilies stressed the insolubility of the divine edict of predestination and the perseverance of the saints.[41] At the same time, he preached that the Christian was helpless in the hands of God, devoid of any voluntary control over his own soteriological destiny. 'A man or woman may have free choise in thing's evil and indifferent,' Denison was prepared to concede. However, the power to act morally, to do good, was given by grace, occasionally, by God, from the 'fountaine of holiness.'[42] At the same time, he stressed the ultimate unknowability of the divine fiat. As he reminded his congregation, the penitent thief—a most unlikely saint—was the first to be admitted to grace by Christ himself.[43] Lake identifies the homiletics of pastors like Denison with the mentality of the Wallingtons of his generation.[44]

We know, from the sermon that Denison preached at the funeral of his parishioner Elizabeth Juxon, that his homiletic style evoked all of the internal tensions of Reformed Protestant theology. Juxon, Denison recalled, 'groaned many a time under the sentence of unbelief.' Nonetheless, she sought out—reflexively—innumerable marks of assurance. Amongst them, Denison listed that 'she loved all God's children and esteemed them the onely excellent people in the world.'[45] Denison added that Juxon was—in this respect—unlike 'the children of this world.'[46]

Denison stressed the centrality of assurance in the reflexive experience of election. 'Know you not that Jesus Christ is in you, except you be reprobate?' he asked. He urged his congregation to examine, to contemplate and to *act* in order to secure the seal and the salve of assurance:

> If we desire to make a comfortable end, we must endeuour betimes to make our calling and election sure. And indeed how can we expect to die with comfort, while we are unresolued what shall become of our soules in the world to come? And that

---

40. Lake, *Boxmaker's Revenge*, 35.
41. Lake, *Boxmaker's Revenge*, 17–48.
42. Denison, *New Creature*, 13.
43. Denison cited in Lake, *Boxmaker's Revenge*, 34.
44. Lake, *Boxmaker's Revenge*, 390.
45. Denison, *Monument*, 102.
46. Denison, *Monument*, 103.

we may make our calling and election sure, we must observe
these rules.[47]

Denison promoted a sense of Godly entitativity and social exclusivity as
a source of assurance.[48] Meanwhile, he invoked the familiar critical inversions of Godly homiletics, cautioning his auditors that being 'hated' was a
hallmark of Godliness.[49]

Denison ministered to a community that was itself a 'hothouse' of
sectarian controversy. London in the pre-civil war era, as Lake has shown,
was a ferment of religious heterodoxy. Within this ferment, the Godly jock-
eyed for positions on consensually agreed (but continuously negotiated)
spectra of heterodoxy and orthodoxy, insiderliness and outsiderliness. One
example of this process was the trial of John Etherington, a parishioner of
Stephen Denison's. When Etherington began to espouse views that smacked
of Familism, Denison had him ritually humiliated. Etherington was forced
to stand at the pulpit of St. Paul's Cross, a paper pinned to his chest 'contayning the chiefe things of the sentence' whilst he was denounced by Denison
in front of the congregation. Denison called Etherington a 'Viper, Serpent,
Heretique, Familist, and many other vile reproachfull and scandalous
names.'[50] Denison's sermon was published under the title 'The White Wolf'
and was dedicated to King Charles. While Denison emphasized that the
correct condition of the Godly was to be 'irregular,' to the 'children of this
world,' he nonetheless stigmatized those who occupied that space in the
community.[51] These exchanges expose the complexities of Puritan divinity,
the experimental and the disciplinary in close and dynamic juxtaposition.
As Lake writes, a tension existed 'between the primacy of spiritual experience and the demands of stern orthodoxy.' This tension provided the basis
for Como and Lake's 'Puritan public sphere': the dynamism of Puritan divinity before as well as during the period of the interregnum. For Como and
Lake, dissent and heterodoxy was not introjected, it was 'dialectically generated' from within Calvinism itself.[52] This interaction between Denison and
Etherington was used by Lake to depict the internal, anxiety-inducing contradictions at the heart of mainline Puritanism. The Godly were urged by
their clergy to seek assurance, which itself could be found in the experience
of marginality. These same clergy, in the disciplinary mode of Puritanism,

47. Denison, *Monument*, 75.
48. Denison, *Exposition*, 27.
49. Denison, *Monument*, 90–91, 111.
50. Etherington, *Defence of Iohn Etherington*, 13–14.
51. Denison, *Monument*, 102–3.
52. Lake, *Boxmaker's Revenge*, 403.

marginalized those who held heterodox opinions. The Godly clergy presented their flocks with an apparent contradiction. Indeed, as the example of Denison shows, they actively 'enlisted the paradoxes, contradictions and tensions at the heart of . . . Calvinism.'[53] It was this contradiction, for Como, that provided the germ for the ultimately fissiparous and sectarian nature of Reformed Protestantism in England.[54]

Totney's experience encapsulates the anxious response to this contradiction. He would write, in 1655, that he had spent many years pondering the true meaning of Romans 9, declaring it 'the one place of Scripture so called, that . . . I my self, in the daies when I knew not God was much troubled at.'[55] For the remainder of his career, he struggled with the doctrine, angrily denouncing it as 'mad,' seeking to demonstrate through his own exegesis that the 'point of election is not in any original.'[56] But the troubling nature of the doctrine marked Totney. In his actions throughout the period of the Civil War and interregnum, he sought ever more innovative ways of self-identifying with the 'irregular people,' in part by antagonizing and inverting the values of 'the children of the world.'

Totney severed his connection with Denison sometime in 1634 when he refused to have his baby baptized. This decision certainly positioned him at odds with the Church and situated Totney on the anti-formalist spectrum of Reformed Protestantism during this period. These two factors combined offer an impression of Totney as—to use Hessayon's term—'confrontationally Godly.'[57] Totney had encountered a similar paradox to that experienced by Etherington: invited to embrace the ethic of singularity in the preaching of Stephen Denison, he moved towards the radical modes of Godly divinity which best exemplified singularity, only to find Denison himself standing in judgement. Totney, like Etherington, embodied the tendency within Puritanism, through its 'deep, structural instabilities,' to 'generate dissent and heterodoxy from within.'[58] From that point on, Totney gravitated towards modes of divinity which made claims about the revelatory, ineffable, irreducible knowability of the decree of justification.

53. Lake, *Boxmaker's Revenge*, 20–21.

54. Como, *Blown by the Spirit*, 439; Lake, *Boxmaker's Revenge*, 392.

55. Tany, *Second Part*, 22–23.

56. Tany, *Theauraujohn His Theous Ori Apokolipikal*, 44.

57. London Metropolitan Archive, Manuscript 9274, f. 171; Hessayon, *Gold Tried in the Fire*, 2, 59.

58. Lake, *Boxmaker's Revenge*, 403.

SINGULARITY AND BEHMENISM

Nigel Smith and Ariel Hessayon have both identified a number of elements of Behemenism in Totney's writings.[59] Totney shared this interest in Behmenism with a number of his comrades and co-religionists and it served as a point of continuity between himself, John Pordage (with whom he spent the autumn of 1650) and others within the Pordage milieu: Abiezer Coppe, Elizabeth Poole and William Everard.[60]

'First and foremost,' Nigel Smith writes, 'Böhme was prophesying about a truth which was immanent in creation if only each individual could come to sufficiently pure knowledge to see this.'[61] As such, Böhme divided his readership between the enlightened, who were able to intuit the meaning of his prophesies, and the unenlightened, to whom it would read as unintelligible or heretical. The overarching aesthetic of Böhme's writing is one of contrast—between light and dark, wrath and love—such that Daniel Walker assumed he was a Manichean.[62] His conception of God was of two contrasting principles: the wrath of the Father and the 'meek love' of the Son.[63] His cosmological narrative posited a struggle between these principles, leading to seven different stages or 'fountains' of rupture and repair between them.[64] But underlying this apparent dualism was a deeply dialectical cosmology. Böhme wrote that the Spirit emerges from the interaction between the first and second principles. Wisdom is also produced by this interaction.[65] The 'seven fountains' cosmology posits a productive conflict between the binary elements of the Godhead. The productive element emanates throughout creation.[66] This dialectical approach also informs Böhme's anthropology in two senses. Firstly, he posited the existence of two contending principles, 'two seeds' within each human being (cf. Gen 3:15).[67] A version of this 'two seeds' view recurs throughout the writings of George Fox.[68] The seed of the 'woman' is matched by the 'seed of the serpent.' The former corresponds to

59. For an overview of Böhme's thought and its influence in early-modern England, see Hessayon, 'Jacob Böhme's Writings,' 77–98; Smith, *Perfection Proclaimed*, 56, 190–92, 304–7; Gibbons, *Gender in Mystical and Occult Thought*, 129–39.

60. Brod, 'Radical Network,' 1230–252.

61. Smith, *Perfection Proclaimed*, 192.

62. Walker, *Decline of Hell*, 120.

63. Böhme, *Epistles of Jacob Behmen*, 122, 145; Böhme, *Aurora*, 554–57.

64. Böhme, *Aurora*, 318.

65. Böhme, *Of the Becoming Man*, 76.

66. Böhme, *Mysterium Magnum*, 287.

67. Böhme, *Mysterium Magnum*, 124.

68. Fox, *What Election and Reprobation Is*, 30.

faith whilst the latter is associated with reason. As such, only such as have managed to conquer the seed of the serpent within can truly reach the condition of new humanity, a return to the prelapsarian state. Such as these are able to understand the scriptures in a way that is inaccessible to those who have not reached this transformational stage. In addition, he envisioned a version of the Fall in which the androgynous figure of Adam turns towards his own will and his own imagination, creating the rupture of gender and the conflicts which inhere to the embodiment of the immortal soul.[69]

The extent of Jacob Böhme's influence over English Protestantism in the mid-seventeenth century has been debated by scholars in recent decades. Rufus Jones had suggested that Behmenist thought was a stimulus for a range of inward, radical, Godly movements in the period of the interregnum, including the Quakers and the Diggers.[70] This thesis was refuted in the middle of the last century by Geoffrey Nuttall, who contended that Quakerism was a distinctively English, Protestant phenomenon.[71] A happy medium was struck by Gibbons who—identifying no substantial Behmenist impact on the Digger movement and only a half-hearted interaction with Behmenism amongst Quakers—claimed that 'interest in Böhme was widespread, but his influence is exaggerated.'[72] More recently, Ariel Hessayon has suggested that the influence of Behmenism played a 'crucial' part in the emergence of Quaker thought. 'Among those that were influenced by Böhme,' he writes 'were several important figures . . . at a time when Quakerism was taking shape.'[73]

Jacob Böhme's influence can be deduced, not only from how many people read his writings, but also *how* his works were read. Lodowick Muggleton apparently read and was intrigued by Böhme, seeing him as a prophetic voice, but he would also claim that Böhme was 'utterly ignorant.'[74] Lichtenberg is reported to have said of Böhme that '*when he philosophizes, he throws* as a rule an agreeable moonlight over things, which pleases in general but shows no single thing clear.' As such, his writings were a 'picnic in which the author provided the words and the reader provided the sense.'[75] At least in terms of the circle within which Thomas Totney moved, it appears that Lichtenberg's description was valid. Totney, Roger Crab,

69. Boehme, *Mysterium Magnum*, 79.

70. Jones, *Spiritual Reformers*, 208–35.

71. Nuttall, *Holy Spirit in Puritan Faith and Experience*, 16–18.

72. Gibbons, *Gender in Mystical and Occult Thought*, 129.

73. Hessayon, 'Jacob Boehme and the Early Quakers,' 191–223 (quotation at 216).

74. Reeve and Muggleton, *Verae Fidei Floria est Corona Vitae*, 45.

75. Freud, *Jokes and their Relation to the Unconscious*, 86.

John Reeve and John Pordage certainly shared some cosmological and soteriological principles with Böhme but none of them adopted Böhme's systematic thought wholesale. Totney himself 'borrowed' from Böhme with 'little consistency in his borrowing.'[76] As such, tracing Totney's thought to Behmenism as a source would be as schematic as tracing it to a scriptural source. Just as Totney sought out and glossed elements in the scriptures that guaranteed his own *analogia fidei*, so he engaged as creatively with the Behmenist literature that he was aware of. To the extent that there is any pattern to his borrowings, it appears the Totney was most beguiled by those elements in Böhme's thought that emphasized the irreducible contrast between the world of light and dark, flesh and spirit and those elements that emphasized the physical transformation of the enlightened.

John Pordage was already espousing views that savored of Behmenism by 1650, when Totney went to stay with him in Bradfield. Pordage presented a cosmology of contrasts, a 'light world' and a 'dark world' populated by light and dark angels.[77] In the condition of enlightenment, the believer was able to perceive these distinctions. The inward eye was able to perceive, in the world around it, light spirits and dark spirits.[78] Whilst the former were linked—in Pordage's vision—to joy and delight, the latter were linked with the forces of authority: 'pomp, powers, principalities, dignities.'[79] Pordage accounted the struggle of the believer to be an inward and an outward one, the struggle between the forces of persecution and the remnant, echoing in the inward struggle between the seed of the serpent and the seed of the woman.[80] The latter, however, was clear only to those given the mystical gift of inward vision. As such, Pordage, like his contemporary Lawrence Clarkson, presented a prophetic barrier to understanding both external and internal conflicts. Like Böhme, he believed that there were no ways to ever attain certainty that any one Church could guarantee salvation.[81] Like his Behmenist contemporaries Thomas Bromley and John Sparrow, he avowed an ecclesiological scepticism which echoed John Traske's earlier writing.[82]

In Thomas Totney's writing we find the persistent claim of spiritual transformation which underpins Behmenist thought and, in which, Behmenism shares a common legacy with the Familism of Traske's generation. God

76. Smith, *Perfection Proclaimed*, 214.

77. Pordage, *Innocencie Appearing*, 15, 73.

78. Pordage, *Innocencie Appearing*, 73.

79. Pordage, *Innocencie Appearing*, 73, 106, 107.

80. Pordage, *Innocencie Appearing*, 74; *Mundorum Explication*, 72.

81. Pordage, *Innocencie Appearing*, a2v.

82. Bromley, *Way to the Sabbath of Rest*, x; Sparrow 'Preface,' in Böhme, *Aurora*, b1r.

emanates through creation and is present in his creatures.[83] The realization of this in-dwelling of the divine, facilitates a transformation in the individual, allowing him or her to transcend the carnality of post-lapsarian condition. Transformation, in Totney's thought is perennially linked with language. Language, meanwhile, comes to form a kind of 'transcendant signifier.' In this way, language is exposed as useless—as a rational form of communication—but it also becomes a conduit to prophetic truth, since elements of human language themselves have their origins in divine expression.[84]

Totney also maintained the 'radical religious dualisms' that characterise Behmenist literature.[85] The flesh was a prison, the post-lapsarian condition a kind of hell.[86] Like Pordage, Totney created a close association between the social and the cosmological in his reading of Böhme. 'There must be enmity between light and darkness,' he wrote, 'Christ and his Apostles were one truth and the dark world persecuted them.'[87] 'God,' meanwhile was described by Totney as 'uncomixed.'[88]

Like Böhme, Totney accentuated the notion of a divine dialectic in which opposites converge to produce perfection. This informed Totney's claim that, in the prelapsarian state, Adam was genderless.[89] Only in the presence of the darkness could the light be visible. As such, the interaction between the light world and the dark world rendered the Gospel life. Only the enmity of the dark world showed that the Gospel caused the Godly to 'act strangely.' As such, Totney's thought offers a cosmological iteration of Walsham's historical claim: that the enmity of the wicked world—the obloquy of the mob—was necessary for the emergence of Godly identity.[90]

Gibbons notes a tendency amongst those influenced by Behmenism to combine the spiritualist solipsism of the Quakers with an embrace of ceremonies.[91] In this, Behmenism provided a middle course between outward ceremonies and inward rituals. This provides context to Totney's embrace of outward circumcision and inward circumcision—the former anathema to the Quakers, the latter a trope of their writings. For those like Everard

83. Tany, *Second Part*, 50–53.

84. Smith, *Perfection Proclaimed*, 299–307.

85. Smith, *Perfection Proclaimed*, 300.

86. Tany, *Theauraujohn His Theous Ori Apokolipikal*, 15.

87. Tany, *Theauraujohn His Theous Ori Apokolipikal*, a2v; Smith, *Perfection Proclaimed*, 216.

88. Tany, *Law Read*, 6.

89. Tany, *Theauraujohn his Theous Ori Apokolipikal*, 22.

90. Walsham, 'Happiness of Suffering,' 59.

91. Everard, *Some Gospel Treasures Opened*, 522–24.

and Coppe (and later the Philadelphian society), who also embraced both traditions, the ceremonies of baptism and the Eucharist retained some of their shadowy significance but took on new grandeur when employed in the context of a spiritual conversion.[92] There is, moreover, a third layer of prophetic singularity in this tendency. Totney's writing is replete with juxtapositions which denote radical contradictions. 'The virgin is Jesus,' he wrote, 'Christ the son is the Virgin.'[93] 'The lesse learned,' he wrote, are 'the best schollers.'[94] As such, Totney demanded a suspension of logic in order to adduce the prophetic claim. 'The gnomic,' as Smith writes, 'enhances the prophet's personal power.'[95]

There is an important conflation of the intrinsic elements of Behmenism in the thought of Pordage and Totney and the circumstantial effects of prophetic, Behmenism in the context of Bradfield in 1650. Behmenism provided an iteration of Godliness as a condition in which the enlightened individual saw himself in a new light, separate from the evils of the world. But the avowal of Behmenist ideas, and the behaviors which the Bradfield Behmenists exhibited, *also* acted as a mode of resistance, demonstrating their distinctiveness from, their separation from their apparently unenlightened peers. They were prone to prophetic excesses, Pordage himself 'bellowing *like a Bull*, saying that he was called, and must be gone.'[96] The behavior of the Pordage community led to the perception that they were 'beyond the Pale.' They were 'shunned,' as though they 'stank above the ground.' They were compared to Anabaptists, Montanists and Jews. In short, as Christopher Fowler would later write, they were 'monsters.'[97]

TOTNEY'S EXODUS

In 1642, Cromwell was at Huntingdon. Thomas Totney heard him speak. Over a decade later, Totney recalled Cromwell's words and pleaded, in print, for Cromwell to make good on the promises that he had made to his audience that day:

> My Lord *Oliver Cromwel,* I claim protection from you, by vertue
> of the Oath you have sworn unto the People, and confirmed it

92. Gibbons, *Gender in Mystical and Occult Thought,* 5.

93. Tany, *Theauraujohn His Theous Ori Apokolipikal,* 8.

94. Tany, *Theauraujohn His Aurora in Tranlagorum,* 6.

95. Smith, *Perfection Proclaimed,* 303.

96. *Most Faithful Relation of Two Wonderful Passages,* 2.

97. Fowler, *Daemonium Meridianum,* 61, 115.

by many reitterations, vowes, and protestations, as that protest at *Huntington* in the Market-house, my SELF there present, and those words I challenge you to make good which you declared, the words were these: You sought not ours, but us; and our welfare, and to stand with us for the liberty of the Gospel, and the Law of the Land.[98]

Totney had seen the fight against Charles as a fight for the liberty of the Gospel. But in victory, the fight continued. Totney believed that onerous taxation represented 'incroaching' by the state. Christians have a duty, he argued to 'pull down' such tyranny.[99] For Totney, the three principles of Christianity were 'the Gospel, the Law and the liberty of the subject.'[100] In his invasion of parliament, Totney enacted his vision of Godly enslavement in a performative protest. He attached a lock and chain to his own leg, to signify the enslavement of the English people. England featured centrally in Totney's thought, as did the emblematic figure of the Magna Carta. Magna Carta was the foundation that 'gives being to us all.'[101] The 'Norman yoke' functioned as a cipher for the notion of aristocratic oppression and enslavement in a number of Totney's writings.[102] The wealthy are portrayed as conspiratorial in their exploitation of the poor. Liberation from enslavement figured heavily in Totney's eschatological thought also. He was a 'king of Seven Nations' who would lead the Jews out of the exile and towards their restoration.[103] As Hessayon notes, this draws together strands from the Exodus and from the Revelation, to form a kind of 'liberation theology.'[104]

This was not an innovation. The Levellers expressed particular concern for the poor and criticized the wealthy. They couched this position in confessional terms. The 'Norman yoke' was also central to the thought of Totney's contemporaries, the Diggers. They too portrayed 'forraign oppression' as a conspiracy of popery and aristocracy, mounted against Protestantism, anti-clericalism and liberty.[105] For Morrill, the desire for political insurrection was rooted in the Godly's profound affinity with the enslaved Israelites and he cites Cromwell's exuberant correspondence with Robert Hammond

98. Tany, *Theauraujohn High Priest to the Iewes*, 6.

99. Tany, *Nations Right in Magna Charta*, 5.

100. Tany, *Nations Right in Magna Charta*, 4.

101. Tany, *Nations Right in Magna Charta*, 1.

102. Tany, *Theauraujohn High Priest to the Iewes*, 1.

103. Muggleton, *Acts of Witnesses of the Spirit*, 44.

104. Hessayon, 'Thomas Totney,' in *Oxford Dictionary of National Biography*.

105. Winstanley, *Watchword to the City of London*, 7–8; *Appeal to the House of Commons*, 4.

as evidence.[106] The commonality between the two is perhaps most evident in the frequent appeals made by both modern Liberation Theologians and radicals like Totney to the exemplar of the Israelite deliverance from Egypt. For Coffey, it was the shared belief that 'redemption had a socio-political as well as a spiritual dimension.'[107]

There is, when it comes to Totney, an additional point of similarity. The work of Liberation Theologians like Segundo and Gutierrez speaks to the underlying concern with holy nationhood in the New Testament context. The concept of the Kingdom of God that these thinkers engaged with was a transformative but earthly condition. The Liberation Theologians did not desire (only) *political liberation* from the oppressors of the people. Rather, in John Segundo's words, they sought to facilitate the emergence of 'a new humanity.'[108] The deliverance of workers from the condition of alienation would have, they believed, a transformative effect.

Both Totney and Segundo's understandings of liberation have a common root in Exodus. While the Exodus narrative is concerned—as Walzer and Coffey note—with national manumission, it is also concerned with the *separation* of Israel from the contamination of Egypt, the rendering of Israel as singular. The Israelites were ordered to inaugurate and maintain ethnic identifiers. The penalty for refusing to maintain these markers—imperilling the unity, cohesion and particularity of Israel within Egypt—was death. Liberty begat purity, whilst purity begat liberty (Exod 12). 'Let my people go,' said the Lord 'that they may worship me' (Exod 7:16). Those who compromized the coherence of Israel or who threatened Israel with miscegenation would be 'cut off' (Exod 12:15, 19; 31:14). The combination of freedom with purity and of enslavement with miscegenation would be rehearsed in the narratives of Ezra and Nehemiah. This symbiosis, implicit in the text, was recognized by the Godly. The inhabitants of the Massachussets Bay Colony understood their project as mirroring the experience of the Israelites, partly in the sense of escaping enslavement, but also in their desire to establish impermeable boundaries between the saints and their enemies: 'liberty and purity of Worship.'[109]

For Totney, 'liberation' constituted the throwing off of the yoke of tyranny. This figure was closely associated in Totney's thought, not only with 'liberation,' but with a broader trope of separation and refinement. By this logic, 'tirany' constituted, not only an invasion, but also a kind of *mixture*. In

106. Morrill, 'Liberation Theology?,' 27–48.

107. Coffey, *Exodus and Liberation*, 10.

108. Segundo, *Theology for Artisans of a New Humanity*, 2:6–8, 12–14, 33–42.

109. Gregory, *Puritanism in the Old World and in the New*, 251.

his claims about over-reaching autocracy, Totney argues that 'tirany' represents both an 'incroachment' and 'a conjoining.' Charles was 'a Conjoiner to himself of that, that is not his.'[110] As such, it was the duty of Christians to 'cut off' Charles and to 'cut off' all forms of 'tirany.' Charles being 'cut off'—like the head of Israel, the palm branch—purified Israel, in Totney's thought.[111] Eventually, Cromwell, too, was 'cut off' from Israel.[112]

Purification and the eradication of filth was an overarching concern of every aspect of his writing. The 'Hebrew' that he claimed to be able to speak was distinguished from the Hebrew studied at the universities in that it was free from 'handling, and mingling . . . adding and adjoining.'[113] Totney was a goldsmith. He worked to eradicate impurities in gold. When he envisioned God, he envisioned a goldsmith who—as Malachi predicted—would refine humanity as gold is refined, 'burning away the dross.'[114] Totney—as Hessayon has shown—was also immersed in the literature of alchemy, and adopted a range of terms which described the purification and 'rectification,' of substance.[115] In a more Behmenist mood, he would refer to the separation of the light world from the dark. Tyranny was an impurity in the lives of the saints, an invasion, an uninvited presence, just as the serpent was an uninvited presence in Eve's womb, according to the Behemist creation mythology. The role of the saints, therefore, was to celebrate their liberation in the Gospel, not necessarily by *defeating* tyranny, or *critiquing* tyranny, but by *separating* from tyranny.

Separation undergirds all of Totney's thought. 'If [the Godly] separate not they will all fall,' he wrote. Ethical miscegenation was associated with contagion. 'Depart their places and company lest ye be partakers in their plague,' he wrote.[116] Nowhere is this ethos of separation more evident than in Totney's perseverative lament for London, which appends his *Edict Royal* of 1654:

> Separate, Separate, Separate, Separate, Separate, Separate, Separate. Come out of her, Come out of her, Come out of her, Come out of her, Come out of her, Come out of her, Come out of her, least ye be partakers of her plague . . . flye out of her Cities, flye out of her Cities, flye out of her Cities, flye out of her Cities, flye

---

110. Tany, *Nations Right in Magna Charta*, 5.

111. Tany, *Nations Right in Magna Charta*, 1–6.

112. Tany, *My Edict Royal*, 5, 14.

113. Tany, *Theauraujohn His Aurora*, 5.

114. Tany, *Theauraujohn His Theous Ori Apokolipikal*, 34.

115. Hessayon, *Gold Tried in the Fire*, 344.

116. Tany, *My Edict Royal*, 11–12.

out of her Cities, flye out of her Cities, flye out of her Cities.
... Touch not her trading, touch not her trading, touch not her
trading, touch not her trading, touch not her trading, touch not
her trading, touch not her trading.[117]

BY LEARNING TO MADNESS

At the start of 1653, upon being released from prison, Totney took a vow
of silence, refusing to communicate for twenty-one days. For Totney, separation was not simply a matter of physical relocation. Alongside physical
sequestration, Thomas Totney engaged in a discursive endeavor, rendering
himself—by his words and deeds—as alien, deviant, irreducibly other in the
eyes of his peers.

Totney refused—like Traske before him and his contemporaries in the
Quaker tradition—to accept consensual, value-laden binaries of good/bad,
strong/weak. For Totney, the most familiar forum for this lay in his repudiation of learnedness. Totney accounted himself as 'unskilled.' In 1652, he
offered a 'disputative challenge' to the *'universities of Oxford and Cambridge,
and the whole hirach. of Roms clargical priests.'*[118] 'Take notice scholars,' he
wrote. 'I am not book-learned, but I am heart-knowledged.'[119] He railed
against those who held university education to be a demarcation of superiority. This, of course, correlates with the broadly class-conscious elements of
Totney's thought. But it also had a theological component. For Totney—as
for Fox—lack of formal education guaranteed a *tabula rasa* upon which
revelatory knowledge could be projected. 'I had no learning,' Totney wrote,
*'but in seven daies when I was a part I received my divine learning by inspira-
tion so that my light is over all languages.'*[120] This contention draws implicit
parallels between Totney's experience and that of the apostles at Pentecost.
The apostles were also privy to divine knowledge which appeared to their
auditors as eccentricity (Acts 2:15). Totney claimed to have 'knowledge
without any books.'[121] Böhme wrote that his 'work came not from *Reason*,
but from the impulse of the Spirit.'[122] But Totney also believed that unlearnedness was an intrinsic good. He promised to 'unlearn the learning' of the

---

117. Tany, *My Edict Royal*, 28.

118. Tany, *Theauraujohn High Priest to the Iewes*, 1.

119. Tany, *Theauraujohn His Aurora*, a2r.

120. Tany, *Theauraujohn His Aurora*, 3.

121. Tany, *Second Part*, 20.

122. Tany, *Second Part*, 20.

'priests.'[123] Totney believed his unlearnedness placed him in a favourable position in relation to St. Paul's prophetic claim that 'Gods glory would confound the learned wise men.'[124] In this, Totney made seemingly contradictory claims. Conversely, the Gospel made him 'act strangely.'[125]

One of the most notable elements of Totney's writing is his idiosyncratic use of language. His writings are populated with bursts of—what Totney claimed to be—Hebrew. Totney claimed that *his* Hebrew was different from the kind spoken by the Hebraists of the day. Totney elaborated in great detail on a mode of linguistics which bore little relation to any academic study of the period. He made assertions about the ancient origins of different letters and sounds, even attributing ethical significance to different pronunciations:

> I write in Mophes, that is in the Medish method then I write k
> for coffe which is strong now from a radax.[126]

Indeed, he even disputed the refinement of Menasseh ben Israel's Hebrew. In this regard, Totney's ministry bares comparison with that of his contemporary John Robins. When Robert Bacon was led into the guest-room of a merchant's house in Fleet street, he found

> In the Room was a Bed, and [John Robins] sitting up in it, speaking as I said before, and claping his hands with exceeding seeming height of confidence; but the words he spake I did not understand, only they seemed to me, to be a mixture of Latine, and some other tongues, (they said Hebrew) and all other Languages) I confess, I remembred he mentioned oft Melchise deck, the High Priest, or Priest-hood, the name Judah, and Jesus, with such zeal, that the fire seemed to me, even to sparkle out of his eyes.[127]

This tendency is also evident in the work of Joshua Garment, who referred to himself as 'Josherbah, tauquan, tauquan, tauquarden, pistauvah, Jah, pahstauvah, Jah, achor, ab, sha, bah, Jah.'[128]

This use of language attests to yet another fixation with purity and separation. It was 'refined,' Totney wrote. The revelatory source of his knowledge of 'Hebrew' rendered it superior to the Hebrew of learned academics.

123. Böhme, *Aurora*, 54; Tany, *Second Part*, 20.

124. Tany, *Second Part*, a3v.

125. Tany, *Theauraujohn His Theous Ori Apokolipikal*, a2r.

126. Tany, *Second Part*, 7; *Nations Right in Magna Charta*, 7.

127. Bacon, *Taste of the Spirit*, 42.

128. Garment, *Hebrew Deliverance at Hand*, 7.

Their Hebrew, he claimed, was 'the tenth derivacy of and from the Hebrew radiases.'[129] But at the same time, his use of an impenetrable language ('a quest for an Adamic language which ended in solipsism') facilitated the erection of insurmountable barriers between himself and his unenlightened peers. This use of 'garbled' and 'glossolalian' language as a mode of resistance is a familiar theme of other religious and social movements.[130]

Indeed, the excesses of Totney's behavior could be accounted a kind of antic disposition. This was certainly the view of some of his contemporaries. Smith describes Totney's behavior as the mark of an 'annointed madman,' the 'pose of a divinely instituted madness.'[131] In this respect, Smith compares Totney with Abiezer Coppe. Richard Baxter was able to penetrate Coppe's 'pose,' and wrote that 'some will say he is a mad man: It is otherwise as may be known by those that will speak with him.' The process of situating oneself as the 'fool' served to produce 'a penetrating satire on orthodox learning.'[132] But for those who wished it, it also offered the opportunity to be the object of scorn in a wicked world. This, as Bauman has suggested, played *some* part in the development of Quaker piety.[133]

For Thomas Coryat, outsiderliness, Jewishness and madness were deeply enmeshed. Totney, at times (at least) appeared to court the suggestion that he was 'lunatick.' Totney explicitly and implicitly made reference to his own madness. 'Know I am mad,' he wrote. 'And ye declare me so to be.'[134] But he also understood and negotiated with the tradition within Christianity of the holy fool, juxtaposing sanctity and insanity. 'Faith and obedience was and is madness unto the world,' he wrote.[135] 'What will this mad man do?' Totney imagined the people saying of Noah. 'Will he cause this Vessel to go upon the dry Land?'[136] Paul too was accounted mad: 'much learning doth make thee mad,' Festus told him. Totney saw himself in this image.[137] But (typically) he inverted the trope. 'By madness I came to knowing,' he wrote.[138]

---

129. Tany, *Theauraujohn His Aurora*, 4–5.

130. Tenneson, *Authority and Resistance in Language*; Condé, 'Creolite without the Creole Language,' 101–10; Pollard, *Dread Talk*, xiii.

131. Smith, *Perfection Proclaimed*, 56, 217.

132. Smith, *Perfection Proclaimed*, 345.

133. Baumann, *Let Your Words Be Few*, 43.

134. Tany, *Nations Right in Magna Charta*, 8.

135. Tany, *High News for Hierusalem*, 2.

136. Tany, *High News for Hierusalem*, 2.

137. Tany, *High News for Hierusalem*, 2.

138. Tany, *Theous Ori Apokolipikal*, 62–63.

This strategy of ethical unlearnedness (or even of lunacy), as a way of resisting, of denoting difference, was effective. Moses Wall despaired of Totney, writing:

> I skill not the man, nor his spirit; in his writing he offends against all rules of Grammar, Geography, Genealogy, History, Chronology, Theology &c so far as I understand them.[139]

Basset Jhones observed that he was 'the accounted madman of the times.'[140] And yet, at other times, it appeared that he was cogent, rational and thoughtful. He was widely read and had at least some facility with languages. On this basis, Hessayon has questioned the widely assented view that he was a 'madman.' Nicholas McDowell's work *The English Imagination*, has drawn attention to instances in which apparently subaltern groups or individuals can actually be read as participants in highly intellectual and academic discourses, satirizing and defining themselves against constructed ideals of learnedness. In a number of instances, he claims, those who were apparently 'illiterate mechanick persons' in fact demonstrated their aptitude for 'scrambling and misapplying' the 'languages of the dominant culture . . . for the purposes of parody and subversion.'[141] These contortions of language and logic, in fact, were sometimes apprehended by contemporary commentators as attempts to evade meaning or—in another sense—to widen the epistemic gulf between the Godly and the ungodly majority. Describing Totney and his kind, John Tickell, wrote:

> They will put themselves on all expressions, ways and windings, to keep themselves from being known . . . but their own shall know their meaning, and so may you when you have once got their Key.[142]

If we read Totney's divinity as being rooted in a sense of the value of outsiderliness, McDowell's analysis takes on new, 'religious' significance. The contention that Totney was nothing more than a madman—and the location of Totney outside of the parameters of sensible discussion—has persisted up to the present day. Most historians who have addressed the Totney scandal have offered the weighty caveat that Totney was 'clearly mentally deranged.'[143]

---

139. Letter from Moses Wall to Samuel Hartlib, June 18, 1652, Sheffield, 34/4/1A (Setright, 'Moses Wall,' 206).

140. Jones, 'Letter of Queries to Theaurau John Tanniour,' 1.

141. McDowell, *English Radical Imagination*, 9.

142. Tickell, *Bottomles Pit Smoaking in Familisme*, 39.

143. Hill, 'John Reeve and the Origins of Muggletonianism,' 69.

If this was the intention behind Totney's actions, then it appears he was an even better strategist than tactician.

Totney followed the familiar path of Reformed Protestants of this era, seeking out and occupying the discursive locus of the oppressed, persecuted and enslaved. He offered a Beatitudes based 'preferential option for the poor,' writing that 'ye poor, ye weak, ye nothings in your selves … the Spirit of God doth rest upon yee.'[144] Totney posited a Foxean dichotomy between the learned leaders of the Church and the 'poor members of Christ,' the 'poor upright, simple Innosent and harmless men.'[145] He counted himself amongst the latter. As Walsham has pointed out, for those who believed that God's favor rested on the poorest and meanest sort—that with the cross came the crown—it became incumbent to cultivate 'crises.' This need required some to generate acts of 'symbolic suffering.'[146] Perhaps the most notable example of this tendency in the life of Thomas Totney occurred in the aftermath of his invasion of the House of Commons and the subsequent arrest. After his examination, Totney attached shackles to his own foot, asserting that it represented the captivity of the English people. He was, apparently, instructed so to do by Jehovah:

> The Lord commanded me for to buy a lock and a chain, saying, I do binde thee to stand by them, and as this chain and lock is my burden upon thee, so are them assembled rebells against me and also against the Gospel, Law, and all good mens liberty: thou shalt keep the lock and give them the key, and I will bring again by thee Englands liberty: so the lock is on my legg night and day till approach our liberty.[147]

This passage is intriguing for two reasons. Firstly, it provides one example of Totney's use of his own body as the locus for acts of resistance. Second, it provides a dramatic and conspicuous example of Totney's self-presentation as the beleaguered, embattled, pariah: he places the shackles, after all, upon himself.

These were familiar themes. But while Totney asserted that he was of the poor, he also constructed a fantastical genealogy for himself, linking himself—genealogically—with the aristocracy and even with royalty. It is to the genealogical theme in Totney's writing that we turn next.

144. Tany, *Second Part*, 52.
145. Tany, *Second Part*, 8.
146. Walsham, 'Happiness of Suffering,' 59.
147. Tany, *My Edict Royal*, 20.

DEMOLISHED FAMILIES

Totney claimed a lineage which guaranteed his inheritance of the seat of the Viscounsie of Northumberland, the throne of Naples and Sicily and Jerusalem. He used this constructed lineage as the basis for a wider, eschatologically inflected history of England. He suggested that, as a disenfranchized nobleman, his lot was reflective of a wider and more pernicious history. His family, he contended, were of true Saxon stock, but had fallen victim to Norman tyranny. His parents 'were poor through the Tyrannical power reigning in the *Norman* Yoak, [which] subdued the Noble *Saxon* Line.'[148] The 'Noble Saxon line', meanwhile, could be traced back to Biblical Israel, through:

> Media, Persia, and Egypt; then into Captivity by Titus Vespasian, and so to Rome, from Rome to France in Charlemaigne, from that descent to Henry the seventh.[149]

Here, the Normans serve as a surrogate for the timeless forces of tyranny described in the prophetic texts of the Hebrew Bible. The Saxons, meanwhile appear in the mode of Biblical Israel: noble, Godly and persecuted. All of this served, in the thought of Thomas Totney, to delineate an eschatological struggle: the struggle against the great, monolithic, atemporal force of 'Babylon.'[150] Ethnicity is grounded in ethics. Tyranny is associated with miscegenation. The purity of the English people is corrupted by the interpolation of the Norman line, and the result is enslavement, mendacity and persecution. Here again, manumission and purity interact.

In one sense, it is understandable that the disappointment Totney felt with the outcome of the great Godly struggles of the 1640s would be redressed by a reconfiguration of the purpose and manner and locus of the Godly struggle. Retreat into myth and euphemism is a well trodden route for those disappointed in their expectation of transformational, eschatological events.[151] For Totney, though, the narration of a counter-factual history served a valuable function in fostering an identity of resistance. To those who would accuse him of fabricating his lineage, Totney was ready with a reply: the Norman conspirators had destroyed the records of his aristocratic genealogy, 'demolishing whole Families.'[152]

This apocalyptic narrative, supplanting Normans and Saxons in the roles of Babylon and Israel, shared similarities with the apocalyptic writing

148. Tany, *Theauraujohn High Priest to the Iewes*, 1.

149. Tany, *Theauraujohn His Aurora*, 27.

150. Tany, *Law Read*, 1–3; *Second Part*, 10, 29.

151. Festinger, *When Prophecy Fails*, 4–5.

152. Tany, *Theauraujohn High Priest to the Iewes*, 8.

of Gerard Winstanley. Winstanley's writing reflects an allochronic sense of history, associating the struggle of the plebeian Englishman with the struggle of the Israelite slaves in Egypt; William the Conqueror with Pharaoh and with Charles I; the task of digging St. George's Hill with the building of the Temple.[153] In doing this, Totney and Winstanley created a kind of guerilla rhetoric, undermining and rendering contingent those absolute, unconditional, totalizing truths at the heart of the feudal society. Totney went further than Winstanley. The Anglocentric eschatology which situated the Normans as the great oppressors was a jumping off point. Totney unraveled the conventional story of England, moving through centuries of history, and establishing an entirely contrasting counter-discourse. Princes are rendered as paupers, paupers as princes. Within *this* narrative, Totney claimed kingship for *himself*, and not only kingship of England. He demanded:

> the Crown of FRANCE, as lineally descended from CHARLES of Castile, who was son-in-law unto CHARLES the Great. Next, I demand the Crown both of REME and ROME, from my ancient Parent Pope NICOLAS of the House of AUSTRIA, who married the Flamina of Flandriah; in whose RIGHT lies included the TITLE unto NAPLES, SISSILIAH, and JERUSALEM.[154]

Prophetic literature, and in particular apocalyptic literature, is often hallmarked with a muddling of chronology. Totney—like Winstanley—located himself, simultaneously, in the context of the struggle against Stuart autocracy, in the eleventh-century struggle against Norman oppression, in the struggle against Egypt, and in the ultimate, eschatological restoration of the Jews. The authors of Daniel spoke of the struggle against Seleucid hegemony by inhabiting the figure of an anti-Babylonian struggle. The author of Revelation inhabited the role of the authors of Daniel. Successive generations of apocalyptic revolutionaries have occupied the role of Israel as described in Revelation. As Thomas Luxon has demonstrated, the allegorical self which situated the justified Christian in the space between the foreshadowings of the Hebrew Bible and a future, fully realized, elect being, was particularly prominent in the soteriological thinking of Totney's period. For Luxon, this explained the emergence of strategies for the reassertion of *tangible*, concretized distinctions between the elect and the Godly. For both William Franklin and Thomas Totney, this included an assertion of spiritual

153. Winstanley, *Watchword to the City of London*, 7–8; *Appeal to the House of Commons*, 4.

154. Tany, *ThauRam Tanjah*, br.

transformation. For Totney, it also appears to have included the wearing of exotic clothing, circumcision and the avowal of a fantastical genealogy.[155]

There are the shades of the skimmington in Totney's use of genealogy. Using himself as the locus of the parody, Totney confronted his reader and his auditor with the unsettling possibility that the crowned heads of Europe and of the world could fall to the condition of a mad, and 'brain-sick' beggar.[156] In the context of the regicide, the contingency of earthly authority was already a troubling realization for many of Totney's contemporaries. As such, his claims were more of an assault, a confrontation and an auto-anathematization than they may appear at first glance. But for Totney, assaulting and unsettling his peers was more than madness and more than mere crankishness. It was a labor in the vineyard of Gospel liberty.

MAKING HOLES IN CHURCH WINDOWS

On March 8, 1652, Thomas Totney 'sealed an edict to the people' entitled *High News for Hierusalem*. The text included some guidelines for the Godly on how they were to greet each other. Kissing was strictly banned:

> For by kissing is caused a fermentation whereby the body is diseased or disquieted by the breath received from any one or other. . . . For breathing in one another and to one another is the mother Begetrix of all lustful brutishness. So much for your Salutes or kissing one another.[157]

As an alternative mode of greeting, Totney proposed the following:

> The woman shall stand upright if her body wil bear it, and with her hands hanging down upon her hips, that is the woman's posture alwaies and all times; if the womans body will not bear uprightness, then she is but to move that way prescribed; the man in his Salute unto the woman, when he meeteth her, he shall a little bow himself in his head and body a little, and he shall lay both his hands upon the womans arms above the elbows, and so shall bear the woman a little on his left side; and this is thy manner.[158]

155. Luxon, 'Not I, but Christ,' 899–937.

156. *Perfect Diurnall* 265 (1655) 4061 (Hessayon, *Gold Tried in the Fire*, 376).

157. Tany, *High News for Hierusalem*, 14.

158. Tany, *High News for Hierusalem*, 13.

The microscopic actions which made up the Puritan character or the Puritan culture infrequently reached the page. Nonetheless, from those infrequent references that survive, it is clear that Godly men and women of the seventeenth century were 'set apart' from their neighbors in their 'behaviour, dress and speech.'[159] Behaviors as microscopic as 'faces, gestures, motions, salutations' functioned as non-verbal exhibitions of Godly self-identification.[160] The goal of these practices was to dramatise the separation from the unregenerate. As such, unusual, idiosyncratic behavior served an instrumental function: to create distinguishing features, to create a Godly identity. Totney himself articulated an awareness that mere words were not sufficient to constitute an ideological position, nor an identity. Recalling the days of the Civil War in Shelford, he described the process by which an attitude of resistance was manifested in deed and action:

> Have we not all ingaged against Popery, and to show the zeal we
> have against it, we have made holes in all our Church Windows,
> in show of abolishment.[161]

Totney often 'made holes in Church windows.' On December 30, 1654, in response, perhaps, to attempts by Parliament to crown Cromwell, Totney tried to storm the Palace of Westminster single-handed. He was apprehended whilst flailing a rusty sword. Disarmed, he was taken away to be interrogated by the Speaker. From there he was taken to the Gatehouse and was later examined by the Committee for the regulation of printing.[162] His armed attack on the Cromwellian state was as brief as it was ignominious. But Totney's resistance was not limited to the kind that required a rusty sword.

Throughout the accounts (both first person and third person) of Totney's career, we find numerous references to quotidian acts of resistance. When brought before the Speaker, for example, Totney refused to remove his hat. In this regard he exemplified the 'rhetorical impoliteness' which is identifiable in the behavior of his contemporaries: the Quakers, and the Diggers.[163] Inviting this comparison was, itself, a choice to self-identify with a marginalized group. At times, Totney's actions enraged and outraged public morality. He stated that the purpose of his preaching was to 'smite' his auditor.[164] This is most evident in his treatment of scripture. Totney was

159. Como, *Blown by the Spirit*, 29.

160. Earle, *Microcosmographie*, h6r; Thurloe, *State Papers*, 5:371; Crouch, *Posthuma Christiana*, 153; Thomas, 'Introduction', 1–15.

161. Tany, *Theauraujohn his Theous Ori Apokolipikal*, 77.

162. Tany, *My Edict Royal*, 12; *Perfect Diurnall* 265 (1655) 4061.

163. Baumann, *Let Your Words Be Few*, 43.

164. Tany, *My Edict Royal*, 14.

regularly equivocal about the impeachability of scripture. He argued that translation had eroded the meaning of the sacred words.[165] Moreover, fixation on the translated (and therefore non-sacred) word of scripture resulted—according to Totney—in idolatry.[166] These assertions served to provoke antagonism from a Christian perspective (since Totney was undermining the sacrality of the Bible) and also from a Protestant perspective (since Protestantism vaunted the vernacularization of scripture as its founding success). Totney was called upon, by Jehovah, to destroy his earthly possessions. This he proceeded to do:

> The Lord commanded me to burn his Tent onely save the Tent
> staff, and burn the Priests garments, with all that I had; where-
> upon I began to burn many things, and my own books.[167]

When Totney began to burn his Bible, 'the multitude began to rage.'[168] Totney was forced to escape via boat. Onlookers hurled stones at him as he was rowed across the Thames.

For all that Totney protested a doctrinal validation for his burning of the Bible (he feared that it had become 'an idol'), he knew that this act would lead to public outrage.[169] In retelling the story, Totney revelled in the detail surrounding his rejection by his peers *moreso* than in the detail of the act itself. For Totney, this act—a demonstrative act of sacrilege and public indecency—served as an assertion of his refusal to be governed either by King or convention. When Totney attempted to co-opt the services of a bystander, to help him to burn his possessions, Jehovah altered his instruction:

> Then the Lord said: Stay thine hand thy sacrifice is accepted;
> then I burnt no more.[170]

This is a direct echo of the words addressed to Abraham in Genesis 22. Totney saw this action—the destruction of his property including the Bible—as an echo of the sacrifice of Isaac. Totney knew that God's instruction contravened the conventional, earthly, ethical norms. In this sense, and in the violent nature of the act, Totney's experience called across the ages to the *Akedah*. The call to sacrifice Isaac was a call to Abraham to move beyond

---

165. Tany, *Theauraujohn His Aurora*, 26.
166. Tany, *My Edict Royal*, 6.
167. Tany, *My Edict Royal*, 9.
168. Tany, *My Edict Royal*, 10.
169. Tany, *My Edict Royal*, 6.
170. Tany, *My Edict Royal*, 10.

the Pale of social acceptability.[171] When God called Totney to burn his Bible, the call had that same quality. Unlike Abraham, however, Totney was not fully spared.

THE JEW OF THE TRIBE OF REUBEN

'Hear *O ye Iewes my Brethren*,' Thomas Totney wrote. 'I am a Jew of the Tribe of *Reuben*.'[172] The genealogical significance of this statement is expounded elsewhere in the Totney corpus. Totney traced his lineage back to ancient Israel:

> My radax was Aaron, Moses his brother, the Lords Priest; then Zachariah was my Radax, whom they slew betwixt the Temple and the Altar; after this I was carried away with Jeconiah into Babylon in that seventy yeers captivity, then I was Priest in Jerusalem in Hosha my Radax, and continued in the Priests Office till the second Captivity, then I was carryed into Egypt by Pharaoh Necho, and returned with Zorobabel in the time of Salmanasser, not Jeconiah but Hosai; but the Hebrew is translated wrong in that state, as I shall make appear when I come to unfold the patched Translations, vilifying some Genealogies, and Deifying some, and some left quite out, that are extant in other Records in the Eastern Countries.[173]

Still, one could argue, these contentions about Totney's lineage may be read as metaphorical or mythological, not relating to any literal meaning of descent. But Totney addresses this issue too. At several junctures, he makes a clear reference to 'the Jews by line' in order, specifically, to distinguish contemporary Jewry from the metaphorical estate of 'spiritual Israel.'[174] More explicitly still, Totney writes in sympathy to 'the Jews my brethren according to the flesh.'[175] He makes explicit his association not only with Biblical Israel but precisely with the Jews in the condition of diaspora. 'I that have been scattered with you,' he wrote 'am sensible of our estate.'[176] Elsewhere, in the *High News for Hierusalem*, Totney regularly uses the word 'our' to refer to

---

171. Kierkegaard, *Fear and Trembling*, 28; Kafka, 'Abraham,' 40.

172. Tany, *I Proclaime*, brs; *High News for Hierusalem*, 1; *Theauraujohn His Aurora*, 58.

173. Tany, *Theauraujohn His Aurora*, 26.

174. Tany, *Theauraujohn His Aurora*, 11.

175. Tany, *Theauraujohn His Theous Ori Apokolipikal*, 42.

176. Tany, *Theauraujohn His Aurora*, 26.

'our Elokim,' 'our tribes,' 'our fathers.'[177] In this instance, it should be remembered that Totney was addressing the Jewish community in Amsterdam. He was *not* referring tangentially or metaphorically to a Biblical trope. He was talking directly to Jews who were his contemporaries, who followed the rabbinic tradition, who were in diaspora and (perhaps most importantly) who were familiar with but not convinced by the message of the Gospel.

What did Thomas Totney mean when he said that he was a Jew? A Jew was one who was born of Jewish stock. A Jew also meant one who observed the rituals of the ceremonial law. But in the seventeenth century, and particular in the years leading up to the tacit readmission of the Jews, the question 'what is the Jew?' became more pressing. Philo-semites like Dury attempted to untangle the confessional from the genealogical definition of the Jew, in doing so to rescue something like a Protestant, 'rational reformed,' Jew: the Caraite.[178] A Jew, to Thomas Coryat, meant 'a *weather beaten warp-faced* fellow, sometimes a phrenticke and lunaticke person, sometimes one discontented.'[179] For some of those engaged in the readmission debate, it was an opportunity to reconstitute the thousand-year old spectre of the evil Jew. For William Prynne, a Jew was—on the one hand—'murmuring, mutinous, rebellious, seditious' and—on the other—'the saddest spectacle of divine justice and humane misery.'[180] For some, the holiness and the reprobation of the Jew intertwined to form a helix of singularity.[181] For Return Hebdon, the Jews were the people who 'for their Creators sake are hated and afflicted of all other people.'[182] These dichotomous claims provide some context to Totney's own definition of a Jew.

Race was a concept that was still in its early infancy during the period of Totney's ministry. But the development of a concept of racial difference during this period had a profound, hegemonic function. Racial thought emerged, in part, from an attempt to create greater ideational distance between 'barbarian' humanity and 'civilized' humanity in the era of European imperialism.[183] Colin Kidd makes the important point that theology provided the grammar for negotiating perceived differences that Christians encountered during this period.[184] The identification of racial, 'blood' dis-

---

177. Tany, *High News for Hierusalem*, 5, 7.

178. Popkin, *Third Force*, 365; Dury, 'Epistolicall Discourse,' C2r–3r.

179. Coryat, *Coryat's Crudities*, 232.

180. Prynne, *Short Demurrer*, 1, 79.

181. Selden, *Table Talk*, 69.

182. Hebdon, *Guide to the Godly*, 80.

183. Arendt, *Origins of Totalitarianism*, 134; Poliakov, *Aryan Myth*.

184. Kidd, *Forging of the Races*, 19.

tinctions between Jews and Christians served to assuage anxieties about the potential for ethical parity between Jews and Christians, which may have been heightened during periods of awareness of other, more radically different groups.[185]

The Biblical account of racial distinction and—in particular—the ethnic distinctiveness of the Jews played a crucial role in Totney's understanding of what it meant to be a Jew. Here again, Totney could find an account of race which enmeshed ethics and ethnicity. The Bible, as Kidd points out, is largely 'colour-blind.' The basis for the racial interpretations of scripture in the seventeenth century 'collapsed race into lineage.' This opened the door to 'the importation of divinely authorized categories of blessed and cursed.'[186] The curse of Adam, after all, was generational. Lineage was a central concern of Totney's writings. In reading the Old Testament he was compelled by the notion that special privileges—most obviously those associated with priesthood—descended generationally. On the same basis, he saw the ethical character of the Jews as being a matter of descent. From this point, he believed it possible to derive knowledge about lineage, ethnicity and descent from the ethical conduct and the social condition of himself and others. One clue as to what Totney *meant* when he claimed that he was a Jew can be found in his references to other people whom he identified as Jews. In one challenging passage he made explicit his understanding that the 'Quakers' were 'Jews.' Totney wrote that the Quakers:

> ARE the Children of Abraham, Isaac, and Jacob; who ARE circumcised in Heart; the JEWISH Race in descent, unto whom the Promise was made.[187]

Other references to the Quakers in the same text provide some important insight into this question. Totney wrote that the Quakers were 'scorned' by men. He referred to them as his 'weak brethren,' 'weak babes' and 'Lambs.'[188] Totney saw the disparagement of the Quakers at the hands of the majoritarian culture to be a designation of Quaker sanctity but also of their 'Jewishness.'

In early modern England, the notion that Jews had physically distinctive racial characteristics still prevailed. 'I knew you to be a Jew,' says the character of Christian to the character of Jew in Sebastian Munster's *The Messias of the Christians and the Jewes*, 'from the form of your face.' Jews

---

185. Adelman, *Blood Relations*.

186. Kidd, *Forging of Races*, 21.

187. Tany, *Tharam Taniah*, 1.

188. Tany, *Tharam Taniah*, br.

were believed to be 'black,' to have 'a peculiar colour of face.' But the physical soma of the Jews was believed to be determined, not by their lineage or genetics, but rather by their religion and morality. Immoral figures were described as being 'black of face,' and 'of evil shape.'[189] In Robert Daborne's *A Christian Turn'd Turk*, Voada wonders whether 'Religion move any thing in the shapes of men.' Rabshake replies:

> Altogether. What's the reason else that the Turke & Iew is troubled (for the most part) with gowty legges, and fiery nose, to express their heart-burning: whereas the Puritan is a man of vpright calfe, and cleane nosthrill.

As such, early modern Englishmen could expect that a change of religion might change their physiology. 'You should turne Christian,' says Voada to Rabshake, 'then your calfe swels vpward mightily.'[190] With a change of ethical conduct, perhaps a 'black-moore' could be 'turned white.'[191] The infrequency with which people were witnessed to have been physiologically transformed was attributed to the obduracy of the Jews.[192] Anxiety about the contagiousness of Judaism informed the debate on the readmission. The fear that prominent figures could mysteriously 'turn Jew' invaded the nightmares of English Protestants.[193]

This was particularly pertinent for those Protestants who were focused on the irreducible differentiation between the justified and the unregenerate. John Traske believed that the experience of conversion had a physically transformative effect on the justified. William Franklin, a contemporary of Totney's, believed that—in justification—his body had been destroyed and replaced with a glorified body, his tent replaced with a temple.[194] Drawing clear, unproblematized distinctions between the topos of 'the Jew' as an ethnic or as an ethical category in Totney's thought, in other words, is not possible.

189. Guevara, *Chronicle*, 110.

190. Daborne, *Christian Turn'd Turk*, c4r.

191. Calvert, *Blessed Jew of Morocco*.

192. Holmberg, *Jews in the Early Modern English Imagination*, 115–17.

193. Josselin, *Diary of Ralph Josselin*, 337.

194. Luxon, 'Not I, but Christ,' 899–937.

CIRCUMCISED IN FLESH AND SPIRIT

'I am a Jew,' wrote Thomas Totney. 'begotten by the Gospel, Circumcised both in flesh and spirit.'[195] That Totney was convinced of the validity of circumcision was corroborated by John Crouch.[196] The act of circumcision brought together a number of themes in Totney's thought. Firstly, he was compelled by the Protestant onus on the allegorical nature of postlapsarian experience and by the corollary that our earthly bodies were merely the foreshadowings of a future, perfect, consummation of the justified Christians elect identity. He, furthermore, was compelled by the notion that the Jews were members of an ethnicity whose benediction was linked to their outsiderliness. Thirdly, he was drawn to any action which denoted an attitude of dissent from conventional norms, which 'broke church windows.' In various ways, the act of circumcision fulfilled all of these expectations of Godliness. Indeed, the act of circumcision in its foundation was *intended* to fulfil these expectations of Godliness.

The Biblical description of circumcision identifies the process as a designation of distinctiveness. Brueggeman writes that the 'strangeness' of the act functioned as a synechdoche for the 'strangeness' of the 'scandalous promise' of the covenant. This 'scandalous promise' required 'a mark of distinctiveness' which the circumcision offers. Brueggeman relates this tradition, this mentality, to the experience of exile, arguing that 'circumcision helped give identity to the 'insiders' of faith who had been declared outsiders by Babylon.'[197]

The notion that circumcision represented a 'cutting off' of the unclean from Israel, and that the action in itself functioned as a symbolic enactment of the process of 'cutting off' would not have been lost on Totney. He referred again and again to the process of 'cutting off' in contexts which echoed the injunctions of Genesis 17.[198] The other touchstone text with regards to the process of circumcision, for Totney, was Galatians 6.[199] Typically, this text was used by supersessionist apologetes as a precedent for the claim that the covenant of the Law had been abrogated. But an alternative reading of the text would highlight the reason for the *maintenance* of the topos of circumcision in the context of the newly established spiritual covenant. As N. T. Wright and James Dunn have shown, the discourse that surrounded the

195. Tany, *Theaurajohn His Theos-ori Apokolipikal*, 9, 28, 42.

196. *Mercurius Democritus* 7 (1652) 49–50 (Hessayon, *Gold Tried in the Fire*, 367).

197. Brueggeman, *Genesis*, 155.

198. Tany, *Law Read*, 3; *High News for Hierusalem*, 1, 13; *I Proclaime*, br; *My Edict Royal*, 2, 5, 12, 14, 15, 18, 23.

199. Tany, *Theauraujohn His Aurora*, 37.

discussion of circumcision in Paul was not laden with categories of moral conduct, imputed righteousness or of soteriological efficacy. Primarily, circumcision was understood as a marker of ethnicity, the 'primary boundary marker for Jewish minorities in the cities of the diaspora.' Paul's use of the topos of circumcision, they claim, *maintains* this core, tropological meaning: the maintenance of the distinctiveness of a minority.[200] Many of Totney's contemporaries understood and revived the notion that circumcision was functionally and discursively interlinked with the 'cutting off' of impurity. Isaac Pennington would write of the flesh being 'cut off by the circumcising knife of the Spirit.'[201] Thomas Bromley, Totney's Behmenist contemporary, envisioned the 'entrance' of the 'highest heaven' where 'the sharp Sword of Circumcision is placed':

> On the left hand there's a Gulf of Fire, on the right hand a deep Water; at the end there stands a Cherubin with a flaming Sword, whose Office is to cut off the Reliques of all Corruption.[202]

That the act of circumcision would locate the early-modern Englishman in the pejorative space 'beyond the Pale'—and that, as such, it acted as a form of separation and resistance, circumstantially as well as necessarily—is evident from Robert Bacon's account of his interaction with a group of 'Jews' on the road outside Marlborough. Bacon was a chaplain in the Parliamentary forces who became known for 'preaching down presbytery' in the early years of the interregnum.[203] He describes how he came upon a group of men and women, travelling together:

> I willingly went softly to have some speech with them, they telling me in effect they were Jews, and that the time of their gathering together, out of all Lands, especially this, was come, and that they should away for Hierusalem; yea, that they must be circumcised, and so forth: To all which I replyed, that in a sence I approved of all this, but not in their sence, or as they applied it; but they said, that he is a Jew, and of the seed of Abraham that believs, whose praise is not of men, but of God.[204]

This juxtaposition of the ethic of singularity—the determination that the praise of God was antithetical to the praise of man—and their

---

200. Dunn, *New Perspective on Paul*, 162, 165; Wright, *What Paul Really Said*, 120–22.

201. Pennington, *Babylon the Great Described*, 20.

202. Bromley, *Way to the Sabbath of Rest*, xii.

203. *Mercurius Elencticus* 8 (1648) 59.

204. Bacon, *Taste of the Spirit*, 41.

self-identification, not only as Jews but as candidates for circumcision, suggests that (at least for these individuals) circumcision functioned as a rejection of earthly authority and of the 'praise' of men—that is to say societal, normative designations of value. This sensibility is mirrored in the writings of John Pordage, who associated circumcision with necessary, Godly suffering:

> Wisdom that eternal virgin as a leading star, invited us, calling to follow her in the way of Circumcision, Resignation, and the Cross, in the way of total self-denyal and forsaking of all for her sake in the way of annihilation and conformity to Christ's death.[205]

This was hardly an unreasonable assumption. The covenant of circumcision was considered by Christians in early-modern England to constitute the carnal foreshadowing of the spiritual covenant.[206] The negation of physical circumcision was all the more pressing in the context of the Protestant refusal of carnality and ceremony. Those who observed circumcision as a 'sacrament,' Richard Baxter wrote 'did plainly deny, that Christ was come, and therefore Christ could profit them nothing.'[207] 'Circumcision is taken off,' wrote William Addamson, 'to all that believe that the Lord Jesus Christ suffered for mans redemption.'[208] The act of renouncing circumcision *was* the act of choosing Christ.

An unacknowledged league existed between the concern for singularity within Judaism and the desire to render to Jews 'singular' in Christian discourse. The act of circumcision, by its very nature, was a centerpiece of this interaction. This dynamic was especially heightened, for a variety of reasons, during the period of Totney's flourishing. In his circumcision and—more importantly—in his self-unveiling as a 'Jew ... circumcised both in flesh and spirit,' Totney openly engaged and invited the 'singularity' which this act denoted.[209]

---

205. Pordage, *Innocencie Appearing*, 77; Fowler, *Daemonium Meridianum*, 114.

206. Pennington, *New-Covenant of the Gospel Distinguished*, 6; Adams, *Commentary or Exposition*, 1341; Airay, *Lectures upon Philippians*, 597.

207. Baxter, *Catholick Unity*, 320.

208. Addamson, *Answer to a Book*, 25.

209. Tany, *Theaurajohn His Theos-ori Apokolipikal*, 9, 28, 42.

YEAST DOTH HINDER OUR RISING

On the June 10, 1656, Totney made a speech before 'the people of Israel' at 'the tent of Judah.' Totney offered an unusual reflection on the significance on Leviticus 17. Since the text abjured the consumption of the 'life giving' substance, Totney asserted that the same principle should be extended to other 'life-giving' substances. 'Bread with yist,' Totney wrote 'doth hinder our rising into steadfastness.' Beer is also alive, for the 'yist doth give the beer life,' and 'the yist is the life, conteining the strength of it.'[210] The consumption of cheese, too, is seen as a corollary of man's fallen nature, with the caveat that 'the people having gained strength in obedience to the Law, Cheese shall be altered.'[211]

Thomas Totney was not alone, in this period, in seeking to renovate and indeed innovate dietary laws. John Traske would not consume unlawful meats. His wife Dorothy Coome ate not flesh nor wine.[212] And Roger Crab, with whom Totney at least had friends in common, adopted a form of vegetarianism.

Totney and Crab shared some characteristics. Crab's *Dagon's-downfall* begins with a jeremiad against the 'whorish stonehouses' of the 'common-prayerbook' Church.[213] It is subtitled 'The great idol digged up root and branch.'[214] Moreover, Crab exemplifies the same Liberationist theology that we find in Totney's work. Crab declared himself to be 'in liberty . . . above all ordinances.'[215] He railed against the tyranny of the priesthood and of moralism.[216] He advocated a spiritual, inward turn ('turn in, turn in' he wrote) and drew on the Clarksonian image of the 'eye,' an internal source of divinity. And yet, as with Totney, we find an assiduous commitment to apparently adiaphorous or abrogated practices—in this instance vegetarianism.[217] Like Totney, this was met with ridicule and bafflement from Crab's contemporaries. His singularity, indeed, was seen by his peers as a defining characteristic. One wrote, 'He is the more to be admired that he is alone in this opinion of eating, which though it be an error, it is an harmelesse error.'[218]

---

210. Tany, *Law Read,* 8.

211. Tany, *Law Read,* 9.

212. Pagitt, *Heresiography,* 210.

213. Crab, *Dagon's-downfall,* 2–6.

214. Crab, *Dagon's-downfall,* 1.

215. Crab, *English Hermite,* a2v.

216. Crab, *English Hermite,* 6.

217. Crab, *English Hermite,* a4v.

218. Crab, *English Hermite,* a2v.

Like Totney, Crab appears to have anticipated and even invited this marginalization. The observation of dietary laws was part of a pattern of cultivating a condition of 'symbolic suffering.'[219] Crab addressed his writings to 'the despised remnant.' He implicitly associated himself with the figure of John the Baptist, claiming that 'if *John* the Baptist should come forth againe, and call himself *Leveller,* and take such food as the wildernesse yeelded, and such cloathing,' that he would be treated 'scornfully' by 'our proud Gentlemen and Gallants.'[220] Like Totney, Crab appears to have been concerned in these actions to facilitate and maintain the passive role of separation from the ungodly majority. Crab saw the persecution of the Godly as evidence of 'the gross darkness and filthiness in the People.' They 'had been purified by their violence,' he wrote.[221]

As with circumcision, the observation of dietary laws functioned intrinsically as well as circumstantially to denote separation. Douglas believed that they came to the fore at moments when the salience of the group was particularly threatened. The enactment of rituals of separation—whether of food or of times—served as a reassertion of divine order and control in the face of chaos. Totney's adoption of dietary laws relating to the consumption of yeast clearly called to mind the Passover injunctions of Exodus 12. Yeast in the Exodus narrative was *closely* associated with the process of purification of the exilic polity. All those who used leaven were to be 'cut off.' Those who did *not* use leaven went on to form the purified, priestly nation. But the Exodus narrative is not the only Biblical text in which the use of yeast is governed. In Leviticus 2, the use of honey and leaven is precluded from any cereal offering. Some commentators have claimed that this injunction results from a preconception that fermentation was linked with putrefaction. As such—like all things which connote mortality and decay—it must remain separate from the holy of holies.[222] Totney certainly associated 'fermentation' with filth.[223] Douglas elaborated on this claim, linking the figures of leaven and honey with the trope of 'teeming creatures,' spontaneously and rapidly reproducing. The teeming creatures which facilitate the fermentation process stand for the 'natural mode of generation'—valuationally neutral but necessarily differentiated from the 'divine mode of generation' which is facilitated by the covenant and therefore by the sacrificial order.[224]

219. Walsham, 'Happiness of Suffering,' 59.

220. Crab, *English Hermite,* 12.

221. Crab, *Tender Salutation,* 1.

222. Milgrom, *Leviticus 1–16,* 189.

223. Tany, *High News for Hierusalem,* 14.

224. Douglas, *Leviticus as Literature,* 163–65.

The inclusion of cheese, another example of teeming life, alongside yeast, is an innovation of Totney's. Cheese is not mentioned in Leviticus. But it denotes the same underlying concern: the separation of things holy and things profane.

CONCLUSION

It is easy to read 'Totneyism' as a farrago: a jarring combination of Jewish ceremonies, dietary regulations, and circumcisions alongside prophetic, mystical reflections on the in-dwelling of God. To follow J. C. Davis, we might expect that the latter sensibility would lead to an abandonment of the former.[225] But for Totney, the realization of the inner light led to renewed enthusiasm for distinctive, devotional, and even ethnic markers. In this respect he shared basic presumptions with his predecessor, John Traske.

There are three ways of interpreting this combination of apparently discrepant elements. Firstly, it could be taken as a mark of eccentricity. This was clearly the view of Christopher Hill, who described Totney as deranged, of Nabil Matar, who thought him 'insane,' of David Katz, who believed that Totney was 'confused,' and even Nigel Smith who believed that there was 'no logic,' to his influences.

Secondly Totney's devotional practices could be read as an efflorescence of a Behmenist impulse. As Smith notes, it was typical for Behmenists to incorporate sacramental and formal elements along with more occult elements. This speaks in one sense to the dialectical character of Böhme's own thought. Opposing and conflicting elements, for Böhme, had a productive power and would ultimately lead to the emergence of the new humanity.

Thirdly, Totney's actions could be seen as demonstrative of a commitment to political liberation: the impression left by a typological reading of the book of Exodus, associated with his experiences as a combatant in a national war of liberation, leading to a confluence of the literary and the real, a desire to mimic, emulate and inhabit the bodies of the biblical figures that he had read about and in which he saw the model of Christian liberty.

If we focus on one, underpinning concern of Totney's thought, new light can be cast on all three of these interpretations. For Totney, the need to separate godly from ungodly elements—the light and the dark, the wheat

225. Davis, 'Against Formality,' 265–88. Mario Caricchio, more recently, has identified an additional analytical layer to Davis's analysis, drawing on the typology of 'supra-formalism' described in the work of Brian Gibbons. For Caricchio—as for Gibbons—many of the 'radicals' of the 1630s and 1640s were less concerned with the rejection of forms and were more convinced that revelation *transcended* formal difference (Caricchio, 'Giles Calvert and the Radical Experience,' 82–84).

from the chaff, the gold from the dross, the saints from the tyrants—was a paramount concern. This concern was stimulated by Totney's exposure to the 'vibrantly *open-ended* and violently evangelical,' soteriology of the Reformed Protestant homiletics of his day.[226] Denison called to mind the necessity of differentiating the peculiar people from the 'children of the world' in his sermons and stressed the use of reflexive modes of morality in this endeavor. Totney's self-identification as one enlightened, to whom the 'perfect knowledge' of creation had been revealed, *facilitated* this separation. In light of this realization, Totney erected innumerable epistemic barriers between himself and his peers, mediated through the 'pose of divinely instituted madness' and the 'gnomic' formulations of perfect, linguistic solipsism. But the ceremonies Totney renovated *also* performed this function. They did so by demonstrating Totney's own critical inversion of the value-laden binaries of his day, and by situating Totney himself 'beyond the pale': a 'Jew,' a 'monster.' Moreover, the practices Totney renovated served, in an intrinsic sense, as *markers* and *symbols* of separation, ceremonies inaugurated to point towards the divine ordering of things within which sacred and profane are refined and distinguished from one another.

This reading of Totney's thought and action offers a different perspective on his understanding of the concept of liberty, one that compliments but extends the claim—made by Coffey—that Totney represented an offshoot of the Puritan 'liberation theology.' It is undoubtedly the case that Totney was heavily invested in the notion of liberty. As such, he combined elements of the political philosophy of the Parliamentary campaign with millenarian conceptions of eschatological manumission. A third element, though, comes from the shared concern that Totney had with the *authors* of the eschatological, exilic texts. He, like them, was concerned with maintaining the separation of the Godly and the tyrants in the interests of maintaining the purity of the former. The goal, for Totney, was not *solely* the critique of power (as Hill would have it), nor the foundation of a 'free' state (as Skinner would), nor the symbolic realization of the liberty of the atonement (as Coffey would) but *also* the separation of the impure elements of worldly power from the godly elements of the priestly nation. The renovation of Jewish practices facilitated this separation. Indeed, the impetus for these practices, at their inception, was to 'call to mind' the separation of the holy from the profane. As such, each element of Totney's thought conforms to an attitude of resistance, the passive fulfilment of Totney's own, self-imposed

---

226. Lake, *Boxmaker's Revenge*, 31

injunction: 'separate, separate, separate, separate, separate, separate, separate, separate, separate, separate, separate.'[227]

227. Tany, *My Edict Royal*, 27.

CHAPTER 5

The Tillamites, Judaizing, and the 'Gospel Work of Separation'

IN 1667, WHILST TRAVELLING in the Rhineland, the English traveller Edward Browne encountered a curious community:

> Two English men came kindly to me (Mr. Villers and Timothy Middleton) belonging to the Lobensfeldt cloister, a convent formerly of the Jesuits but since let out to about an hundred English who left the country in 1661, came up the Rhine and settled themselves a few miles from hence, living altogether men, women and children in one house and having community of many things. They are of a peculiar religion calling themselves Christian Jews and one Mr. Poole formerly living at Norwich is their Head. They cut not their beards and observe many other ceremonies and duties which they either think themselves obliged to from some expression of the Old Testament or from the exposition of their leader.[1]

These were the Tillamites, a congregation of exiles who had left England in the aftermath of the Restoration led by Christopher Pooley and Thomas Tillam.

Thomas Tillam attained a significant degree of notoriety within the Baptist milieu during the period of the Civil War and the interregnum. He was characterized by more than one contemporary as a 'turbulent spirit,' with a tendency towards fomenting sectarian strife. He travelled across England during the 1640s and 1650s. He 'set the house on fire where ever he came,'

---

1. Browne, *Account of Several Travels*, 56.

wrote Thomas Weld.[2] For Robert Eaton, he was 'a ball of wild-fire, tossed from one end of the nation to the other, scattering pestilent error.'[3] Tillam travelled to America in the 1630s but by his own testimony fell out with prominent figures in New England and promptly returned. He preached for the Separatist congregation at Hill Cliffe near Warrington during the mid-1640s.[4] Whilst at Warrington he also preached at the separatist chapel in Wrexham.[5] From Wrexham he moved to Chester where he preached at the Dukinfield chapel. Dukinfield had recently been embroiled in a controversy due to the anti-Trinitarian tendencies of its pastor John Knowles.[6] At Chester, Tillam ran afoul of Samuel Eaton and 'incurred his displeasure.'[7] By 1650, he had become attached to Hanserd Knollys's Baptist congregation at Coleman Street in London. Whilst in London, he penned a work of millenarian Republicanism entitled *Two Witnesses*. It was published by Giles Calvert.[8] Hanserd Knollys sent Tillam to Hexham as a 'messenger' to help establish a Baptist community there.[9] At Hexham, he became embroiled in a scandal: falling for the ruse of a 'Jew' who Tillam 'converted' to Christianity. It transpired that 'the Jew' was in fact a Scottish Catholic named Thomas Ramsay. Tillam gave his side of the story in a book published in 1654 entitled *The Banners of Love*.[10] This misadventure was just one of a number of controversies between Tillam and his co-religionists at the Baptist community in Newcastle. Tillam's commitment to the 'fourth principle'—the imposition of hands—was a point of division between him and the leadership of the Newcastle Baptists (Thomas Gower and Paul Hobson).[11] He defended this practice in a third volume but, despite his best efforts, he was ejected from the Hexham congregation in 1655. The following year he was preaching in Colchester and by this stage was advocating for the observation of the Seventh-Day Sabbath.[12]

2. Weld, *Mr. Tillam's Account Examined*, A3r.

3. Eaton in Weld, *Mr. Tillam's Account Examined*, 1.

4. Kenworthy, *History of the Baptist Church at Hill Cliffe*, 43–49.

5. Nuttall, 'New Letter to George Fox,' 222–24.

6. For Knowles career, see McLachlan, *Socinianism in Seventeenth-Century England*, 263–73.

7. Weld, *Mr. Tillam's Account Examined*, 15.

8. Tillam, *Two Witnesses*, A1v.

9. Underhill, *Records of the Churches of Christ*, 289.

10. Tillam, *Banners of Love*, a2r–3r; Weld, *False Jew*, b2r–3v.

11. Underhill, *Records of the Churches of Christ*, 295, 320–323; Tillam, *Fourth Principle of Christian Religion*.

12. Tillam, *Seventh-Day Sabbath*; Josselin, *Diary of Ralph Josselin*, 368.

Tillam was imprisoned at Colchester in 1656 and, during his incarceration, wrote a fourth book entitled *The Seventh-Day Sabbath Sought Out and Celebrated*.[13] Released from prison, he wrote a fifth text entitled *A Christian Account of Some Passages of Providence*.[14] In this text, Tillam articulated some of his more heterodox beliefs including that only those called to ministry in dreams or visions should be allowed to preach and that he had the power to replicate the blessing of Christ by the practice of the laying on of hands. His arguments were contested by Thomas Weld.[15]

From Colchester, Tillam moved to Norwich. There, in 1658, he met Christopher Pooley. Pooley was a Norfolk clergyman who had advocated for Fifth-Monarchist principles in East Anglia in the years following the Civil War.[16] Pooley was counted amongst those who were 'tending to bloud' in the latter years of the interregnum. As a 'dipper' and a suspected conspirator, he had drawn the attentions of Thurloe's informants.[17] Both men were, by this point, avowed proponents of the Seventh-Day Sabbath. After a short period of preaching in the city, Tillam was banned and Pooley was imprisoned. Pooley accused the magistrates of the city of Norwich of being 'the limbs of the beast.'[18] Whilst he was in prison, Pooley wrote one work of his own and a foreword to a text by Tillam who was, by that point, also imprisoned in the Gatehouse of Lambeth palace. The former was *Unwarranted principles leading to unwarranted practices, sought out and examined*.[19] The latter was *The Temple of Lively Stones*.[20]

The Temple was written in the summer of 1660. Tillam attested that he could hear the ceremony of the installation of the new Archbishop of Canterbury, William Juxon, as he was writing.[21] It argued for the validity of several 'ceremonial laws,' generally understood to be abrogated by the supersession of the Mosaic covenant. Tillam argued, amongst other things, that observation of Levitical dietary restrictions remained valid and that men were bound by Leviticus 19 to grow their beards.[22]

13. Tillam, *Seventh-Day Sabbath*, 1.

14. Weld, *Mr. Tillam's Account Examined*, A1r.

15. Weld, *Mr. Tillam's Account Examined*, 19–20

16. Thurloe, *State Papers*, 5:220–21.

17. Thurloe, *State Papers*, 5:220.

18. Blomefield, *Essay Towards a Topographical History*, 3:401.

19. Pooley, *Unwarranted Principles*.

20. Tillam, *Temple of Lively Stones*, 1.

21. Tillam, *Temple of Lively Stones*, 19.

22. Tillam, *Temple of Lively Stones*, 215–16, 293.

With the restoration of the monarchy, Tillam was arrested and imprisoned in Ipswich but managed to escape.[23] Tillam and Pooley, along with several followers, fled England. They travelled to Rotterdam in 1661 where they encountered the exilic community of English Quakers and Baptists.[24] Between 1661 and 1663, they moved back and forth between the continent and England.[25] Their stated intention was to establish a community of the Godly on a plantation in the Palatinate and they travelled around England during these years in order to publicize their project.[26] At some point they joined forces with Edmund Skipp, a former Baptist vicar from Herefordshire who had written an excoriating criticism of Quakerism in the mid-1650s.[27] According to contemporary accounts they made 'many converts'.[28] The scholarship of Bryan W. Ball supports these claims.[29]

During the 1660s the Tillamites adopted a range of other Judaizing practices. In the summer of 1661, Pooley and Tillam returned to England.[30] Four-thousand Quakers were in prison and nearly three-hundred Baptists were in Newgate.[31] Pooley and Tillam began proselytizing a new form of Christianity. Perhaps as an evangelical aid, they had brought with them, from Rotterdam, a convert. This convert travelled under the alias of 'Dr. Love.' Their arrival at Lowestoft provoked consternation in some quarters. William Killigrew reported that the three emissaries were forthcoming about their designs in England: 'They give out that they have been in the Palatinate to settle one hundred plantations there for so many families as would remove out of England.'[32]

Later developments proved that they were in earnest. In the summer of 1664, they travelled to Heidelberg. They took ownership of a property on the outskirts of Lobbach in August 1664. The arrival of the Tillamite retinue in the town of Lobbach is noted in the parish archives. It records that on

23. Whitehead, *Light and Life of Christ Within*, 4.

24. Friends' House Library, Swarthmore Manuscript, 1:328. This citation comes from a transcribed version of the text in Hull, *Benjamin Furly and Quakerism in Rotterdam*, 221. For the Baptist community in Holland during this period, see Hutton, *Benjamin Furly*; Greaves, *Deliver Us from Evil*, 94–97.

25. National Archives, SP 29/41, f. 1–2; Calendar of State Papers Domestic, 1663–1664, 521.

26. National Archives, SP 29/236, f. 28.

27. Cowell, *Snare Broken*, 2; Coke, *Discourse of Trade in Two Parts*, 53.

28. Coke, *Discourse of Trade*, 53; Brewster, *Essays on Trade*, 23.

29. Ball, *Seventh-Day Men*, 292.

30. National Archives, SP 29/40, f. 131.

31. Sewel, *History of the Rise, Increase, and Progress of the Christian*, 2:3.

32. National Archives, SP 29/41, f. 1–2.

August 10, a caravan drawn by six horses arrived at the convent. The passengers included both men and women of both high and low birth. Having arrived late on Tuesday night, the Englishmen slept. They lunched together, 'masters and servants,' on Wednesday.[33] Some documents survive which describe the layout of the convent as it was in Tillam's time there. Tillam himself, it appears, occupied his own bedroom in the space that had previously been used as a guard-house or lookout. The other occupants occupied the roof space of the convent.[34] On a final trip to England in 1666, Pooley brought with him a copy of the Tillamite manifesto, a 'covenant' which included a number of commitments to the Mosaic law.[35] These included a commitment to the reintroduction of sacrificial worship at Jerusalem, an injunction against marriage with 'gentiles' and the reintroduction of the rite of circumcision.[36] Silas Taylor saw the Tillamites depart England for the last time, and mentioned their maintenance of circumcision, the Jewish Sabbath and common ownership of goods.[37]

These innovations inflamed the ire of their erstwhile colleagues in the English, Seventh-Day Baptist community. A number of Sabbatarian luminaries subscribed to a text entitled *A Faithful Testimony Against the Teachers of Circumcision Who Are Lately Gone into Germany*, distancing themselves from the conclusions made by the Tillamites.[38] Despite the condemnation of their peers, the Tillamite congregation appeared to flourish in the later years of the 1660s.[39] In 1674, Thomas Tillam's death was reported. Apparently Tillam had died without renouncing his opinions.[40]

Tillam and Pooley's careers could be seen in the context of a millenarian drift towards a Judeo-Christian irenicism. They were millenarians and they were 'Judeocentrists,' after all. Popkin makes the claim that a spirit of philo-semitism during this era helped to usher in a new period of enlightened, nomothetic morality. Philo-semites sought to facilitate greater interaction between Jews and Christians. This in turn informed newly emerging discussions concerning Natural Law.[41] John Selden, amongst oth-

---

33. Heimatarchiv Lobbach, Jahresrechnungen Schaffnei Lobenfeld 1664, f. 186 (I am grateful to Dr. Ludger Syre and Ms. Doris Ebert for helping me to identify these documents).

34. Heimatarchiv Lobbach, Kloster Bauakten 1662–1671, GLA 229/62019, f. 52–56.

35. National Archives, SP 29/181, f. 150r–151v

36. Cowell, *Snare*, 2–7.

37. National Archives, SP 29/236, f. 28.

38. Squibb et al., 'Faithful Testimony,' 45–47.

39. Coke, *Discourse of Trade*, 53; Brewster, *Essays on Trade*, 23.

40. Hubbard, *Samuel Hubbard's Journal*, 74–76.

41. Katz, *Jews in the History of England*, 112; Popkin, 'Christian Jews and Jewish

ers, contended that the principles of the Law were revealed to Adam and communicated through social structures, thereby providing the basis for civic law. However, at the forefront of Tillam and Pooley's thought was *not* consensus but division and separation. The observation of the law functioned as a demonstration of distinctiveness. 'The Law cuts off the filthy adulterer,' Tillam wrote.[42] Pooley denounced the Grotian concept of Natural Law. 'By nature a man knows not God, nor his Law,' he wrote. The Law of Nature as understood by Pooley was in common amongst humans and 'brute beasts.'[43] Nor did Pooley recognise the claim that the Law was revealed initially to Adam and that civic laws were corollaries of this Law. For Pooley, the Law was recognized *exclusively* by the elect. The justified elect were obedient 'not under the Law,' but rather 'under the precious assisting power of grace.'[44]

Biblicism and literalism are often cited as the roots of Puritan Judaizing. And yet, in the context of Tillamism, the problems intrinsic to these terms are even more profound. Tillam was not noted as a literalist (in its modern usage) by his peers. Indeed, Thomas Weld dubbed Tillam 'a notorious abuser of scripture.'[45] According to Samuel Eaton's description, Tillam convinced his followers that his teachings were directly revealed to him, 'oracles of God,' which must be 'taken without any consulting others.'[46] Eaton, of course, was a hostile observer. But elements of Tillam's own account of his career attest to this theme. Tillam believed that the Law was enlightened by grace and by revelation, *not* by careful and clear exegesis. 'The path of the Just shines,' he noted, but 'the injust know not why they stumble' (cf. Prov 4).[47] When charged by Jeremiah Ives to produce scriptural basis for his beliefs, Tillam responded that he believed there not to be 'a plain text to prove the proposition.'[48] Indeed, Tillam directly disparaged those who believed that knowledge of God could be derived from 'the dead letter.' He called this position 'meer historical faith,' worthy only of 'Agrippa.' In this comparison, Tillam associated the Godly with Paul, who questioned the scriptures on

---

Christians,' 57–72; Sutcliffe, *Judaism and the Enlightenment*, 42–58.

42. Tillam, *Temple of Lively Stones*, 189.

43. Pooley, *Unwarranted Principles*, 35–36.

44. Pooley, *Unwarranted Principles*, 36.

45. Weld, *Mr. Tillam's Account Examined*, 18.

46. Eaton in Weld, *Mr. Tillam's Account Examined*, a3v.

47. Tillam, *Temple of Lively Stones*, 1.

48. Ives, *Saturday No Sabbath*, 37.

the basis of direct revelation—the Damascene conversion—and who was accused of insanity on this basis at the court of Agrippa (Acts 26).[49]

Tillam might be seen as an exemplar of 'philo-semitism' on the basis of his revival of ceremonies. Certainly he was intrigued by Jews and dispensed with a number of anti-Jewish canards in his writings.[50] Nonetheless, Tillam believed that the justified Christian, endowed with grace, was superior in his closeness to the divine to any Jew. Christians could not learn from Jews about correct worship. 'The lowest minister,' he wrote, 'is greater than Moses.'[51] Elsewhere he associated 'Jews' with 'infidels, Turks and Papists.'[52] As such, suggesting that Tillamism was a form of mimetic philo-semitism is not justified.

The Tillamites could be counted amongst the arch-primitivists. This would support Smith's contention that Judaizing sated 'a desire to return to the simple modes of prayer and worship which characterized early Christianity.'[53] Certainly Tillam and Pooley referred regularly and with admiration to the primitive church.[54] But the Godly did not understand the disciples to be practitioners of irenic, Jewish-Christianity. On the contrary, Tillam venerated the disciples as the proto-separatists. They 'removed all ceremonial rites from Judaism,' he wrote.[55] Indeed, for Tillam, the Disciples were to be commended for 'separating *out of* Judaisme.'[56] On this basis, Tillam's revival of ceremonies is an awkward fit, rather than a natural bedfellow, with his veneration of the early church. Only the fact that ethical separation—as Tillam recognized—was a process which was contingent in its character on the context in which it was enacted, allowed Tillam to avow an affinity between the disciples (who he saw as renouncers of ceremony) and himself and his followers (as revivers of those same ceremonies).

I want to argue that Tillam's millenarianism and Pooley's legalism both interacted with their interest in ceremonialism and Judaizing. But rather than suggesting that the one *caused* the other, I argue that all three phenomena—ceremonialism, legalism and millenarianism—were manifestations of a single, fundamental concern: separation, singularity and resistance.

49. Tillam, *Temple of Lively Stones*, 55.

50. Tillam, *Seventh-Day Sabbath*, 51.

51. Tillam, *Fourth Principle*, 34.

52. Tillam, *Temple of Lively Stones*, 66.

53. Smith, 'Christian Judaizers in Early Stuart England,' 131.

54. Tillam, *Temple of Lively Stones*, 74; Pooley, *Unwarranted Principles*, 26.

55. Tillam, *Temple of Lively Stones*, 25.

56. Tillam, *Temple of Lively Stones*, 120.

PURITANISM, SINGULARITY, AND THOMAS TILLAM

Thomas Tillam lived during a period of political and sectarian factionalism and confessional disintegration. He was a prominent figure in the Baptist milieu of revolutionary and post-revolutionary England, which intersected with Fifth-Monarchist and Saturday Sabbatarian elements. He was an advocate of the Parliamentary cause. Towards the end of his life he accrued a similar degree of infamy amongst the Clarendonian exiles in Holland and in Germany. All of these experiences left their marks on his thought.

Like many of his contemporaries, Tillam oscillated between assurance and anxiety in his understanding of salvation and he evoked these oscillations in his congregants and readers. These oscillations were heightened by a lack of ecclesiastical stability. The 1640s was witness to the cracks and fissures emerging in consensual religious practice in Cheshire, which would soon lead to a profound fracturing in the Church. The establishment of small, separatist congregations was coupled with violent interruptions of Laudian liturgy. This was met with horror from sections of the lay population, in both the plebeian and aristocratic tier. In 1642, the signatories of the 'Cheshire petition for Establishing the Common Prayer-Book' complained of 'present disorders of many turbulent and ill-disposed spirits.' They attested that these 'spirits' were prone to 'many tumultuous (if not sacrilegious) violences both by day and by night upon divers churches.' They worried further that the separatists 'menace some great alteration.' The most acute fear expressed by the petitioners was of

> the true Reformed Protestant Religion, established by so many Acts of Parliament, and so harmoniously concurring with the confessions of all other Reformed Churches, being tainted with the Tares of divers Sects and Schismes lately sprung amongst us.[57]

The petition was signed by over nine-thousand people, approximately 10 percent of the population of Cheshire.[58] At the same time, Sir Thomas Aston wrote his *Remonstrance Against Presbiterie*. He, too, warned of the gradual disintegration of consensual worship in Cheshire. Where the petitioners used the analogy of a malign spiritual possession to describe the 'schmismaticks,' Aston described them as noxious. He spoke of 'popular poysons,' spread amongst the population of Cheshire 'under the pretext of pietie and Reformation.' For Aston, this process spoke to a more tectonic

57. *Cheshire Petition*, br.
58. Phillips and Smith, *Lancashire and Cheshire*, 64.

movement towards general social disintegration.[59] The toxic influence of separatism, he suggested, would 'corrupt or dissolve the Nerves & Liga-ments of Government.' He believed that if 'the presbiterie' got their way, the results would be catastrophic for English society as a whole. '*Sampson* like in their full strength,' he wrote 'they will wilfully burie themselves and us in the rubbish of that *Chaos,* which they so pull upon their owne heads.'[60] As-ton warned that the 'schismatickes' would elicit 'the totall subversion of the Fabrick of a Church and State.'[61] His fears about social decline would soon be vindicated. He was captured and imprisoned by Parliamentary forces and died from head-wounds sustained from a bludgeoning at the hands of his guards.[62]

For some, the vacuum left by the disintegration of social and soterio-logical structures during the Civil War was filled by the Godly cause. Morrill has argued that engagement of the Godly in the popular overthrow of a seemingly anti-Christian tyranny galvanized a cultural demographic that otherwise had a profound tendency to fracture and milliformity.[63] Tillam, it is clear, found some sort of assurance in his ideological alignment with the Parliamentary forces. For Tillam, as for many others, the Godly army functioned as a surrogate for the Godly church, the invisible made visible. In 1651, he called Cromwell's parliament 'the joy of Saints and the honour of Christ.'[64] He commended the Acts for the Propagation of the Bible of that year. Tillam presented a diagrammatic account of the forces of Anti-Christ and of the true Church, within which Parliament and its allies represented the latter camp:

> *Their Enemies beheld them,* and would gladly have pulled them down; which they endeavored by all possible industry, policy and violence; they never beheld them but as Enemies; King, Prelates, and Papists.[65]

He believed that this parliament, the Rump, was to play an eschatological role, as the 'Great voice' prophesied in Revelation, which would call the Godly towards heaven. Tillam came close to believing—as Edward Symons wrote—'the *Elect* being all on the Parliament side, or well affected at least to

59. Aston, *Remonstrance*, M3r–N1r.

60. Aston, *Remonstrance*, K1v.

61. Aston, *Remonstrance*, c4r.

62. Vernon, 'Aston, Sir Thomas, First Baronet,' in *Oxford Dictionary of National Biography.*

63. Morrill, 'Puritan Revolution,' 84.

64. Tillam, *Two Witnesses*, 92.

65. Tillam, *Two Witnesses*, 91.

their cause, the rest must needs be all damned creatures.'[66] As for many of his contemporaries, the Revolution offered Tillam an opportunity to explore the deeply allegorical anthropology of Reformed Protestantism. Here at last was Brinsley's prayer answered: the Godly and 'Satan's slaves' marshalled against each other in battalions.[67]

By the mid-1650s, Tillam was disappointed, disillusioned and disoriented by the Commonwealth. At a lecture in Colchester in 1656, he exhorted his auditors to strive against the 'rising oppressions, appearing persecutions: and manifold enormities of a revolting nation.'[68] By December he had apparently lost all patience with the 'good old cause' and had begun to see the Protectorate as yet another agent of Anti-Christian conspiracy. He made a thinly-veiled jibe at Cromwell, promising that God would 'eminently punish' those 'clothed in the strange apparel' of the monarchy.[69] Parliament fared no better. Tillam was prepared, by this point, to equate 'Parlements' and 'Princes,' as the promised victims of providential justice.[70]

Tillam's *Temple of Lively Stones*, written as the Commonwealth began to flag, exhibited a conscience in the throws of uncertainty. The soul would not be satisfied, he wrote, without assurance.[71] Like Traske, he returned to the prophecy of ecclesiological uncertainty in Matthew 24. 'The Kingdom is much in the mouths of most professors,' he wrote. 'They cry lo here and lo there' (Matt 24:23).[72] He cautioned his reader against reliance on exterior signs of salvation. They must not rely on membership of parish congregations.[73] They must not rely on obedience to scripture, which Tillam called 'meer historical faith.'[74] Nor should they rely on providential signs and wonders. Such as resorted to the latter were no better than Doubting Thomases.[75] Membership of the Godly elect, Tillam claimed, was irreducible fact, discernible only through the self-authenticating experience of conversion. 'None is able to discern the Gospel church,' he wrote, 'except they be born again.'[76]

---

66. Symmons, *Vindication of King Charles*, 85.

67. Brinsley, *Second Part of the True Watch*, 60.

68. Tillam, *Seventh-Day Sabbath*, a3v.

69. Tillam, *Seventh-Day Sabbath*, a3v.

70. Tillam, *Seventh-Day Sabbath*, 94.

71. Tillam, *Temple of Lively Stones*, 167.

72. Tillam, *Temple of Lively Stones*, 6.

73. Tillam, *Temple of Lively Stones*, 176.

74. Tillam, *Temple of Lively Stones*, 55.

75. Tillam, *Temple of Lively Stones*, 138.

76. Tillam, *Temple of Lively Stones*, 62.

But whilst Tillam understood that the elect church of the saints was invisible, he—like John Brinsley—looked forward with great ardour to the point of its unveiling. In that day all of the uncertainties incumbent on the Godly professor would be alleviated. 'The life hid with Christ,' he wrote, 'will be made visible in him.'[77]

THE SPECIAL DESIGN OF GOSPEL SEPARATION

Writing in 1659, as the era of Godly rule panted towards an undignified end, Tillam wrote wistfully of the 'Gospel Church of true believers':

> It is a Kingdom of all Divine perfections, compact of Kings and Priests, who by one pure offering are for ever perfected. Here's perfection of Beauty, shining from the presence of God. Here's perfect order, which compleats the joy of Saints, who are distinguished by the Character of faith and order. Here's perfect Peace, within these gracious walls.[78]

Walls, built to separate the Godly from the reprobate, to protect the 'perfect' from defilement, *and* to imprison the Godly, were prominent in the imagination of Thomas Tillam. From the earliest stages of his career as a minister and pastor, he had urged his flock to maintain 'separation' between themselves and the reprobate majority. During the period of the Civil War, he cautioned his co-religionists in Warrington and Wrexham to separate from the 'King, Prelates, Papists, and the whole rabble of Cavalliers, restless in their spirits, from the first ascending of the Witnesses into Heaven to this very day.'[79] During the period of his ministry in Hexham, he warned his flock to be separate from the Quakers—including George Fox—who were proselytizing in the area.[80] Hexham was a largely rural community. In 1651, it was still on the front line of the Third Civil War and neighboring Newcastle had been occupied by the invading Scots.[81] Tillam stoked feelings of embattlement. 'All Sion's towers should be planted with sentinels to warn the inhabitants thereof of their enemy's approaches,' his congregants wrote, 'to excite them to a holy watchfulness, and an earnest looking for the return of the Captain of our salvation.'[82] During the last years of the interregnum,

---

77. Tillam, *Temple of Lively Stones*, 228.

78. Tillam, *Temple of Lively Stones*, 237.

79. Tillam, *Two Witnesses*, 91.

80. Fox, *Journal of George Fox*, 119.

81. Howell, *Newcastle upon Tyne*, 163–69, 248–50.

82. Underhill, *Records of the Churches of Christ*, 316.

he warned his followers in Essex and East Anglia to separate 'from this un-
toward nation wherein they have lived so long in pollution.'[83] But for Tillam,
the process of separation was an intrinsic rather than an instrumental good.
He did not believe that the Godly should 'separate' solely in order to avoid
falling into the errors of one particular group or another. Rather, he believed
that the Godly condition was one of 'separation from the world.'[84] Separation, he claimed, 'was the ultimate use and end' of right worship. It was 'the
only duty of the disciple.'[85]

The 'Gospel work of separation' was most fulsomely described by Tillam in his final book, *The Temple of Lively Stones*. *The Temple* is a text that
describes the correct condition of a Godly congregation, defined—from
within and without—by the coherence of the saints and the enmity of the
dross. The eponymous image is of the Temple, the tabernacle of the covenant Law, as described in Revelations 15. The Temple—Tillam reminds
his reader—is filled with smoke so that none can see clearly within it.[86] The
Temple stood as an edifice of holiness, a centerpiece of the work of separation. But for Tillam the carnal temple had been destroyed. The walls of the
Temple had been burst.[87] As such, the *people of God* now took on the role
of the Temple. The Temple was not made of masonry, but of 'lively stones.'
The text offers a detailed description of church governance. But its central
theme is separation. Through grace, he claimed, the elect were 'solemnly
separated.'[88] The atonement itself—the death of Christ and its mirror-image
in Baptism—was a 'separation.'[89]

Tillam was beset with uncertainty about the source of assurance. But
the experience of separation, he believed, was identical to assurance. 'The
Saints may be notably discerned,' he wrote, 'by their resorting together in
Gospel society and strengthening one another.' They are bound together by
'ligatures.'[90] The metaphor of the temple, built of the fleshly bodies of the
Godly, signified the mutual interdependency of the Godly in supporting and
maintaining assurance in one another. The Temple, Tillam wrote, was 'com-
pact of lively stones, separated from the world in peculiar union with the
Lord and mutual communion together.' This juxtaposition—sequestration

83. Tillam, *Temple of Lively Stones*, 85.

84. Tillam, *Temple of Lively Stones*, 119.

85. Tillam, *Temple of Lively Stones*, 228.

86. Tillam, *Temple of Lively Stones*, a2v.

87. Knohl, *Divine Symphony*, 67.

88. Tillam, *Temple of Lively Stones*, 16.

89. Tillam, *Temple of Lively Stones*, 33.

90. Tillam, *Temple of Lively Stones*, 34–35.

from the world and 'mutual communion' with each other—provided each member of the Godly with assurance. There was, as he wrote, perfect peace within the walls.[91]

Like a number of Baptist thinkers of the period, Tillam considered himself and his followers to be members of 'the remnant of the woman's seed.'[92] But for Tillam, like Traske, separation from the world was a step that was required of the Godly believer before he or she was justified. Separation formed part of a tripartite process leading from repentance, to faith, to baptism.[93] The regenerate soul would be 'engaged by grace to separate from the world to the Lord.'[94] Only when the Christian had 'gotten one step out of the pollutions of the world' would he be given 'help, handed from the everlasting hills.'[95]

Tillam's self-conception as a member of the Godly interacted with his apprehension of his identity in the eyes of his peers and specifically his antagonists. The saints must be visible, he believed, in order for assurance of Godly identity to be secured. 'There is a faithful remnant,' he wrote, 'who are visible in view and are therefore persecuted by the world.'[96] '*Only* the separation from the world brings a soul into visible sonship,' and '*only*' when the saint 'is really and visibly separated from the world,' can he 'profess to live onely and alone to God.'[97] As such, Tillam and his justified readers were marked as 'God's peculiar people,' not only in the eyes of the Almighty, but more immediately in the eyes of their peers.[98]

'Separate the precious from the vile leprosy,' wrote Tillam.[99] The metaphor of illness was a commonplace of heresiography during this period.[100] Presbyterian discipline of the kind espoused by Edwards and Brinsley was considered an 'antidote' to heterodoxy, to 'the Swarmes of sectaries that infect the air of the land with their erroneous, blasphemous opinions.'[101] The Traskites were described as a 'plaguy people.'[102] Tillam describes the way of

---

91. Tillam, *Temple of Lively Stones*, 235, 237.

92. Tillam, *Temple of Lively Stones*, a3v; Bell, *Apocalypse How?*, 245.

93. Tillam, *Temple of Lively Stones*, 42.

94. Tillam, *Temple of Lively Stones*, a3v.

95. Tillam, *Temple of Lively Stones*, 52.

96. Tillam, *Temple of Lively Stones*, 4.

97. Tillam, *Temple of Lively Stones*, 171, 95.

98. Tillam, *Temple of Lively Stones*, 112.

99. Tillam, *Temple of Lively Stones*, 176.

100. Hughes, *Gangraena*, 85, 106, 194–95.

101. D. P. P., *Antidote Against the Contagious Air*, 24.

102. Falconer, *Briefe Refutation*, 6.

Babylon as leprous, and cautions that the Godly should avoid them.[103] The condition of apostasy, for Tillam, was associated with the condition of being 'plaguy', of being 'deprived of human society'.[104]

The facilitation of 'separation' went hand in hand, in Tillam's career, with the formenting of sectarianism. Lake writes that the phenomenon of Puritanism, with its vision of correct worship and the attachment of virtue to the minority experience was an unstable phenomenon. Dissent, as such, was not a 'semi-autonomous' tradition, an interpolation of latter-day Lollardry, of the kind envisioned in Hill's *The World Turned Upside Down*. Rather it came from *within* the devotional culture of the Godly.[105] Nowhere is this more evident than in the career of Thomas Tillam. Everywhere he went, Weld wrote, his churches 'fell into pieces'.[106] Weld was bemused by Tillam's apparent tendency to antagonize not only his doctrinal adversaries, but also his own peers and co-religionists. 'This man is opposed by men of his own judgment and practice in doctrine and discipline,' Weld wrote.[107]

Tillam constantly sought newer and more extraordinary ways of alienating his peers, of sowing the seeds of distrust amongst his congregation about all outsiders, separating the Godly from the ungodly, whittling and cuppeling and off-scouring, seeking out a remnant, a 'holy huddle'.[108] This task led Tillam and his followers to the restoration of practices which functionally and intrinsically facilitated separation.

FLEE FROM PARISH STREETS AND LANES

From his prison cell in 1660, Thomas Tillam recalled a walk that he had taken in Halifax some years earlier:

> Informed that my certain way to my wife or friends lay through very narrow stony rugged lanes and other parts of it through wild Moors up hill and down hill. . . . Should I pass through a broad pleasant even road, I must needs conclude that I were out of my way, so that the beauty of my passage would greatly aggravate my fears. . . . The more foul and ill-favoured the way and

---

103. Tillam, *Temple of Lively Stones*, 380.

104. Tillam, *Temple of Lively Stones*, 381.

105. Lake, *Boxmaker's Revenge*, 403.

106. Weld, *Mr. Tillam's Account Examined*, 9.

107. Weld, *Mr. Tillam's Account Examined*, 10.

108. Collinson, 'Shearmen's Tree', 219.

weather were, the more pleasant and sweet would my thoughs of home be.[109]

In the aftermath of the Restoration, Tillam would lead his congregation to establish a community in a place inaccessible to the reaches of ungodly Babylon. The work of separation had several practical concerns. First and foremost, the Godly were to separate from conventional worship. They were to build a house on a high mountain.[110] They were not to take positions or 'benefices' from any Parish provision.[111] They were not to sin by worshipping with 'Parish worshippers.'[112] They were to flee from 'the Parish streets and lanes,' wrote Pooley.[113] 'We must not, like unconstant Christians mingle with carnal interests,' Tillam wrote.[114]

But refusing affiliation with these groups was not sufficient. The Godly were enjoined to avoid *all* contact, to 'foresake all Anti-Christian persons and places.' All people who had been ordained or even baptized according the 'Parish-worshipper' practices were to be shunned.[115] To eat with apostates was a mark of ungodliness.[116] 'We must eschew their haunts,' wrote Tillam.[117] These boundaries were to be carefully policed. It could not be left to the individual conscience to maintain 'Gospel separation.' It was the job of the Elder to investigate the conduct of each member in public and in private. 'It is not sufficient to be watchful over the flock when all are assembled,' he wrote. 'The Elders who desire to be informed must be frequently visiting their houses to inquire after their private conversation.'[118]

Nor would the process of maintaining the separation of the Godly from the profane end at death. The great 'design of separation' would not 'cease with our breath,' Tillam wrote.[119] The Godly would follow Abraham's example, not burying one another amongst the uncircumcised (Gen 23). They would be buried separately. Nor could the Godly mourn at the graves of the ungodly or follow a body to a 'common burial place.'[120]

109. Tillam, *Temple of Lively Stones*, 93.

110. Tillam, *Temple of Lively Stones*, 172.

111. Tillam, *Temple of Lively Stones*, 31.

112. Tillam, *Temple of Lively Stones*, 222.

113. Pooley, 'Epistolary,' in Tillam, *Temple of Lively Stones*, a5v.

114. Tillam, *Temple of Lively Stones*, 172.

115. Tillam, *Temple of Lively Stones*, 175 (incorrectly numbered 125).

116. Tillam, *Temple of Lively Stones*, 377, 176.

117. Tillam, *Temple of Lively Stones*, 178.

118. Tillam, *Temple of Lively Stones*, 338–39.

119. Tillam, *Temple of Lively Stones*, 222.

120. Tillam, *Temple of Lively Stones*, 222–25.

With the Restoration, Tillam saw the duty of the separating saint as being to physically separate from Babylon–England. The Lord would raise the wings of an Eagle, he believed 'to preserve his persecuted saints.'[121] The eagle here denoted the German electors.[122] The Tillamites removed first to Holland and then to Lobbach on the outskirts of Heidelberg in August of 1664.[123] They claimed that removal from England was a requirement of the Godly:

> They that are willing to depart out of their own Country and to
> follow the example of Father Abraham seeking their inheritance
> in his land as being right heirs thereunto, resolving to separate
> themselves from all persons, even their nearest relations.[124]

But whilst physical separation gave the Godly some assurance of their righteousness, it was only through a process of spiritual and psychological separation that they could truly know justification. They must 'get an hatred,' Tillam cautioned, of Babylon, they must have 'her high places in contempt.'[125] 'This,' he claimed, 'is an assured prophecie of God's mercie to his elect lambs.' Without it, they would never attain 'thorough separation.'[126]

WALK TOGETHER AND THOROUGHLY SEPARATE

> The outward ordinances—like walls, rooves and bulwarks—surround the prince.[127]

Tillam wrote that the 'four foundation principles'—repentance, faith, baptism and the laying on of hands—attained the task of separation.[128] But the Godly professor should seek to 'improve the separation.'[129] This could be accomplished by the observation of a number of practices. Like many of the Godly, acts of voluntary religion provided 'improved separation' for the Tillamites. Tillam wrote: 'By prayer, fasting and conference we have agreed

121. Tillam, *Temple of Lively Stones*, 195.

122. Tillam, *Temple of Lively Stones*, 195.

123. Heimatarchiv Lobbach, Jahresrechnungen Schaffnei Lobenfeld 1664, f. 186 (I am grateful to Dr. Ludger Syre and Ms. Doris Ebert for helping me to identify these documents). Friends' House Library quoted in Hull, *Benjamin Furly*, 221.

124. National Archives, SP 29/181, f. 150r.

125. Tillam, *Temple of Lively Stones*, 183, 220.

126. Tillam, *Temple of Lively Stones*, 220.

127. Tillam, *Temple of Lively Stones*, 234.

128. Tillam, *Temple of Lively Stones*, 171 (incorrectly numbered 121).

129. Tillam, *Temple of Lively Stones*, 172.

to walk together and thoroughly to separate.'[130] As Collinson recognized, for the Godly, the (often anti-social) 'concomitants' of these practices performed a social function which exceeded their doctrinal significance. They were *seen* by the neighbors of the Godly, and as such functioned as a communication, a divisive identification.[131] This was recognized by Tillam himself. These practices served an *instrumental* purpose he thought, in more 'really' rendering the 'visible separation' of the saints.[132]

The 'virgin train of separated saints,' meanwhile, had their own practices, which departed significantly from conventions of Puritan 'voluntary religion.'[133] Their eucharists took place during the hours of the night. 'Tread not in the ways of the time-changing horn,' Tillam warned, 'by communicating in any part of the day.'[134] Christopher Pooley attests to the observation of this practice.[135] Nocturnal rituals were identified with Puritan, dissenting excess during this period.[136] Rather than being baptized in white, the Tillamites were baptized in red. This practice was designed by Tillam as a reminder to the baptized of the 'scornful strippings of their dying redeemer.'[137] Tillam encouraged his followers to engage in the practice of a Holy Kiss.[138] He advocated for the celebration of 'Holy Feasts' amongst believers. All of these practices, Tillam claimed, facilitated a greater sense of Christian society, of Godly entitativity. Tillam noted that 'joynt singing' was a practice for the encouragement of fellowship amongst the saints.[139] By 'sitting cheerfully together' and performing these practices, the Godly could expect to 'build up in one another a holy faith.'[140] Indeed, they could expect to reach the point of having 'the same mind.'[141]

Whilst they developed their own devotional practices, the Godly were also expected to renounce any practices that were associated with the wicked world. James I was joking when he asked the assembled divines at

130. Tillam, *Temple of Lively Stones*, 242.

131. Collinson, 'Puritanism as Popular Religious Culture,' 48.

132. Tillam, *Temple of Lively Stones*, 171 (incorrectly numbered 121).

133. Tillam, *Temple of Lively Stones*, 220; Collinson, 'Puritanism as Popular Religious Culture,' 48.

134. Tillam, *Temple of Lively Stones*, 282.

135. Pooley, *Unwarranted Principles*, 6.

136. *Calendar of the Manuscript of the Marquis of Salisbury*, 10:450–51.

137. Tillam, *Temple of Lively Stones*, 72.

138. Tillam, *Temple of Lively Stones*, 251.

139. Tillam, *Temple of Lively Stones*, 273–74.

140. Tillam, *Temple of Lively Stones*, 284, 260.

141. Tillam, *Temple of Lively Stones*, 271.

Hampton if they would wear shoes, given that shoes were worn in Popery, but Tillam came close to conforming to this stereotype. 'The whole design of Gospel separation must be affected,' he wrote. In order to achieve this, the Godly must 'foresake all unChristian expressions, seasons, provisions.'[142] They must 'separate from sinners,' in their 'hearts, habits, wedlock, word, oath, offices, all things possible.'[143] They must 'beware of bowing to the traditions of men.'[144] As language played a prominent role in erecting and changing the boundaries between the Godly and ungodly in Totney's thought, so it was with Tillam's. The Tillamites were enjoined to 'destroy the Dragon's dialect.'[145] Conformity with social norms was a form of defilement: it 'defiled the beautiful garments of Godly innocency.'[146] The Godly were enjoined to avoid deference and terms of courtesy. 'To compliment rulers with if it please your worship, your honour, your excellency,' was—for Tillam—'extremely below the believer.'[147] Similarly, the Godly were to avoid 'anti-Christian expressions,' and 'escape all the customary ridiculous oaths of corrupt courts.'[148] Refusing oaths and deploying 'rhetorical impoliteness' were staples of practical divinity for Quaker and other dissenting groups.[149] For Tillam it explicitly constituted a form of 'escape.'[150] However, the 'escape' of 'separation' was not a single *act*, but rather a 'constant' *process*.[151]

It was on this basis that Tillam believed the 'separated seed of Sion' should observe different times and calendars to the ungodly.[152] They must 'overturn and destroy all the times and laws of the little horn,' he wrote.[153] The first hour of the day, should be called 'one' rather than 'six.'[154] The Sabbath should be observed on the Saturday rather than the Sunday. Meanwhile, the 'Bachanalian' festivities of Christmas and Easter were to be abandoned.[155]

142. Tillam, *Temple of Lively Stones*, 174.

143. Tillam, *Temple of Lively Stones*, 199.

144. Tillam, *Temple of Lively Stones*, a4r.

145. Tillam, *Temple of Lively Stones*, 203.

146. Tillam, *Temple of Lively Stones*, 188.

147. Tillam, *Temple of Lively Stones*, 192.

148. Tillam, *Temple of Lively Stones*, 184.

149. Penn, *Briefe Account*, 43–44; Higginson, *Brief Relation*, 29; Greaves, *Society and Religion*, 522–25; Walsham, *Charitable Christian Hatred*, 144; Davies, *Quakers in English Society*, 49.

150. Tillam, *Temple of Lively Stones*, 184.

151. Tillam, *Temple of Lively Stones*, 228.

152. Tillam, *Temple of Lively Stones*, 206.

153. Tillam, *Temple of Lively Stones*, 28.

154. Tillam, *Temple of Lively Stones*, 202–3.

155. Tillam, *Temple of Lively Stones*, 208

So too were the 'Whitsun Ales, heathenish maypoles, plays, wakes, and wassail bowls.'[156] Weld depicted Tillam's doctrinal innovations as 'designs to divide the church.'[157] Of course, Weld was an opponent of Tillam's, but in this respect Tillam agreed. In these practices, Tillam believed that he and his followers would be 'intirely separated.'[158]

If they were to be efficacious in exhibiting the difference between the Godly and the reprobate, Tillam cautioned that the marks of Godliness were to be superficially *visible* to the ungodly. The profession of separation from the world was a 'publick profession.'[159] In one passage, he describes the performative nature of Godly prayer:

> Bow, fall down in reverence fear and dread, only be sure that your affections be first in motion without which your bodily exercise will profit little . . . this will have such a powerful influence on those unbelievers who shall see your assemblies.[160]

But if they were intended to be *seen*, Tillam also intended these 'divisive identifications' to attract the obloquy of the mob.[161] He assured his followers that, by following his lead, their 'parents and rulers' would 'hate their profession.'[162] Nonetheless, he urged his reader that they should 'hate such relations, shake off that yoak according to the apostolicall liberty.'[163] 'Shun, avoid and detest': these were Tillam's watchwords.[164]

For Tillam, the eliciting of antagonism between the Godly and the ungodly was not only divinely mandated, it was providential. In acts of separation, Tillam believed, the Godly were providentially marked, identified. Those who were baptized in running water would not be afflicted with colds. Those who failed to observe the Sabbath correctly would 'have their bones shaken.'[165] In 1658, Tillam was prevented by the magistracy of Norwich from preaching the observation of the Saturday Sabbath. Tillam described his response:

156. Tillam, *Temple of Lively Stones*, 200–210.

157. Weld, *Mr. Tillam's Account Examined*, 2.

158. Tillam, *Temple of Lively Stones*, 221.

159. Tillam, *Temple of Lively Stones*, 129.

160. Tillam, *Temple of Lively Stones*, 301.

161. Lake and Stephens, *Scandal and Religious Identity*, 123.

162. Tillam, *Temple of Lively Stones*, 360.

163. Tillam, *Temple of Lively Stones*, 360.

164. Tillam, *Temple of Lively Stones*, 357.

165. Tillam, *Temple of Lively Stones*, 80.

> At my departure so soon as I was without their City, I did sol-
> emnly in the name of our Lord Jesus Christ, shake off the dust
> of my feet against them.[166]

He was pleased to discover, soon afterwards, that the mayor of Norwich was struck dead by Almighty God for the sin of working on the Sabbath.[167]

Tillam's pastoral style enlivened the sense that the Godly were a sancti-fied, isolated, separated remnant. At Hexham, he warned his followers to be mindful not *only* of the threats of professed enemies, but also of professed friends. Writing to his congregation at the height of the Newcastle-Hexham split, Tillam euphemistically associated the Newcastle congregation and their leaders with the forces of anti-Christ, lamenting that

> opposition hath been great which wee have met with from
> all hands, ever since wee first made a visible profession of ye
> despised truths of the Lord Jesus . . . those conflicts have been
> most sad which we have had with ye bretheren of a neighbour-
> ing church.[168]

He drew comparisons between the pretended allies of the Godly and other examples of this phenomenon in the history of God's people—the intrigues of the dissembling Gibeonites in Joshua 9 and the undermining of attempts to rebuild the temple in Ezra 4:

> They say: we are not of the Prelatical Faction, we are the Par-
> liaments friends, that rejoice in the ruin of their Enemies, by
> these and the like expressions, many a crafty Gibeonite got both
> protection and provision. . . . But they secretly conspire against
> the Jews, endeavouring by all means to hinder the work.[169]

Like Totney and Traske before him, Tillam believed the truth of his doctrinal innovations were revealed by the Spirit and that, as such, were discernible 'to few.'[170] For those to whom knowledge was revealed, it was— Tillam invariably claimed—'unspeakable.'[171] Pneumatological 'literalism,' in the case of the Tillamites, led to precisely the conflicts and sectarianism that

166. Tillam, *Temple of Lively Stones*, 31–32.

167. Tillam, *Temple of Lively Stones*, 32. For other examples of providential retribu-tion, meted out by God on behalf of the Godly, see *Blazing Starre*. For commentary on the role of providence in the popular imagination of the period, see Walsham, *Provi-dence in Early Modern England*, 326–27; Burns, *Age of Wonders*, 12–57.

168. Underhill, *Records of the Churches of Christ*, 349.

169. Tillam, *Two Witnesses*, 93.

170. Tillam, *Temple of Lively Stones*, 4.

171. Tillam, *Temple of Lively Stones*, 18.

Como's analysis predicts. It led to 'fragmentation,' and threatened 'not only the institutional power of the church but the very notion of centralized and centralizing order.'[172] 'It is a usual thing with him,' wrote Thomas Weld, 'to set his own single testimony against all that contend with him.' This tendency served to antagonize those who Tillam sought to separate *from*. He was a 'Church-divider.'[173] 'He cast down to hell all that opposed him,' Weld wrote, 'and lifted up to Heaven all that sided with him.'[174] Those who were his 'proselites,' he described as 'refined spirits.' Those who disagreed with him, he described as 'base born muck-worms.'[175] Underlying this expression was a presumption of the irreducible, binary opposition of the Godly and the ungodly. This binary opposition allowed Tillam to reconfigure hatred of the 'dross' as love of the saints. 'Hate the high places of Babylon,' he urged and 'get an hatred for yourself.'[176] Some years later, the critics of the Tillamites would co-operate with Tillam's desire. 'We exhort those that tremble at God's word,' they wrote 'to hate with a perfect hatred these men.'[177] Moreover, this oppositional anthropology allowed Tillam to reconfigure the enmity of the ungodly as a mark of sanctity. For Tillam, being hated by the world was a mark of sanctity. 'Getting an hatred,' was a work of holiness.[178]

Some of Tillam's peers accused him of Popishness.[179] They believed that Tillam believed in the efficacy of works. This was a misapprehension. Tillam believed that the justified believer had to endure a period of penitence and personal reformation in anticipation of the experience of conversion. This was not dissimilar to the Traskite conception of repentance. 'The penitent must work through every tittle of the second table,' Tillam wrote, before he can attain 'the second step.'[180] But like Traske, the work of attaining knowledge of one's sanctity *had* to originate in the passive mood. 'Affections' had to be 'in motion' before the professor could exhibit an act of piety.[181] The enmity of the ungodly, as a passively experienced indication of Godliness, played a vital role in the emergence of Tillamite divinity.

---

172. Como, *Blown by the Spirit*, 439.

173. Weld, *Mr. Tillam's Account Examined*, 17.

174. Weld, *Mr. Tillam's Account Examined*, 16.

175. Ives, *Saturday No Sabbath*, a3v.

176. Tillam, *Temple of Lively Stones*, 183, 220.

177. Squibb et al., 'Faithful Testimony Against the Teachers of Circumcision,' 45–49.

178. Tillam, *Temple of Lively Stones*, 183.

179. Weld, *Mr. Tillam's Account Examined*, 17.

180. Tillam, *Temple of Lively Stones*, 51–52.

181. Tillam, *Temple of Lively Stones*, 301.

THE DESPISED RAMS HORNS

> The Remnant have passed already through the Baptismal streams of Jordan and have made such progress towards the land of promise, that they are at this instant sounding with their despised Rams horns about the lofty walls of cursed Jericho.[182]

Tillam believed that the world was largely reprobate. As such, that which was 'despised' in the eyes of the world was considered, by extension, to be holy. That which menaced and antagonized the majority was therefore a holy act. This informed the way that he presented many aspects of his theology. Valuational binaries relating to learning, happiness and success were inverted in order to denote the singularity of the Godly enclave.

True knowledge, for Tillam, was discernible only through the intercession of the Holy Spirit and, as such, reliance on carnal reason was a mark of hubris. Only those who had been 'sent' rather than 'educated' had the right to preach.[183] Those who had attained education were treated with suspicion rather than approbation. The merchants of Babylon 'bought their abilities for money at universities.'[184] The 'schools and colledges' themselves were 'corrupt.'[185] The Godly must not be educated in 'rational universities' Tillam wrote, but rather in 'separated schools and nurseries of prophets.'[186] Learning, for Thomas Tillam, was not an indication of superiority or sanctity. God chose the 'weak and the foolish' for his vessels. At the same time, He 'turned the counsel of wise men backward.'[187] Pooley, meanwhile, believed that 'the Lord would hide from the wise and prudent and reveal to babes, making use of these foolish, poor, weak, despised, base things.'[188] Faith and obedience were *directly* contrary to the use of reason. For Tillam: 'As a saint is known by his Rule, so a man is known by his reason.'[189] In 1659, at the Stone-Chapel in London, Thomas Tillam engaged in a debate with Jeremiah Ives. The event was characterized by a failure of Tillam's to engage with Ives according to the conventional rubric of discussion. 'Mr Tillam refuses to observe any logical method,' one commentator noted.[190] This was not solely a disparage-

---

182. Tillam, *Temple of Lively Stones*, 4

183. Tillam, *Temple of Lively Stones*, 29.

184. Tillam, *Temple of Lively Stones*, 175 (incorrectly numbered 125).

185. Tillam, *Temple of Lively Stones*, 238.

186. Tillam, *Temple of Lively Stones*, 21.

187. Tillam, *Temple of Lively Stones*, 84.

188. Pooley, *Unwarranted Principles*, a2v; Tillam, *Temple of Lively Stones*, 8.

189. Tillam, *Temple of Lively Stones*, 197.

190. Ives, *Saturday No Sabbath*, 1.

ment of Tillam by a hostile observer. Tillam openly declared himself 'against syllogistical ways of disputation,' and 'devices of men's wisdom.'[191] At other times, he refused to answer Ives's questions.[192]

The potential fragility of Reformed Protestant epistemology was evident to Tillam. 'At present every man's way is right in his own eyes,' he wrote.[193] The milliform nature of the church created 'the confused noise of many streams.'[194] The Tillamites were enjoined to avoid reliance on learned counsel. Nor could they rely on the 'meer historical faith,' which depended on scripturalism.[195] Tillam cautioned against reliance on the 'inner light.'[196] He also cautioned against reliance on providential signs.[197] Those who were the vessels of providence, meanwhile, were not certain to be justified. 'Even a Judas can perform a miracle,' Tillam wrote 'and can go to hell afterward.'[198] Without the doctrines of Thomas Tillam, to paraphrase Perry Miller, the Tillamites confronted chaos.[199]

'They sow in tears,' wrote Tillam, 'who reap in glory.'[200] Tillam believed that separation, and therefore justification, was identifiable with suffering. 'What measure have you and I met with, from unreasonable and wicked men?' he asked his Hexham congregation.[201] Recalling the ordeals of the Waldensians, he wrote:

> They undoubtedly *know their God and understand his will*, and therein instruct many thousands both by doctrine and sufferings, by the sword, by flame, by spoyl, and by Captivity, whereunto they know they were appointed with the rest of their brethren for many days.[202]

He warned his reader that the 'baptized person hazards the loss of friends, parents.' Tillam called this process, the 'Baptism of sufferings.'[203] Af-

---

191. Ives, *Saturday No Sabbath*, 22.

192. Ives, *Saturday No Sabbath*, 25.

193. Tillam, *Temple of Lively Stones*, 6.

194. Underhill, *Records of the Churches of Christ*, 322.

195. Tillam, *Temple of Lively Stones*, 55.

196. Tillam, *Temple of Lively Stones*, 144.

197. Tillam, *Temple of Lively Stones*, 138.

198. Tillam, *Temple of Lively Stones*, 140.

199. Miller, *New England Mind*, 1:19.

200. Tillam, *Temple of Lively Stones*, 52.

201. Tillam, *Banners of Love*, a2v.

202. Tillam, *Two Witnesses*, 64.

203. Tillam, *Temple of Lively Stones*, 95.

ter all, the Godly had always been an 'afflicted poor people.'[204] The Godly must pursue 'the praise not of men but of God,' wrote Christopher Pooley.[205] The Godly could hope to be 'appointed' not by providential favor, but rather 'by the sword, by flame, by spoyl, and by Captivity.'[206] The word 'poverty' referred to both a spiritual and an economic condition in Tillam's thought. 'Many are the precious people baptized in poverty,' wrote Tillam. The rich, meanwhile, were disparaged as 'the merchants of Babylon.'[207] Separation was a 'self-denying work' and in Tillam's own experience it had landed him poor, homeless and in prison.[208] Pooley's own account of his career described a refusal of 'profits, reputations and pleasures after the which my flesh lusted.'[209]

Those who recognized the true nature of the relationship between God and humanity suffered spiritually as well as physically. They saw themselves as 'shattered sinners,' as 'dead dogs.' The Godly 'groaned under the weight of their newly awakened consciences.'[210] Like many of this period, Tillam saw the Godly as passive in relation to their discovery of their own justification. Involuntary behaviors therefore were good sources of assurance. 'Penitential tears' were 'not to be wanting.' 'Heart bleedings,' he believed, 'would divert the cataracts.'[211]

'Let not crosses or losses deter you,' Christopher Pooley wrote. But the Tillamites were equally prepared to cultivate these crosses.[212] The Godly professor was to 'expose himself to all kinds of sufferings, dangers and reproches.'[213] The Sabbath keepers of Colchester, led by Tillam during the winter of 1656, met in a 'steeple-house' without windows. The windows had been broken in the war. Tillam saw the experience of meeting in the cold, particularly without wearing a cap, as a mark of Godliness, of faith that God would provide and protect.[214] If the Tillamites did 'appear with no hat upon their heads,' then the 'concomitant' unconventionality of this sartorial choice would certainly have functioned as a divisive identification.[215]

---

204. Tillam, *Temple of Lively Stones*, a2v.

205. Pooley, *Unwarranted Principles*, a2r.

206. Tillam, *Two Witnesses*, 65.

207. Tillam, *Temple of Lively Stones*, 175.

208. Tillam, *Temple of Lively Stones*, 229.

209. Pooley, *Unwarranted Principles*, 59.

210. Tillam, *Temple of Lively Stones*, a6v.

211. Tillam, *Temple of Lively Stones*, 51.

212. Pooley, *Unwarranted Principles*, a2v.

213. Tillam, *Temple of Lively Stones*, 17.

214. Tillam, *Temple of Lively Stones*, 296

215. Shakespeare, *Hamlet* 2.1.77; Webster, 'Early Stuart Puritanism,' 54.

Colds or the lack thereof may seem a trivial source of assurance of salvation. But Tillam saw evidence of his justification and the justification of others in more dramatic events. His own imprisonment at the time of writing *The Temple* was one. The 'Baptism of Blood'—which he celebrated in the Waldensians and which he wholeheartedly expected for himself—was another. 'Let us prepare for some great affliction,' he wrote. The disciples 'must sacrifice their lives rather than swear to support the laws of a nation which are contrary to the laws of God.'[216] Tillam certainly experienced the obloquy of the mob. In the years between 1645 and 1660, he was excommunicated from four separate congregations and was arrested several times. His character was variously attacked by Robert Eaton, George Fox, Thomas Weld, Arthur Squibb, Edward Stennet and John Cowell.[217] He was loathed and despised. It seems that Tillam also saw this process as identical with sanctification. 'If your assemblies be abominable in the eyes of the Egyptians,' he wrote, 'rather leave your country than stain your souls.'[218]

Tillam's peers clearly *understood* and were eager to repudiate the implicit connection between the plight of the Tillamites and their Godliness. 'Whereas Godly men suffer as Christians for well doing,' Weld wrote 'this man is buffered for fault, scandal, pride and slander.'[219] These hardships, he suggested, were constructive, cultivated crises.[220] This was a 'black mark' and a 'flesh brand' for Tillam. He had 'exposed' his congregation in Hexham 'to reproaches, temptations and sufferings of several sort.' The condition of suffering was similar to the exposure of the skin to the sun, which left the Godly 'black, swarthy and sun burnt' in the eyes of the world.[221] The topos of 'blackness,' during this period, denoted otherness, not only of 'Blackamoores,' but also of Jews and those of evil repute.[222] Nonetheless, Tillam believed that the 'blackness' of the saints would render them 'comely in Christ's eye.'[223] Opposition encouraged Tillam of the righteousness of his position. It did not deter him. 'The more I hear the contest of the croud,' he wrote, 'the more concerned I am to advance . . . a doctrine.'[224]

216. Tillam, *Temple of Lively Stones*, 183.

217. Weld, *Mr. Tillam's Account Examined*, 1–30; Fox, *Answer to Thomas Tillams*, 1–30; Squibb et al., 'Faithful Testimony Against the Teachers of Circumcision.'

218. Tillam, *Temple of Lively Stones*, 388.

219. Weld, *Mr. Tillam's Account Examined*, 9.

220. Weld, *Mr. Tillam's Account Examined*, 8–10.

221. Underhill, *Records of the Churches of Christ*, 322.

222. Munster, *Messias of the Christians and the Jewes*, 2–4; Guevara, *Chronicle*, 110.

223. Underhill, *Records of the Churches of Christ*, 322.

224. Tillam, *Temple of Lively Stones*, 95.

Tillam's endeavor in 'publickly' exhibiting his distinctiveness from his peers, and advancing doctrines which actively courted 'the contest of the croud' was to maintain the separation of 'Israel' from 'Babylon.' The threat of cultural miscegenation, which residence in Babylon presented to the saints was a cause of sorrow and anxiety. The saints hung their harps upon the willow trees. Tillam adopted the role of Ezra, refining the gold of Israel from the dross of Babylon. Like the prophet, Tillam warned the people to 'beware of bowing to the traditions of men.'[225] But he also urged them to participate in ceremonies which ritualized, symbolized and brought to life, in Tillam's own words, the Gospel work of separation.

THE DESPISED DUTY OF BAPTISM

'In Baptism,' Tillam wrote, 'the disciple is separated from the unbaptized world.'[226] For Tillam, Christ's death represented a separation, and the baptism of believers mirrored this separation. This was a radical revision, thematically, of the Pauline understanding of baptism. For Paul, the act of Baptism represented an annihilation of ethnic or genealogical particularity, the substitution of a 'literal genealogy' for an 'allegorical genealogy.' Marks of difference, in the act of baptism 'are effaced.' In part, for this purpose, baptism supplanted circumcision in Paul's thought.[227] In Tillam's reading, however, Baptism *reinforced* the distinction between the minority and majority, rather than annihilating it.

At the same time, Tillam was concerned that the act of baptism itself was a 'pure' act, in which the constituent symbolic elements were not tarnished, polluted or mixed. On this basis, he favored the use of 'self-cleaning' running water rather than stagnant water.[228] On this basis, also, he expressed his aversion to the 'popish' practice of baptizing with a combination of 'water, spittle, oyl and salt.'[229]

Tillam looked to the Old Testament, as well as the New, for scriptural precedent for the practice of Believers Baptism. He referred to the story of the immersion of Naaman in 2 Kings 5.[230] For Naaman, the Baptism was a physical transformation, a cure. Tillam also believed that the act of baptism was curative. Tillam negatively compared the practice of

225. Tillam, *Temple of Lively Stones*, a4r.

226. Tillam, *Temple of Lively Stones*, 95.

227. Boyarin, *Radical Jew*, 22–25.

228. Tillam, *Temple of Lively Stones*, 71

229. Tillam, *Temple of Lively Stones*, 70.

230. Tillam, *Temple of Lively Stones*, 77, 85.

'sprinkling'—conventional infant baptism—with the immersion practiced by *contemporary* Jews in the *mikveh*.[231]

The Tillamite baptism, therefore, was intrinsically associated with the Tillamite concern for separation. But it was also *circumstantially* an act which denoted singularity. It was a 'despised duty,' Tillam wrote.[232] This 'separating' quality of the act of baptism was corroborated by the reception of 'dipping' by Tillam's contemporaries. The conversion of Fifth-Monarchists to Baptist practices was reported by Hezekiah Haynes to Thurloe in the summer of 1656: 'At Norwich-our fifthe monarchy party there have many of them turned anabaptists and submitted to the ordinance.'[233]

An anonymous letter to Haynes in that month, notified him that a parish meeting had been called to assert the validity of paedobaptism. The meeting culminated in confrontation.[234] Haynes's anonymous correspondents relayed rumours of Baptist-Fifth-Monarchist plottings afoot, warning that: 'that party does intend disturbance.' At North Walsham, Pooley and his acolytes were making equally alarming noises, apparently in the vanguardist tenor of John Tillinghast. Haynes reported to Thurloe in July:

> Our North Walsham fifth monarchy bretheren, who weare lately
> dipped, are synce growen exceeding high in their expressions,
> and that tending to bloud, as by the enclosed your honor will
> perceive; and Buttephant of the lyfe guard, Rudduck, and Pooly
> the cheiftanes of them. Buttephant is come to London: some
> horses better then usualy such persons had, and some pistolls I
> am informed they have.[235]

Adopting practices which savored of Anabaptism was, in light of the meaning attached to that term, a form of deviance during this period. It called to mind the chaos of Münster and the various, infamous, anti-Anabaptist slanders of the sixteenth century. In these complex ways, Tillam saw the act of baptism as being a fertile source of separation. The separateness which Believers' Baptism denoted was guaranteed by a number of factors, not least its association with political and religious dissent and—for Tillam—its association with Judaism.

---

231. Tillam, *Temple of Lively Stones*, 78.

232. Tillam, *Temple of Lively Stones*, 72.

233. Thurloe, *State Papers*, 5:188.

234. Thurloe, *State Papers*, 5:219.

235. Thurloe, *State Papers*, 5:219.

THE FOURTH PRINCIPLE

One contentious aspect of Tillam's liturgical thought was the adoption of the practice of the laying on of hands. Tillam attested that the 'fourth principle' was an act of obedience to Christian doctrine as described in Hebrews 6. This echoed the standard formula for the defence of the rite.[236] For Tillam, though, there was a further purpose and further utility to the practice. He claimed that his reader could 'witnesse the Gospell light that lightneth every man that cometh out of the world, by religious separation' and that 'this light is communicated through the Word and Ordinances, and particularly, through this holy Ordinance of Laying on of hands.'[237] It allowed the Godly to 'gather out of the world into the Gospel church state.'[238] This 'Gospel duty' was 'of singular concernment' since it functioned within Tillam's liturgical thought as a 'solemn separating ordinance.'[239] Tillam suggested that the Church was 'neglecting her duty' when she did not use the rites and rituals mandated by the Gospels to 'separate such persons by it, as are fit for the Lords harvest.'[240]

The laying on of hands was 'by nature a separation.' The laying on of hands in violence, separated the saints from their persecutors. The laying on of hands in healing separated the sick from their sickness.[241] In this sense, Tillam pointed to the innovative conclusion that hands—as the agents of separation in human activity—were intrinsically related to 'separation' and, as such, to purity.

It is clear, though, that Tillam himself understood that the laying of hands *also* constituted a form of Judaizing. He saw the renewed practice of the fourth principle as a renewal or an echo of the *shemikhah*. 'On this wise were the Levites of old brought before the Law,' he wrote.[242] The laying on of hands is described in Numbers 8 as a process of ordination, used to separate and to sanctify (הִתְקַדִּשׁוּ) the priestly class. The priests are then presented before the Lord as a 'shake offering.' As such, the priests take up a role between the sanctuary and the people, an embodiment of the holiness of the temple rite. The complexity of the notion of קדוש is fully explored in this short text: the priesthood are to be anointed as קדוש in the sense that

236. Grantham, *Christianismus Primitivus*, 133–39.

237. Tillam, *Fourth Principle*, a3v.

238. Tillam, *Temple of Lively Stones*, 19.

239. Tillam, *Temple of Lively Stones*, 95.

240. Tillam, *Fourth Principle*, 36.

241. Tillam, *Temple of Lively Stones*, 129.

242. Tillam, *Temple of Lively Stones*, 129.

they are to bear the burden of Israel's shame. Their קדוש status is described as one of self-abnegation and starvation, atonement for the collective sins of the people. Tillam makes explicit reference to the *sanctity* of the role conferred on the priesthood by this process, emphasizing the separateness of the priesthood, identified by laying on of hands. If the Temple stood for 'separation,' the priesthood were marked by their ability to enter the sanctuary: 'a peculiar priviledge.'[243]

Ultimately, the adoption of the practice served as a mode of separation circumstantially as well as intrinsically. Tillam adopted the practice after visiting Peter Chamberlen in 1654. He was upbraided for his persistence in the practice by Thomas Gower and Paul Hobson. Apparently Paul Hobson visited Coleman Street in 1655 and complained about Tillam's use of the practice, which—he claimed—'sets up *Moses* above Christ.'[244] The Coleman Street congregation agreed and asked Tillam to leave his position in 1655 along with all others who 'were in the practice of the laying on of hands.'[245] Tillam responded with the publication, in 1655, of *The fourth principle of Christian religion: or, the foundation doctrine of laying on of hands.* The controversy in Northumberland was a microcosm of controversies which wracked the Baptist communities of England during the Civil War period. In 1646, Francis Cornwell had attempted to revive the fourth principle within the General Baptist Congregation at White's Alley. This controversy led to a schism and to the founding of a separate congregation at Dunning's Alley.[246] The laying on of hands, when described in Judaizing terms, became a source of division and schism within Baptist circles. For this reason, Tillam understood the laying on of hands to be 'a publick profession of separation from the world.'[247]

THE PURCHASED, PECULIAR SPOUSE

Ezra and his fellow exiles gathered in Jerusalem upon their return and offered burnt sacrifices to the God of Israel. When this was completed, the leaders of the community came to Ezra and confessed:

> The people of Israel have not kept themselves separate from the nations. They have taken some of their daughters as wives for

243. Tillam, *Fourth Principle*, 34.

244. Hobson, *Fallacy of Infants Baptisme Discovered*, 8.

245. Underhill, *Records of the Churches of Christ*, 295.

246. Payne, 'Baptists and the Laying on of Hands,' 203–15.

247. Tillam, *Temple of Lively Stones*, 130.

themselves and their sons, and have mingled the holy race with
the peoples around them. (Ezra 9)

When Ezra found out about the miscegenation of Israel he tore his
clothes, pulled his hair from his head and sat down, appalled until the
evening sacrifice.

Joseph Blenkinsopp identified this text—and the corpus within which
it sits—as an inauguration of the 'first phase of Judaism.' For Blenkinsopp,
this phase facilitated the reification of Judaism as a 'proto-sectarian' group.
As Blenkinsopp notes, intermarriage during this period was not just a matter of individual preference. It was a carefully developed political culture, favored by a ruling elite in order to facilitate political stability in the Satrapies
of the Persian controlled region. Moreover, Ezra's injunction was a break
with tradition: Abraham, Moses and Joseph had all taken foreign wives. As
such, Ezra's 'remarkable intervention' was scandalous. But it set a tone of
sectarianism within Judaism which facilitated a symbolic historiography. In
the Qumran documents, the notion of a remnant, rescued from the wrath
of an angry God is symbolically associated with the precious and separated
remnant, the *bene-haggola*, who returned with Ezra.[248]

Tillam characterized all kinds of ethical mixing, and the pollutions of
Babylon in sexual terms. God had, in the eternal decree of the predestination
of the elect, 'purchased a peculiar spouse.'[249] To renege on this covenantal
relationship by indulging in Popish practices was a form of 'adultery.' The
saints should flee from 'the fornications of Babylon,' Tillam wrote, for 'it
must be made a burnt mountain.'[250]

Alongside these symbolic formulations, *actual* miscegenation was as
central to the separation of the Tillamites as it was to the separation of the
returning Israelites. 'We must not mingle,' wrote Tillam, 'marrying with the
daughters of Moab.'[251] The leadership of the community were to provide
guidance about whether potential conjugal partners were legitimate or
not. 'Secret marriages' which were pursued 'without advice' were considered, by Tillam, to be grievous acts of disobedience.[252] 'Sensual mixtures in
Anti-Christian marriages' were further restricted.[253] 'We will never give our

---

248. Blenkinsopp, *Judaism*, 67–71, 221.

249. Tillam, *Temple of Lively Stones*, 173.

250. Tillam, *Temple of Lively Stones*, 174 (misnumbered as 124).

251. Tillam, *Temple of Lively Stones*, 172.

252. Tillam, *Temple of Lively Stones*, 352.

253. Tillam, *Temple of Lively Stones*, 178.

daughters to sons of strangers,' the Tillamites wrote, 'nor take their daughters for our wives.[254]

Their conjugal practices were perceived by the Tillamites' contemporaries as scandalous. The authors of the 'Faithful Testimony' corroborated the suggestion that the Tillamites maintained separation from the ungodly in matters of marriage. In addition, the authors suggest that the Tillamites excommunicated those spouses who were not prepared to participate in the Lobenfeld project. 'They make it lawful, nay a duty,' claimed the authors, 'for women to leave their husbands to go with them, if their husbands be not willing':

> And if any of them should covet a believers wife then it is her duty to separate and go to Germany and if they should have unbelievers for their wives, then have them away to Germany and convert them there.[255]

There is also some evidence of a polygamist tendency within the Tillamite community. Silas Taylor thought that the Tillamites believed in the communion of goods and the communion of 'concubines,' and lamented the loss of English 'mayds' to the Palatinate settlement.[256] One anti-Tillamite tract asserts that the Tillamites 'hold it lawfull to multiply wives to themselves, pleading the example of the saints of old for their so doing.'[257] In 1663 Benjamin Furly, the English Quaker, wrote from Rotterdam of a scandal that had gripped the English community there. Tillam had become embroiled in a romantic affair during his time in the city. When Furly, who was the postmaster to the English community in Rotterdam discovered his infidelities, he exposed Tillam as a hypocrite. Tillam was reported to have called his illegitimate son 'the root of Jesse.'[258] When Pooley returned on a proselytizing mission to Rotterdam in the winter of 1664, he met and spoke to one John Pigeon, who relayed the details of his conversation to Pooley's wife Frances, at home in England, in a letter of November 20, 1664:

> There is a fiery and masterfull woman with whom Christopher Pooly had such shamefull and open familiarity, that many who had not abandoned all modesty were stounded at and left them and are now dwelling in this city.[259]

254. National Archives, SP 29/181, f. 150r–151v.

255. Squibb et al., 'Faithful Testimony,' 45.

256. National Archives, SP 29/236, f. 28.

257. Squibb et al., 'Faithful Testimony,' 45.

258. Reiger, *Ausgeloschte Chur-Pfalz-Simmerische Stammlinie*, 273–79.

259. National Archives, SP 29/106, f. 14.

Polygamy, as a demonstrative rejection of conventional sexual ethics, has functioned as a mode of resistance for many religious groups. In her study of Mormonism, Merina Smith has suggested that 'by reworking marriage norms, Mormons [set] themselves up for a confrontation with their fellow citizens.'[260] The utility of polygamy as a practice that would inflame public ire, and thereby promote the distinctiveness and entitativity of the Tillamites, was just as significant in early modern England as it was in nineteenth-century America. Polygamy was variously associated with Islam, Paganism, Anabaptism and Judaism in early modern England.[261] The interaction between the Tillamites and the authors of the *Faithful Testimony* therefore, functioned as a negotiation of resistance. The Tillamites adopted practices which were deemed deviant by the wider society. They courted the disapproval and anathematization of their peers. Their peers (the authors of the *Faithful Testimony*) responded by treating them 'with a perfect hatred.' Tillam, meanwhile, had already anticipated this response.

THE MASTERPIECE OF THE MAN OF SIN

The returning Israelites, in Nehemiah's account, close the doors to the city of Jerusalem and renew the practice of the Sabbath. Here again, 'the Law' and 'the wall' are juxtaposed. In the text of Nehemiah, the account of the renewal of the Sabbath is juxtaposed with Nehemiah's injunction against inter-marriage. Tillam looked to this text, rather than to the Genesis account or the decalogue, for the ultimate exemplar of Sabbath observation—a pre-eminent work of 'separation.'[262]

The observation of the Saturday Sabbath presented an opportunity for separation. Sabbath-keepers 'by their entire separation,' he wrote 'are become victors over the Beast, his image, his mark, and the numbers of his name.'[263] Tillam conceded and accepted the perennial description of the Saturday-Sabbath as a Jewish Sabbath. Nevertheless, he argued, since Jesus was Jewish and celebrated the Saturday-Sabbath, this designation should not deter Christians. Tillam stressed that Christ was both 'a Jew indeed' and was also 'Lord of the Sabbath.' The celebration of a 'Jewish Sabbath' should not 'startle us anymore then a Jewish Saviour.'[264] 'Odium of the

260. Smith, *Revelation, Resistance, and Mormon Polygamy*, 42

261. Abbot, *Christian Family Builded by God*, 28–30; Loughead, *Perception of Polygamy*, 114–16; Charron, *Of Wisdom Three Books*, 427.

262. Tillam, *Seventh-Day Sabbath*, 133.

263. Tillam, *Temple of Lively Stones*, 2.

264. Tillam, *Seventh-Day Sabbath*, 52.

Jewish Sabbath,' Tillam counselled, was the work of Satan since it tempts Christians away from righteous celebration of the true Sabbath.[265] Moreover, Tillam contended that the opposition of the majority to the practice (on the grounds that it was a form of Judaizing) should *encourage* the Godly to participate, rather than discouraging them:

> The saints set long since to the sanctification of Gods seventh-day Sabbath, according to the fourth commandement, upon which the Dragon was wroth with the woman, and went to make war with the remnant of her seed, which keep the commandements of God, and have the testimony of Jesus.[266]

As such, any compliance with a matter of doctrine on the basis of societal pressure, particularly in matters of Sabbath observation, was, for Tillam, a designation of reprobation. Conversely, the obloquial gaze of the ungodly, directed towards the celebrants of the true Sabbath was a sign of Godliness. 'Let but a scoff drive thee to disdain what was given to the Jews,' he wrote 'and so living and so dying, thou shalt assuredly be damned.'[267] Tillam saw these liturgical practices as functional, not in terms of intrinsic value, but as facilitating the separation of the holy and the profane. On issues like the Sabbath, the decision to conform or resist provided the acid-test for salvation. The magnitude of the issue of the Sabbath took on eschatological proportions for Tillam. It was, he believed, 'the last great controversie between the Saints and the Man of sin.'[268]

Similar themes emerged in the debate held at the Stone-Chapel between Tillam and Jeremiah Ives. Tillam's approach, described by Ives, attached singularity to true Sabbath-observance, merging all that objected to the Seventh-Day Sabbath into one 'mass':

> branding all that differ from thee as Law-breakers and denyers of Scriptures, calling all Ranters, Quakers, Papists, Atheists, &c. that deny the truth of thy opinion. . . . But no wonder Mr. Tillam speakes at this rate, since as he confesseth in his Book, that sometimes his affection did out-run his judgement.[269]

The same attitude is evident in the work of Christopher Pooley. Pooley believed that through true observation of the law, the elect would be demarcated, not only in an eschatological but in a revelatory sense. The

265. Tillam, *Seventh-Day Sabbath*, 52.

266. Tillam, *Seventh-Day Sabbath*, 133.

267. Tillam, *Seventh-Day Sabbath*, 49.

268. Tillam, *Seventh-Day Sabbath*, 1.

269. Ives, *Saturday No Sabbath*, a4r.

sanctification of the saints, Pooley claimed, was evidenced by their opposition to the authorities and acolytes of the state and the national church:

> Consider what was written of old time, especially it calls to the people of God that are stepping out of Babylon, alas wherefore you are put in Prison holes and none saith diliver, and robbed of all your honours.[270]

By designating the observation of the Sabbath as a mark of resistance—a symbolic refusal to accept the ideas of the majority—Tillam and Pooley were recognizing both intrinsic and circumstantial valences of the practice. The word used in Genesis 2:3 to describe the nature of the Sabbath (וַיְקַדֵּשׁ) contained within it that same tension: sacred, separate, sanctified, other and aberrant. The observation of the Sabbath constituted an imposition of Divine Time which cut off the observer from 'natural' time. This understanding of the identity-defining nature of the observation of seasons and times informed the assertion in Daniel 7 that times and days would mark the distinction between the saints and the beast. Tillam made a similar claim, contending that the linking of the names of days and months to heavenly bodies was a Baalish practice, and should be abominated in the interests of preserving the 'sanctified seasons.' The renewed interest in the Sabbath which arose in the context of the destruction of the Temple has been ascribed by Amit to an effort to 'set apart and preserve Israelite society' under the threat of miscegenation. By establishing the 'holiness calendar,' the Israelites sought to 'cut themselves off from the time rhythm of the environment and connect to a new understanding of time.' 'It is doubtful,' Amit contends 'whether a more effective technique of separation than that of the Sabbath could have been invented.'[271] For the Israelites, as for the Tillamites, the natural represented the nomothetic, whereas those elements which conflicted with the natural represented the 'separate' and idiographic. As far as Pooley was concerned, that which was 'natural' was for the beasts. God—His grace, His unveiling—*interrupted* the natural, to create a space—in history—for the sanctified saints to occupy.[272]

But at the same time, the observation of the Sabbath *did* set up—in an immediate, historical sense—the conflict between the Tillamites and the 'man of sin.' In celebrating the Seventh-Day Sabbath, the Tillamites attracted the ire of their peers. They were imprisoned and banished. They were scorned by learned interlocutors. 'His wickedness is well noted,' wrote

---

270. Pooley, *Unwarranted Principles*, 57 (misnumbered as 49).

271. Amit, *Hidden Polemics in the Biblical Narrative*, 239.

272. Pooley, *Unwarranted Principles*, 41.

Edward Burroughs of Thomas Tillam, 'and for wickedness and filthiness, he was cast out and denied of the Assembly whereof he was the Pastor; and stands this day as one cast off.'[273] Once again, therefore, the social and soteriological functions of these practices were intertwined with one another.

SWINES FLESH AND STRONG CHRISTIANS

> Alas the Land is full of Idols! The great city of our Nation hath almost at every door the sight of an idolater.[274]

In this passage, Tillam draws on the imagery of Ezekiel 8. Ezekiel is led by the Sovereign Lord, around the city of Jerusalem. There he sees the wicked and detestable things of Israel portrayed: 'all kinds of crawling things and unclean animals and all the idols of Israel' (Ezek 8). Dietary impurity and idolatry are assimilated in these texts. The separation of Israel from the idols of the nations and the separation of unclean meat and clean meats are interlinked. For Douglas, the pig itself served as a potent symbol of mixture, an anomaly which defied the 'whole' categories within which meats and animals were categorized. The intrinsic concern for separation, which informed the dietary restrictions of Leviticus, would gradually become entangled with a secondary discourse—the othering of Jews on the basis of their refusal to consume pork—creating a helix of factors centring around pork and separation.

Thomas Tillam understood the observation of dietary restrictions, and the separation of clean and unclean meats, to denote purity and singularity. Demonstrating a continuity between the concerns of the redactors of the Levitical laws and those of the separated saints, Tillam identified the consumption of pork with the condition of exile. He wrote that the consumption of 'swine's flesh' was 'a Babylonish custom rather than any Gospel allowance.'[275]

Tillam made the argument that the observation of Levitical dietary requirements was a designation of Christian virtuosity. He argued that anyone who did not observe these injunctions was 'no strong Christian,' since 'stronger Christians are straitly charged to avoid censures.' Any individual who was 'offended' by Tillam's proposals was also 'discovered to be no strong Christian.'[276] In these claims, Tillam pursued the idea of an

---

273. Burroughs, *Memorable Works of a Son of Thunder*, 167.

274. Tillam, *Temple of Lively Stones*, 39.

275. Tillam, *Temple of Lively Stones*, 216–20.

276. Tillam, *Temple of Lively Stones*, 215–17.

'improved separation.'[277] Whilst the act of abstaining from pork is not ethical *per se*—since this would be dangerously close to Popish pelagianism—it was functionally good as a marker of 'strong Christianity.'

Tillam wrote that the attraction of the observation of dietary laws lay in its *distinctiveness* as a practice. Abstaining from 'swines flesh' showed that one was 'firmly fixed upon this great work of separation (which so many do by halves)'; that one was 'making sure of escaping all popish Pollutions.' A key purpose of dietary observations, therefore, was to facilitate the separation of the 'strong Christian' from the 'Popish Pollutions' of Babylonish society.[278] 'Where fore as we must carefully avoid Babylons provision,' Tillam wrote, 'so faithfully must we refuse what God hath prohibited in the heights of Sion.'[279] For an action to denote resistance and singularity, it required the gaze of the majoritarian other. For Tillam, the ethical value of the action (in this instance observation of dietary law) was not *only* predicated on its distinctiveness from the conventions of (Babylonian) society, but also on its *perceived* distinctiveness. The act of refusing pork was to be *seen* by others. 'Undoubtedly such shall do ill who reject and oppose them and cast aspersions upon them,' Tillam wrote.[280]

Tillam was in good company, of course. Philo had been mocked for his refusal to consume pork. John Traske had been forced to eat pork as a method of eroding the troubling and seditious 'singularity' of his teachings. In fact, the 'false Jew,' Thomas Ramsay was tested by his interrogators to prove that he was not Jewish by eating pork. But, as the authors of the midrash of Leviticus 18 had written, the refusal of pork was *especially* precious in that it exhibited the separateness of the Jews from the gentiles.[281] This, then, is the endpoint, the proof of election: to conform to an ethical code that results in rejection and opposition and aspersion at the hands of the massed reprobate, 'the heathen of the land.'

THE STRANGE ACT OF CIRCUMCISION

The most eye-catching element of Tillam's thought emerged only in the context of the self-imposed exile in Lobbach. The Solemn Covenant that Tillam and Pooley brought with them on their second mission to England

277. Tillam, *Temple of Lively Stones*, 172.

278. Tillam, *Temple of Lively Stones*, 215–17.

279. Tillam, *Temple of Lively Stones*, 215.

280. Tillam, *Temple of Lively Stones*, 214.

281. Sifra, *Acharei Mot*, 13:9–10.

in 1666 contained within it several references to the practice of physical circumcision.

> It proveth Abraham's spiritual seed to be his seed, inasmuch as
> that was one of the steps of his faith, in which step of circumci-
> sion his seed ought to walk, and that would prove themselves
> to be such.

Referring to their projected eschatological inheritance in Zion, Pooley and
Tillam located circumcision at the center of their doctrine:

> They are not fitted by the Lord to follow him, knowing that no
> uncircumcised in heart and flesh shall inherit that possession of
> Canaan.[282]

Nowhere is the tension—the paradoxical relationship of 'sacred' and 'aberrant'—more acutely evident than in the topos of circumcision. In Genesis
17, the notion of the 'cutting-off' (יִכָּרֵת) of the uncircumcised is juxtaposed
with the image of God 'cutting' a covenant with Israel (Gen 17). This, in turn,
is juxtaposed with the image of the polity of Israel as תָמִים, 'unblemished' or
'perfect' or 'blameless.' These ideas of perfection, sanctification and separation are all intrinsically bound up in the practice as described in the Hebrew
Bible. Furthermore, through the injunction of Genesis 17:12 to circumcise
those foreign born members of the nation, it is apparent that the process of
circumcision is not only for the purpose of *maintaining* the nationhood of
Israel but that it is also nation-*forming*. The historical context for the genesis of these passages adds another layer of complexity. Some scholars have
contended that these texts and the holiness code of Leviticus were produced
by the authors of the 'Priestly source' in the sixth century and that they
reflect anxieties about the maintenance of the nation of Israel in the face
of diaspora, exile and colonization. Underlying these texts, therefore, is a
desire to stress and define the separateness of Israel, to *resist*, in an ongoing,
discursive, indeed a 'constant' way.[283] The practice of circumcision was identified as both noxious and as a potent identity-marker in the ancient world.
The practice was banned by Hadrian in an attempt to establish a '*varius,
multiplex, multiformis*' Roman identity. This endeavor was the stimulus for
the Bar Kochba revolt.[284] In Spain in the seventh century, the penalty for
participating in a circumcision ritual was castration.

---

282. National Archives, SP 29/181, f. 150r–151v.

283. Albertz, *Israel in Exile*, 107; Bandstra, *Reading the Old Testament*, 88; Houston, *Purity and Monotheism*, 14; Carr, *Reading the Fractures of Genesis*, 138; McKenzie
Covenant, 48.

284. Rizzi, 'Introduction,' 3–4; Bazzana, 'Bar Kochba Revolt,' 85–110.

As Boyarin has shown, circumcision became a forum within which the early rabbinic scholars could demonstrate their refusal of the 'inner/outer, visible/invisible, body/soul' distinctions of the Hellenistic hermeneutic. The hermeneutic of the latter was intimately linked with anthropology. Thus, we find the nexus of carnality, literalism and circumcision in the writings of Philo and of St. Paul. Allegoresis, the soul and 'spiritual circumcision' form the opposite hermeneutic system. These concerns, Boyarin writes, stem from an underlying pursuit of univocity, of 'the one.' It leads Paul towards the radical conclusions of Galatians 3, the annihilation of difference, and of Jewish particularity specifically. Galatians 3 and Romans 3—on this reading—form the antithesis, or perhaps the shadow figure, of Genesis 17. According to the 'maximalist' account of the genesis of rabbinic Judaism, the latter emerged as a reaction to this discourse. At very least, it is clear that 'the extravagant praise heaped upon circumcision by the Mishnah and other early rabbinic documents may have been intended as a response to Paul.'[285] Some contemporary texts also remove or elide the requirement for the circumcision of non-Jewish slaves and of black people in general.[286] As such, from the earliest moment of the cleavage between Christianity and Judaism, circumcision was re-constructed as a mark of distinctiveness.

The echoes of this dynamic were redolent in early-modern Europe. Circumcision functioned primarily as a mark of Jewish identity, but secondarily as a mark of non-Christian identity. Menasseh ben Israel described the importance of circumcision in his *Thesouro dos Dinim*, a guide for reverting marranoes. Almost half of the length of the book is given over to the discussion of circumcision.[287] Thomas Coryat claimed that the Jews at Istanbul were 'desirous that we should attend their ceremony.'[288] Eva Frojmovic suggests that this was a 'projection' of Coryat's. But the alternative—that Jews of Istanbul actively wished to demonstrate and celebrate their distinctiveness in the presence of a curious observer—is equally possible.[289] Once again, as the practice became more invested with the function of determining Jewish distinctiveness, it simultaneously was identified as a centerpiece for Jewish otherness within Christian discourse. As Frojmovic has shown, even (seemingly) curious observers of Jewish life in Europe—like Fynes Moryson—upheld traditional, anti-Judaic biases. Moryson's description of circumcision in Prague surreptitiously included a conflation of the ritual with elements of

285. Cohen, *Why Aren't Jewish Women Circumcised?*, 102.

286. Schorsch, *Jews and Blacks in the Early Modern World*, 172–75, 75n.

287. Schorsch, *Jews and Blacks in the Early Modern World*, 175.

288. Coryate, 'Master Thomas Coryates,' 1825.

289. Frojmovic, 'Christian Travelers to the Circumcision,' 137.

the blood libel.[290] That the mark of circumcision for a *Christian* was considered an act of especial deviation and aberrance is testified to by Menasseh ben Israel himself. Describing the conversion of Diego d'Assumeaon—'who was born a Christian and made a Jew'—ben Israel writes that it was a case that 'all wondered at.'[291] Another figure, Lord Lope de Vera 'imbraced' Judaism in 1644. He circumcised himself in prison. 'O strange act! And worthy of praise,' wrote Menasseh ben Israel.[292]

Strangeness and praiseworthiness intersected in the thought of all of the figures discussed above, not least Thomas Tillam. The overarching concern with the preservation of particularity, the separation of the sacred and the profane, which is so redolent in the text of Genesis 17, is a mirror image of the concern expressed in the manifesto of the Lobbach community. The Tillamite covenant makes several mention of 'strangers,' with whom the Tillamites foreswear contact, particularly in matters of marriage. The text also determines that the Godly will 'obey all the laws, statutes and Judgements . . . of Israel,' asserting that God 'is the onely judge, law giver and King.' The Tillamites in exile assented to a theocratic system of government and rejected earthly jurisdiction, much in the same way that Israel was called upon to do. The document contains a positivist statement of singularity:

> By a distinct people dwelling alone and not reckoned among the nations we understand that every person is bound to keep close to all as respect this.

The manifesto describes the Tillamites' decision to 'chuse for our God with our whole hearts.'[293] As one might expect, the adoption of circumcision by the Tillamites served precisely the purpose with which it was ordained in both Genesis 17 and in the Tillamite manifesto. By their actions, the Tillamites were designated as 'separate' from their own kindred within the Sabbatarian community: they were labelled as 'monstrous' by Squibb et al in the *Faithful Testimony*, as 'marvellously corrupted' by John Cowell.[294]

---

290. Moryson, *Unpublished Chapters of Fynes Moryson's Itinerary*, 494–96; Frojmovic, 'Christian Travelers to the Circumcision,' 134–35.

291. Israel, *Hope of Israel*, 71.

292. Israel, *Hope of Israel*, 72.

293. National Archives, SP 29/181, f. 150r–151v.

294. Cowell, *Snare Broken*, 2; Squibb et al., 'Faithful Testimony Against the Teachers of Circumcision,' 45.

CONCLUSION

'Thomas Tillam is a man boared in the ear, branded and stigmatized in the forehead,' wrote Thomas Weld.[295] Whether or not Weld was deliberately calling to mind the comparable figure of John Traske, he echoed the scorn with which Bacon recalled Traske's punishment. Like Traske before him, Tillam appeared to have cultivated such a hatred in others that it had rendered him amongst the stigmatized. But for Tillam (as for Traske) the distinction between stigma and stigmata was not always clear. Tillam was *unlike* Traske in that he more openly avowed the necessity of schism and ecclesiological separatism. Nor did Tillam have any affinity with the esotericism of Thomas Totney. He harangued those who paid undue attention to the inner light.

And yet, like Traske and Totney, Tillam saw the facility of Judaizing as a mode of separation. Like Traske and Totney he understood that those practices were circumstantially and intrinsically related to resistance, and to the maintenance of impermeable boundaries between the Godly and the ungodly. The practice of circumcision, the renovation of dietary laws and the celebration of the Saturday Sabbath, Tillam openly declared, were marks of separation between the 'virgin train of separated saints' and the 'man of sin.' Tillam openly declared that the facility of these practices was dependent on their visibility. In the disapproving gaze of the other, the Godly found their sanctity. They could hope, as such, to attain the stigmata of a boared ear or a branded forehead.

For the Tillamites there was a third, more clearly avowed dimension. As Pooley wrote, the Law was not a 'natural' thing. It was an idiographic, historical, scandalous thing, an *interpolation* in the natural human experience. Moreover, it defied reason. It was the privilege and the preserve of 'weak base things,' rather than 'rational universities.' Nowhere was the *unnatural* and idiographic nature of the Law more apparent—in the seventeenth century and in general—than in the celebration of the elements of the ceremonial Law.

Perhaps more than anything, the Tillamites were millenarians. They believed that they stood at the threshold of a great unveiling. And whilst the anticipated unveiling would reveal the world, it would also—as John Brinsley prophesied—reveal the long awaited division between the saints and the slaves of satan. These figures stood in history, but with a foot in the eternal. They knew themselves to be at once temporal and atemporal.

---

295. Weld, *Tillam's Account Examined*, 8.

These acts, these marks, these ceremonies separated them from their historical context, and located them amongst the number of another atemporal polity: the Jews.

Conclusion

'LET US GO UP to the Mountain of the Lord,' wrote Thomas Tillam:

> Where we may behold the Labourers at their work digging deep
> through all the Jewish customs, traditions and administrations,
> for old things are passed away and all things become new. That
> is new framed, new formed, for we must not imagine that Christ
> doth totally cast away the old creature, but he heweth, squareth
> and polisheth. . . . Neither are the old elements of Moses house
> utterly rejected, but onely new moulded and fashioned. And al-
> though our Lord's Kingdom is not meat and drink, yet he takes
> their chief meat and drink, he finds in that old building whereof
> he institutes a new feast. And on this wise did those skilful care-
> ful builders dig through and demolish that old heap of Tradi-
> tions, Rites and Ceremonies, yea and all their carnal interests,
> and of the very same materials do they form and frame a new
> and living temple to the Honour of the Everlasting God.[1]

The Judaizers did not deny the supersession of the Mosaic covenant. The
Temple had been destroyed. The old ways had been abolished. They were
Protestants, and they did not believe in the efficacy of forms or rites or sacraments. But from the old heap of 'traditions, rites and ceremonies' they
were able to rescue and repurpose a host of new practices, with new meaning for the specific context in which they were living. As Tillam noted, for
the disciples, the abandonment of the ceremonies served the function of
separation. For the 'strong Christians' it was the renovation of ceremonies
that served this same function.

---

1. Tillam, *Temple of Lively Stones*, 26.

PURITANISM AND IDENTITY

In describing Judaizing as a form of resistance, it could be argued, we simply attach a new label to a familiar phenomenon. But the purpose of this study, at least in part, has been to identify the ways in which the specifically Puritan concern with—what they would have called—'singularity' could become a dynamo for developing new religious practices and movements. More than that, the rise of Judaizing shows us that groups and individuals, during this period, were able to co-opt, repurpose, reconfigure and invert the cultural materials that their society provided.

This could only have been possible in a culture that habitually generated binaries and polarities. All things were in pairs, in early modern England. Good versus evil. Elect versus reprobate. Moderate versus extremist. Popery versus Puritanism. Christians versus Jews. It was only in this context that the *meaning* of these critical inversions—as well as the meaning of other cultural tropes like the skimmington and the rhetoric of paradiastole—could have been clearly understood. Thomas Tillam was able to find 'the contest of the croud,' which he found so encouraging, in the regular inversions of these consensually accepted binaries.[2]

This was Lake's insight when he noted that Puritanism—and indeed all religious controversies of the pre-Civil war period in England—placed individuals in orbit around certain consensually agreed types and ideals. Far from being entirely separate from these ideals, Godly individuals perpetually engaged in processes of self-definition *in relation to* them. As Lake pointed out in his debate with Collinson regarding the 'invention of Puritanism,' the process of identity formation by alterity could never be stable or inert. The Puritan identity was never a concrete thing, but nor was it a construct.[3] It was a constant series of interactions and exchanges. The Godly—to a certain degree—needed to be hated by the world. In order to *be* hated, they needed to watch the ungodly, watching them.[4] They needed to learn *from* the ungodly, from what the ungodly hated.

When Thomas Tillam described right worship, in the *Temple of Lively Stones*, he described the response that the wicked world would have to seeing the Godly pray.[5] It was only, he knew, if the Godly behaved in ways that demonstrated their *distinctiveness* that they could be sure of their difference from the dross of Satan's slaves. But he also knew that awareness of

---

2. Tillam, *Temple of Lively Stones*, 95.

3. Lake, 'Anti-Puritanism,' 86–87.

4. Lake, 'Charitable Christian Hatred,' 145–83.

5. Tillam, *Temple of Lively Stones*, 301.

this distinctiveness could only be found in the disapproving gaze *of* Satan's slaves. This was a masterpiece of Godly divinity. For not only could the Godly derive the satisfaction of assurance from these experiences, they were also able to deny the voluntary nature of this attainment of assurance. As such, they could be absolved of the stain of Pelagianism. The hatred of the mob, after all, was something that happened *to them*, not something they *did*. Tillam recognized this too. 'Be sure that your affections are in motion,' he warned, or 'your bodily exercise will profit little.'[6]

Of course, not just *any* practice would work to project that diplopic view of the Godly, as saintly and despised. Unlearnedness and the 'pose of divinely appointed madness' could do it, because Paul and Noah and the disciples at Pentecost had been good men who were derided for their madness and unlearnedness. Rhetorical impoliteness could do it, because it could be couched in terms of a refusal to give to Caesar that which is God's—that is deference. Even turning one's eye upwards could do it, because it was—at least on one level—a mark of prayerfulness. That it also appeared to denote sanctimony and as such could make one the object of derision was a happy accident.

Judaizing also appeared to do the trick. My analysis is indebted, in this regard, to the work of scholars like Nicholas McDowell and Eliane Glaser (and further back to James Shapiro) who have shown how the topos of Judaism provided discursive materials, which were used and manipulated for the purpose of stigmatizing and locating groups and individuals beyond the Pale of acceptability.[7] I have sought to apply some of their insights in a different direction. I think that the preceding chapters have demonstrated that, if the topos of Judaism was used by early-modern writers to *confine* their antagonists in a pejorative space, it was also used by some to *occupy* that same space. Of course, these processes were far from mutually exclusive. In fact they were complementary. If conformists knew that they could render John Traske as 'singular,' by *labelling* him a Judaizer, Ockham's razor would demand we concede that Traske *himself* knew that by *Judaizing* he could render *himself* as 'singular.'

THE JUDAIZERS AND THE BIBLE

It has been almost unanimously claimed that the Judaizing phenomenon within Puritanism was caused by the shift towards a more literal

6. Tillam, *Temple of Lively Stones*, 301.

7. McDowell, 'Stigmatizing of Puritans as Jews,' 125–33; Glaser, *Judaism without Jews*, 66, 76.

understanding of scripture. I have claimed that this is not a viable explanation, at least with regards to the deeds and words of Thomas Totney, John Traske and Thomas Tillam. All of these figures wrote openly of the need for a pneumatological approach to the Word. Traske relied on dreams and visions in order to come to doctrinal conclusions. Totney derided those who relied on 'verses' to form their arguments. Thomas Tillam, when called upon to defend his claims on the basis of scripture, conceded that he could not. And apparently it didn't matter. Faith based on the letter of the Law, he wrote, was a 'meer historical faith.'

This should not, perhaps, be surprising. As Crome has demonstrated, the Godly tended to read the Bible in accordance with an *analogia fidei*. Ian Green's depiction of the Godly as Certeauzian 'nomads,' searching the text for validation of pre-established beliefs is perhaps cynical.[8] But even if we do not take our analysis to that extent, it is clear that different figures, with different sensibilities and different opinions on matters of ecclesiology and soteriology during this period proposed radically different accounts of what the text *said*. The first advocates of Protestant-style scripturalism *may* have believed that this development would lead to greater consensus and less controversy. If they did, they would have been dismayed by the English experience. As Como has demonstrated, the fundamental claims of Protestantism in relation to scripture carried the germ of chaos, which would ultimately lead to the milliformation of Protestantism and to the disintegration of Puritanism.[9]

The Bible was absolutely central to the emergence of Judaizing. This cannot be denied. But to claim that Judaizers were simply those Puritans who took the principles of literalism and *sola scriptura* 'too far' or who took them too seriously, suggests an understanding of this phenomenon which places too great an emphasis on its quantitative rather than its qualitative distinctiveness from other modes of divinity. The Judaizers read the Bible differently. This does not only apply to their reading of the Law. It also applies to their reading of the history of the Jewish people, of the prophets and of the apocalyptic literature.

UNCERTAINTY AND EXTREMISM IN THE PURITAN CONTEXT

Collinson, Walsham, Bozeman, Lake and many other historians of this period have expressed a belief in the utility of psychological models for

8. Green, *Print and Protestantism*, 130.

9. Como, *Blown by the Spirit*, 439–40.

examining the experiences of the Godly of this period.[10] I think that this study points out the value in considering the role which psychological uncertainty played in the development of widespread and long-lasting themes within English Protestant culture.

If Michael Hogg's research is correct, then the feelings of uncertainty which followed from the absolute denial of volition in the task of salvation, and in the debasement of reason in servitude to the theology of the cross, would lead to greater desire for entitativity, and to the development of small, highly entitative, sect-like groups. Any number of factors could be pointed at to demonstrate the potential anachronism of using contemporary, experimental psychology to describe tendencies in the early-modern world. Certainly, however, Michael Hogg believes that his findings have something to say about cultural and political shifts that have taken place throughout history.[11]

I believe that the applicability of these theories is particularly apparent in the study of the Puritan era. All of the figures with whom this study is concerned expressed, at one point or another, great uncertainty about the future. And more often than not they related these feelings of uncertainty, explicitly, to matters of soteriology. They lived through a time of teeming prophecy and it recalled, for them, Christ's warning concerning the false messiahs that would emerge in the end times. Where the structures of sacramentalism had guaranteed assurance for a hundred generations of English Christians, the Godly who developed the greatest fixation on Romans 9 were left with very few tools to investigate their own salvation. Neither princes, nor Churches, nor reason, nor common sense morality, as Leif Dixon put it, could help the Godly to fetch the warrant from within.[12]

Hogg's model would suggest that in this context Godly men and women would seek to form or join small, highly entitative groups. The entitativity of these groups would be informed by their sense of togetherness and uniformity of behavior. It would also be informed by their sense of the obloquy of the majority. The previous chapters have shown how these dynamics played out in the specific context of Judaizing. But I believe that the same pattern could be demonstrated to have played out in innumerable contexts across the panorama of Godly divinity during the seventeenth century.

10. Collinson, *Puritan Character*, 21; Bozeman, *Precisianist Strain*, 51; Lake, 'Anti-Popery', 80.

11. Hogg et al., 'Uncertainty and the Roots of Extremism', 409.

12. Dixon, *Practical Predestinarians*, 91, 101.

ALLOSEMITISM AND JUDAIZING

In the 1980s and 1990s, David S. Katz and James Shapiro offered starkly different accounts philo-semitism and antisemitism in early modern England. Whilst Shapiro described England as being immersed in anti-Judaic bias—such that the nation itself was defined in opposition to a host of Jewish bogeymen—Katz conversely presented a culture awakening to a new era of 'philo-semitism.'[13] These accounts informed the narratives which both authors offered for the emergence of Judaizing amongst the Godly.

Katz has expressed the view that these two visions are irreconcilable, or at least that Shapiro's is false. Here I have tried to suggest that this is not necessarily the case. I believe that the topos of the Jew stood for otherness in English culture, but not entirely in a pejorative sense. Rather, the understanding of the Jew as other, was informed by a vast array of cultural materials, some anti-Judaic, some philo-Semitic; some Christian, some Jewish. In this respect, Zygmunt Bauman's theoretical claims about allosemitism hold true. In early modern England, Jews were different, their difference mattered, and—whether for good or bad reasons—they could not be allowed to melt, inconspicuously, into the crowd. Nowhere is the proteophobic nature of early-modern Protestant allosemitism more evident—as Andrew Crome has demonstrated in his recent work—than in the apparently philo-Semitic, Judeocentric millenarianism of Brightman and Finch. 'The Jew,' represented a complex (and ultimately uncanny) helix of positive and negative characteristics. These distinctive, singular characteristics, would render the Jew as irreducibly other, until the very end of days.[14]

As Crome has suggested, in the context of the readmission discussion, to portray the English as anti-Semitic—at least to the degree that Shapiro does—would probably be an overstatement. Equally, to portray the English as philo-semitic—at least to the degree that Katz does—would be an overstatement.[15] Nonetheless, for both the 'philo-semites' and the 'antisemites,' the figure of the Jew was reduced to a totem, or a fetish. This perhaps explains the curious and characteristic interactions between Jews and Christians when they did encounter each other. Whether it be Coryat's meeting with the Jews in Venice, or Whitehead at 'Bevers Marks' or Broughton in Amsterdam, we find Christians and Jews talking at each other, rather than to each other.[16] As Crome has it, the Jew can never be interacted with 'on his

13. Katz, *Philo-Semitism*, 7; Shapiro, *Shakespeare and the Jews*, 8.

14. Crome, *Christian Zionism and English National Identity*, 60–62.

15. Crome, 'English National Identity,' 284.

16. Whitehead, 'For the Jews,' 63; Coryat, *Coryates Crambe*, D4r; *Coryate's Crudities*, 236.

own terms.'[17] The otherness—or in Buberian terms the 'itness'—of the Jew, a perennial of English culture up to this point, sits uneasily in Katz's account of the rise of Judaizing. In fact, Katz believed that the Judaizing phenomenon was irreconcileable with Shapiro's vision of a broadly anti-Judaic culture. By identifying the reasons why 'otherness', or 'singularity' may have held an intrinsic, cultural value for the Godly who gravitated towards apparently Jewish practices, I have also sought to demonstrate that both the anti-Judaic *and* philo-Semitic valences of English culture can be accommodated within an account of Judaizing.

In doing so, I have also tried to attribute a greater role to Judaism itself, suggesting that the otherness of the Jews, as separate from the nations, was a persistent component of the Jewish experience and one which was carefully crafted *within* Judaism, rather than being simply foisted upon Jews by supersessionist ideologues. In this I have drawn from the insights of Daniel Boyarin. Boyarin sought to replace the kinship model of Judeo-Christian history—suggesting that a single model of Judaism branched off into two scions called Christianity and Rabbinic Judaism—with a wave model. According to the latter, Judaism and Christianity continue to interact with one another, the one supervening on the other, changes in one occasionally effecting changes in the other. As such, different iterations of Judaism, Christianity and Jewish-Christianity appear along a spectrum, like dialects within a language.

JEWISH CHRISTIANITY

A significant, underlying issue, throughout this study has been the question of what makes a Jew. This was an extremely fraught question in the early modern period as those diverse elements, which would eventually develop into a modern conception of race, began to emerge. Was Judaism a matter of lineage? Of race? Of religion? Of ethics?

These questions have not become more straightforward to answer in the intervening centuries. I have sought, here, to add another dimension to this discussion, by employing some aspects of John Howard Yoder's understanding of Judaism. I chose to do so, in part, because Yoder's perspective on radical Reformed Protestantism was (in some sense) an emic one. In other words, he read the Bible, and the literature of the radical Reformed Protestants from the perspective of a radical Reformed Protestant (albeit a twentieth-century one). I believe this offers some insight into the understanding of what 'a Jew' is, from a perspective which shares some similarities with the

17. Crome, *Christian Zionism and English National Identity,* 23.

subjects of this study. For Yoder, the Jewish character of Christianity came to efflorescence in the development of 'free Churches,' during the post-Reformation period.[18] It stood not for any specific set of practices, nor of genealogy, but rather for an understanding of the nexus of relationships that existed between God, his people and the world. For Yoder, the Jewishness of Christianity lay in its avowal of a truly historical sense of God, a genuine renunciation of power and a corresponding epistemology of powerlessness.

It is difficult not to recognize that figures like Returne Hebdon and Thomas Totney and their peers shared—in some respects—Yoder's understanding of what it meant to be Jewish. For Hebdon, to be Jewish was to be amongst the people of 'least esteeme,' 'hated and afflicted . . . for their Creator.'[19] For Thomas Totney, the Quakers were Jews in that they were 'lambs,' 'weak brethren,' 'scorned by men.'[20] For Christopher Pooley, obedience to the Law was not natural or moral or 'religious'—to use Yoder's parlance. Rather it was scandalous, anachronistic, historical. It called the Godly out of the world, Tillam wrote, and 'cut off the filthy adulterer.'[21]

PURITANS AND DANGER

This all points to a fundamental claim that Puritans were primarily concerned with separating. 'Separatism'—with a capital S—was only one component of this tendency. Innumerable acts, beliefs and practices spoke to the separation of the Godly from the profane world. This could take the form of a passive assertion of difference in the form of resistance, that is to say actions which invited the opprobrium of their peers. In each of these acts the Godly were seeking to 'sort out company.'[22]

I have suggested here that this tendency also spoke to the development of devotional practices within the Godly sphere. As Douglas and others have suggested, the rituals and practices associated with Biblical Judaism often focused on the importance of maintaining separation. The Sabbath itself was the pre-eminent exemplar of this. But the division of meats, the act of circumcision and the maintenance of temple rites all spoke to the same concern. For Douglas, these practices were most prominent when the cohesion of the polity was threatened. Anxiety about mixing and confusion elicited a desire to perform acts of separation within the ritual sphere.

18. Yoder, 'Jewishness of the Free Church Vision,' 105–20.
19. Hebdon, *Guide to the Godly*, 80.
20. Tany, *Tharam Taniah*, br.
21. Tillam, *Temple of Lively Stones*, 189.
22. Collinson, *Puritan Character*, 32.

As we have seen, the Godly were also focused on purity and on the separation of things sacred from things profane. This was as much a function of the Johannine, 'light/dark' imagery of Traske's anti-legalism, or of Totney's Behmenism, as it was a function of the Jewishness of either of their traditions. I have argued here, on that basis, that anxiety about separation may have contributed to the appeal of practices which were themselves inaugurated in order to formalise separation, purification and rectification. From a non-religious perspective, it is tempting to seek an instrumental reason for these acts of separation. Kristeva believed that acts of separation were inaugurated in order to eliminate those things which elicited disgust.[23] Modern and ancient writers have sought 'medical materialist' explanations for these practices: the rejection of pork in the interests of avoiding trichinosis for example.[24] Douglas, and those who have later refined her work, have moved the emphasis of these rituals from the object of the act, to the act itself. Separation *itself* was good, whether or not that which was being separated was good or not. I believe that by focussing on the Godly desire to separate things from one another into coherent categories, we can open up a vista towards the understanding of those practices most commonly associated with voluntary religion during this period.

JUDAIZING, SINGULARITY, AND RESISTANCE

At this point in our history, more than any other, it is clear that identities are not built on the solid ground—on the beliefs and convictions, on the shibboleths and truths—that we perhaps once thought they were. On the contrary, we belong to cultures that supervene, for their own existence, on idealized projections of alterior and antagonistic 'others.' When they change, we change and vice versa.

Without an antagonist or an antipode, as Collinson once pointed out, the Godly mind was in trouble.[25] The obloquial gaze of the reprobate critic, the 'contest of the croud,' allayed those feelings of anxiety, that one might be amongst the rabble of the reprobate. For this, amongst other, reasons, the Godly required the ungodly, just as the ungodly required the Godly. All things go in pairs. Everything completes the goodness of something. The on-going, feedback loop of interactions between the Godly and the ungodly, between the Judaizers and those who accused them of Judaizing, provided the material from which both could create their own identities, their own

23. Kristeva, *Powers of Horror*, 3.
24. Douglas, *Purity and Danger*, 30.
25. Collinson, 'Cohabitation of the Faithful with the Unfaithful,' 55–57.

cultures. What was said for Puritans and anti-Puritans could also be said, in this respect, for Jews and Christians.

For all of its ancient grandeur, the Law, in the first instance, is a thing felt. This is the endpoint of our academic pursuit of religion. Ultimately, therefore, to question *why* an individual or group pursues a particular religious practice is to reach a dead-end. David Como attempted to explain what it felt like for the Traskites to worship in the way that they chose to. It was a sense of electricity, he thought.[26] They had stepped outside of the world, and they had been unveiled as creatures not of the world. For Tillam, this was true peace, within the walls.[27] For Traske, it was

> The fellowship of the Father, and the Son [and] such unspeakable comfort of the saints in light.[28]

26. Como, *Blown by the Spirit*, 148.

27. Tillam, *Temple of Lively Stones*, 235, 23.

28. Traske, *Heaven's Joy*, 75.

Bibliography

PRIMARY SOURCES

Manuscript

Cambridge University Library
Ely Diocesan Records B/2/35.

Guildhall Library
Manuscript 5576/1.

Lincolnshire Archives Office
Bishop's Transcripts, South Hykeham, Lady Day 1608.

London Metropolitan Archives
Manuscript 9274.
Manuscript 10091/17.

National Archives
SP 14/180.
SP 18/102.
SP 29/40.
SP 29/41.
SP 29/106.
SP 29/181.
SP 29/236.
SP 63/237.

Somerset Records Office
D/D/Ca 204.
D/D/Ca 140.

D/D/Ca 189.

Westminster City Archives
STC/B, mf. 2.

Printed Books

Abbot, Robert. *A Christian Family Builded by God.* London, 1653. British Library, Wing A68.

Adams, Thomas. *A Commentary or, Exposition upon the Divine Second Epistle.* London, 1633. British Library, STC 108.

Addamson, William. *An Answer to a Book Titled Quakers Principles Quaking.* London, 1656. British Library, Wing A501.

Ainsworth, Henry. *Annotations upon the First Book of Moses, Called Genesis.* Amsterdam, 1616. Cambridge University Library, STC 210.

———. *An Apologie or Defence of Brownists.* Amsterdam, 1604. Cambridge University Library, STC 238.

———. *An Epistle Sent Unto Two Daughters of Warwick from H. N.* Amsterdam, 1608. British Library, STC 18553.

Ainsworth, Henry, et al. *A Seasonable Treatise for this Age Occasioned by a Letter Written by one Thomas Woolsey Prisoner in Norwich.* London, 1657. Cambridge University Library, Wing S2245.

Airay, Henry. *Lectures upon the whole Epistle of St. Paul to the Philippians.* London: n.p., 1618.

Ambrose, Isaac. *The Doctrine & Directions but More Especially the Practice and Behavior of a Man in the Act of the New Birth.* London, 1605. Henry E. Huntington Library, Wing A2955.

Andrewes, John. *Andrewes Repentance, Sounding Alarum to Returne from His Sins Unto Almightie God.* London, 1631. Pepys Library, STC 589.5.

Andrewes, Lancelot. *A Sermon Preached before His Maiestie at Whitehall, on Easter Day Last.* London, 1618. British Library, STC 623.

———. *Two Answers to Cardinal Perron and Other Miscellaneous Works of Lancelot Andrewes.* Oxford: Parker, 1854.

Askew, Anne. *The First Examinacion of Anne Askewe Latelye Martired in Smythfelde, by the Romyshe Popes Upholders.* London, 1548. Folger Shakespeare Library, STC 852.

Aston, Thomas. *A Remonstrance, Against Presbytery.* London, 1642. British Library, Wing S2775.

Bacon, Francis. *Sylva Sylvarum.* London, 1627. Henry E. Huntington Library, STC 1168.

Bacon, Robert. *A Taste of the Spirit.* London, 1652. British Library, Wing B371.

Bancroft, Richard. *A Sermon Preached at Paules Crosse.* London, 1588. British Library, STC 1347.

Bampfield, Thomas. *An Enquiry Whether the Lord Jesus Christ Made the World.* London, 1692. British Library, Wing B629.

Barlow, Thomas. *Several Miscellaneous and Weighty Cases of Conscience Learnedly and Judiciously Resolved.* London, 1692. British Library, Wing B843.

Barlow, William. *The Summe and Substance of the Conference Which, It Pleased His Excellent Maiestie to Haue with the Lords, Bishops, and Other of His Clergie.* London, 1604. Folger Shakespeare Library, STC 1456.5.

Barrow, Henry. *A Brief Discoverie of the False Church.* Dordrecht, 1590. Yale University Library, STC 1517.

Basset, William. *A Sermon at the Warwick-Shire Meeting.* London, 1679. Cambridge University Library, Wing B1053.

Baxter, Richard. *Certain Disputations of Right to Sacraments, and the True Nature of Visible Christianity.* London, 1658. St. John's College Library, Wing B1212.

———. *The Church Told of Mr. Ed Bagshaw's Scandals and Preached to the Right Worshipfull Companie of the Haberdashers Warned of the Dangerous Snares of Satan.* London, 1672. Union Theological Seminary, Wing B1226.

———. *Reliquiae Baxterianae.* London, 1696. British Library, Wing B1370.

———. *A Treatise of Episcopacy Confuting by Scripture.* London, 1681. British Library, Wing B1427.

Becon, Thomas. *The Reliques of Rome Contayning All Such Matters of Religion, as Haue in Times past Bene Brought into the Church by the Pope and His Adherents.* London, 1563. Folger Shakespeare Library, STC 1754.

Bedford, Thomas. *Luthers Predecessours: Or an Answere to the Question of the Papists.* London, 1624. Emmanuel College Library, STC 1787.

Bentham, Joseph. *The Christian Conflict.* London, 1635. Cambridge University Library, STC 1887.

Bernard, Richard. *A Weekes Worke.* London, 1616. Sion College Library, STC 1965.

Beza, Theodor. *A Briefe and Piththie Summe of the Christian Faith.* Translated by R. F. London: n.p., 1565.

———. *Master Bezaes Sermons upon the Three Chapters of the Canticles.* Translated by John Harmar. Oxford: n.p., 1587.

A Blazing Starre Seen in the West at Totneis in Devonshire. London, 1642. British Library, Wing B3182.

Blount, Charles. *The Oracles of Reason.* London, 1693. Cambridge University Library, Wing B3312.

Böhme, Jakob. *Aurora.* London, 1656. British Library, Wing B3397.

———. *The Epistles of Jacob Behmen.* London, 1649. British Library, Wing B3404.

———. *Mysterium Magnum.* London, 1656. British Library, Wing B3411.

———. *Of the Becoming Man or Incarnation of Jesus Christ, the Sonne of God.* London, 1659. British Library, Wing B3405.

Bolton, Robert. *A Discourse on the State of True Happiness.* London, 1611. Bristol Public Libraries, STC 3228.

———. *Instructions for a Right Comforting Afflicted Consciences.* London, 1631. British Library, STC 3238.

Bourgchier, Henry. 'Henry Bourgchier to Dr. James Ussher.' In vol. 16 of *The Works of the Reverend James Ussher*, edited by Charles Elrington, 359. London: n.p., 1864.

Brabourne, Theophilus. *A Defence of That Most Ancient and Sacred Ordinance of Gods, the Sabbath Day.* London, 1632. Cambridge University Library, STC 3473.

Bradford, William. *Of Plymouth Plantation.* New York: Knopff, 2004.

———. *William Bradford's Books.* Baltimore: Johns Hopkins University Press, 2003.

Brewster, Francis. *Essays on Trade and Navigation in Five Parts*. London: Cockerill, 1695. British Library, Wing B4434.

Bridges, Francis. *Gods Treasurie Displayed: Or, the Promises, and Threatnings of Scripture*. London, 1630. Bodleian Library, STC 3733.

Brightman, Thomas. *A Commentary on the Canticles*. London, 1644. Union Theological Seminary, Wing B4681.

———. *A Revelation of the Apocalypse*. Amsterdam, 1611. University of Illinois, STC 3754.

Brinsley, John. *The Second Part of the True Watch*. London, 1607. Bodleian Library, STC 3776.

Bromley, Thomas. *A Way to the Sabbath of Rest*. London, 1692. British Library, Wing B4888A.

Browne, Edward. *An Account of Several Travels through a Great Part of Germany*. London, 1677. British Library, Wing B5109.

Browne, Robert. *An Answere to Master Cartwright His Letter for Joyning with the English Churches*. London, 1585. Bodleian Library, STC 3909.

———. *A Treatise of Reformation without Tarying Anie*. Middleburg: Painter, 1582. Bodleian Library, STC 3910.3.

Burroughs, Edward. *The Memorable Works of a Son of Thunder*. London: n.p., 1672.

Burroughs, Jeremiah. *The Excellency of a Gracious Spirit Deliuered in a Treatise upon the 14 of Numbers, Verse 24*. London, 1639. Union Theological Seminary, STC 4128.

Byfield, Nicholas. *A Cure for the Fear of Death*. London, 1618. British Library, STC 4213.

———. *The Marrow of the Oracles of God*. London, 1630. British Library, STC 4225.

———. *The Signes*. London, 1614. Bodleian Library, STC 4236.

Calvert, Thomas. *The Blessed Jew of Morocco; or, the Blackamoor Made White*. London, 1648. British Library, Wing S545.

Calvin, John. *Institutes of the Christian Religion*. Translated by Henry Beveridge. Edinburgh: Calvin Translation Society, 1845.

Capel, Richard. *Tentations: Their Nature, Danger, and Cure*. London, 1633. British Library, STC 4595.

Carter, Richard. *The Schismatick Stigmatised*. London, 1641. British Library, Wing C664.

Cartwright, Thomas. *A Replye to an Answere Made of M. Doctor Whitgifte against the Admonition to the Parliament*. London, 1573. Henry E. Huntington Library, STC 5711.

———. *The Second Replie*. London, 1575. Henry E. Huntington Library, STC 4714.

Chapman, George. *Gyles Goosecap Knight*. London, 1606. British Library, STC 12050.

The Cheshire Petition for Establishing of the Common-Prayer-Booke, and Suppression of Schismatiques, Presented to the Kings Majestie, and from Him Recommended to the House of Peers by the Lord Keeper. London, 1642. British Library, Wing C3783.

Clarke, Samuel. *The Lives of Sundry Eminent Persons*. London, 1683. British Library, Wing C4538.

Coke, Roger. *A Discourse of Trade in Two Parts*. London, 1670. Henry E. Huntington Library, Wing C4976.

Collier, Thomas. *A Brief Answer to Some of the Objections and Demurs Made Against the Coming in and Inhabiting of the Jews in this Common-wealth*. London, 1655. British Library, Wing C5269.

Coppe, Abiezer. *Some Sweet Sips, of Some Spirituall Wine Sweetly and Freely Dropping from One Cluster of Grapes, Brought between Two upon a Staffe from Spirituall Canaan.* London, 1649. Henry E. Huntington Library, Wing C6093.

Coryat, Thomas. *Coryats Crudities.* London, 1611. Henry E. Huntington Library, STC 5808.

Cotton, John. *Christ the Fountaine of Life: Or, Sundry Choyce Sermons on Part of the Fifth Chapter of the First Epistle of St. John.* London, 1651. Library of Congress, Wing C6417.

Cowell, John. *The Snare Broken.* London, 1677. Cambridge University Library, Wing C6647.

Crab, Roger. *Dagon's-Downfall; Or the Great Idol Digged up Root and Branch.* London, 1657. British Library, Wing C6735.

———. *The English Hermite.* London, 1655. British Library, Wing E3089.

———. *A Tender Salvation.* London, 1659. British Library, Wing C6738.

Crowley, Abraham. *Visions and Prophecies Concerning England, Scotland, and Ireland of Ezekiel Grebner.* London, 1660. British Library, Wing C6696.

Crowley, Robert. *The Voyce of the Laste Trumpet Blowen by the Seventh Angel.* London, 1549. Henry E. Huntington Library, STC 6094.

Culverwell, Ezekiel. *Time Well Spent in Sacred Meditations.* London, 1634. British Library, STC 6112.

D. P. P. *An Antidote against the Contagious Air of Independency.* London: n.p., 1645.

Daborne, Robert. *A Christian Turn'd Turk.* London, 1612. British Library, STC 6184.

Davenport, Robert. *A New Tricke to Cheat the Divell.* London, 1639. Henry E. Huntington Library, STC 6315.

Davies, William. *A True Relation of the Travailes and Most Miserable Captivitie of William Davies.* London, 1614. Henry E. Huntington Library, STC 6365.

Dawbeny, Henry. *Historie and Policie Reviewed, in the Heroick Transactions of His Most Serene Highnesse, Oliver, Late Lord Protector.* London, 1659. British Library, Wing D448.

Dell, William. *The Tryal of Spirits Both in Teachers & Hearers Wherein Is Held Forth the Clear Discovery and Certain Downfal of the Carnal and Antichristian Clergie of These Nations.* London, 1660. British Library, Wing D933.

Denison, Stephen. *An Exposition upon the First Chapter of the Second Epistle of Peter.* London, 1622. British Library, STC 6603.

———. *The Monument or Tombe-stone.* London, 1620. British Library, Wing 6604.

———. *A New Creature.* London, 1619. Bodleian Library, STC 6607.

Dent, Arthur. *The Plaine Man's Pathway to Heaven.* London: n.p., 1607.

———. *The Ruine of Rome: Or an Exposition upon the Whole Revelation.* London, 1628. Bodleian Library, Wing 6644.

A Distinct and Faithful Accompt of All the Receipts, Disbursments, and Remainder of the Moneys Collected in England, Wales & Ireland, for the Relief of the Poor Distressed Protestants in the Valleys of Piemont. London, 1658. British Library, Wing D1694.

Dowsing, William. *The Journal of William Dowsing.* Woodbridge: Boydell, 2001.

Dury, John. *A Case of Conscience.* London: n.p., 1656.

———. *An Information Concerning the Present State of the Jewish Nation in Europe.* London: n.p., 1658.

Earle, John. *Microcosmographie.* London, 1628. British Library, STC 7439.

Eaton, John. *The Discovery of the Most Dangerous Dead Faith.* London, 1642. British Library, Wing E114.

———. *The Honey-Combe of Free Justification by Christ Alone.* London, 1642. Union Theological Seminary, Wing E115.

Edwards, Thomas. *Antapologia.* London: n.p., 1644.

Elidad. *A Good and Fruitfull Exhortation Unto the Famelie of Love.* London, 1574. British Library, STC 7573.

Estwick, Nicholas. *Mr. Bolton's Last and Learned Work.* London: n.p., 1639.

Etherington, John. *The Defence of Iohn Etherington against Steven Denison.* London, 1641. British Library, Wing E3384.

Evelyn, John. *The Diary of John Evelyn.* Woodbridge: Boydell, 1995.

Everard, John. *Some Gospel Treasures Opened.* London: n.p., 1653.

Everyman, a Morality Play. London, 1515. Bodleian Library, STC 10604.

'The Examination of John Pecke.' National Library of Scotland, MS Adv. 33.1.6, vol. 20, f. 60.

Fairfax, Ferdinando. *A Fuller Relation of that Miraculous Victory.* London, 1643. British Library, Wing F2491A.

Falconer, John. *A Briefe Refutation of John Traske's Judaical and Novel Fancyes.* London, 1618. British Library, STC 10675.

The Family of Love. London, 1608. British Library, STC 17879.

Fawcet, Samuel. *A Seasonable Sermon for these Troublesome Times.* London, 1641. British Library, Wing F562.

Felltham, Owen. *Resolves, Divine, Moral, and Political.* London, 1660. Henry E. Huntington Library, Wing F655A.

Field, John. *A Godly Exhortation.* London, 1583. Bodleian Library, STC 10844.8.

Finch, Henry. *The Worlds Great Restauration or the Calling of the Jews.* London, 1621. British Library, STC 10874.5.

Fowler, Christopher. *Daemonium Meridianum, Satan at Noon. Or, Antichristian Blasphemies, Anti-Scripturall Divelismes, Anti-Morall Uncleanness, Evidenced in the Light of Truth, and Published by the Hand of Justice.* London, 1655. British Library, Wing F1692.

Fox, George. *Journal of George Fox.* London, 1694. British Library, Wing F1854.

———. *A Looking-Glass for the Jews.* London, 1674. Bodleian Library, Wing F1859.

———. *What Election and Reprobation Is.* London, 1679. British Library, Wing F1989.

Foxe, John. *Actes and Monuments.* London, 1583. Cambridge University Library, STC 11222a.

Fry, John. *The Clergy in Their Colours.* London, 1650. British Library, Wing F2255.

Fuller, Thomas. *The Church History of Britain: From the Birth of Jesus, Until the Year MDCXLVIII.* London, 1655. British Library, Wing F2416.

———. *The Infants Advocate of Circumcision on Jewish and Baptisme on Christian Children.* London: n.p., 1653.

G. H. *The Declaration of John Robins, the False Prophet, Otherwise Called the Shakers God, and Joshua Beck, and John King, the Two False Disciples.* London, 1651. British Library, Wing H28.

Gardiner, Stephen. *Reports of Cases in Courts of Star Chamber and High Commission.* London: Camden Society, 1886.

Garment, Joshua. *The Hebrew Deliverance at Hand.* London, 1641. British Library, Wing G261.

Gerree, John. *The Character of an Old English Puritan, or Non-Conformist*. London, 1659. Bodleian, Wing G592.

Gibbons, Nicholas. *Questions and Disputations Concerning the Holy Scripture*. London, 1601. Henry E. Huntington Library, STC 11814.

Gifford, George. *A Briefe Discourse of Certaine Points of the Religion Which Is among the Common Sort of Christians, Which May Bee Termed the Countrie Diuinitie with a Manifest Confutation of the Same*. London, 1582. British Library, STC 11846.

Goodwin, Thomas. *The Works of Thomas Goodwin*. London: n.p., 1863.

Gouge, William. *The Progresse of Divine Providence*. London, 1645. British Library, Wing G1393.

Grantham, Thomas. *Christianismus Primitivus*. London: n.p., 1674.

———. *The Fourth Principle of Christs Doctrine Vindicated*. London, 1674. Bodleian Library, Wing G1533.

Greenwood, Henry. *A Treatise of the Great and Generall Daye of Iudgement Necessarie for Euerie Christian That Wisheth Good Successe to His Soule*. London, 1606. British Library, STC 12337.

Griffith, John. *A Declaration of Some of Those People in or near London, Called Anabaptists, That Own, and Beleeve, That Gods Love, in the Death of His Son, Is Extended to All Men*. London, 1660. British Library, Wing G2001.

Grindal, Edmund. *The Remains of Edmund Grindal*. Cambridge: n.p., 1843.

Guevara, Antonio. *A Chronicle*. London: n.p., 1577.

Hall, Joseph. *Fanatick Moderation, Exemplified in Bishop Hall's Hard Measure, as It Was Written by Himself*. London, 1680. British Library, NUC 3272.

Haller, William. *Tracts on Liberty in the Puritan Revolution, 1638–1647*. New York: Columbia University Press, 1934.

Harrington, James. *Oceana*. London: n.p., 1656.

Harris, Alexander. *Œconomy of the Fleete*. London: n.p., 1879.

Harvey, Richard. *Theologicall Discourse of the Lamb of God and His Enemies Contayning a Briefe Commentarie of Christian Faith and Felicitie*. London, 1590. Bodleian Library, STC 12915.

Hebdon, Returne. *A Guide to the Godly*. London, 1646. Henry E. Huntington Library, Wing H1347.

Herbert, George. *A Priest to the Temple or the Country Parson*. London, 1652. Union Theological Seminary, Wing H1513.

Heylyn, Peter. *The History of the Sabbath*. London, 1636. British Library, STC 13274.

Hickman, Henry. *The Believer's Duty Towards the Spirit*. London, 1665. Bodleian Library, Wing H1906.

Higden, Ranulf. *Polychronicon*. London: 1482. British Library, STC 13438.

Higginson, Francis. *A Brief Relation of the Irreligion of Northern Quakers*. London: n.p., 1653.

Hobson, Paul. *The Fallacy of Infants Baptisme Discovered*. London, 1645. British Library, Wing H2272.

Holyday, Barten. *Against Disloyalty Fower Sermons Preach'd in the Times of the Late Troubles*. London, 1661. Bodleian Library, Wing H2530.

Holyoake, Francis. *A Sermon of Obedience Especially Unto Authoritie Ecclesiasticall*. Oxford, 1613. Bodleian Library, STC 13623.

Hooker, Richard. *Of the Lawes of Ecclesiasticall Politie Eight Books*. London, 1604. British Library, STC 13712.

————. *The Works of Mr. Richard Hooker That Learned and Judicious Divine.* London, 1666. Henry E. Huntington Library, Wing H2631.

Howell, James. *Instructions for Forreine Travel.* London, 1642. British Library, Wing H3082.

Israel, Menasseh ben. *The Hope of Israel.* London, 1650. British Library, Wing M377.

Ives, Jeremiah. *Saturday No Sabbath.* London, 1659. Cambridge University Library, Wing I1104.

J. J. *The Resurrection of Dead Bones.* London: n.p., 1655.

Jewel, John. *A Replie to M. Hardinge.* London, 1565. British Library, STC 424:03.

Jones, John. *The Arte and Science of Preserving Bodie and Soule in Healthe, Wisedom, and Catholike Religion: Phisically, Philosophically, and Divinely.* London, 1579. British Library, STC 14724.

Jonson, Benjamin. *Bartholomew Fair.* Manchester: Manchester University Press, 2000.

Josselin, Ralph. *The Diary of Ralph Josselin.* London: Oxford University Press, 1976.

Kellet, Edward. *Tricoenivm Christi: In Nocte Proditionis Suae.* London, 1641. Bodleian Library, Wing K238.

Knewstub, John. *A Confutation of Monstrous and Horrible Heresies.* London, 1579. British Library, STC 15040.

Laud, William. *Seven Sermons.* London, 1651.

Ley, John. *A Discourse Concerning Puritans.* London, 1641. British Library, Wing L1875.

Lightfoot, John. 'Preface Giving Some Accompt of the Authours Life.' In *The Works of the Great Albionean Divine Mr. Hugh Broughton*, a1v–d1v. London, 1662.

A List of Some of the Grand Blasphemers and Blasphemies. London, 1654. British Library, Wing L2406.

Ludlow, Edmund. *Memoirs.* Oxford: Clarendon, 1854.

Luther, Martin. *The Annotated Luther.* Edited by Timothy J. Wengert et al. 6 vols. Philadelphia: Fortress, 2015.

M. P. *The Mystery of the Deity in the Humanity or the Mystery of God in Man.* London: n.p., 1649.

Manton, Thomas. *A Fourth Volume Containing One Hundred and Fifty Sermons.* London, 1693. Henry E. Huntington Library, Wing M524.

Marana, Giovanni. *Letters Writ by a Turkish Spy Who Lived Five and Forty Years Undiscovered at Paris.* Vol. 5. London, 1692. Bodleian Library, Wing M565CL.

Marshall, Stephen. *Meroz Curse for not Helping the Lord Against the Mightie.* London, 1641. British Library, Wing M761A.

Mather, Samuel. *The Figures or Types of the Old Testament.* London, 1683. Union Theological Seminary, Wing M1279.

Matthew, Henry. *An Account of the Life and Death of Mr. Philip Henry.* London, 1698. Harvard University Library, Wing B1100A.

Mede, Joseph. *The Key of the Revelation, Searched and Demonstrated Out of the Natural and Proper Characters of the Visions.* Translated by Richard More. London, 1643. British Library, Wing M1600.

Moryson, Fynes. *Unpublished Chapters of Fynes Moryson's Itinerary.* London: Sherratt and Hughes, 1903.

A Most Faithful Relation of Two Wonderful Passages. London: n.p., 1650.

Muggleton, Lodowicke. *Acts of the Witness.* London, 1699. Henry E. Huntington Library, Wing M3040.

———. *A True Interpretation of All the Chief Texts and Mysterious Sayings and Visions Opened of the Whole Book of the Revelation of St. John.* London, 1665. Henry E. Huntington Library, Wing M3049.

Munster, Sebastian. *The Messias of the Christians and the Jewes.* London, 1655. British Library, Wing M3039A.

Nalson, John. *An Impartial Collection of the Great Affairs of State.* London, 1682. National Library of Scotland, N107.

Naogeorg, Thomas. *The Popish Kingdome.* London, 1570. British Library, STC 15011.

Niclaes, Hendrik. *Dicta HN, Documentall Sentences Eaven as Those Same Were Spoken Fourth by HN.* Cologne, 1574. British Library, STC 18551.

Norden, John. *A Mirror for the Multitude.* London, 1589. Cambridge University Library, STC 18613.

Norris, Edward. *The New Gospel, Not the True Gospel.* London, 1638. British Library, STC 18645.

Norton, John. *The Heart of N-England Rent at the Blasphemies of the Present Generation.* Boston, 1659. Henry E. Huntington Library, Wing N1318.

Norwood, Robert. *The Case and Trial of Captain Robert Norwood, Now Prisoner in Newgate.* London: n.p., 1651.

———. *The Form of an Excommunication.* London, 1651. British Library, Wing N1382.

Ockford, James. *The Doctrine of the Fourth Commandement, Deformed by Popery, Reformed & Restored to Its Primitive Purity Objections Answered, and the Truth Cleared, by Gods Unworthy Servant, J. O.* London, 1640. Christ Church Library, Wing O128A.

Ofwod, Stephen. *An Advertisement to Ihon Delecluse, and Henry May the Elder.* Amsterdam, 1632. Marsh's Library, STC 18789.

Ormerod, Oliver. *The Picture of a Puritane.* London, 1605. British Library, STC 18851.

Paget, John. *An Arrow against the Separation of the Brownistes.* Amsterdam, 1618. British Library, STC 19098.

Pagitt, Ephraim. *Heresiography, or, a Description and History of the Hereticks and Sectaries Sprang up in These Latter Times.* London, 1662. University of Illinois, Wing / P182.

Parnell, James. *The Watcher.* London, 1655. British Library, Wing P541.

Parker, Henry. *A Discourse Concerning Puritans.* London, 1641. British Library, Wing L1875.

Penn, William. *A Briefe Account of the Rise and Progress of the People Call'd Quakers.* London: n.p., 1694.

———. *The Sandy Foundation Shaken.* London, 1668. National Library of Wales, Wing P1356.

Pennington, Isaac. *Babylon the Great Described.* London: n.p., 1659.

———. *The New-Covenant of the Gospel Distinguished.* London, 1660. British Library, Wing P1180.

Perkins, William. *The Arte of Prophecying.* London, 1607. Harvard University Library, STC 19735.4.

———. *A Discourse of the Damned Art of Witchcraft So Farre Forth as It Is Reuealed in the Scriptures, and Manifest by True Experience.* London, 1610. British Library, STC 19698.

———. *A Godlie and Learned Exposition upon the Whole Epistle of Iude.* London, 1606. British Library, 19724.3.

————. *Of the Calling of the Ministerie, Two Treatises.* London, 1605. British Library, 19733a.

Pinke, William. *The Triall of a Christians Sincere Love unto Christ.* London, 1636. Bodleian Library, STC 19944.

Playfere, Thomas. *Hearts Delight: A Sermon Preached at Paul's Cross.* London, 1603. Bodleian Library, STC 20012.

Pooley, Christopher. *Unwarranted Principles Leading to Unwarranted Practises, Sought Out and Examined.* London, 1660. Beinecke Library, Wing P2859A.

Pordage, John. *Innocencie Appearing, through the Dark Mists of Pretended Guilt. Or, a Full and True Narration of the Unjust and Illegal Proceedings of the Commissioners of Berkshire.* London, 1655. British Library, Wing P2967.

————. *Mundorum Explication.* London: n.p., 1663.

Primrose, Gilbert. *The Christian Mans Teares and Christs Comforts.* London, 1625. Bodleian Library, STC 20389.

Prynne, William. *Canterburies Doome.* London: n.p., 1646.

————. *Short Demurrer to the Jewes Long Discontinued Remitter into England.* London, 1656. British Library, Wing P4079.

Purchas, Samuel. *Purchas His Pilgrimage.* London, 1626. Henry E. Huntington Library, STC 20508.5.

Reeve, John, and Lodowick Muggleton. *Verae Fidei Floria est Corona Vitae.* London: n.p., 1755.

Reeve, Thomas. *God's Plea for Nineveh.* London: n.p., 1657.

'Recognizances and Indictments from the Sessions of the Peace Rolls: Temp. Charles I.' In *1625–67,* edited by John Cordy Jeaffreson, 160–87. Vol. 3 of *Middlesex County Records.* London: n.p., 1888.

Rogers, Francis. *A Visitation Sermon.* London, 1633. British Library, STC 21176.

Rogers, John. *An Answere unto a Wicked and Infamous Libel.* London: n.p., 1579.

————. *To His Highnesse Lord Generall Cromwell.* London, 1653. British Library, Wing R1817.

Rollock, Robert. *Lectures, upon the History of the Passion, Resurrection, and Ascension of Our Lord Iesus Christ.* London, 1616. Bodleian Library, STC 21283.

Sacristan, T. T. *The Whetstone of Reproofe.* London, 1632. British Library, STC 23630.

Salmon, Joseph. *A Rout.* London, 1649. British Library, Wing S416.

Saltmarsh, John. *Sparkles of Glory.* London, 1647. British Library, Wing S504.

Sanderson, John. 'Sundry the Personal Voyages Performed by John Sanderson of London.' In vol. 2.9 of *Purchas His Pilgrimes,* by Samuel Purchas, 1614–40. London: n.p., 1625.

Sanderson, Robert. *Sermons.* London: Ball, 1841.

Sclater, William. *An Exposition with Notes upon the First Epistle to the Thessalonians.* London, 1619. Bodleian Library, STC 21834.

Scudder, Henry. *The Christians Daily Walke in Holy Securitie and Peace.* London, 1631. Folger Shakespeare Library, STC 22117.

————. *Gods Warning to England by the Voyce of His Rod.* London, 1644. British Library, Wing S2139.

Sedgwick, John. *Anatomie of Antinomianism.* London, 1644. Thomason Collection, Wing S2359.

————. *Antinomianism Anatomized.* London: n.p., 1644.

Selden, John. *Table Talk.* London, 1696. Bodleian Library, Wing S2438.

———. *Tyth-gatherers, No Gospel Officers*. London, 1646. British Library, Wing T1037B.

Sewel, William. *The History of the Rise, Increase, and Progress of the Christian*. York: Baker, 1844.

Smith, John. *Memoirs of Wool*. London. 1747. British Library, ESTCT 140550.

Squibb, Arthur, et al. 'A Faithful Testimony against the Teachers of Circumcision.' In *The Royal Law Contended For*, by Arthur Squibb et al., 45–47. London, 1667. National Library of Scotland, Wing S5403.

Stennet, Edward. 'Letter from the Bell Lane Church to the Church in Rhode Island.' *The Seventh Day Baptist Memorial* 1 (1852) 24.

———. *The Royal Law Contended For*. London, 1667. Exeter College Library, Wing S5402B.

Stubbes, Phillip. *The Anatomie of Abuses Contayning a Discoverie*. London, 1583. British Library, STC 1755.

A Supplication of the Family of Love. London, 1606. British Library, STC 10683.

Symmons, Edward. *A Vindication of King Charles*. London, 1647. British Library, Wing S6350.

Tany, Thomas. *Hear, O Earth, Ye Earthen Men and Women the Heavens Have Given Fire to Lighten the Cabbal in Man*. London, 1653. British Library, Wing T153.

———. *High News for Hierusalem*. London, 1653. Lambeth Palace Library, Wing T153A.

———. *I Proclaime from the Lord of Hosts the Returne of the Jewes from Their Captivity*. London, 1650. British Library, Wing T154.

———. *The Law Read June the 10, 1656, unto the people Israel*. London, 1656. British Library, Wing P3993A.

———. *My Edict Royal*. London, 1655. Henry E. Huntington Library, Wing T152C.

———. *Tharam Taniah, Leader of the Lords Hosts, Unto His Brethren the Quakers*. London, 1654. Lambeth Palace Library, Wing T158B.

———. *The Nations Right in Magna Charta Discussed with the Thing Called Parliament*. London, 1651. British Library, Wing T154A.

———. *Theauraujohn High Priest to the Jewes, His Disputive Challenge to the Universities of Oxford and Cambridge and the Whole Hirach of Roms Clargical Priests*. London, 1652. British Library, Wing T152B.

———. *Theauraujohn His Aurora in Tranlogorum in Salem Gloria*. London 1650. Folger Shakespeare Library, Wing T152A.

———. *Theauraujohn His Theous Ori Apokolipikal: Or, Gods Light Declared in Mysteries Salem Ori Ad Te Israel*. London, 1651. British Library, Wing T158.

———. *Theauraujohn Tani His Second Part of His Theous-Ori Apokolipikal*. London, 1654. Cambridge University Library, Wing T156.

———. *Thauram Tanjah His Speech in His Claim, Verbatim*. London, 1654. British Library, Wing T157.

Taylor, Thomas. *Circumspect Walking Describing the Severall Rules*. London, 1619. Cambridge University Library, STC 23823.5.

Taylor, John. *Three Weekes, Three Daies, and Three Houres Obseruations and Trauel*. London, 1617. British Library, STC 23807.

Thorowgood, Thomas. *Digitus Dei: New Disoveryes with Such Arguments to Prove That the Jews Inabite Now in America*. London, 1652. Trinity College Library, Wing T1066.

———. *Iewes in America*. London, 1650. British Library, T1067.

Thurloe, John. *A Collection of the State Papers of John Thurloe*. London, 1742.

Tickell, John. *The Bottomles Pit Smoaking in Familisme*. London, 1652. British Library, Wing T1153.

Tillam, Thomas. *Banners of Love Displaied over the Church of Christ, Walking in the Order of the Gospel at Hexham*. London, 1653. British Library, Wing T1164.

———. *The Fourth Principle of Christian Religion*. London, 1655. British Library, Wing T1165.

———. *The Seventh-Day Sabbath Sought Out and Celebrated*. London, 1657. Union Theological Seminary, Wing T1166.

———. *The Temple of Lively Stones*. London, 1661. Cambridge University Library, Wing T1167.

———. *The Two Witnesses Their Prophecy, Slaughter, Resurection and Ascention*. London, 1651. British Library, Wing T1168.

Toland, John. *Nazarenus: Or Jewish, Gentile and Mahometan Christianity, Containing the History of the Ancient Gospel of Barnabas*. London: 1718. British Library, ESTC T139629.

Trapnel, Anna. *A Legacy for a Saint*. London, 1654. British Library, Wing 2032.

Traske, John. *Christ's Kingdome Discovered*. London, 1615. Union Theological Seminary, STC 24175.3.

———. *Heauens Joy, Or, Heauen Begun upon Earth Wherein There Is Discouered More Plainely Than Euer Formerly*. London, 1616. Folger Shakespeare Library, STC 13019.

———. *A Pearle for a Prince*. London, 1615. Bodleian Library, STC 24176.

———. *A Treatise of Libertie from Iudaisme*. London, 1620. Henry E. Huntington Library, STC 24178.

———. *The True Gospel Vindicated*. London, 1636. Henry E. Huntington Library, STC 24178.5.

Turner, William. *The History of All Religions in the World*. London, 1695. British Library, Wing T3347.

Udall, John. *A True Remedy against Famines and Warres*. London, 1588. British Library, STC 24507.

Ussher, James. *The Whole Works of the Reverend James Ussher*. London: 1864.

Vaughan, Edward. *A Plaine and Perfect Method for the Understanding of the Whole Bible*. London, 1617. British Library, STC 24599.5.

Walker, George. *The Doctrine of the Sabbath*. Amsterdam, 1638. British Library, STC 24957.

Wallington, Nehemiah. *The Notebooks of Nehemiah Wallington*. Aldershot: Ashgate, 2007.

Walsall, John. *A Sermon Preached at Pauls Crosse*. London, 1578. Bodleian Library, STC 24995.

Walwyn, William. *The Compassionate Samaritane Unbinding the Conscience*. London, 1644. British Library, Wing W681B.

Ward, Richard. *The Vindication of Parliament and their Proceedings*. London, 1642. British Library, Wing W808aA.

Warren, Edmund. *The Jews Sabbath Antiquated*. London, 1659. British Library, Wing W955.

Weemes, John. *Exercitations Divine.* London, 1632. Henry E. Huntington Library, STC 25212.5.

———. *A Treatise of the Four Degenerate Sons.* London, 1636. British Library, STC 25218.

Weld, Thomas. *A False Jew, or, a Wonderfull Discovery of a Scot.* London, 1653. British Library, Wing W1267.

———. *Mr. Tillam's Account Examined.* London: n.p., 1657.

Whately, Wiliam. *A Bride-Bush: Or, a Direction for Married Persons Plainely Describing the Duties Common to Both, and Peculiar to Each of Them.* London, 1619. Bodleian Library, STC 25297.

Whitehead, George. 'For the Jews Who Assemble in Bevers Marks.' In *A Looking-Glass for the Jews,* by George Fox, 62–78. London, 1674. Bodleian Library, Wing F1859.

Wilkinson, William. *A Confutation of Certain Articles Deliuered Unto the Family of Love.* London, 1579. British Library, STC 25665.

Winstanley, Gerrard. *An Appeal to the House of Commons.* London, 1649.

———. *Fire in the Bush. The Spirit Burning, Not Consuming but Purging Mankind.* London, 1649.

Whitehead, George. *The Light and Life of Christ Within.* London, 1668. British Library, Wing W1941.

Whitelock, Bulstrode. *Memorials of the English Affairs.* London, 1682. British Library, W1986.

Widdowes, Giles. *The Schismaticall Puritan.* London, 1630. British Library, STC 25595.

Wilcox, Thomas [T. W.]. *A Glasse for Gamesters.* London, 1581. Bodleian Library, STC 25623.

Woodford, Robert. *Diary of Robert Woodford.* Cambridge: Cambridge University Press, 2012.

Young, Robert. *A Breviary of the Later Persecutions of the Professors of the Gospel of Christ Jesus.* London, 1674.

Young, Thomas. *Dies Dominicas.* Leiden: n.p., 1639.

Zanchius, Jerome. *Doctrine of Absolute Predestination.* Translated by Augustus Toplady. London: n.p., 1769.

SECONDARY SOURCES

Achinstein, Sharon. 'John Foxe and the Jews.' *Renaissance Quarterly* 54.1 (2001) 86–120.

Ackroyd, Peter. *Exile and Restoration.* Philadelphia: Westminster, 1968.

Adelman, Janet. *Blood Relations: Christian and Jew in 'The Merchant of Venice.'* Chicago: University of California Press, 2008.

Adkins, Mary. 'The Genesis of Dramatic Satire against the Puritan, as Illustrated in *A Knack to Know a Knave.*' *The Review of English Studies* 22.86 (1946) 81–95.

Albertz, Rainer. *A History of Israelite Religion in the Old Testament Period.* Louisville: Westminster John Knox, 1994.

———. *Israel in Exile: The History and Literature of the Sixth Century BCE.* Translated by David Green. Atlanta: SBL, 2003.

Almond, Philip. 'Thomas Brightman and the Origins of Philo-Semitism: An Elizabethan Theologian and the Return of the Jews to Israel.' *Reformation and Renaissance Review* 9.1 (2007) 3–25.

Amit, Yaira. *Hidden Polemics in the Biblical Narrative*. Leiden: Brill, 2000.

Arendt, Hannah. *The Origins of Totalitarianism*. New York: Harcourt, 1968.

Atkin, Malcolm. *Worcestershire Under Arms*. Barnsley: Pen and Sword, 2004.

Auerbach, Erich. *Scenes from the Drama of European Literature*. Manchester: Manchester University, 1984.

Babington Macaulay, Thomas. *History of England*. 1848. Reprint, London: Heron, 1967.

Baden, Joel. *The Composition of the Pentateuch: Renewing the Documentary Hypothesis*. New Haven: Yale University Press, 2012.

Bale, Anthony. 'Framing Antisemitic Exempla: Locating the Jew of Tewkesbury.' *Mediaevalia* 20 (2001) 19–47.

———. *The Jew in the Medieval Book: English Antisemitisms 1350–1500*. Cambridge: Cambridge University Press, 2006.

Balfour, Reid. *English Epicures and Stoics*. Oxford: Oxford University Press, 1998.

Ball, Bryan. *The English Connection: The Puritan Roots of Seventh-Day Adventist Belief*. Cambridge: James Clarke, 1981.

———. *A Great Expectation: Eschatological Thought in English Protestantism to 1660*. Leiden: Brill, 1975.

———. *The Seventh-Day Men*. Cambridge: James Clark, 2009.

Bandstra, Barry. *Reading the Old Testament*. Belmont: Wadsworth, 2009.

Barbelet, Jack. 'Power and Resistance.' *British Journal of Sociology* 36 (1985) 531–48.

Barr, David L. *The Reality of Apocalypse: Rhetoric and Politics in the Book of Revelation*. Atlanta: SBL, 2006.

Barr, James. *Bible and Interpretation*. Oxford: Oxford University Press, 2013.

Barrell, John. *Imagining the King's Death: Figurative Treason, Fantasies of Regicide, 1793–1796*. Oxford: Oxford University Press, 2000.

Bartels, Emily. *Spectacles of Strangeness: Imperialism, Alienation, and Marlowe*. Philadelphia: University of Pennsylvania Press, 1993.

Bauckham, Richard. *Tudor Apocalypse: Sixteenth-Century Apocalypticism, Millenarianism, and the English Reformation from John Bale and John Foxe to Thomas Brightman*. Oxford: Sutton Courtenay, 1978.

Bauman, Zygmunt. 'Allosemitism: Premodern, Modern, Postmodern.' In *Modernity, Culture and 'The Jew'*, edited by Bryan Cheyette and Laura Marcus, 143–56. Cambridge: Polity, 1998.

Baumann, Richard. *Let Your Words be Few: Symbolism of Speaking and Silence Among Seventeenth-Century Quakers*. Cambridge: Cambridge University Press, 1983.

Bayley, James E. 'A Jamesian Theory of Self.' *Transactions of the Charles S. Peirce Society* 12.2 (1976) 148–65.

Bazzana, Giovanni. 'The Bar Kochba Revolt and Hadrian's Religious Policy.' In *Hadrian and the Christians*, edited by Marco Rizzi, 85–110. Gottingen: Gruyter, 2010.

Beeke, Joel. *Assurance of Faith: Calvin, English Puritanism, and the Dutch Second Reformation*. New York: Lang, 1991.

Bell, Dean. 'Jews, Ethnicity, and Identity in Early Modern Hamburg.' *Transit* 3 (2007) 1–16.

Bell, Mark Robert. *Apocalypse How? Baptist Movements During the English Revolution*. Macon: Mercer University Press, 1994.

Berg, Johannes van den. *Religious Currents and Cross Currents*. Leiden: Brill, 1999.

Berkovitz, Jay. 'Rabbinic Culture and the Historical Development of Halakhah.' In *The Early Modern World, 1500–1815*, edited by Jonathan Karp and Adam Sutcliffe, 349–78. Vol. 7 of *The Cambridge History of Judaism*. Cambridge: Cambridge University Press: 2018.

Berry, Helen, and Elizabeth Foyster. *Marriage and the Family in Early Modern England*. Cambridge: Cambridge University Press, 2007.

Biddick, Kathleen. *The Typological Imaginary: Circumcision, Technology, History*. Philadelphia: Pennsylvania University Press, 2003.

Bieringer, Reimund, et al. 'Wrestling with Johannine Anti-Judaism: A Hermeneutical Framework for the Analysis of the Current Debate.' In *Anti-Judaism and the Fourth Gospel*, edited by Reimund Bieringer et al., 3–41. London: Westminster: 2001.

Bird, Phyllis. 'The Place of Women in the Israelite Cultus.' In *Women in the Hebrew Bible: A Reader*, edited by Alice Bach, 3–21. London: Routledge, 2013.

———. 'Prostitution.' In *The Oxford Companion to the Bible*, edited by Brue Metzger and Michael Coogan, 623–24. Oxford: Oxford University Press, 2004.

Blenkinsopp, Joseph. *Judaism: The First Phase*. Cambridge: Eerdmans, 2009.

———. *The Pentateuch*. New Haven: Yale University Press, 2007.

Blomefield, Francis. *An Essay Towards a Topographical History of the County of Norfolk*. London, 1806.

Blumer, Herbert. 'A Note on Symbolic Interactionism.' *The American Sociological Review* 38.6 (1973) 797–98.

Bourdieu, Pierre. *Outline of a Theory of Practice*. Cambridge: Cambridge University Press, 1977.

Boyarin, Daniel. *Border Lines: The Partition of Judaism and Christianity*. Philadephia: University of Pennsylvania, 2004.

———. *Carnal Israel*. London: University of California Press, 1995.

———. *A Radical Jew: Paul and the Politics of Identity*. Berkeley: University of California Press, 1997.

———. 'Rethinking Jewish Christianity: An Argument for Dismantling a Dubious Category.' *Jewish Quarterly Review* 99 (2009) 7–36.

Bozeman, Theodore. 'The Glory of the "Third Time": John Eaton as Contra-Puritan.' *Journal of Ecclesiastical History* 47 (1996) 638–54.

———. *The Precisianist Strain: Disciplinary Religion and Antinomian Backlash in Puritanism to 1638*. Chapel Hill: University of North Carolina Press, 2004.

———. *To Live Ancient Lives*. Chapel Hill: University of North Carolina Press, 1988.

Brachlow, Stephen. 'John Smyth and the Ghost of Anabaptism: A Rejoinder.' *Baptist Quarterly* 30.7 (1984) 296–300.

Bremer, Francis J. *Congregational Communion*. Boston: Northeastern University Press, 1994.

———. *Lay Empowerment the Development of Puritanism*. Basingstoke: Palgrave Macmillan, 2015.

Brod, Manfred. 'A Radical Network in the English Revolution: John Pordage and His Circle, 1646–1654.' *English Historical Review* 119.484 (2004) 1230–52.

Brook, Benjamin. *The Lives of the Puritans*. London: James Black, 1813.

Brown, Andrew. *Popular Piety in Late Medieval England*. Oxford: Clarendon, 1995.

Brown, John. 'Landscapes of Drink.' PhD diss., University of Warwick, 2007.

Brown, Peter. 'Person and Group in Judaism and Early Christianity.' In *A History of Private Life: From Pagan Rome to Byzantium*, edited by Philippe Ariès and Georges Duby, 253–67. Cambridge: Harvard University Press, 1987.

Brownslow, F. W. *Shakespeare, Harsnet, and the Devils of Denham*. Newark: University of Delaware Press, 1993.

Brueggeman, Walter. *Genesis: Interpretation*. Louisville: Westminster, 1982.

Burke, Bernard. *Index to Burke's Dictionary of the Landed Gentry of Great Britain & Ireland*. London: Colburn, 1853.

Burnett, Stephen G. *From Christian Hebraism to Jewish Studies: Johannes Buxtorf*. Leiden: Brill, 1996.

———. 'The Regulation of Hebrew Printing in Germany, 1555–1630: Confessional Politics and the Limits of Jewish Toleration.' In *Infinite Boundaries: Order, Re-Order, and Disorder in Early-Modern German Culture*, edited by Max Reinhart, 329–48. Kirksville: Sixteenth-Century Journal, 1998.

Burns, William. *An Age of Wonders: Prodigies, Politics, and Providence in England, 1637–1727*. Manchester: Manchester University Press, 2002.

Cambers, Andrew. *Godly Reading: Print, Manuscript, and Puritanism in England, 1580–1720*. Cambridge: Cambridge University Press, 2011.

Campbell, David T. 'Common Fate, Similarity, and Other Indices of the Status of Aggregates of Persons as Social Entities.' *Behavioral Science* 2 (1958) 202–4.

Carlebach, Elisheva. 'The Status of the Talmud in Early Modern Europe.' In *Printing the Talmud: From Bomberg to Schottenstein*, edited by Sharon Liberman Mintz and Gabriel M. Goldstein, 79–89. New York: Yeshiva University Museum, 2005.

Caricchio, Mario. 'Giles Calvert and the Radical Experience.' In *Varieties of Seventeenth-and Early Eighteenth-Century English Radicalism in Context*, edited by Ariel Hessayon and David Finnegan, 69–87. Farnham, VT: Ashgate, 2011.

Carleton Paget, James. *Jews, Christians, and Jewish Christians in Antiquity*. Tubingen: Mohr Siebeck, 2010.

Carr, David. *Reading the Fractures of Genesis: Historical and Literary Approaches*. Louisville: Westminster, 1996.

Carson, Leland, and Albert Peel. *The Writings of Robert Harrison and Robert Browne*. Abingdon: Routledge: 2014.

Cassidy, Irene. 'The Episcopate of William Cotton, Bishop of Exeter, 1598–1621, with Special Reference to the State of the Clergy and the Administration of the Ecclesiastical Courts.' BLitt. thesis, University of Oxford, 1964.

Castells, Manuel. *The Power of Identity*. Vol. 2 of *The Information Age: Economy, Society, and Culture*. London: Wiley, 2009.

Carter, Warren. 'James C. Scott and New Testament Studies.' In *Hidden Transcripts and the Arts of Resistance: Applying the Work of James C. Scott to Jesus and Paul*, edited by Richard Horsley, 81–94. Leiden: Brill, 2004.

Caughey, Christopher. 'Anti-Christs and Rumours of Anti-Christs.' In *Prophecy and Eschatology in the Transatlantic World, 1550–1800*, edited by Andrew Crome, 105–27. London: MacMillan, 2016.

Cefalu, Paul. *The Johannine Renaissance in Early Modern English Literature and Theology*. Oxford: Oxford University Press, 2017.

———. *Moral Identity in Early Modern English Literature*. Cambridge: Cambridge University Press, 2004.

Cesaro, Cristina. 'Consuming Identities: Food and Resistance Among the Uyghur in Contemporary Xinjiang.' *Inner Asia* 2 (2002) 225–38.

Chapman, Alister, et al. *Seeing Things Their Way: Intellectual History and the Return of Religion.* Notre Dame: University of Notre Dame Press, 2009.

Christianson, Paul. *Reformers and Babylon: English Apocalyptic Visions from the Reformation to the Eve of the Civil War.* Toronto: University of Toronto Press, 1978.

Chryssides, George. *Exploring New Religions.* London: Continuum, 2001.

Cobbett, Lawrence. 'The Hospitals of St. John the Baptist and St. Mary Magdelene at Ely and the Remains of Gothic Buildings Still to Be Seen There at St. John's Farm.' *Proceedings of the Cambridge Antiquarian Society* 36 (1936) 34–37.

Coffey, John. 'England's Exodus: The Civil War as a War of Deliverance.' In *England's War of Religion Revisited,* edited by Charles Prior and Glen Burgess, 253–80. Farnham: Ashgate, 2011.

———. *Exodus and Liberation.* Oxford: Oxford University Press, 2014.

———. *Persecution and Toleration in Protestant England 1558–1689.* London: Routledge, 2000.

Coffey, John, and Paul Lim. *The Cambridge Companion to Puritanism.* Cambridge: Cambridge University Press, 2008.

Cogley, Richard W. 'The Fall of the Ottoman Empire and the Restoration of Israel in the "Judeocentric" Strand of Puritan Millenarianism.' *Church History* 72.2 (2003) 304–32.

Cohen, Alfred. 'Two Roads to the Puritan Millenium.' *Church History* 32 (1963) 322–38.

Cohen, Kitty. *The Throne and the Chariot: Studies in Milton's Hebraism.* Michigan: Mouton, 1975.

Cohen, Shaye. *Why Aren't Jewish Women Circumcised?* Berkeley: University of California Press, 2005.

Cohn, Norman. *The Pursuit of Millennium.* Oxford: Oxford University Press, 1970.

Collins, John. *The Apocalyptic Imagination.* Cambridge: Eerdmans, 1998.

Collinson, Patrick. *Archbishop Grindal, 1519–1583: The Struggle for a Reformed Church.* California: University of California Press, 1979.

———. 'The Beginnings of English Sabbatarianism.' *Studies in Church History* 1 (1964) 207–21.

———. 'Ben Johnson's *Bartholomew Fair:* The Theatre Constructs Puritanism.' In *The Theatrical City: Culture, Theatre, and Politics in London, 1576–1649,* edited by David L. Smith et al., 157–69. Cambridge: Cambridge University Press, 1995.

———. *The Birthpangs of Protestant England.* Basingstoke: Macmillan, 1988.

———. 'The Cohabitation of the Faithful with the Unfaithful.' In *From Persecution to Toleration: The Glorious Revolution and Religion in England,* edited by Ole Peter Grell et al., 51–76. Oxford: Oxford University Press, 1991.

———. 'Ecclesiastical Vitriol: Religious Satire in the 1590s and the Invention of Puritanism.' In *The Reign of Elizabeth I: Court and Culture in the Last Decade,* edited by John Guy, 150–70. Cambridge: Cambridge University Press, 1995.

———. *The Elizabethan Puritan Movement.* London: Cape, 1967.

———. *From Cranmer to Sancroft.* London: Bloomsbury, 2007.

———. *Godly People: Essays On English Protestantism and Puritanism.* London: Hambledon, 1983.

———. *The Puritan Character.* Los Angeles: University of California Press, 1989.

————. 'Puritanism as Popular Religious Culture.' In *The Culture of English Puritanism*, edited by Christopher Durston and Jacqueline Eales, 32–57. London: Macmillan, 1996.

————. *Richard Bancroft and Elizabethan Anti-Puritanism*. Cambridge: Cambridge University Press, 2013.

————. 'Sects and the Evolution of Puritanism.' In *Puritanism: Transatlantic Perspectives on a Seventeenth-Century Anglo-American Faith*, edited by Francis J. Bremer, 147–66. Boston: Massachussets Historical Society, 1993.

————. 'Separation In and Out of the Church: The Consistency of Barrow and Greenwood.' *Journal of the United Reformed Church History Society* 5.5 (1994) 239–58.

————. 'The Shearmen's Tree and the Preacher: The Strange Death of Merry England in Shrewsbury and Beyond.' In *The Reformation in English Towns*, edited by Patrick Collinson and John Craig, 205–20. Basingstoke: Macmillan, 1998.

————. *This England: Essays on the English Nation and Commonwealth in the Sixteenth Century*. Manchester: Manchester University Press, 2011.

Collinson, Patrick, et al. 'Religious Publishing in England, 1557–1640.' In vol. 4 of *The Cambridge History of the Book in England*, edited by John Barnard and D. F. McKenzie, 29–67. Cambridge: Cambridge University Press: 2002.

Como, David. *Blown by the Spirit*. Stanford: Stanford University Press, 2004.

————. 'The Kingdom of Christ, the Kingdom of England, and the Kingdom of Traske.' In *Protestant Identities: Religion, Society and Self-Fashioning in Post-Reformation England*, edited by Muriel McClendon and Joseph Ward, 63–85. Stanford: Stanford University Press, 1999.

Como, David, and Peter Lake. 'Puritans, Antinomians, and the Laudians in Caroline London: The Strange Case of Peter Shaw and its Context.' *Journal of Ecclesiastical History* 50.4 (1999) 684–715.

Condé, Maryse. 'Creolite without the Creole Language.' In *Carribean Creolisation*, edited by Kathleen Balutansky and Marie Agnes Sourieau, 101–10. Gainesville: University of Florida Press, 1998.

Coolidge, John. *The Pauline Renaissance in England*. Oxford: Clarendon, 1970.

Cressy, David. 'Different Kinds of Speaking: Symbolic Violence and Secular Iconoclasm in Early Modern England.' In *Protestant Identities: Religion, Society, and Self-Fashioning in Post-Reformation England*, edited by Muriel McClendon and Joseph Ward, 19–43. Stanford: Stanford University Press, 1999.

Crome, Andrew. *Christian Zionism and English National Identity*. London: MacMillan, 2018.

————. 'English National Identity and the Readmission of the Jews, 1650–1656.' *The Journal of Ecclesiastical History* 66.2 (2015) 280–301.

————. '"The Proper and Naturall Meaning of the Prophets": The Hermeneutic Roots of Judeo-Centric Eschatology.' *Renaissance Studies* 24.5 (2010) 725–41.

————. *The Restoration of the Jews: Early Modern Hermeneutics, Eschatology, and National Identity in the Work of Thomas Brightman*. Dordrecht: Springer, 2014.

Dalton, Margaret. *Laud's Laboratory, the Diocese of Bath and Wells in the Early Seventeenth Century*. Lewisburg: Bucknell University Press, 1982.

Damrosch, Leo. *The Sorrows of the Quaker Jesus: James Nayler and the Puritan Crackdown on the Free Spirit*. Cambridge: Harvard University Press, 1996.

Danner, Dan. *Pilgrimage to Puritanism*. New York: Lang, 1999.

Davies, Adrian. *Quakers in English Society*. Oxford: Oxford University Press, 2000.

Davies, Brian. *Thomas Aquinas's Summa Theologiae: A Guide and Commentary*. Oxford: Oxford University Press, 2014.

Davies, James. *Fear, Myth, and History: The Ranters and the Historians*. Cambridge: Cambridge University Press, 1986.

Davis, Colin. 'Against Formality: One Aspect of the English Revolution.' *Transactions of the Royal Historical Society* 3 (1993) 265–88.

DeCerteau, Michel. *The Practice of Everyday Life*. Translated by Steven Rendall. Los Angeles: University of California Press, 1984.

Despres, Denise. 'Cultic Anti-Judaism and Chaucer's Litel Clergeon.' *Modern Philology* 91 (1994) 413–27.

Dever, Mark. *Richard Sibbes: Puritanism and Calvinism in Late Elizabethan and Early Stuart England*. Macon, GA: Mercer University Press, 2000.

Dickens, Arthur. *The English Reformation*. London, 1964.

Dietz Moss, Jean. 'Godded with God': Henrick Niclaes and His Family of God. Philadelphia: Transactions of the American Philosophical Society, 1981.

Dixon, Leif. *Practical Predestinarians*. Farnham: Ashgate, 2014.

Doelman, James. *King James and the Religious Culture of England*. Cambridge: Brewer, 2000.

Dorsten, Jan van. *The Anglo-Dutch Renaissance*. New York: Brill, 1988.

Douglas, Mary. *Leviticus as Literature*. Oxford: Oxford University Press, 1999.

———. *Purity and Danger*. 1966. London: Routledge, 2003.

Duffy, Eamonn. *The Stripping of the Altars*. London: Yale University Press, 1992.

Dundes, Alan. *The Blood Libel Legend: A Casebook in Anti-Semitic Folklore*. Madison: University of Wisconsin Press, 1991.

Dunn, James. *The New Perspective on Paul*. Cambridge: Eerdmans, 2005.

Durston, Christopher. 'The Puritan Ethos.' In *The Culture of English Puritanism*, edited by Christopher Durston and Jacqueline Eales, 1–31. London: Macmillan, 1996.

Durston, Christopher, and Jacqueline Eales. *The Culture of English Puritanism*. London: Macmillan, 1996.

Duschinsky, Robbie, et al. *Purity and Danger Now: New Perspectives*. London: Routledge, 2016.

Edmonds, Ennis Barrington. *Rastafari*. Oxford: Oxford University Press, 2003.

Eire, Carlos. *War against the Idols: The Reformation of Worship from Erasmus to Calvin*. Cambridge: Cambridge University Press, 1986.

Elliot, Mark. 'Calvin and the Ceremonial Law of Moses.' *Reformation & Renaissance Review* 11.3 (2009) 275–93.

Endelman, Todd. *The Jews of Britain, 1656 to 2000*. London: University of California Press, 2002.

Eveden, Elizabeth. *Religion and the Book in Early Modern England*. Cambridge: Cambridge University Press, 2011.

Fenton, Paul. 'The European Discovery of Karaism in the Sixteenth to Eighteenth Centuries.' In *Karaite Judaism: A Guide to Its History and Literary Sources*, edited by Meira Polliack, 3–7. Leiden: Brill, 2003.

Ferreira-Ross, Jeanette. 'Religion and the Law in Jonson's *Bartholomew Fair*.' *Renaissance and Reformation* 18.2 (1994) 45–66.

Feselstein, Frank. *Anti-Semitic Stereotypes: A Paradigm of Otherness in English Popular Culture*. Baltimore: Johns Hopkins University Press, 1995.

Festinger, Leon. 'A Theory of Social Comparison Processes.' *Human Relations* 7 (1954) 117–40.

————. *When Prophecy Fails.* Minneapolis: University of Minnesota Press, 1956.

Fincham, Kenneth. *The Early Stuart Church, 1603–1642.* Basingstoke: Macmillan, 1993.

————. *Prelate as Pastor: The Episcopate of James I.* Oxford: Clarendon, 1990.

————. *Religious Politics in Post-Reformation England.* Woodbridge: Boydell, 2006.

Firth, Katherine. *The Apocalyptic Tradition in Reformation Britain, 1530–1645.* Oxford: Oxford University Press, 1979.

Fish, Stanley. *Self-Consuming Artifacts: The Experience of Seventeenth-Century Literature.* London: University of California Press, 1972.

Fletcher, Anthony, and Peter Roberts. *Religion, Culture, and Society in Early Modern England.* Cambridge: Cambridge University Press, 1994.

Fohrer, Georg. *Introduction to the Old Testament.* Translated by David Green. Nashville: Abingdon, 1968.

Foster, Stephen. 'New England and the Challenge of Heresy.' *The William and Mary Quarterly* 38.4 (1981) 624–60.

Foxley, Rachel. *The Levellers: Radical Political Thought in the English Revolution.* Manchester: Manchester University Press, 2015.

Frank, Joseph. *The Levellers.* Cambridge: Harvard University Press, 1955.

Fredriksen, Paula. *Augustine and the Jews.* New Haven: Yale University Press, 2008.

————. *Jesus of Nazareth, King of the Jews.* New York: Knopf, 2012.

Freud, Sigmund. *Jokes and their Relation to the Unconscious.* London: Routledge, 1960.

Frojmovic, Eva. 'Christian Travelers to the Circumcision.' In *The Covenant of Circumcision*, edited by Elizabeth Wyner Mark, 128–42. London: Brandeis, 2003.

Fulbrook, Mary. *Piety and Politics: Religion and the Rise of Absolutism in England, Wurtenberg, and Prussia.* Cambridge: Cambridge University Press, 1983.

Garrett, Christina. *The Marian Exiles.* Cambridge: Cambridge University Press, 1938.

Geertz, Clifford. *The Interpretation of Cultures.* New York: Basic, 1975.

George, Charles. *The Protestant Mind of the English Reformation 1570–1640.* Princeton: Princeton University Press, 1961.

George, Henry. *The Cambridgeshire Visitation, 1619.* Gilmour: n.p., 1840.

George, Timothy. 'War and Peace in the Puritan Tradition.' *Church History* 53 (1984) 492–503.

Gibbons, Brian. *Gender in Mystical and Occult Thought: Behmenism and its Development in England.* Cambridge: Cambridge University Press, 1996.

Ginther, James R. *The Westminster Handbook to Medieval Theology.* Louisville: John Knox Press, 2009.

Glaser, Eliane. *Judaism without Jews.* Basingstoke: Palgrave, 2007.

Glassman, Bernard. *Anti-Semitic Stereotypes without Jews: Images of the Jews in England 1290–1700.* Detroit: Wayne State University Press, 1975.

Goadby, James. *Bye-Paths in Baptist History.* London, 1871.

Goffman, Erving. *The Presentation of the Self in Everyday Life.* New York: Doubleday, 1959.

Goldish, Matt. 'The Battle for "True" Jewish Christianity.' In *Everything Connects: In Conference with Richard Popkin*, edited by Richard Popkin and James E. Force, 143–62. Leiden: Brill, 1999.

Grabbe, Lester. *Leviticus.* London: Bloomsbury, 1993.

Greaves, Richard. *Deliver Us From Evil: The Radical Underground in Britain 1660–1663.* Oxford: Oxford University Press, 1986.

———. *Society and Religion in Elizabethan England.* Minneapolis: University of Minnesota Press, 1981.

Green, Ian. *Print and Protestantism in Early Modern England.* Oxford: Oxford University Press, 2000.

Greene, Charles. 'Trask in the Star-Chamber, 1619.' *Transactions of the Baptist Historical Society* 5 (1917) 8–14.

Gregory, John. *Puritanism in the Old World and in the New.* London: Revell, 1896.

Grell, Ole, et al. *From Persecution to Toleration.* Oxford: Clarendon, 1991.

Gribben, Crawford. *The Puritan Millennium: Literature & Theology, 1550–1682.* Portland, OR: Four Courts, 2000.

Groeneveld, Leanne. 'Mourning, Heresy, and Resurrection in the York Corpus Christi Cycle.' In *Response to Death: The Literary Work of Mourning,* edited by Christian Riegel, 1–23. Edmonton: University of Alberta Press, 2003.

Guadagno, Rosanna E., et al, 'Social Influence in the Online Recruitment of Terrorists and Terrorist Sympathizers: Implications for Social Psychology Research.' *Revue Internationale de Psychologie Sociale* 23.1 (2010) 25–56.

Guibbory, Achsah. *Christian Identity, Jews, and Israel.* Oxford: Oxford University Press, 2010.

———. 'England, Israel, and the Jews in Milton's Prose, 1649–1660.' In *Milton and the Jews,* edited by Douglas Brooks, 13–34. Cambridge: Cambridge University Press, 2006.

Gunther, Karl. *Reformation Unbound.* Cambridge: Cambridge University Press, 2014.

Haigh, Christopher. 'The English Reformation: A Premature Birth, a Difficult Labour, and a Sickly Child.' *The Historical Journal* 33.2 (1990) 449–59.

———. *English Reformations.* Oxford: Oxford University Press, 1993.

———. *The Plain Man's Pathway to Heaven.* Oxford: Oxford University Press, 2007.

———. 'Puritan Evangelism in the Reign of Elizabeth.' *The English Historical Review* 92.362 (1977) 30–58.

———. *The Reign of Elizabeth I. Basingstoke.* Basingstoke: Macmillan, 1984.

Haller, William. *Foxe's Book of Martyrs and the Elect Nation.* London: Jonathan Cape, 1963.

Halsam, Alex, et al. 'Social Categorisation and Group Homogeneity: Changes in the Perceived Applicability of Stereotype Content as a Function of Comparative Context and Trait Favourableness.' *British Journal of Social Psychology* 34 (1995) 139–60.

———. 'Social Identity, Self-Categorisation, and the Perceived Homogeneity of Ingroups and Outgroups: The Interaction between Social Motivation and Cognition.' In *The Interpersonal Context,* edited by R. M. Sorrentino and E. T. Higgins, 182–222. Vol. 3 of *Handbook of Motivation and Cognition.* New York: Guilford Press, 1996.

Hanbrick Stowe, Charles. *The Practice of Piety.* Chapel Hill: University of North Carolina, 1982.

Haran, Menahem. 'The Holiness Code.' In vol. 9 of *Encyclopedia Judaica,* edited by Michael Berenbaum and Fred Skolnik, 318–21. Detroit: Macmillan, 2007.

Hardman Moore, Susan. 'Reformed Theology and Puritanism.' In *The Cambridge Companion to Reformed Theology*, edited by Paul Nimmo and David Ferguson, 199–215. Cambridge: Cambridge University Press, 2016.

Harrison, William Bagshaw *The Elizabethan Journals*. Prescott: Anchor, 1965.

Hartley, Thomas. *Proceedings in the Parliaments of Elizabeth I.* Leicester: Leicester University Press, 1995.

Haynes, Douglas, and Gyan Prakash, 'Introduction: The Entanglement of Power and Resistance.' In *Contesting Power: Resistance and Everyday Social Relations in South Asia*, edited by Douglas Haynes and Gyan Prakash, 1–23. Berkeley: University of California Press, 1991.

Hendel, Ronald. *Remembering Abraham: Culture, Memory, and History in the Hebrew Bible*. Oxford: Oxford University Press, 2005.

Heng, Geraldine. 'Jews, Saracens, "Black Men," Tartars: England in a World of Racial Difference.' In *A Companion to Medieval English Literature, c. 1350–1500*, edited by Peter Brown, 247–72. Oxford: Blackwell, 2006.

Hessayon, Ariel. *'Gold Tried in the Fire': The Prophet TheaurauJohn Tany and the English Revolution*. Aldershot: Ashgate, 2007.

Hessayon, Ariel, and Sarah Apetrei. *An Introduction to Jacob Boehme*. Abingdon: Routledge, 2014.

Hessayon, Ariel, and David Finnegan. *Varieties of Seventeenth- and Early Eighteenth-Century English Radicalism in Context*. Farnham, VT: Ashgate, 2011.

Hill, Christopher. 'The Norman Yoke.' In *Democracy and the Labour Movement: Essays in Honour of Dona Torr*, edited by John Saville, 11–67. London: Lawrence and Wishart: 1954.

———. *Puritanism and Revolution: Studies in Interpretation of the English Revolution of the Seventeenth Century*. London: Secker and Warburg, 1965.

———. *Society and Puritanism in Pre-Revolutionary England*. London: Penguin, 1964.

———. *The World Turned Upside Down*. London: Penguin, 1991.

Hill, Christopher, and Barry Reay. *The World of the Muggletonians*. London: Temple Smith, 1983.

Hoak, Dale. 'A Tudor *Deborah*? The Coronation of Elizabeth I, Parliament, and the Problem of Female Rule.' In *John Foxe and His World*, edited by Christopher Highley and John N. King, 73–99. Burlington: Ashgate, 2002.

Hodgkin, Katherine. *Women, Madness, and Sin in Early Modern England*. Abingdon: Routledge, 2010.

Hogg, Michael. *Extremism and the Psychology of Uncertainty*. Sussex: Wiley-Blackwell, 2012.

———. 'From Uncertainty to Extremism.' *Current Directions in Psychological Science* 23 (2010) 338–42.

———. 'Social-Identity Theory.' In *Contemporary Social Psychological Theories*, edited by Peter Burke, 111–37. Stanford: Stanford University Press, 2006.

———. 'Uncertainty-Identity Theory.' *Advances in Experimental Social Psychology* 39 (2007) 69–126.

———. 'Uncertainty-Identity Theory.' In *Handbook of Theories of Social Psychology*, edited by Paul A. M. van Lange et al., 62–81. London: Sage, 2011.

Hogg, Michael, et al. 'Religion in the Face of Uncertainty: An Uncertainty-Identity Theory Account of Religiousness.' *Personality and Social Psychology Review* 14.1 (2009) 72–83.

————. 'Uncertainty, Entitativity, and Group Identification.' *Journal of Experimental Social Psychology* 43 (2005) 135–42.

Holmberg, Eva. *Jews in the Early Modern English Imagination: A Scattered Nation.* Farnham: Ashgate, 2011.

Hotson, Howard. *Paradise Postponed: Johannes Alsted and the Birth of Calvinist Millenarianism.* Dordrecht: Kluwer, 2000.

Houston, Walter. *Purity and Monotheism.* Sheffield: Sheffield Academic, 1993.

Howell, Roger. *Newcastle upon Tyne an the Puritan Revolution.* Oxford: Clarendon, 1967.

Hughes, Ann. *Causes of the English Civil War.* London: MacMillan, 1998.

————. *Gangraena and the Struggle for the English Revolution.* Oxford: Oxford University Press, 2004.

Hulston, James. *Ehud's Dagger: Class Struggle in the English Revolution.* London: Verso, 2002.

Hunt, Arnold. *The Art of Hearing.* Cambridge: Cambridge University Press, 2010.

Hunter, Michael. 'The Problem of "Atheism" in Early Modern England.' *Transactions of the Royal Historical Society* 5.35 (1985) 135–57.

Hurowitz, Victor. 'P-Understanding the Priestly Source.' *Bible Review* 12.3 (1996) 30–37.

Israel, Jonathan. *European Jewry in the Age of Mercantilism: 1550–1750* Oxford: Clarendon, 1989.

Jacob, Walter. 'The Primacy of Diaspora.' In *Israel and the Diaspora in Jewish Law,* edited by Walter Jacob and Moshe Zemer, 149–65. Pittsburgh: Rodef Shalom, 1997.

James, William. *The Principles of Psychology.* New York: Dover, 1950.

Jewson, Charles. 'The English Church in Rotterdam and its Norfolk Connections.' *Norfolk Archaeology* 30 (1952) 324–37.

————. 'St. Mary's, Norwich.' *Baptist Quarterly* 10.5 (1941) 282–88.

————. 'Transcript of Three Registers of Passengers from Great Yarmouth to Holland.' *Publications of the Norfolk Record Society* 25 (1954) 30.

Johns, Adrian. 'Coleman Street.' *The Huntington Library Quarterly* 71.1 (2008) 33–54.

Jones, Rufus. *Spiritual Reformers in the Sixteenth and Seventeenth Centuries.* New York: Macmillan, 1928.

Jowitt, Claire. "'The Consolation of Israel': Representations of Jewishness in the Writings of Gerrard Winstanley and William Everard." In *Winstanley and the Diggers 1649–1999,* edited by Andrew Bradstock, 87–100. London: Cass, 2000.

Kamerick, Kathleen. *Popular Piety and Art in the Late Middle Ages: Image Worship and Idolatry in England, 1350–1500.* Basingstoke: Palgrave, 2002.

Karant Nunn, Susan. *The Reformation of Ritual: An Interpretation of Early Modern Germany.* London: Routledge, 1997.

Karp, Jonathan, and Adam Sutcliffe. *A Brief History of Philo-Semitism.* Cambridge: Cambridge University Press, 2012.

Katchen, Aaron. *Christian Hebraists and Dutch Rabbis: Seventeenth-Century Apologetics and the Study of Maimonides's Mishneh Torah.* Cambridge: Harvard University Centre for Jewish Studies, 1984.

Katz, David S. 'English Redemption and Jewish Readmission in 1656.' *Journal of Jewish Studies* 34 (1983) 73–91.

————. *God's Last Words: Reading the English Bible from the Reformation to Fundamentalism.* London: Yale University Press, 2004.

————. 'Jewish Sabbath and Christian Sunday in Early Modern England.' In *Jewish Christians and Christian Jews*, edited by Gordon Weiner and Richard Popkin, 119–30. Dordrecht: Kluwer, 1994.

————. *The Jews in the History of England*. Oxford: Clarendon, 1996.

————. 'Menasseh ben Israel's Christian Connection: Henry Jessey and the Jews.' In *Menasseh ben Israel and his World*, edited by Henry Mechoulan et al., 117–38. Leiden: Brill, 1989.

————. *Philo-Semitism and the Readmission of the Jews to England*. Oxford: Clarendon, 1982.

————. 'The Restoration of the Jews: Thomas Tany to the World Jewry (1653).' In *Jewish-Christian Relations in the Seventeenth Century*, edited by Johannes van den Berg, 189–90. London: Kluwer, 1988.

————. *Sabbath and Sectarianism in Seventeenth-Century England*. Leiden: Brill, 1987.

————. 'Shylock's Gender: Jewish Male Menstruation in Early Modern England.' *The Review of English Studies* 50.200 (1999) 440–62.

Katz, Stephen, and Steven Bayme, eds. *Continuity and Change: A Festschrift in Honor of Irving Greenberg's 75th Birthday*. Lanham, MD: University Press of America, 2010.

Kendall, Robert. *Calvin and English Calvinism to 1649*. Oxford: Oxford University Press, 1981.

————. 'The Puritan Modification of Calvin's Theology.' In *John Calvin, His Influence in the Western World*, edited by W. Stanford Reid, 199–214. Grand Rapids: Zondervan, 1982.

Kenny, Anthony. *Wyclif*. Oxford: Oxford University Press, 1985.

Kenworthy, James. *History of the Baptist Church at Hill Cliffe*. London: n.p., 1899.

Kepel, Gilles. *Muslim Extremism in Egypt*. Berkeley: University of California Press, 1984.

Kidd, Colin. *The Forging of the Races: Race and Scripture in the Protestant Atlantic World, 1600–2000*. Cambridge: Cambridge University Press, 2006.

Killeen, Kevin. *Biblical Scholarship, Science, and Politics in Early Modern England*. Farnham: Ashgate, 2009.

Klawans, Jonathan. *Impurity and Sin in Ancient Judaism*. Oxford: Oxford University Press, 2000.

Knohl, Israel. *The Divine Symphony*. Philadelphia: Jewish Publication Society, 2003.

Knoppers, Laura. *Puritanism and Its Discontents*. Newark: University of Delaware Press, 2003.

Knott, John. *Discourses of Martyrdom in English Literature, 1563–1694*. Cambridge: Cambridge University Press, 1993.

————. *The Sword of the Spirit*. Chicago: University of Chicago Press, 1980.

Knox, R. Buick. *Reformation Conformity and Dissent: Essays in Honour of Geoffrey Nuttall*. London: Epworth, 1977.

Kraemer, David. *Jewish Eating and Identity Through the Ages*. London: Routledge, 2007.

Kristeva, Julia. *Powers of Horror: An Essay on Abjection*. Translated by Leon Roudiez. New York: Columbia University Press, 1982.

Kumar, Krishan. *The Making of English National Identity*. Cambridge: Cambridge University Press, 2003.

Kümin, Beat. 'Sacred Church and Worldly Tavern: Reassessing an Early Modern Divide.' In *Sacred Space in Early Modern Europe*, edited by W. Coster and A. Spicer, 17–38. Cambridge: Cambridge University Press, 2005.

Lachter, Hartley. 'Israel as a Holy People in Medieval Kabbalah.' In *Holiness in Jewish Thought*, edited by Alan Mittleman, 137–59. Oxford: Oxford University Press, 2018.

Lake, Peter. *Anglicans and Puritans?* London: Hyman, 1988.

———. *The Antichrist's Lewd Hat*. New Haven: Yale University Press, 2002.

———. 'Anti-Popery: The Structure of a Prejudice.' In *Conflict in Early Stuart England*, edited by Ann Hughes and Richard Cust, 72–107. London: Routledge, 1989.

———. 'Anti-Puritanism, the Structure of a Prejudice.' In *Religious Politics in Post-Reformation England*, edited by Kenneth Fincham, 80–98. Woodbridge: Boydell, 2000.

———. *The Boxmaker's Revenge: 'Orthodoxy,' 'Heterodoxy,' and the Politics of a Parish in Early Stuart London*. Manchester: Manchester University Press, 2001.

———. 'Calvinism and the English Church, 1570–1635.' *Past and Present* 114 (1987) 32–76.

———. 'Defining Puritanism: Again?' In *Puritanism: Trans-Atlantic Perspectives on a Seventeenth-Century Anglo-American Faith*, edited by Francis J. Bremer, 3–29. Boston: Massachusetts Historical Society, 1993.

———. *Moderate Puritans and the Elizabethan Church*. Cambridge: Cambridge University Press, 1982.

———. 'Puritanism, Familism, and Heresy in Early Stuart England: The Case of John Etherington Revisited.' In *Heresy, Literature, and Politics in Early Modern English Culture*, edited by David Loewenstein and John Marshall, 82–107. Cambridge: Cambridge University Press, 2006.

———. 'William Bradshaw, Antichrist and the Community of the God.' *Journal of Ecclesiastical History* 36.4 (1985) 570–89.

Lake, Peter, and Michael Questier. *Conformity and Orthodoxy in the English Church 1560–1642*. Woodbridge: Boydell, 2000.

Lake, Peter, and Isaac Stephens. *Scandal and Religious Identity in Early Stuart England*. Woodbridge: Boydell, 2015.

Lamont, William. *Godly Rule*. London: Macmillan, 1969.

———. 'The Two National Churches of 1691 and 1829.' In *Religion, Culture and Society in Early Modern Britain*, edited by Anthony Fletcher and Peter Roberts, 335–53. Cambridge: Cambridge University Press, 1994.

Langum, Virginia. 'Discerning Skin.' In *Reading Skin in Medieval Literature and Culture*, edited by Katie L. Walter, 141–60. New York: Palgrave, 2013.

Leverenz, David. *The Language of Puritan Feeling: An Exploration in Literature, Psychology, and Social History*. New Brunswick: Rutgers University Press, 1980.

Levering, Matthew. *Reading Romans with St. Thomas Aquinas*. Washington, DC: Catholic University of America Press, 2012.

Lewalski, Barbara. *Protestant Poetics and the Seventeenth Century Religious Lyric*. Princeton: Princeton University Press, 1979.

Lipton, Sarah. *Images of Intolerance: The Representation of Jews and Judaism in the Bible Moralisée*. Berkeley: University of California Press, 1999.

Loach, Jennifer. *Edward VI*. London: Yale University Press, 1999.

Loewenstein, Rudolph. *Christians and the Jews*. New York: Delta, 1951.

Loughead, Lisa. *The Perception of Polygamy in Early Modern England*. Halifax: Dalhousie University Press, 2008.

Luomanen, Petri. *Recovering Jewish-Christian Sects and Gospels*. Leiden: Brill, 2012.

Luxon, Thomas. *Literal Figures: Puritan Allegory and the Reformation Crisis in Representation*. London: University of Chicago Press, 1995.

———. "'Not I, but Christ': Allegory and the Puritan Self." *ELH* 60 (1993) 899–937.

Lynch, Joseph. *The Medieval Church*. London: Routledge, 2014.

Macculloch, Diarmaid. *Thomas Cranmer: A Life*. London: Yale University Press, 1997.

———. *The Tudor Church Militant*. London: Penguin, 1999.

MacCallum, Hugh. 'Milton and the Figurative Interpretation of the Bible.' *The University of Toronto Quarterly* 31 (1967) 397–415.

Mach, Michael. 'Justin Martyr's *Dialogus cum Tryphone Iudaeo* and the Development of Christian Anti-Judaism.' In *Contra Iudaeos: Ancient and Medieval Polemics Between Christians and Jews*, edited by Guy Stroumsa and Ora Limor, 27–85. Tubingen: Mohr, 1996.

Mack, Phyllis. *Visionary Women: Ecstatic Prophecy in Early Modern England*. London: University of California Press, 1992.

Maltby, Judith. *Prayer Book and People in Elizabethan and Early Stuart England*. Cambridge: Cambridge University Press, 1998.

Manningham, John. *The Diary of John Manningham of Middle Temple, 1602–1603*. Hanover, NH: University Press of New England, 1976.

Marsh, Christopher. *The Family of Love in English Society, 1550–1630*. Cambridge: Cambridge University Press, 1994.

———. "'A Gracelesse, and Audacious Companie'? The Family of Love in the Parish of Balsham, 1550–1630." *Studies in Church History* 23 (1986) 191–208.

———. *Popular Religion in Sixteenth-Century England*. London: Palgrave, 1998.

Martin, Dale B. *New Testament History and Literature*. London: Yale University Press, 2012.

Martin, John. 'Christopher Vittell: An Elizabethan Mechanick Preacher.' *The Sixteenth Century Journal* 10.2 (1979) 15–22.

Matar, Nabil. *Islam in Britain 1558–1685*. Cambridge: Cambridge University Press, 1998.

McClachan, Herbert. *Socinianism*. Oxford: Oxford University Press, 1951.

McDowell, Nicholas. 'The Ghost in the Marble: Jeremy Taylor's *Liberty of Prophesying* and Its Readers.' In *Scripture and Scholarship in Early Modern England*, edited by Ariel Hessayon and Nicholas Keene, 176–92. Aldershot: Ashgate, 2006.

———. 'The Stigmatizing of Puritans as Jews in Jacobean England: Ben Jonson, Francis Bacon, and the Book of Sports Controversy.' *Renaissance Studies* 19.3 (2005) 348–63.

McGee, James Sears. *The Godly Man in Stuart England: Anglicans, Puritans, and the Two Tables*. New Haven: Yale University Press, 1976.

McGowen, Randall. 'A Well-Ordered Prison.' In *The Oxford History of the Prison: The Practice of Punishment in Western Society*, edited by Norval Morris, 71–99. Oxford: Oxford University Press, 1998.

McGrath, Alister. *Iustitia Dei: A History of the Christian Doctrine of Justification*. Cambridge: Cambridge University Press, 1986.

McKenzie, Steven L. *Covenant*. St. Louis: Chalice, 2000.

McKim, Donald. 'The Function of Ramism in Perkins' Theology.' *The Sixteenth Century Journal* 16.4 (1985) 503–17.

———. *Ramism in William Perkins Theology*. New York: Peter Lang, 1987.

McManus, Edgar. *Law and Liberty in Early New England*. Amherst: University of Massachusetts Press, 1993.

Mead, George Herbert. *The Individual and the Social Self: Unpublished Essays*. Chicago: University of Chicago Press, 1982.

Meeks, Wayne. *The Origins of Christian Morality*. New Haven: Yale University Press, 1993.

Meens, Robert. *Penance in Medieval Europe: 600–1200*. Cambridge: Cambridge University Press, 2014.

Milgrom, Jacob. 'Priestly ("P") Source.' In vol. 5 of *The Anchor Bible Dictionary*, edited by David Noel Freedman, 454–61. New York: Doubleday, 1992.

Miller, Daniel. 'The Limits of Dominance.' In *Domination and Resistance*, edited by Daniel Miller et al., 63–79. London: Unwin Hyman: 1989.

Miller, Perry. *The New England Mind*. Cambridge: Belknap, 1939.

Milton, Anthony. 'Religion and Community in Pre-Civil War England.' In *The English Revolution*, edited by Nicholas Tyacke, 62–80. Manchester: Manchester University Press, 2007.

Milward, Peter. *Religious Controversies of the Jacobean Age*. Los Angeles: Scolar, 1978.

Mitchell, Timothy. 'Everyday Metaphors of Power.' *Theory and Society* 19.5 (1990) 545–77.

Mittleman, Alan. *Holiness in Jewish Thought*. Oxford: Oxford University Press, 2018.

Moltmann, Jürgen. 'The Liberation of the Future and it Anticipation in History.' In *God Will Be All in All*, edited by Richard Bauckham, 269–72. Edinburgh: T&T, 1999.

Morgan, Edmund. *Visible Saints: The History of Puritan Idea*. Ithaca: Cornell University Press, 1965.

Morgan, John. *Godly Learning: Puritan Attitudes Towards Reason, Learning, and Education, 1560–1640*. Cambridge: Cambridge University Press, 1988.

Morrill, John. 'The Church in England.' In *Reactions to the English Civil War 1642–1649*, edited by John Morrill, 89–114. Basingstoke: Macmillan, 1982.

———. 'A Liberation Theology? Aspects of Puritanism in the English Revolution.' In *Puritanism and Its Discontents*, edited by Laura Lunger Knoppers, 27–48. Newark: University of Delaware Press, 2003.

———. *The Nature of the English Revolution*. London: Routledge, 1993.

———. 'The Puritan Revolution.' In *The Cambridge Companion to Puritanism*, edited by John Coffey and Paul Lim, 67–88. Cambridge: Cambridge University Press, 2008.

———. *Reactions to the English Civil War*. London: Macmillan, 1982.

———. 'The Religious Context of the English Civil War.' *Transactions of the Royal Historical Society* 34 (1984) 155–78.

Morton, A. L. *The World of the Ranters*. London: Wishart, 1970.

Mozley, James. *John Foxe and His Book*. Octagon: London, 1970.

Murrell, Samuel, and Lewin Williams. 'The Black Biblical Hermeneutics of Rastafari.' In *Chanting Down Babylon: The Rastafari Reader*, edited by Nathaniel Samuel Murrell et al., 326–49. Philadelphia: Temple University Press, 1998.

Muslow, Martin. 'The Third Force Revisited.' In *The Legacies of Richard Popkin*, edited by Jeremy Popkin, 109–21. Dordrecht: Springer, 2008.

Neale, John. *Elizabeth I and Her Parliaments*. London: Cape, 1953.

Neusner, Jacob. *Judaism: A Textbook and a Reader*. Louisville: Westminster, 1991.

Newman, Paul. *Atlas of the English Civil War*. London: Routledge, 2005.

Nirneberg, David. 'The Politics of Love and its Enemies.' In *Religion: Beyond a Concept*, edited Hent de Vries, 120–60. New York: Fordham, 2009.

Nuttall, Geoffrey. *The Holy Spirit in Puritan Faith and Experience*. Chicago: University of Chicago Press, 1943.

———. 'A New Letter to George Fox.' *The Journal of the Friends' Historical Society* 57.3 (1996) 222–24.

Ogbu, John. *Minority Education and Caste: The American System in Cross-Cultural Perspective*. San Diego: Academic, 1978.

———. *Minority Status and Schooling: A Comparative Study of Immigrant and Involuntary Minorities*. New York: Garland, 1991.

Olsen, Viggo. *John Foxe and the Elizabethan Church*. Berkeley: University of California Press, 1973.

Parker, Kenneth. *The English Sabbath: A Study of Doctrine and Discipline from the Reformation to the Civil War*. Cambridge: Cambridge University Press, 1988.

Parkes, James William. *Judaism and Christianity*. London: Gollancz, 1948.

Patai, Raphael. *The Myth of the Jewish Race*. Detroit: Wayne State University Press, 2008.

Patterson, William. *William Perkins and the Making of Modern England*. Oxford: Oxford University Press, 2014.

Payne, Ernest. 'Baptists and the Laying on of Hands.' *The Baptist Quarterly* 15 (1954) 203–15.

Perkins, Judith. *The Suffering Self: Pain and Narrative Representations in the Early Christian Era*. London: Routledge, 1995.

Pettegree, Andrew. *Marian Protestantism*. London: Scolar, 1996.

Phillips, Christopher, and John Smith. *Lancashire and Cheshire from AD 1540*. London: Routledge, 2014.

Poliakov, Leon. *The Aryan Myth*. London: Heinemann, 1974.

Pollard, Velma. *Dread Talk: The Language of Rastafari*. Kingston: Queen's University Press, 2000.

Poole, Kristen. *Radical Religion From Shakespeare to Milton*. Cambridge: Cambridge University Press, 2006.

Popkin, Richard H. 'Can One Be a True Christian and a Faithful Follower of the Law of Moses? the Answer of John Dury.' In *Secret Conversions to Judaism in Early Modern Europe*, edited by Martin Muslow and Richard H. Popkin, 33–50. Leiden: Brill, 2004.

———. 'Christian Interest and Concerns about Sabbatai Zevi.' In *Jewish Messianism in the Early Modern World*, edited by Matt Goldish and Richard Popkin, 91–107. Vol. 1 of *Millenarianism and Messianism in Early Modern European Culture*. Dordrecht: Springer, 2001.

———. 'Christian Jews and Jewish Christians in the Seventeenth Century.' In *Jewish Christians and Christian Jews*, edited by Richard Popkin, 57–72. Dordrecht: Kluwer, 1994.

———. 'Could Spinoza Have Known Bodin's *Colloquium Heptaplomares*?' *Philosophia* 16.3 (1986) 307–14.

———, ed. *Jewish Christians and Christian Jews*. Dordrecht: Kluwer, 1994.

———. 'Rabbi Nathan Shapira's Visit to Amsterdam in 1657.' In *Dutch Jewish History: Proceedings of the Symposium on the History of the Jews in the Netherlands*, edited by Jozeph Michman and Tirtsah Levie, 185–205. Jerusalem: Hebrew University Press, 1984.

————. 'Spinoza and Samuel Fisher.' *Philosophia* 15.3 (1985) 219–36.

————. *The Third Force in Seventeenth Century Thought.* Leiden: Brill, 1992.

Portier-Young, Anathea. *Apocalypse Against Empire: Theologies of Resistance in Early Judaism.* Eerdmans: Cambridge, 2011.

Powell-Williams, Todd. 'Social Control and the Westboro Baptist Church.' PhD diss., Southern Illinois University: 2008.

Prior, Charles. *Defining the Jacobean Church.* Cambridge: Cambridge University Press, 2005.

Prior, Charles, and Glen Burgess. *England's War of Religion Revisited.* Farnham, VT: Ashgate, 2011.

Reay, Barry. 'Quakerism and Society.' In *Radical Religion*, edited by J. F. McGregor and B. Reay, 141–64. Oxford: Oxford University Press, 1984.

Reed, Annette Yoshiko, and Adam Becker. 'Introduction.' In *The Ways That Never Parted: Jews and Christians in Late Antiquity and the Early Middle Ages*, edited by Annette Yoshiko Reed and Adam H. Becker, 1–35. Heidelberg: Mohr Siebeck, 2003.

Reynolds, Matthew. *Godly Reformers and Their Opponents in Early Modern England: Religion in Norwich c. 1560–1643.* Woodbridge: Boydell, 2005.

Richardson, Robert. *Puritanism in North-West England: A Regional Study of the Diocese of Chester.* Manchester: Manchester University Press, 1972.

Rodwell, Warwick. *The Coronation Chair and Stone of Scone.* Oxford: Oxbow, 2013.

Roper, Lyndal. *Martin Luther.* London: Bodley, 2016.

Rosenblatt, Jason. 'John Selden's *De Jure Naturaliis.*' In *Hebraica Veritas*, edited by Allison Coudert and Jeffrey Shouldson, 102–59. Philadelphia: University of Pennsylvania Press: 2004.

————. *Renaissance England's Chief Rabbi: John Selden.* Oxford: Oxford University Press, 2006.

Rosenblum, Joshua. *Food and Identity in Early Rabbinic Judaism.* Cambridge: Cambridge University Press, 2010.

Roth, Cecil. *History of the Jews in England.* Oxford: Oxford University Press, 1964.

Rowley, Matthew. 'From Fratricide to Revival: The Creation and Evolution of a Theological War Slogan, 1642–1917.' Lecture delivered at Ecclesiastical History Society Postgraduate Colloquium, Magdalene College, Cambridge University, March 4, 2016.

Rubin, Miri. *Gentile Tales: The Narrative Assault on Late Medieval Jews.* Philadelphia: University of Pennsylvania Press, 1999.

————. 'Identities.' In *A Social History of England 1200–1500*, edited by Rosemary Horrox, 383–412. Cambridge: Cambridge University Press, 2004.

Rubright, Marjorie. *Doppelganger Dilemmas: Anglo-Dutch Relations in Early-Modern English Literature and Culture.* Philadelphia: University of Pennsylvania Press, 2014.

Ruether, Rosemary. *Faith and Fratricide.* Eugene, OR: Wipf & Stock, 1995.

Ryrie, Alec. *Being Protestant in Reformation Britain.* Oxford: Oxford University Press, 2013.

————. *The Gospels and Henry VIII.* Cambridge: Cambridge University Press, 2003.

Samuel, Edgar. 'Sir Thomas Shirley's Project for Jewes: The Earliest Known Proposal for the Resettlement.' *Transactions and Miscellanies of the Jewish Historical Society of England* 24 (1973) 195–97.

Samuel, Walter. *The First London Synagogue of the Resettlement*. London: Jewish Historical Society, 1924.

Sanders, Julie. *Ben Jonson in Context*. Cambridge: Cambridge University Press, 2010.

Scarisbrick, John. *Henry VIII*. Yale: Yale University Press, 2011.

———. *Reformation and the English People*. London: Blackwell, 1985.

Scheil, Andrew. *The Footsteps of Israel*. Ann Arbor: University of Michigan Press, 2004.

Schmidt, Francis. *How the Temple Thinks: Identity and Social Cohesion in Ancient Judaism*. Translated by J. Edward Crowley. Sheffield: Sheffield Academic, 2001.

Schmidt, Jeremy. *Melancholy and the Care of the Soul*. Aldershot: Ashgate, 2007.

Scholem, Gershom. *Sabbatai Sevi, The Mystical Messiah*. Translated by Raphael Judah Zwi Werblowsky. Princeton: Princeton University Press, 1973.

Schorsch, Jonathan. *Jews and Blacks in the Early Modern World*. Cambridge: Cambridge University Press, 2004.

Schwartz, Baruch J. 'Leviticus.' In *The Jewish Study Bible*, edited by A. Berlin and M. Z. Brettler, 203–80. New York: Oxford University Press, 2004.

Scott, James C. *The Art of Not Being Governed: An Anarchist History of Upland South-East Asia*. New Haven: Yale University Press, 2009.

———. *Domination and the Arts of Resistance: Hidden Transcripts*. New Haven: Yale University Press, 1990.

———. *Weapons of the Weak: Everyday Forms of Peasant Resistance*. New Haven: Yale University Press, 1985.

Seaver, Paul. 'Puritan Preachers and their Patrons.' In *Religious Politics in Post-Reformation England*, edited by Kenneth Fincham, 128–43. Woodbridge: Boydell, 2000.

———. *Wallington's World: A Puritan Artisan in Seventeenth-Century London*. Stanford: Stanford University Press, 1985.

Segundo, Juan. *Theology for Artisans of a New Humanity*. Maryknoll, NY: Orbis, 1973.

Semaj, Leahcim. 'Race and Identity and the Children of the African Diaspora.' *The Caribe* 4.4 (1980) 14–18.

———. 'Rastafari: From Religion to Social Theory.' *Caribbean Quarterly* 26.4 (1980) 22–31.

Seters, John van. *A Law Book for the Diaspora*. Oxford: Oxford University Press, 2003.

Setright, Helen. 'Moses Wall.' PhD diss., University of Leicester, 2003.

Shagan, Ethan. *The Rule of Moderation*. Cambridge: Cambridge University Press, 2011.

Shapiro, James. *Shakespeare and the Jews*. New York: Columbia University Press, 1996.

Sharpe, Kevin. *Remapping Early Modern England*. Cambridge: Cambridge University Press, 2000.

Shea, Daniel. *Spiritual Autobiography in Early America*. Stanford: Stanford University Press, 1966.

Simon, Marcel. *Verus Israel*. Translated by Henry McKeating. Oxford: Oxford University Press, 1986.

Skinner, Patricia. *The Jews in Medieval Britain: Historical, Literary, and Archaeological Perspectives*. Woodbridge: Boydell, 2003.

Skinner, Quentin. 'Classical Liberty and the Coming of the English Civil War.' In *The Values of Republicanism in Early Modern Europe*, edited by Martin van Walderen, 9–29. Vol. 2 of *Republicanism*. Cambridge: Cambridge University Press, 2002.

———. *Liberty Before Liberalism*. Cambridge: Cambridge University Press, 1998.

———. 'Paradiastole: Redescribing the Vices as Virtues.' In *Renaissance Figures of Speech*, edited by Sylvia Adamson et al., 149–67. Cambridge: Cambridge University Press, 2007.

———. *Regarding Method*. Vol. 1 of *Visions of Politics*. Cambridge: Cambridge University Press, 2002.

Slack, Paul. 'The Public Conscience of Henry Sherfield.' In *Public Duty and Private Conscience in Seventeenth-Century England: Essays Presented to G. E. Aylmer*, edited by John Morrill et al., 151–71. Oxford: Oxford University Press, 1993.

Smith, Daniel. *Religion of the Landless*. Bloomington: Meyer Stone, 1989.

Smith, Merina. *Revelation, Resistance, and Mormon Polygamy*. Denver: University Press of Colorado, 2013.

Smith, Nigel. *Perfection Proclaimed*. Oxford: Clarendon, 1989.

Smith, Robert. 'Christian Judaizers in Early Stuart England.' *The Historical Magazine of the Protestant Episcopal Church* 52.2 (1983) 125–33.

Snyder, Susan. 'The Left Hand of God: Despair in Medieval and Renaissance Tradition.' *Studies in the Renaissance* 12 (1965) 18–59.

Somerville, Johann. 'John Selden, the Law of Nature, and the Origins of Government.' *The Historical Journal* 27.2 (1984) 437–47.

Spraggon, Julie. *Puritan Iconoclasm*. Woodbridge: Boydell, 2003.

———. 'Puritan Iconoclasm in England: 1640–1660.' PhD diss., University of London: 2000.

Sprunger, Keith. *Dutch Puritanism: A History of English and Scottish Churches of the Netherlands in the Sixteenth and Seventeenth Centuries*. Leiden: Brill, 1982.

———. 'English and Dutch Sabbatarianism and the Development of Puritan Social Thought, 1600–1660.' *Church History* 51 (1982) 24–28.

———. *Trumpets from the Tower: English Puritan Preaching in the Netherlands 1600–1640*. Leiden: Brill, 1994.

Spufford, Margaret. 'Can We Count the Godly and the Conformable in the Seventeenth Century?' *Journal of Ecclesiastical History* 36 (1985) 428–38.

———. *Contrasting Communities*. Cambridge: Cambridge University Press, 1974.

———. *The World of Rural Dissenters 1520–1725*. Cambridge: Cambridge University Press, 1995.

Spurr, John. *English Puritanism 1603–1689*. London: Macmillan, 1998.

Stanchiewski, John. *The Persecutory Imagination: English Puritanism and the Literature of Religious Despair*. Oxford: Oxford, 1991.

Stacey, Robert. 'Anti-Semitism and the Medieval English State.' In *The Medieval State: Essays Presented to James Campbell*, edited by J. R. Maddicott and D. M. Palliser, 163–77. London: Hambledon, 2000.

Stieg, Margaret. *Laud's Laboratory, the Diocese of Bath and Wells in the Early Seventeenth Century*. Lewisburg: Bucknell University Press, 1982.

Stoever, William. *A Faire and Easie Way to Heaven*. Middletown: Wesleyan University Press, 1978.

Stone, Bailey. *The Anatomy of Revolution*. Cambridge: Cambridge University Press, 2014.

Stone, Lawrence. 'The Bourgeois Revolution of Seventeenth-Century England Revisited.' *Past and Present* 109 (1985) 44–54.

Stretton, Tim. 'Marriage, Separation, and the Common Law.' In *The Family in Early Modern England*, edited by Helen Berry and Elizabeth Foyster, 18–40. Cambridge: Cambridge University Press, 2007.

Sun, Henry. 'Holiness Code.' In vol. 3 of *Anchor Bible Dictionary*, edited by David Noel Freedman, 254–57. New York: Doubleday, 1992.

Sutcliffe, Adam. *Judaism and the Enlightenment*. Cambridge: Cambridge University Press, 2003.

———. 'The Philo-Semitic Moment? Judaism and Republicanism in Seventeenth-Century European Thought.' In *Philo-Semitism in History*, edited by Adam Sutcliffe and Jonathan Karp, 67–89. Cambridge: Cambridge University Press, 2011.

Tait, James. 'The Declaration of Sports for Lancashire.' *English Historical Review* 32 (1917) 561–68.

Tajfel, Henri. 'Cognitive Aspects of Prejudice.' *Journal of Social Issues* 25.4 (1969) 79–97.

———. *Differentiation between Social Groups: Studies in the Social Psychology of Intergroup Relations*. London: Academic, 1978.

———. 'Experiments in Intergroup Discrimination.' *Scientific American* 223.5 (1970) 96–102.

———. *Human Groups and Social Categories*. Cambridge: Cambridge University Press, 1978.

———. 'Social Psychology of Intergroup Relations.' *Annual Review of Psychology* 33.1 (1982) 1–39.

Taylor, Charles. *A Secular Age*. Cambridge: Harvard University Press, 2007.

Tenneson, Carol. *Authority and Resistance in Language*. Milkwaukee: University of Winsconsin Press, 1985.

Termini, Cristina. 'Philo's Thought within the Context of Middle Judaism.' In *The Cambridge Companion to Philo*, edited by Adam Kamesar, 95–123. Cambridge: Cambridge University Press, 2009.

Thomas, Keith. *Religion and the Decline of Magic*. London: Penguin, 1991.

Todd, Margo. *Christian Humanism and the Puritan Social Order*. Cambridge: Cambridge University Press, 1987.

———. *The Culture of Protestantism in Early Modern Scotland*. London: Yale University Press, 2002.

———. *Reformation to Revolution*. London: Routledge, 1995.

Toon, Peter. 'The Latter Day Glory.' In *The Puritans, The Millennium & The Future of Israel: Puritan Eschatology 1600–1660*, edited by Peter Toon, 23–42. Cambridge: James Clarke, 1970.

Turner, John C. *Rediscovering the Social Group: A Self-Categorization Theory*. Oxford: Blackwell, 1987.

———. 'Social Categorization and the Self-Concept: A Social Cognitive Theory of Group Behavior.' In vol. 2 of *Advances in Group Processes*, edited by E. J. Lawler, 77–122. Greenwich: JAI, 1985

———. 'Social Identification and Psychological Group Formation.' In vol. 2 of *The Social Dimension: European Developments in Social Psychology*, edited by Henri Tajfel, 518–38. Cambridge: Cambridge University Press, 1984.

Tyacke, Nicholas. *Anti-Calvinists: The Rise of English Arminianism 1590–1640*. Oxford: Oxford University Press, 1990.

———. *The English Revolution*. Manchester: Manchester University Press, 2007.

———. 'Puritanism, Arminianism and Counter-Revolution.' In *The Origins of the English Civil War*, edited by Conrad Russell, 119–43. London: Macmillan, 1973.

Tyerman, Christopher. *England and the Crusades*. Chicago: University of Chicago Press, 1988.

Underdown, David. *Revel, Riot, and Rebellion*. Oxford: Clarendon, 1985.

Underhill, Edward. *Records of the Churches of Christ, Gathered at Fenstanton, Warboys, and Hexham, 1644–1720*. London: Hanserd Knollys Society, 1854.

VanderKam James C. *Calendars in the Dead Sea Scrolls: Measuring Time*. New York: Routledge, 1998.

Vauchez, Andre. *The Laity in the Middle Ages*. Translated by Margery Schneider. Notre Dame: University of Notre Dame Press, 1996.

Vivian, John. *The Visitation of the County of Devon Comprising the Herald's Visitations of 1531, 1564, and 1620*. Exeter: n.p., 1895.

Wagner, Hans-Peter. *Puritan Attitudes toward Recreation in Early Seventeenth-Century New England*. New York: Lang, 1982.

Walker, Daniel. *The Decline of Hell*. Chicago: University of Chicago Press, 1964.

Wallace, Dewey. *Puritans and Predestination*. Chapel Hill: University of North Carolina Press, 1982.

Walraven, Klaas van, and Jon Abbink. 'Rethinking Resistance in African History: An Introduction.' In *Rethinking Resistance: Revolt and Violence in African History*, edited by John Abbink, 1–42. White Plains, NY: M. E. Sharpe, 1978.

Walsham, Alexandra. *A Charitable Christian Hatred*. Manchester: Manchester University Press, 2006.

———. 'The Happiness of Suffering.' In *Suffering and Happiness in England 1550–1850* edited by Michael Braddick and Joanna Innes, 45–65. Oxford: Oxford University Press, 2017.

———. *Providence in Early Modern England*. Oxford: Oxford University Press, 1999.

Walzer, Michael. *Exodus and Revolution*. New York: Basic, 1985.

———. *The Revolution of the Saints: A Study in the Origins of Radical Politics*. Cambridge, MA: Harvard University Press, 1965.

Watkins, Carl. *History and the Supernatural in Medieval England*. Cambridge: Cambridge University Press, 2007.

Watkins, Owen. *The Puritan Experience*. London: Routledge, 1972.

Watt, Tessa. *Cheap Print and Popular Piety, 1550–1640*. Cambridge: Cambridge University Press, 1994.

Watts, Matthew. *The Dissenters: From the Reformation to the French Revolution*. Oxford: Clarendon, 1985.

Webster, Tom. 'Early Stuart Puritanism.' In *The Cambridge Companion to Puritanism*, edited by John Coffey and Paul Lim, 48–66. Cambridge: Cambridge University Press, 2008.

Weinfeld, Moshe. *Deuteronomy and the Deuteronomic School*. Oxford: Oxford University Press, 1972.

Weiss, Daniel H. 'Impurity without Repression: Julia Kristeva and the Biblical Possibilities of a Non-Eliminationist Construction of Religious Purity.' In *Purity and Danger Now: New Perspectives*, edited by Robbie Duschinsky et al., 205–21. London: Routledge, 2016.

Westermann, Claus. *Isaiah 40–66*. Philadelphia: Westminster, 1969.

White, Barrington. *The English Separatist Tradition*. Oxford: Oxford University Press, 1971.

White, Peter. *Predestination, Policy, and Polemic: Conflict and Consensus in the English Church from the Reformation to the Civil War*. Cambridge: Cambridge University Press, 1992.

Whitely, John. 'Church Discipline in the Loughwood Records.' *Baptist Quarterly* 31.6 (1986) 288–94.

———. 'Loughwood Baptists in the Seventeenth Century.' *Baptist Quarterly* 31.4 (1985) 148–58.

Whitley, William. 'The Rev. Colonel Paul Hobson.' *Baptist Quarterly* 9 (1939) 307–10.

Willen, Diane. '"Communion of the Saints": Spiritual Reciprocity and the Godly Community in Early Modern England.' *Albion* 27 (1995) 19–41.

Williams, Penry. *The Late Tudors*. Oxford: Oxford University Press, 1995.

Wilson, Charles *The Anglo-Dutch Contribution to the Civilization of Early Modern Society*. Oxford: Oxford University Press, 1976.

Withington, Phil. 'Intoxicants in the Early Modern City.' In *Remaking English Society: Social Relations and Social Change in Early Modern England*, edited by Steve Hindle et al., 135–63. Woodbridge: Boydell, 2013.

Wolf, Lucien. 'Jews in Tudor England.' In *Essays in Jewish History*, edited by Cecil Roth, 71–90. London: Jewish Historical Society of England, 1934.

———. *Menasseh ben Israel's Mission to Oliver Cromwell*. Cambridge: Cambridge University Press, 1901.

Wright, Nicholas. *What Paul Really Said*. Cambridge: Eerdmans, 1997.

Wrighton, Keith. *English Society 1580–1680*. London: Routledge, 2013.

———. *Poverty and Piety in an English Village: Terling, 1525–1700*. Oxford: Clarendon, 1995.

Yoder, John Howard. *The Jewish-Christian Schism*. Grand Rapids: Eerdmans, 2003.

———. 'On Not Being Ashamed of the Gospel.' *Faith and Philosophy* 9.3 (1992) 285–300.

———. *To Hear the Word*. Eugene, OR: Wipf and Stock, 2001.

Zacher, Samantha. 'Judaism and National Identity in Medieval England.' In *The Routledge Companion to Religion and Literature*, edited by Mark Knight, 367–75. London: Routledge, 2016.

Zachman, Randall C. *The Assurance of Faith: Conscience in the Theology of Martin Luther and John Calvin*. Louisville: Westminster John Knox, 2005.

Zafirovski, Milan. 'The Most Cherished Myth: Puritanism and Liberty Reconsidered and Revised.' *The American Sociologist* 38.1 (2007) 23–59.

———. *The Protestant Ethic and the Spirit of Authoritarianism*. Denton: Springer, 2007.

Zaret, David. *Origins of Democratic Culture: Printing, Petitions, and the Public Sphere in Early Modern England*. Princeton: Princeton University Press, 2000.

Index

London, 1, 5, 6, 7, 108, 129, 130, 131,
146, 149, 151, 153, 162, 168, 177,
201, 221, 226
Luther, Martin, 8, 26, 28, 60, 115

Marlowe, Christopher, 110
Mather, Samuel, 29
Mede, Joseph, 18, 22

Napier, John, 18
Niclaes, Heinrich, 132, 134
Norden, John, 57
Norwood, Robert, 161, 163

Pagitt, Ephraim, 120, 125, 137, 147,
151, 153
Paget, John, 6, 8, 109
Parker, Henry, 84
Passover, 1, 54, 100, 120, 156, 157,
160, 196
Paul, Saint, 24, 67, 105, 106, 152, 179,
180, 193, 205, 225, 237, 243
Penington, Isaac, 86, 193
Perkins, William, 27, 43, 62, 67, 75,
135
Pharisaism 17, 107, 108, 121
Philosemitism 3, 9, 10, 14–18, 18–24,
35, 40, 54, 98, 105, 121, 163, 189,
204, 206, 246–47
Playfere, Thomas, 76
Pooley, Christopher, 200–206, 214,
216, 221, 223, 226, 230, 232, 233,
235, 236, 239, 248, 260
Pordage, John, 161, 170–74, 194
Prynne, William, 10, 33, 34, 98, 110,
111, 112, 189

Quakerism, 85, 129, 144, 145, 146,
171, 173, 178, 180, 186, 190, 203,
210, 217, 230, 232, 248
Quartodecimanism, 156–57

Ramsay, Thomas, 7, 201, 235
Reeve, John, 172
Rogers, Francis, 95
Rogers, John, 31, 35
Rollock, Robert, 83
Rotterdam, 60, 203, 230

Sabbath, 1, 3, 11, 54, 55, 100, 103, 109,
115–18, 119–20, 127, 151–53,
158, 160, 201–2, 204, 207,
217–19, 223, 231–33, 239, 248
Salmon, Joseph, 43
Sanderson, Robert, 6, 90
Sands, Christopher, 119, 120, 151, 158
Sclater, William, 140, 141, 147, 149
Selden, John, 5, 14, 16, 18, 204
Sermon-gadding, 79, 82, 127
Shapira, Nathan, 14
Shirley, Thomas, 5
Somerset, 7, 128, 129, 131
Stephen, Saint, 37–38
Stubbes, Philip, 109

Taylor, John, 113
Thurloe, John, 112, 202, 226
Tickell, John, 181
Tillam, Thomas, 1–7, 15–19, 23, 29,
34, 36, 48, 53, 55, 103, 105, 118,
200–238, 239–44, 248, 250
Tillinghast, Thomas, 22, 226
Totney, Thomas, 2, 3, 4, 7, 16, 18, 19,
21, 23, 27, 29, 34, 36, 48, 53, 55,
103, 105, 118, 142, 161–99, 217,
219, 239, 244, 248, 249
Trapnel, Anna, 75, 76, 77
Traske, John, 1, 2, 3, 4, 6, 7, 11, 16, 17,
18, 19, 29, 34, 48, 53, 54, 55, 103,
118, 119–60, 166, 172, 178, 191,
195, 197, 209, 212, 219, 220, 235,
239, 242, 244, 249, 250

Vitell, Christopher, 132, 139

Wallington, Nehemiah, 44, 75, 77, 79,
137, 167
Weemes, John, 22, 25, 27
Weld, Thomas, 201, 202, 205, 213,
218, 220, 224, 239
Whitaker, William, 25, 85
Whitgift, John, 42, 65, 73, 128, 135
Wightman, Edward, 156
Wilcox, Thomas, 64
Winstanley, Gerard, 184
Woolsey, Thomas, 1, 8

www.ingramcontent.com/pod-product-compliance
Lightning Source LLC
Chambersburg PA
CBHW060329100426
42812CB00003B/921